THE GOSPEL IN THE EARLY CHURCH

THE GOSPEL IN THE EARLY CHURCH

A STUDY OF THE EARLY DEVELOPMENT OF CHRISTIAN THOUGHT

BY

JAMES MACKINNON, 1860 –

Ph.D., D.D., D.Th., LL.D.

Regius Professor-Emeritus of Ecclesiastical
History, University of Edinburgh

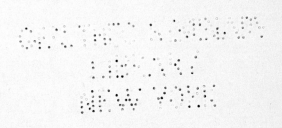

LONGMANS, GREEN, AND CO.

LONDON :: NEW YORK :: TORONTO

1933

LONGMANS, GREEN, AND CO. LTD.

39 PATERNOSTER ROW, LONDON, E.C.4
6 OLD COURT HOUSE STREET, CALCUTTA
53 NICOL ROAD, BOMBAY
36A MOUNT ROAD, MADRAS

LONGMANS, GREEN, AND CO.

55 FIFTH AVENUE, NEW YORK
221 EAST 20TH STREET, CHICAGO
88 TREMONT STREET, BOSTON
128-132 UNIVERSITY AVENUE, TORONTO

Made in Great Britain

To

THE UNIVERSITY OF EDINBURGH

ON THE OCCASION OF THE 350TH
ANNIVERSARY OF ITS FOUNDATION (1583)

IN TOKEN

OF DEEP INDEBTEDNESS, DURING A LONG
ASSOCIATION WITH IT, AS STUDENT,
LECTURER, EXAMINER, AND PROFESSOR

PREFACE

In my " Historic Jesus," published two years ago, I attempted to depict the Gospel as it appears in the authentic record of his mission and teaching. In this volume, which is a continuation of that work, I have endeavoured to trace its development from his death onwards to, approximately, the middle of the second century, as this development is reflected in the apostolic and subapostolic writings, and in those of the early Fathers.

I use the term " Gospel " as equivalent to Christianity, in its early form, as a proclamation or teaching which centres in Jesus Christ, the Revealer of God, and the divinely ordained Redeemer of mankind. The term does not embrace, except in a secondary degree,[1] other aspects of early Christianity, considered as a religious movement, such as the Christian mission and the rise of the Christian Church as an organised institution. It is with the Christian message concerning Christ and his redemptive significance, rather than with the Christian movement, that the work is mainly concerned.

In the sub-title, I have indicated the character and scope of the work as " A Study of the Early Development of Christian Thought." I use the term " development " advisedly. In the New Testament and other documents, from which our knowledge of the period is derived, this developing thought is clearly discernible. This fact is now increasingly recognised, and its recognition is, it seems to me, essential to an adequate treatment of the subject. Important elements of the Gospel were present from the outset in the teaching of Jesus and his personal disciples, and the common faith in him as Revealer and Redeemer is there throughout the period. At the same time, it is evident that the common faith underwent a process of development in the minds of a succession of outstanding

[1] See, for instance, the section on the " Beginnings of Catholicism," in Chapter III., and Chapter V. on " The Appeal of the Gospel."

vii

personalities—known and unknown by name—and in the Christian communities themselves. The Apostle Paul, the writer of the Epistle to the Hebrews, the author of the Fourth Gospel, Clement of Rome, Ignatius of Antioch, for instance. These and others added their quota, in more or less distinctive degree, in accordance with their culture and their Christian experience. Moreover, there were, in the environment of the Gospel in the ancient world, factors of an impersonal kind at work in moulding this development. If the Gospel exerted an influence on its Græco-Roman environment, it is no less evident that this environment exerted an influence on the Gospel. As it expanded into the Gentile world, the inter-action of the one on the other was inevitable. It has impressed itself on the documents throughout the period. The question of this mutual influence is not one of fact, but only of degree.

In view of the cumulative evidence for this development within the period, it is a mistake to ignore or minimise it, if it is equally a mistake to exaggerate or unduly enlarge it, with the more extreme representatives of the critical-historical school. For a general survey of it, I may refer the reader to the first section of the concluding chapter.

A striking feature of this development appears in the diversity in the apprehension of the Gospel, which the documents more or less reveal. With the common faith these writers combine distinctive variations, which reflect individual culture and experience. In this respect the result of my study of the early development of Christian thought coincides, generally, with that of Dr Streeter in his recent study of the organisation of the early Church. " There was ' one Lord, one faith, one baptism '; but the content of that faith and its outward expression in the life of the local community cannot but have varied enormously from place to place." [2] In virtue of this marked diversity in both cases, the development, if gradual, is not uniform. In some of the documents, even the later ones, Christian thought, as well as organisation, appears at a more primitive stage than in others.

This diversity of view raises, for the historian, the problem how far the subjective element entered into or coloured the

[2] "The Primitive Church," 46 (1929). I should be inclined to substitute "markedly" for "enormously."

developing Gospel. The influence of current thought and
speculation—the Logos theory of the Fourth Gospel, for
instance—in moulding it, is, I think, undeniable. In the
course of the work I have accordingly dealt with the problem
of this subjective influence in its various aspects, and have
discussed a number of important questions arising out of it.
Was, for instance, the variation due to this influence, in accord,
in every respect, with the teaching of Jesus on himself and
his redemptive function ? How far was it a legitimate interpretation or amplification of the faith in him as the exalted
Redeemer and Lord ? In dealing with such questions, I have
applied the critical-historical method, which it is the right
and duty of the historian to do in all questions of evidence
relating to ideas as well as facts. A purely traditional treatment of the subject can no longer meet the demands of an age
in which historic and scientific knowledge has been vastly
enlarged. Hence this attempt critically to delineate and
evaluate, in the light of this enlarged knowledge, the development of Christian thought, in its early phase, apart from
preconceived conclusions. At the same time, I have striven
to elucidate and evaluate, in its own light, the religious and
moral content of the Gospel, in which its real significance
and abiding power lie. In the last chapter, in particular,
I have attempted to show how, and with what effects, the
Gospel as a message and a life appealed to the ancient world,
as well as the difficulties which this appeal encountered in
the progress of the Christian mission.

In the face of the widespread knowledge and the religious
perplexity of the age, many Christian men and women are
striving to rethink their faith and relate it to their own experience and mentality. These men and women are sincere
believers in the Gospel, if they cannot accept the traditional
version of it in its entirety. Their endeavour does not mean
disloyalty to Jesus and his teaching, or to what may be
found to be the legitimate development of it in the thought of
his immediate disciples and their early successors. It means
the retention of the imperishable truths of the Gospel, which,
apart from the forms in which current thought clothed them,
the larger knowledge and experience of our age only tend to
confirm. If some of the beliefs imported into it have become

obsolete or problematic, the things that really matter are an abiding heritage.

Whilst thus indicating my own standpoint, I readily acknowledge that it is not the only one, and that others may draw from the evidence conclusions differing from mine. I have at least endeavoured to state both sides of any given question, as this is reflected in the large modern literature on the subject, though the list of works referred to in the footnotes is representative, and does not profess to be exhaustive. It does not include even all that I have read on the subject during a long period of academic office. As it was part of my duty, as professor, to lecture on Early Christianity, my former students may detect, here and there, echoes of these lectures. They have, however, been almost entirely rewritten for submission, in book form, to a wider audience—parts of them several times over.

There is room for a monograph in English on the developing faith of the Early Church. Hence the contribution attempted in the present work.

TABLE OF CONTENTS

CHAPTER I

CHAPTER II

CHAPTER III

CHAPTER IV

CHAPTER V

The Gospel in the Early Church

A Study of the Early Development of Christian Thought

CHAPTER I

THE PRIMITIVE GOSPEL

I. THE PRIMITIVE PREACHING

THE primitive Gospel is the glad tidings about Jesus, the Christ, proclaimed by the apostles. In form it is a proclamation[1] ; in content it is good news, and the verb used, in the latter sense, in connection with the preaching of Peter and Philip—" evangelising " or " gospelling "[2]—conveys both meanings. " Proclaiming the glad tidings about Jesus as the Christ." " Proclaiming the glad tidings of the Word." " Proclaiming the glad tidings concerning the kingdom of God and the name of Jesus Christ." " Proclaiming the glad tidings of peace through Jesus Christ." This distinctive term is applied by Luke to the Baptist's proclamation of the Coming One,[3] and by Mark and Matthew to that of Jesus himself.[4] The primitive proclamation is also described as " witnessing," or " testifying "—particularly in reference to the resurrection. The apostles are " witnesses "[5] to Christ. " This Jesus did God raise up, whereof we all are witnesses."[6] " And we are witnesses of these things."[7] It is further described as

---

[1] Κήρυγμα.
[2] εὐαγγελιζόμενοι. Acts v. 42 ; viii. 4, 12 ; x. 36; cf. Peter i. 25.
[3] Luke iii. 18, εὐαγγελίζετο τὸν λαόν.
[4] Mark i. 14; Matt. iv. 23. They use the words κηρύσσων τὸ εὐαγγέλιον. For the sacral use of εὐαγγέλιον in the imperial cult, see Deissmann, " Light from the Ancient East," 366 (4th ed., 1922 ; Eng. trans., 1927).
[5] μάρτυρες.
[6] Acts ii. 32 ; cf. iii. 15.   [7] Ibid.

I

"teaching." "And they continued steadfastly in the apostles' teaching." [8] "Teaching in the temple." "Teaching the people." "Teaching in this name." [9]

This Gospel, this witness, teaching is specifically the glad tidings concerning the earthly mission, the message of the kingdom, the death, resurrection, exaltation, the heavenly existence, the spiritual presence, the visible coming again of Jesus, the Christ. It is a missionary proclamation—an attempt to vindicate and commend Jesus, the Master whom the disciples had known so intimately during his sojourn on earth, and whose Messianic claim and function the resurrection experience had confirmed and placed in a new light. It is at once proclamation and apologetic. It affirms who Jesus was and has become, and why this was so. It professes to be based on the preaching, the teaching of Jesus himself. From this point of view it may be described as the Gospel of Jesus as well as the Gospel about Jesus. Its main ideas obviously reflect those of Jesus himself, who had proclaimed the kingdom of God, present and future, and his part in its realisation, and foretold his death, resurrection, exaltation, and his coming again in the clouds of heaven. There is thus a genetic connection between the Gospel of Jesus and the Gospel of the Apostles. What Peter, Philip, and others proclaim is, in the main, no mere reflection of the ideas of the nascent Christian community, as Wellhausen and other critics maintain. [10]   These ideas go back to Jesus himself, though the apprehension of them may be coloured and rendered more definite by the new spiritual life, consequent on the resurrection and the inspiration of the Holy Spirit connected with it. The viewpoint is from a different angle, in keeping with the altered situation and the enlarged experience of the disciples. But, due allowance made for the difference of angle and outlook, the train of thought is the same. The same also the apocalyptic atmosphere—the intense expectation of the kingdom of God, the elevated ethical ideal befitting its members, the radical change of heart and life in accordance with this ideal, the sublime figure of the suffering Messiah who will overcome death, ascend to his heavenly throne at the right hand of God, and come again in

---

[8] Acts ii. 42, διδαχή.   [9] *Ibid.*, v. 21, 25, 28.
[10] See note at the end of this chapter.

his glory. Given the intimate intercourse of the disciples with their Master on earth, there is nothing essentially different in their preaching from his. It is centred in the historic Jesus. It is not based on the mythological figure of the dying and resurrected God, as some assume, but on the mission and message of Jesus himself, adapted to the changed situation which his death and resurrection have produced. Though the titles applied to him are largely similar to those of the apocalyptic books, they no longer denote an imaginary figure. They are embodied in a real person—the " Jesus of Nazareth " whom they had known on earth, though now exalted to heaven, the God-attested man. Moreover, the proclamation of Jesus as the Christ corresponds to his own conception of himself as the Son of Man, who on earth inaugurates the new age or æon and will come again to accomplish its consummation. In the opening chapters of the Acts, making allowance for the writer's tendency to see some things in a later light, we recognise at once, with " the rulers and elders and scribes," that Peter and John " had been with Jesus." [11] It is not a purely heavenly being that Peter proclaims, no mere " value judgments about Jesus " that he professes to give,[12] though the enhanced estimate of him, in the light of the resurrection, is certainly there, and with it the tendency to view him through the eye-glass of prophecy. It is the Jesus of his earthly career, as well as the Lord exalted to heaven, that he sets before his hearers. He emphasises the wonderful facts of his life on earth.[13] He recounts on occasion the course of his career from the baptism onwards, as he had witnessed it.[14] He appeals again and again to the resurrection as an experienced reality. It is, in fact, largely from this preaching that the Synoptic narratives took shape, as the tradition about Jesus was imparted in the mission preaching and the catechetical instruction of believers. These narratives may betray here and there later reflection about Jesus, in addition to the actual facts of his life and the actual content of his teaching. At the same time, they substantially gave us a faithful account of his mission and his thought, and the primitive Gospel, as outlined in the early chapters of

[11] Acts ii. 13.
[12] J. Weiss, " Das Urchristenthum," 92 (1917).
[13] Acts ii. 22.   [14] *Ibid.*, x. 37 f.

Acts, and discernible to a certain extent in the Epistles of Paul and other apostolic writings, is, in the main, a reliable reflection of what the disciples had learned from the Master himself.

II. The Offence of the Cross

An urgent problem confronting the apostles in the proclamation of the Gospel about Jesus was the death of the Messiah. How could the Jesus who suffered as a common malefactor possibly be the Messiah ? How could the offence of the Cross—so unthinkable to current Jewish thought—be reconciled with the Messianic claim of Jesus himself and with the assertion of this claim by his disciples ? The answer to this problem was found in the appeal to the divine determination and to prophecy. The apostolic preachers had recourse to the Pharisaic doctrine of predestination, which Jesus himself had held, as the prayer in Gethsemane, for instance, and other sayings show.[1] " Not my will, but thine be done." For him it was a needs be, the secret of which lay in the divine will and purpose. It was a tragic inevitability not only because the religious authorities refused to accept his Messianic claim and his spiritual conception of the kingdom, which threatened to supplant the traditional legalism, but because it was a necessary condition of bringing into operation the redemptive purpose which God had ordained him to accomplish. He must lose his life in order to find it, must become the Suffering Servant before he could become the glorified Christ. So also it appeared to Peter and his fellow-apostles in their attempt to explain away the offence of the Cross and maintain, in spite of it, the Messianic claim of the crucified Jesus. " Delivered up by the determinate counsel and foreknowledge of God."[2] The language may savour of the speculative scribal theology, and the writer may be putting this language into the mouth of Peter, but the thought undoubtedly reflects the line of argument which the preacher adopted. The Gentiles, as represented by Pontius Pilate, and the Jews, as represented by the Sanhedrin, in adjudging him to the Cross have done " whatsoever thy hand and thy counsel foreordained to come to pass."[3] Their

---

[1] Luke xxii. 22.
[2] Acts ii. 23 ; cf. 1 Peter i. 20.   [3] Ibid., iv. 27-28.

action is an essential part of God's will and purpose in the salvation of Israel. True, it is a murderous, an inconceivably wicked act of human blindness and brutality. Nevertheless it must be the act of God. There is a problem here which the apostolic preachers, with their traditional interpretation of the will of God, do not envisage. Why did God permit this unspeakably brutal, blind, and wicked act ? Why must the highest and the best of mankind be delivered to a horrible death as the victim of human passion and fury ? Where is the Providence of a merciful God, and why should such a revolting enormity be necessary for man's salvation ? The disciples do not ask, and we, who do ask, cannot find any more satis- factory answer than that, as human life is conditioned, it seems that it must be so, and that, as history shows, God does work by terrible methods in the gradual elevation of humanity and does make use of suffering for great ends, not all known to us. Though they have no such philosophy of suffering, the disciples do recognise the grim fact of this needs must be. They fall back on the Jewish idea of vicarious suffering in accordance with God's eternal determination.

They turn not to philosophy but to prophecy for the demonstration of it. The death of Jesus is the fulfilment of prophecy. It is not only foreordained by God ; it was foreseen and foretold by the prophets. The Cross is visualised in the light of Old Testament passages, and in this light its necessity becomes for them visible and compelling. All the prophets, as the mouthpieces of God's will, have foreshown that the Christ should suffer, and in his death these prophecies have been fulfilled.[4] The classic proof is found in the Servant passages in Second Isaiah, reinforced probably by such Psalms as xxii. and lxix. In the spirit of Isaiah, Jesus is regarded as the Servant or Child of God,[5] and he is explicitly identified with the Suffering Servant of chapter liii. in the interpretation given by Philip to the Ethiopian eunuch.[6] Here also the primitive Gospel is in accord with that of Jesus himself, in which the

---

[4] 1 Peter i. 10-11 ; Luke xxiv. 25 f., 46 ; Acts iii. 18.
[5] ὁ παῖς, Acts iii. 13, 26 ; iv. 27, 30 ; cf. Matt. xii. 18. The title παῖς is taken from the Septuagint version of the Old Testament. It may mean " child " or " servant." In the Hebrew original it means " servant " only.
[6] Acts viii. 38.

figure of the Son of Man is combined with that of the Suffering
Servant of Isaiah. " How is it written of the Son of man, that
he should suffer many things, and be set at nought ? " [7]   The
argument from prophecy for the purpose of invalidating the
offence of the Cross is thus no mere afterthought of the
primitive community—though its significance doubtless came
home with a force which the disciples had been unable to
appreciate when adduced by Jesus himself. Looking backwards in the light of present experience, this apologetic acquired
a new cogency. To us, accustomed to test evidence at its true
historical value, it may, as developed by the apostolic preaching,
seem forced and, therefore, unconvincing. Like statistics,
prophecy can be made to prove anything we like. But it came
with all the force of demonstration to Peter's contemporaries,
to whom, as Jews, it was sufficient proof of an event that it
was assumed to have been predicted. Considering the Jewish
mentality, it was natural for Peter to appeal to prophecy in
support of his contention. Equally natural for the people,
if not for the priestly authority, which was hopelessly biassed
against the victim of its blind bigotry, to accept this kind of
proof. The Christian application of it is only a specific
instance of this Jewish tendency, though the Christian application differs from the Jewish in as far as it centres in a definite,
historic personality, and seeks to prove the claims of the
historic personality as the actual fulfilment of prophecy.[8]

III. THE RESURRECTION OF JESUS

'at contributed to give a heightened force to the argument
from prophecy was the fact of the resurrection. Without the
experience of the resurrection, indeed, no argument of this kind
would have been possible. The Cross would otherwise have
remained for them a hopeless, a crushing enigma. It was this
experience that made the primitive Gospel, of which it was a

---

[7] Mark ix. 12.
[8] On the argument from prophecy as applied in the apostolic preaching,
see the elaborate discussion of Weidel, " Studien über den Einfluss des
Weissagungsbeweisses auf die evangelische Geschichte. Theologische
Studien und Kritiken," 88 f., 163 f. (1910). Weidel contends that the
application of prophecy by Jesus to himself in the Synoptic narratives is
ascribable to the later community. This is too sweeping.

fundamental element, possible. Without it there would have
been no Gospel to preach and no Church to found. The belief
that Jesus was the Messiah involved as a *sine qua non* the
conviction that he had conquered death and was enthroned
in heaven as the participator of the divine dominion or rule,
now and in the coming æon or age. Here the appeal is, in the
first place, to personal experience, and it is in this experience,
not in the appeal to prophecy or the later stories of the empty
tomb, that the strength of the case for the resurrection lies.
" This Jesus did God raise up, whereof we all are witnesses." [1]
" And with great power gave the apostles their witness of
the resurrection of the Lord Jesus." [2] " Him God raised up
the third day and gave him to be made manifest, not to all the
people, but to witnesses that were chosen before of God." [3]
On what experience this witness rested we learn from Paul.
It was the specific appearances to Peter, the Twelve, and many
other disciples, including ultimately Paul himself.[4] Though
in the earliest tradition as recorded by Paul, it was after the third
day that this experience came, it was not based on the belief
in the empty tomb. Like the ascension story, this is evidently
a later accretion in the tradition recorded in the Gospels.[5]
It was the spiritual manifestation of the risen Jesus that underlay
this resurrection Gospel. It belongs to the realm of psychic
experience, not of material things. In the earliest preaching,
as preserved in the opening chapters of the Acts,[6] the resurrection belief means pre-eminently the conviction, gained through
the vision of the risen and exalted one, that the spirit of Jesus
has not been extinguished by death, but has passed through
death into a higher life with God.

For the reality of this manifestation we have the explicit
and detailed evidence of Paul, which goes back to a short interval

[1] Acts ii. 32 ; iii. 15.   [3] *Ibid.*, x. 40-41.
[2] *Ibid.*, iv. 33.   [4] 1 Cor. xv. 4 f.
[5] On this question see my " Historic Jesus," 280 f.
[6] Acts ii. 24, 32, 33 ; iii. 15 ; v. 30, 31. According to Mark and Matthew
the earlier appearances at least took place in Galilee. Luke places them at
Jerusalem and neighbourhood (Emmaus), while the Fourth Gospel, which
attempts a synthesis of the varying traditions, knows of appearances at both
Jerusalem and in Galilee. Mark (which is incomplete, the conclusion being
a later addition) and Matthew seem to give the earlier tradition, which,
in Luke and the Fourth Gospel, is mingled with later legendary matter.
The earlier tradition does not, however, necessarily exclude subsequent
appearances at Jerusalem or elsewhere.

after the crucifixion, and is devoid of all legendary colouring. From all accounts the condition of the disciples after the tragedy of Calvary was that of complete collapse. From this collapse they erelong emerge as the convinced believers in the spiritual existence of their crucified Master. These appearances, which engendered this irrefragable conviction, may indeed have been the illusions of religious excitement, and so some have judged. But this judgment, which ignores or rules out the possibility of spiritual contact with a spiritual world, is arbitrary and subjective. What the record reveals is not religious excitement, but mental shock and disillusion. The assumed condition did not exist. Even the women, who proceed to the tomb to pay the last tribute of love and care to the dead body, evidently do so under the impression that all is over. Nor does the assumed illusory cause adequately account for the effect produced. Besides being a purely arbitrary treatment of the recorded evidence, it fails to account for the rise of the Christian religion in spite of the tragedy of Calvary. That this religion, which ultimately took possession of the Roman Empire and spread beyond its borders, was born in an illusion is an assumption which, in the face of the matter-of-fact Pauline evidence, may in turn be justifiably termed an illusion. On rational grounds alone something must have happened to revive and even intensify the faith in the crucified Jesus. Nothing could have done this except the absolute conviction, which the evidence avers was derived from Jesus himself, that in dying he had conquered death and revealed the fact by the repeated psychic manifestations of his spiritual existence. The credibility of this manifestation is, moreover, strengthened by the uniqueness of the personality and the marvellous life with which the disciples had been in close personal contact throughout Jesus' earthly ministry. Even the tragedy of the Cross could not efface from their minds the unique moral endowment and spiritual elevation of the Master, the divine power which had been attested [7] by his teaching and healing ministry. The profound impression of his personality and life remained in spite of the Cross, as the words of Peter show. " Jesus of Nazareth anointed by God (for his Messianic vocation) with the Holy Spirit and with power,

[7] ἀποδεδειγμένον, Acts ii. 22.

who went about doing good and healing all that were oppressed
of the devil, for God was with him." [8]   They remembered his
ideal life of selfless service and matchless purity which marked
him out as "the Holy and Righteous One," "Thy Holy
Servant Jesus." [9]   These titles reflect their profound estimation of him not only as Messiah, but as the exemplar of the
perfect life, the supremely inspired medium of God's Spirit.
Surely if there is anything at all rational and divine in and
behind the universe, the personality so depicted could not have
vanished into blank nothingness on Calvary.   If so, it is no
vain assumption that it was capable of communicating the fact
to the disciples, as Paul avers.   This averment may, therefore,
be reasonably accepted as an actual experience, by which the
risen Master restored the broken faith in his Messianic claim
and vocation.   Here again, in characteristic Jewish fashion,
Peter and his fellow-disciples seek in Scripture an additional,
if more problematic warrant for their conviction.   Prophecy is,
in this case also, made to confirm conviction, and the prophecy
is sanguinely traced to Moses and all the prophets, especially
to David.[10]   They have foretold his resurrection and his
exaltation to heaven, where he is now enthroned, awaiting
"the times of the restoration of all things," of which they have
also spoken.[11]

IV. Christ and Lord

As the result of the conviction of his resurrection and
exaltation, Jesus has become for the disciples the heavenly or
transcendental Lord and Christ.   "Let all the house of
Israel, therefore, know assuredly that God hath made him
both Lord and Christ, this Jesus whom ye crucified." [1]   They
find the provenance and the precondition of this high vocation
in the life of Jesus on earth.   For this vocation God has
appointed him and anointed him with the Holy Spirit (*i.e.*, at
his baptism), and they appeal to the divine power operating in
his earthly ministry in proof of the fact that God has so
appointed and anointed him as the Christ, the Messiah.   The
conception of him as the Christ in the primitive preaching is

---

[8] Acts x. 38.   [9] *Ibid.*, iii. 14; iv. 27, 30; vii. 52.
[10] *Ibid.*, ii. 25 f., 34; iii. 21 f.   [11] *Ibid.*, iii. 21.   [1] *Ibid.*, ii. 36.

thus what has been called the "adoptionist" one. Jesus is
the man chosen and attested by God to be the Messiah.
" Jesus of Nazareth, a man approved of God unto you by
mighty works and wonders and signs, which God did by him
in the midst of you."[2] " Jesus of Nazareth (whom) God
anointed with the Holy Ghost and with power."[3] " Thy
Holy Servant Jesus, whom thou didst anoint."[4] " The
Christ who hath been appointed for you, even Jesus."[5] This
conception is also reflected in the Synoptic tradition by the
voice at the baptism, which proclaims him the Beloved Son in
the Messianic sense. Even in the preaching of Paul at Pisidian
Antioch and at Athens, as reported in the Acts, it is the man
whom God has ordained and chosen that is emphasised.[6] There
is even a trace in that of Peter of the conception of him as the
prophet of the Galilean ministry. He is the prophet whom
Moses had foretold.[7] He is the Servant or Child of God,
the (Messianic) Holy and Righteous One, the Prince or In-
augurator of Life, whom God has "set up," "sent to bless you,"
" glorified " in the wonderful works of his earthly ministry.[8]

In this respect the primitive Gospel retains its grip of the
historic Jesus. At the same time the resurrection and the exaltation have produced a heightened evaluation of him. The earthly
Messiah has thereby been transformed into the heavenly, the
transcendental Lord and Christ. In virtue of his enthronement
at the right hand of God, he has become the Lord, the partaker
of the divine dominion, the wielder of the kingly function, the
heavenly associate of God as the agent of his purpose in the
destiny of man and the world. In this sense the kingdom of
God has become the kingdom of Christ, though the phrase
" kingdom of God " is used in the early chapters of Acts.[9]

[2] Acts ii. 22.
[3] Ibid., x. 38.
[4] Ibid., iv. 27.
[5] Ibid., iii. 20, προκεχειρισμένον.
[6] Ibid., xiii. 22, 38 ; xvii. 31.
[7] Ibid., iii. 22.
[8] Ibid., iii. 13 f., 26. The term ὁ παῖς (servant) is taken from the
Septuagint, and it has been suggested that it was applied to Jesus in later
Christian Hellenist circles, which used the Greek Translation of the Old
Testament (Foakes-Jackson and Lake, " Beginnings of Christianity," i. 301),
and that it is here read back into the belief of the primitive Palestinian
community, Blunt, " Acts of the Apostles," 149 (1922). In view of Jesus'
emphasis on the Suffering Servant, these suggestions seem superfluous.
There is no reason why Peter and the primitive disciples should not have
applied to him a title which Jesus himself had evidently in mind.
[9] Acts i. 3 ; viii. 12.

Whilst there is a trace of the traditional belief in the restored kingdom of Israel,[10] it erelong disappears in the thought of the kingdom in the ethical, heavenly sense—as in the teaching of Jesus himself—of which Christ is Lord. The recognition of him as Lord implies the recognition of his kingly function. In this sense, too, he is identified with the Messianic Lord in the prophetic saying ascribed to David, " The Lord said unto my Lord," etc.[11] To this Messianic Lordship " all the house of Israel " must be subject. It is reflected in Stephen's vision of the heavenly Son of Man standing at the right hand of God, and in his dying invocations of him as Lord.[12] It is echoed by Paul, " For he must reign till he hath put all his enemies under his feet." [13] It goes back, in fact, to Jesus, who applied to himself the title Son of Man in the future transcendental sense, and quoted, in indirect reference to his Messianic Lordship, the cryptic saying ascribed to David.[14] According to Matthew and Luke,[15] he spoke, as Son of Man, prospectively of the kingdom as his, and there is no reason to doubt his use of this title as its prospective Lord.

The primitive conception of the risen and exalted Lord is preserved in the Aramaic *Maran*, " our Lord " applied to him by Paul [16]—*Maranatha*, " Our Lord, come." The Greek equivalent in the primitive preaching in Acts is κύριος, and in the Septuagint κύριος is applied to Yahweh, God Himself. But in the primitive Jewish Christian usage it stands, not for Yahweh, but for His Servant, the Christ, the Lord in the Messianic sense.

In this sense it undoubtedly forms an essential feature of this preaching, and there is no need to regard it as an importa-

[10] Acts i. 6.
[11] *Ibid.*, ii. 24-25.
[12] *Ibid.*, vii. 56 f.
[13] 1 Cor. xv. 26-28.
[14] Mark xii. 36.
[15] Matt. xiii. 41 ; xvi. 28 ; xxv. 34, 40 ; Luke xxii. 29-30. The term Lord in Mark xii. 36 is indirectly at least applied by Jesus to Himself. In Mark xi. 3, " The Lord hath need of him " (the colt), Lord may denote merely Master, though the term, which is used in connection with the Messianic entry, may be significant of a higher sense. In Matthew, and especially in Luke, Jesus is frequently addressed as Lord. This may be an evidence of its use in the early community as a specific title of the exalted Christ. But according to a number of critics, it is largely a redactional substitute for Master or Teacher, the usual title. Foakes-Jackson and Lake, " Beginnings of Christianity," i. 412 f.
[16] 1 Cor. xvi. 22 ; *cf.* Rev. xxii. 20, where only the Greek translation is given, and in the " Didache," 10, where the original is also given.

tion from the Hellenist-Christian community of Antioch and elsewhere, and see in it a reflection of the Hellenist conception of a God-man, as Bousset and others do.[17] Deissmann has shown from contemporary inscriptions and papyri the prevalence of the view in the Hellenist world that regarded the emperor as " God," " Son of God," and " divine Lord," and the use of the term in the mystery religions of Syria and Asia Minor to denote the object of the worship of the circle of initiates, to whom they owed a religious allegiance.[18] The term Lord in this sense was applied, at an earlier period, to the Seleucid kings of Syria and the Ptolemaic kings of Egypt. But the specific application of the title to Jesus in the primitive community was not derived from this source. It is traceable to the later indirect teaching of Jesus himself, and to the resurrection experience and its sequel. At most the widespread worship, in the eastern Gentile world, of a deified God-man might tend to make the idea of Jesus as Lord more intelligible to the Hellenist-Christian communities, and seems to have ultimately contributed to the accentuated deification of him in these communities.

At the same time, its use in the primitive Jewish-Christian community does betoken an enhanced consciousness of His person as the divinely chosen instrument of salvation for Israel and erelong, as the Gospel expanded into the Græco-Roman Empire, for the world. A certain apotheosis has begun with the conviction of his exaltation to the right hand of God, and it reflects not only the influence of a mere theory about him, but of the impression made by his life and teaching. The relation of the disciples to the risen and exalted Lord has become a more markedly religious one than in the days of the earthly ministry. He has become the object of faith. Of his actual worship there may be no explicit trace. The invocation of Stephen, " Lord Jesus, receive my spirit," [19]

[17] Bousset, " Kyrios Christos " (1913). As the result of a detailed study of the subject, Graf von Baudissin has shown that Christianity took over the divine name κύριος and the conception of God which it expresses from Judaism. See " κύριος als Gottesname im Judenthum," ed. by Eissfeldt. For a recent criticism of Bousset's theory see Rawlinson, " The New Testament Doctrine of The Christ " (1926), 92 f., 231 f.
[18] " Light from the Ancient East," 349 (4th ed., 1922 ; Eng. trans., 1927) ; Jackson and Lake, " Beginnings," i. 411-412. See also Kennedy, " St Paul and The Mystery Religions."
[19] Acts vii. 59.

the description of the disciples as "those that call on his name," and "the prayers" in Acts ii. 42,[20] do not necessarily involve worship. There is only as yet the presupposition of a Christolatry. This enhanced evaluation remains within the circle of Jewish Messianic thought, which saw in Jesus the chosen agent, of the seed of David, of God's purpose in the salvation of Israel. Jesus as Lord and Christ is conceived in the Messianic, not in the later theological or metaphysical sense. The title Son of God does not occur in the early preaching as reported in Acts.[21] It is not used even in the more developed teaching of Peter in the first Epistle ascribed to him, and where it does occur in the early preaching of Paul at Damascus, it is used only in the Messianic sense. "And straightway in the synagogues he proclaimed Jesus that he is the Son of God . . . proving that this is the Christ."[22] Even in the Pauline teaching, as represented in first Thessalonians and in the opening paragraph of the Epistle to the Romans, the term Son has still the primitive Messianic meaning. This primitive teaching does not go beyond a few statements about Jesus of Nazareth as the exalted Lord and Christ. These statements may, indeed, be regarded as a sort of incipient creed—"born, died, risen, exalted."[23] But they are not of the nature of a theology in the later sense, and it is misleading to speak with Weizsäcker[24] and others of "the first Christian theology." They are rather of the nature of a religious experience than of theological reasoning. There is nothing about the supernatural birth of the man Jesus of Nazareth. Paul knows nothing of the supernatural generation, which marks the developing estimate of Jesus in the later birth stories related in Matthew and Luke.

---

[20] ταῖς προσευχαῖς. These were the prayers of the Jewish worship in temple and synagogue, with some adaptation to the celebration of the Agape. In this respect they would have a Christian colouring. A sample may be contained in that given in the "Didache" on the occasion of the celebration of the Eucharist. It is quite primitive in character. See "Didache," ix.

[21] Acts viii. 37 is spurious.

[22] Ibid., ix. 20. This is brought out clearly in verse 22, "proving that this is the Christ."

[23] In the primitive confession of faith two other beliefs found special expression—that of God as Father (Aramaic Abba) and that of the imminent coming of the Lord (Aramaic Maranatha), both stressed by Paul in their original form, Rom. viii. 16 ; Gal. iv. 6 ; 1 Cor. xvi. 22. On these confessional expressions see Fabricius, "Festschrift für R. Seeberg," i. 21 f. (1929).

[24] "Apostolic Age," i. 33 (Eng. trans., 1894).

Jesus is " born of the seed of David, according to the flesh." [25]
He is not as yet a pre-existent being, as in the later Pauline
thought. He is elected, appointed, ordained by God to be the
Messiah. His death is foreknown and determined by God.
His resurrection is foreseen by the prophets. But he is not the
pre-existent Christ of the higher Jewish Apocalyptic, or of Paul
and other later writers. He is not the eternal, incarnate Son
of John. He is the Messianic king and Lord ; not God, or a
second God. The conviction of his Messiahship has entered
into the religious experience of the disciples. But they are
Jewish monotheists who take part in the temple worship as well
as the meetings of their own community, which constitutes
a party within Judaism like the synagogues of the Libertines,
etc., at Jerusalem. The belief in the Messianic Lord is quite
compatible with Jewish monotheism, which could combine
belief in God with that of a God-appointed Messiah. At the
same time, it is easy to see that what was a simple faith in the
primitive Jewish-Christian community might develop, under
Hellenist influence, into the more theological conception of the
God-man as the eternal, divine Logos and Son of God.[26]

V. Salvation

The acceptance of Jesus as Lord and Christ is an essential
condition of the salvation of Israel. In accordance with the
apocalyptic train of thought in the primitive Gospel, salvation
is understood in the Messianic sense. It means primarily
deliverance from the coming judgment, for which the remission
of sin is indispensable. In this sense Jesus is the Saviour,

---

[25] Rom. i. 3.

[26] Feine, who may be taken as a representative of the traditional standpoint,
sees in the attitude of the primitive community to Christ, a proof of the full
recognition of his divinity. " Unbedenklich zollen aber fortan die Christen
Jesus die Verehrung, die Gott gebührt." " Theologie des Neuen Testaments,"
199 (1910). This seems to me to go beyond the evidence. M'Giffert, on
the other hand, concludes that there is no evidence to show that the early
disciples "deified Jesus or thought of him as anything more than God's
servant and anointed. They had known him in the flesh—a man among
men ; with their Jewish traditions, the last thing they could have thought of
was to count him a divine being or identify him with God," " The God of
the Early Christians," 22 (1924). This hardly allows sufficient play to the
influence of the resurrection experience in enhancing their estimation of
him in his exalted state, though it is the case that this estimation did not go
the length of deifying him.

the Prince or Author of Life,[1] and the nature of the salvation
obtainable through him is clearly brought out by the belief
that he is destined to be the judge of the living and the dead.[2]
Hence the appeal to " save yourselves from this crooked
generation," [3] and the declaration that only through him is
this salvation possible.[4] To obtain it faith, in the sense of
" receiving " the proclamation about Jesus—" the word," the
words of this Life " [5]—is indispensable. " Believers " is a
distinctive designation of the members of the community.[6]
This faith, this submissive reception of the word—the fundamental requisite of salvation—involves repentance and baptism
" in " or " into " the name of Jesus Christ unto the remission
of sins. " And they said unto Peter and the rest of the apostles,
Brethren, what shall we do ? And Peter said unto them,
Repent ye and be baptised every one of you in the name of
Jesus Christ unto the remission of your sins." [7] Faith, repentance, baptism, remission—these are the essentials of the
primitive preaching of salvation. The emphasis on repentance,
baptism, remission recalls the message of John the Baptist,[8]
from whom the Christian practice of baptism seems to have
been derived.[9] Only, the Christian message has taken on a
different significance, in accordance with the altered situation
of the disciples, and in the light of their actual knowledge of
the Christ, whom John had foretold, and who, as the exalted
Lord, has become for them the object of faith. It reminds, too,
of Jesus' message, at the outset of his mission, of repentance in
view of the imminence of the kingdom. Jesus, indeed, whilst
submitting himself to baptism, had not practised this rite, and
the parting injunction to his disciples, in Matthew's Gospel,
to baptise in the triune name is not authentic. Nor is it certain
that in the primitive preaching baptism was invariably required
as a condition of salvation. Whilst it is emphasised in Peter's
first discourse and in other accounts of the primitive preaching
in Acts, there are passages in which only faith, repentance,

---

[1] Acts iii. 15, τὸν δὲ ἀρχηγὸν τῆς ζωῆς ; v. 31, καὶ σωτῆρα.
[2] *Ibid.*, x. 42.　　　　[3] *Ibid.*, ii. 40.　　　　　　　[4] *Ibid.*, iv. 12.
[5] *Ibid.*, ii. 41 ; iv. 4 ; v. 20.
[6] *Ibid.*, ii. 44 ; v. 14.　　　　　　　　　　　[7] *Ibid.*, ii. 37-38.
[8] Mark i. 4 ; Luke iii. 3.
[9] Heitmüller controverts this contention, " Im Namen Jesu," " Forschung
zur Religion und Literatur des Alten und Neuen Testaments," I. Heft, ii.
272 f. (1903-1904). In my opinion on insufficient grounds.

and remission are adduced. " Repent ye, therefore, and turn again that your sins may be blotted out." [10] " Through his name every one that believeth in him shall receive remission of sins." [11] These passages appear to have been derived by the writer of the Acts from a different source, in which baptism was apparently not accounted an essential of salvation, as it was not in the ministry of Jesus himself. If so, it erelong became an essential, and in including it in their preaching the disciples evidently inferred that they were acting in accordance with the mind of Jesus.

For Peter's hearers repentance means particularly contrition for the rejection of him " whom ye crucified." [12] Baptism " in " or " into " the name [13] brings out the heightened estimate of him as the exalted Lord, the Prince or Author of Life, though it is not yet a mark of separation from Judaism and could quite well accord with Jewish practice. [14] It is no purely symbolic act, as in the case of the Baptist. " In his name " implies the invocation of the name of Jesus, as the exalted Lord, over the baptised person, who yields himself to him. " Into his name " means the dedication to Jesus as his property, the seal of ownership, like that placed on slaves to mark them as the property of their master, and, in addition, the imparting to the baptised the power for which the name stands. [15] The name stands for the saving power which emanates from Jesus and operates in the healing of the body as well as the salvation of the soul. It is, however, no magical force. Its effective operation presupposes faith, begetting in the believer a real change of heart and the dedication of himself in baptism to Jesus, as his acknowledged Lord. " Faith in the name," on the part of Peter and John, and evidently on the part of the lame man himself, operates the first miracle of healing recorded in the Acts. " And by faith in his name hath his name made this man strong whom ye behold and know ;

---

[10] Acts iii. 19.   [11] Ibid., x. 43.

[12] Ibid., ii. 36 ; iii. 17 f.

[13] ἐπὶ τῷ ὀνόματι, εἰς τὸ ὄνομα. The first phrase is the one used in the early chapters of Acts.

[14] On this point see Pfleiderer, " Das Urchristenthum," i. 21-22 (2nd ed., 1902) ; H. J. Holtzmann, " Neutestamentliche Theologie," i. 421 (2nd ed., 1911).

[15] See Heitmüller, " Im Namen Jesu," 51 f., 106 f., 268. See also Bartlet, " Peake's Com.," 638 (1920).

yea, this faith which is through him (inspired by him) hath given him this perfect soundness in the presence of you all." [16] From it, as similarly conditioned, streams forth to the repentant and baptised sinner, the gift of the Holy Spirit,[17] though, in some instances, baptism " in " or " into " the name does not necessarily convey this gift,[18] and is not the exclusive condition of its bestowal, which may result from the preaching of the Word appropriated by the believer, and may precede baptism.[19]

Whether salvation was specifically connected with his death is not definitely apparent in the early chapters of Acts. It is only from Paul that we learn that in the primitive preaching the remission of sins was vitally related to the death on the Cross. " For I delivered unto you first of all that which also I received, how that Christ died for our sins according to the Scriptures." [20] The Scriptures referring to the Suffering Servant in Acts are more particularly Isaiah liii., and the necessity of the suffering of the Messiah as God's Servant does form a fundamental element in the preaching of Philip.[21] Otherwise, it is the apologetic aspect of the death of Christ that, in view of the offence of the Cross, is emphasised—the fact that, in spite of his death, he is the Messiah, since his death is in accordance with God's will. Moreover, the crucifixion, if in accordance with God's revealed will and purpose in the prophets, is represented as the wicked act of the Jews, which Stephen in particular reprobates as the act of " betrayers and murderers." [22] It is the acceptance of Jesus as the Messiah, coupled with repentance and baptism, that brings remission of sin. The " breaking of bread " [23] has not a sacrificial or sacramental character. It is a social-religious meal, a love feast (the Agape) in which believers nurture their fellowship with Jesus and with one another. Whether it concluded with the celebration of the Eucharist, as many infer, the writer does not say. In view of its institution by Jesus at the Last Supper,

[16] Acts iii. 6 f., 16. [17] Ibid., ii. 38.
[18] Ibid., viii. 16 f. According to the theory of the writer at least, who shows a tendency to confine its bestowal to the laying on of the hands of the apostles.
[19] Ibid., x. 44 ; xi. 15 f.
[20] 1 Cor. xv. 3 ; cf. 1 Thess. v. 10 ; Rom. iv. 25.
[21] Acts viii. 35.
[22] Ibid., vii. 52. [23] Acts ii. 42, 46.

2

and the later evidence of its combination with the Agape,[24] there is some force in the inference.

At the same time marked emphasis is laid in the primitive preaching on the suffering of the Christ, as the Master himself had done in the face of the looming tragedy of his closing career. Besides the apologetic presentation of the death on the Cross, the primitive preachers doubtless had in view its saving or redemptive aspect.

For Jesus himself his death evidently had such a significance. In the later phase of his mission he had on several occasions spoken to the disciples of its redemptive aspect. From Cæsarea Philippi onwards, he had recognised and made known to them its inevitability, and insisted on the necessity of losing one's life in order to save it. He appears to have combined with his conception of the Son of Man that of the Suffering Servant of Isaiah liii.—the martyred Israel who, by vicarious suffering under conquest and captivity, is represented as redeeming the nations. In the face of the imminent Cross, this thought of service by redemptive suffering had become the dominating thought of the closing period of his mission. "The Son of Man came not to be ministered to, but to minister and to give his life a ransom for many,"[25] he had told the disciples in reproof of the striving of the sons of Zebedee for first place in the Messianic kingdom. At the institution of the Eucharist at the Last Supper, he had spoken to them of the shedding of His blood in inauguration of the new covenant with them, which is sealed by it. "This is my blood of the (new) covenant, which is shed for many." The reference seems to be to Jeremiah xxxi. 32 f., in which the new covenant inaugurates the era of the direct and spiritual knowledge of God, coupled with the assurance of the spontaneous forgiveness of his people's iniquity. Jesus' self-sacrifice will thus contribute to the benefit of many. Whilst he sheds his blood on their behalf,[26] he does not definitely indicate in what sense and for what purpose he does so. Matthew, indeed, adds "into remission of sins."[27] But this is almost certainly

---

[24] 1 Cor. xi. 20 f. ; Acts xx. 7, 11.   [25] Mark x. 45 ; Matt. xx. 28.
[26] ὑπὲρ πολλῶν, "for many" in Mark xiv. 24, and Matt. xxvi. 28 ; ὑπὲρ ὑμῶν, "for you" in Luke xxii. 20 and in 1 Cor. xi. 24, where the phrase is used only of the giving of the bread.
[27] εἰς ἄφεσιν ἁμαρτιῶν.

an editorial addition. At the same time, the tradition received
and handed down by Paul [28] shows that the early disciples
believed his death to be in some sense for their sins. This
belief is, however, not based on any saying of Jesus himself,
but on an inference from the teaching of Scripture. It is
" according to the Scriptures," [29] and is in keeping with the
appeal to prophecy in proof of the necessity of his death and
the fact of his resurrection. The only definite saying of Jesus
himself on the nature of his death is that in which he describes
it as a ransom for many. For him it is the price paid for their
deliverance, presumably from the effects of sin. There is no
compelling reason to suppose that this saying, which is peculiar
to Mark and Matthew, is merely a reflection of the later belief
of the community in the redemptive character of the death of
the Christ. Its omission by Luke, who records the saying
in the form, " I am in the midst of you as he that serveth," [30]
suggests that there were two versions of it in the tradition, not
that Mark transformed it under Pauline influence. Still less
reason is there to question the declaration at the Last Supper
that, in dying on the Cross, he was shedding his blood in their
behalf. That the shedding of his blood had an efficacy in relation
to man's salvation from sin and judgment, was for him, we may,
nay must, say, an imperative belief in face of his imminent
doom. Only this belief, coupled with that in the resurrection,
could have given him the resolution and the strength to meet
this doom. This thought appears to have formed a distinctive
element in the primitive Gospel, and in this respect, also, the
primitive Gospel was in keeping with his own utterances on
the redemptive significance of his death. The remission of
sin was, in some sense, associated in the primitive preaching
with the suffering Christ. The blessing of the divine forgiveness is attainable through repentance and faith in the crucified
Messiah, whom God has appointed to accomplish his saving
purpose. His suffering is the means whereby " your sins
may be blotted out," of " turning away every one of you from
your iniquities." [31] It is not only foreseen by the prophets,
it is determined by God for a definite purpose—the remission
of sin, salvation from judgment. " In none other is there

---

[28] 1 Cor. xv. 3.
[29] κατὰ τὰς γραφάς.
[30] Luke xxii. 27.
[31] Acts iii. 18 f., 26.

salvation, for neither is there any other name under heaven that is given among men, wherein we must be saved." [32]

Was the death on the Cross, for Jesus and for the disciples, who preached salvation through his suffering, also an act of expiation, of propitiation for sin? Was the ransom a price paid to God's justice, a sacrifice required by God to cancel the guilt of sin? Was it one in the sense of service, or one in the sense of sin bearing to satisfy God's justice? The answer here is more problematic. Jesus does not tell us, and it is only by inference that we can form a judgment one way or the other. With the idea of bloodshed—at least of animals—in atonement for sin, both he and the disciples, as Jews, were quite familiar. Moreover, the idea of one man dying for the common good of the people, which the Fourth Gospel puts into the mouth of Caiaphas, [33] may also have been known to them, though the saying may be only the reflection of the writer of the Gospel a couple of generations after the crucifixion. In the Fourth Book of Maccabees, which is supposed to have been written some time between 63 B.C. and A.D. 38, [34] the martyr Eleazar, under Antiochus Epiphanes, prays that his death and that of his sons may mercifully be accepted as a satisfaction on behalf of the people, and that his blood may be their purification and his soul a ransom for theirs. [35] The book was possibly known in primitive Christian circles, though the indefinite primitive teaching on the subject does not tend to show that it was. They were certainly familiar with the figure of God's Suffering Servant in Isaiah liii., which contains the idea of an offering for sin (v. 10). Israel, as the Servant of the Lord, bears the pains and sicknesses of the nations, endures suffering at God's hands for their transgressions and iniquities, which have rendered such suffering necessary. In this sense the Servant offers his soul, his life as a guilt offering. He bears the sins of many and justifies many. But the bearing of sin is not penal, but moral. It is not understood in the sense of the sacrificial law,

---

[32] Acts iv. 12 ; *cf.* v. 31 ; x. 42-43.

[33] John xi. 50.

[34] See Townshend, "Apocrypha and Pseudepigrapha of the Old Testament," ed. by Charles, ii. 654.

[35] 4 Macc. vi. 28 ; *cf.* xvii. 31-32, where the same thought is expressed by the writer that through the blood of these righteous men and the propitiation of their death, God delivered Israel. In 2 Macc. vi. and vii. these martyrdoms are not said to be an expiation.

but in the prophetic sense of gratuitous service. It is vicarious
—that of the guiltless for the guilty. It does not seem to be a
propitiation of God's anger, a satisfaction made to God for
sin. The Servant vicariously endures in order that the nations
may thereby turn to God and be received into His love.[36]

If Jesus, in envisaging his death, had in view the Suffering
Servant of Second Isaiah, it does not, therefore, necessarily
follow that he conceived it as a propitiation, a satisfaction of
God's justice. Such a thought is hardly in harmony with the
general tenor of his teaching on the Father-God, whose forgiveness is freely available to the repentant sinner, as in the parable
of the Prodigal Son and other classic utterances. Both the
ransom saying and that on the shedding of his blood are
connected with the establishment of the kingdom of God
and the service rendered in suffering to this end. It was for
the sake of its realisation that he gave his life as a ransom,
shed his blood " for many," as in Isaiah liii. His death would
have a saving efficacy in leading many to repentance and faith
in him, and thereby into the kingdom. Sacrifice unto death
for the purpose of nullifying the effects of sin in frustrating the
realisation of the kingdom is the thought that runs through
his whole teaching on the absolute surrender of the soul to
God in order to attain its true life.[37] Whilst observing the
Jewish ritual, his thought moved in a higher spiritual sphere
than that of the current priestly religion, with its barbarous
practice of shedding innocent blood in atonement for sin. It
is this train of thought that he impressed on his disciples to
the end and exemplified in his own act of supreme sacrifice.
It was in this sense rather than that of a blood propitiation
to God that, in view of his own teaching, they seem to have

[36] Schultz, " Old Testament Theology," ii. 433. G. A. Smith, " Isaiah,"
ii. 363 f., takes the view that it is penal. So also Wade, " Isaiah," 339 (1911),
and Feine, " New Testament Theology," 127 f. Mr Gayford holds the penal
view, but seeks to make out that nevertheless " the death is not regarded in
itself as a satisfaction, a propitiation, an atonement." It is not the death,
but the vicarious offering of the life (the blood) that makes the atonement.
" Sacrifice and Priesthood," 117 f. (1924). Torrey also appears to share the
penal view. " The Servant suffers the penalty of the sin of the world,
and through his woes makes atonement to God for the heathen nations,"
" The Second Isaiah," 146 (1928). According to his interpretation the
Servant suffers vicariously, but he does not die. He only comes nigh to
death (421 f.). He thinks that Second Isaiah is post-exilic, and dates it about
the beginning of the fourth century B.C.
[37] On this subject see my " Historic Jesus," 222 f.

proclaimed that Christ " died for our sins according to the
Scriptures." It is significant that in the passage quoted from
Isaiah liii., in the preaching of Philip, it is the meekness and
the humiliation of the sufferer that are emphasised, though the
words actually quoted do not necessarily represent all that the
evangelist thought on the subject.

Some have, indeed, seen a hint of a propitiating sacrifice
in the reference, in the early preaching, to the slayers of Jesus
as " hanging him on a tree." [38]   The reference is to the passage
in Deuteronomy which adjudges the sinner, who has committed
a sin worthy of death, to be hanged on a tree as accursed
of God.[39]   Obviously the words of Peter refer to the manner,
not the nature of the death of Jesus, and it is only later that
Paul, by an all too arbitrary exegesis, reads into the passage in
Deuteronomy the expiatory inference that Christ, in redeeming
us on the Cross from the curse of the law, became a curse for us.[40]
So also Peter, in the first Epistle ascribed to him, represents
him as bearing our sins in his body upon the tree.[41]   But in so
doing the writer is obviously influenced by the later Pauline
conception of his death. To the actual disciples of Jesus,
at any rate, who composed the first members of the primitive
community, it could not apply. In virtue solely of their
acceptance of the Master's Messianic claim, apart from any
belief in the sacrificial death on the Cross, they were already
in his lifetime members of the kingdom.

The death on the Cross, whereby the sinner attains the
remission of sin, and is assured salvation from judgment,
thus appears in the early preaching to be vicarious in the
sense of rendering the supreme service for others. It does not
seem to be propitiatory.[42]   The apprehension of it is markedly
simpler than in the more developed thought of Paul. In
particular, saving faith in the suffering Christ is strikingly
different from the Pauline conception of it. It does not involve
a complete breach with the Law in order to ensure salvation.
The Pauline conception of it as implying the abolition of the
Law and the traditional religion is not there, and is not to be

[38] Acts v. 30 ; x. 39.   [40] Gal. iii. 13.
[39] Deut. xxi. 22.   [41] 1 Pet. ii. 24.
[42] I find my own conclusion in accord with that of Stevens, " The
Christian Doctrine of Salvation," 55 f. (1905).

read into the primitive Gospel. The Law and saving faith are not yet antagonistic. Saving faith is quite compatible with its observance, as in the Sermon on the Mount. Both co-operate in the life of the primitive disciple. His life is energised by his acceptance of the Christ and the consequent outpouring of the Spirit. So quickened he strives to carry out the Law in the spirit of Jesus in self-denial and well-doing and in loyal obedience to its mandates. There is not yet an antithesis between faith and works, Law and grace. Salvation by faith in Christ, apart from the works of the Law, is not yet on the horizon.

VI. The Coming of the Christ

Bound up with the Messianic conception of salvation is the belief in the coming of the Christ on the clouds of heaven (Parousia). " This Jesus which was received up from you into heaven shall so come in like manner as ye beheld him going into heaven." [1] Such is the assurance of the two men in white apparel, with which Luke concludes the story of the ascension. The story cannot be taken in the literal sense. It is a pictorial accretion. Its later accretion is revealed in the fact that it was evidently written in the light of the expansion of the Gospel as a universal religion in the Gentile world.[2] In like pictorial fashion in the closing chapter of his Gospel, Luke even represents Jesus as leading the disciples through the streets of Jerusalem to a spot looking over to Bethany (the Mount of Olivet), where the ascension takes place.[3] But the belief in the coming, which the two men in white apparel are thus pictorially made to announce, is undoubtedly a genuine trait of the primitive Gospel. The Maranatha of Paul and other reporters of the primitive tradition is a convincing proof of it. In the Acts it appears in Peter's proclamation of the ultimate effect and object of repentance and remission that " the Lord may send the Christ who hath been appointed for you, even Jesus ; whom the heaven must receive until the times of restoration of all things, whereof God spake by the mouth of his holy prophets." [4] Jesus himself had in the

---

[1] Acts i. 11.
[2] *Ibid.*, i. 8.
[3] Luke xxiv. 50 ; *cf.* Acts i. 12.
[4] Acts iii. 20-21.

apocalyptic discourse to the disciples cherished the belief in his return as the heavenly Son of Man and judge in great power and glory, and bidden them watch for this consummation. Peter is here undoubtedly echoing the mind of the Master. " And he charged us to preach unto the people that this is he which is ordained of God to be the Judge of quick and dead." [5]

The coming of the Christ was a current Jewish conception and the announcement of his coming in the primitive preaching was not, in itself, for the Jews something new and incredible. What was new and incredible was the assertion on which it was based—that the Jesus who had suffered death was, or could be, the Messiah, and would reappear from heaven to complete his Messianic function. For them, whilst the forerunner of the Messiah might reappear in the person of Elijah or other prophet, the Messiah himself could only come to reign. For the disciples, on the other hand, he had to come to suffer before he could come to reign. This was the new and incredible thing for current Jewish thought, to which the idea of a suffering Messiah was unthinkable. True, the Servant of the Lord, depicted in the Second Isaiah, was to fulfil the redemptive function by suffering for the nations. But the tragic figure depicted by the prophet was understood to personate the suffering people of Israel in the past, and was not applicable to the expected Messiah of later Jewish Apocalyptic. This Messiah was either a king of the House of David, appointed by God for this vocation, who would deliver the people from their pagan oppressors, or the supernatural figure of the Son of Man, who would appear as the agent of the divine transformation of the present age or order of things. It was this Son of Man idea, combined with that of the Suffering Servant that, as we have seen, Jesus seems to have embodied in his own person. As the Suffering Servant, he dies in the service of the kingdom or rule of God. As the Son of Man he will come on the clouds of heaven to hold the great assize and establish God's rule. This is the great innovation which he had introduced in the current Messianic expectation, and which the disciples proclaimed. The Christ whom God had chosen, who must needs suffer in accordance with his determinate counsel, and who has been

[5] Acts x. 42.

exalted to heaven, will erelong come to judge and reign. In
this proclamation they were undoubtedly echoing the mind of
the Master. The innovation was his, not theirs.

Hence the spirit of tense expectancy which is reflected in
the first Epistle to the Thessalonians and in first Peter and the
Book of Revelation, as well as in the early chapters of Acts,[6]
though, in view of the deferred hope of the passing years, the
warning about " times and seasons " is emphasised [7] and undue
anticipation is discouraged in the second Thessalonian Epistle.
The belief in the speedy spectacular coming might be visionary,
and ultimately, as we shall see, there appears a tendency to
spiritualise it, particularly in the Fourth Gospel. But it
imparted a tremendous energy, a feverish activity to the
incipient Christian mission, and, in this sense, it was of great
practical significance. The belief in the effective establishment of a new order of things, in an impending divine
intervention in history, for which repentance and remission
are preparing the way, accounts, in part at least, for the tidal
wave of conviction which made the primitive Gospel a vital
force within Judaism. Erelong, too, as the result of the
outpouring of the Spirit, it transcends the crasser nationalist
outlook and acquires a pre-eminently ethical and religious
aspect. There is still, indeed, a trace of the lingering belief
in the coming of a victorious king of the house of David to
establish the kingdom in the material sense, and restore Israel.[8]
Whilst the hope of a restored Israel thus survived in certain
Jewish-Christian circles, this feature of it is displaced by the
transcendental conception of the kingdom, which Jesus himself
had taught. Here the coming is associated with " the restoration of all things " and the judgment of the quick and the
dead.[9] Salvation from judgment is, indeed, primarily for
Israel. " To you *first* God has sent his Servant to bless
you," [10] and the expectation is that the coming will supervene

---

[6] 1 Thess. vi. 2 ; 1 Pet. i. 5 ; iv. 7 ; Rev. iii. 3 ; xvi. 15.
[7] Acts i. 7.   [8] *Ibid.*, i. 6 ; Luke i.
[9] *Ibid.*, iii. 21, ἀποκατάστασις πάντων ; x. 42-43. This seems to reflect
a knowledge of the Stoic doctrine of cycles or periods of creation when,
after its destruction at the end of each, the world would be created anew.
Some critics accordingly deny or doubt that Peter could have so spoken,
Foakes-Jackson, " Commentary on Acts," 29 (1931). He appears, however,
to have meant the apocalyptic new creation.
[10] *Ibid.*, iii. 26.

on Israel's repentance and reception of the Christ. But this salvation is evidently available, through Israel, for the Gentiles also. Peter is represented in the conversion of Cornelius and his household, and Philip in that of the Samaritans, as already extending the benefit of the primitive Gospel to those outside the pale of Judaism. The conversion of the Gentile as well as the Jew is to be undertaken before the coming and the judgment take place, though apparently on the understanding that the Gentile shall conform to Jewish religious practice. With his return his Messianic mission will be complete.

VII. The Inspired Community

With the belief in the coming of the Christ is combined the belief in the presence of the Holy Spirit, or simply Holy Spirit,[1] without the article. The outpouring of the Spirit is, in fact, regarded as a sign of, a preparation for " the last days," the near advent of the new age or æon, as Peter's quotation from Joel shows. Its presence and power form for him, as for his fellow Jews, a distinctive feature of the Messianic age. The divine inspiration of the individual and the community is thus one of the striking features of primitive Christianity. Viewed from the standpoint of the present, it is the conviction of the presence of the exalted Christ, through the Spirit, in both. Christ will speedily come in his glory as king and judge. In reality he is already spiritually there with his disciples. The Holy Spirit, or simply Holy Spirit, does not seem to imply a distinct personality, except as far as it is the personality of the exalted Christ reacting on hearts and minds which had been in close fellowship with the earthly Jesus. In the Old Testament the divine Spirit stands, generally, for the creative, enlightening, and inspiring activity of God himself in man and the world, as well as in the prophets. In the early chapters of Acts it is still conceived in the Old Testament sense of a

---

[1] Both phrases are used in the early chapters of Acts. There is no solid reason for assuming, with a number of scholars, that the outpouring of the Spirit and its effects, as depicted in the early chapters of Acts, is a reflection of the later conditions prevailing in the Gentile churches, especially Corinth, which the writer has transferred back to the early period. Given the Old Testament doctrine of the Spirit and the tense religious atmosphere of the early community, the phenomenon is quite credible. See E. F. Scott, " The Spirit in the New Testament," 81 f. (1923).

quickening power, which energises the soul and conveys the prophetic fervour and utterance. This is sufficiently evident from the appeal to the prophet Joel and from the neuter gender used by Peter of the Spirit, in reference to its outpouring on " the day of Pentecost." [2] It is a concrete experience—the link between the exalted Christ and the disciples, forged by the resurrection faith which had restored to them this fellowship in a higher form. From the moment that they attained this faith the disciples must have been conscious of this inspiration.[3] The theory of the writer of the Acts is that it first came to them on Pentecost Day, and this theory he seeks to convey to the reader. The Fourth Gospel, on the other hand, makes Jesus impart the Spirit on his resurrected appearance to them,[4] and it does seem more likely that this vital experience was accompanied by a spiritual exaltation in reaction from the preceding depth of despair. The particular manifestation of it on Pentecost day took the form of the gift of tongues—the Glossolalia, or ecstatic, unintelligible utterance, which Luke mistook for the ability to speak foreign languages. It marks the beginning of the Christian mission in the form of Peter's first missionary discourse, if not, as is usually asserted, of the Church, which was already in existence in the circle of disciples founded by Jesus himself and assembled in the upper room at Jerusalem, after the resurrection and the appearance of the Master.[5]

This dynamic experience was apparently not the only one of its kind. There was at least one repetition of it,[6] though without the gift of tongues, and there is no compelling reason to regard, with Harnack, this similar incident as merely a variant report of that of Pentecost. At a time of religious exaltation such spiritual phenomena are the rule rather than the exception.

In the closing chapter of his Gospel, Luke represents Jesus as promising to the disciples the endowment of this divine power. According to this report, he assures them that they will be " invested with power from on high." [7] In the opening

---

[2] Acts i. 16, 33, " he hath poured forth this " (thing), τοῦτο.

[3] I think that M'Giffert's contention to this effect is correct, " History of Christianity in the Apostolic Age," 48 f. (1897).

[4] John xx. 22.
[5] Acts i. 13.

[6] *Ibid.*, iv. 31.
[7] Luke xxiv. 49.

chapters of Acts, the promise is renewed in the assurance of
the baptism with the Holy Spirit, which is contrasted with
John's baptism with water.[8] It means the transference to
them " of the power " [9] which had operated so mightily in
Jesus himself. The exact historicity of the scene in both cases
may be questionable. But the belief in possession by the
Spirit of God runs through the whole record of his life as the
explanation of the secret power in and behind his ministry
of healing and teaching. In the discourse at Nazareth he had,
according to Luke, inaugurated his mission as the medium
of the Spirit of the Lord by reading the appropriate passage
from Isaiah. It was in the power of this Spirit that the disciples
inaugurated theirs on Pentecost Day, in the attempt to perpetuate
his mission through their activity in healing and teaching, in
preparation for the grand climax of his triumphant coming.

In representing the individual and the community as
inspired by this dynamic Spirit, the writer of the Acts reflects
historic reality, though he misunderstands the character of
the manifestation on Pentecost Day, and shows a tendency to
make the apostles the medium of the conferring of the Spirit,
in accordance with the view current at the time when he wrote.[10]
It is evident from his own narrative in the early chapters of the
Acts that the gift could be experienced as the result of faith and
baptism or faith alone.[11] Not only is the inspiration of the
Spirit in all believers an additional proof of the Messiahship of
Jesus, as in the missionary discourse of Peter, following the
account of its outpouring. It is a vitalising force which
manifests itself, in both the individual and the community,
in the quickening of the natural gifts or charismata of the
believer ; in enthusiastic, self-denying service ; in the healing
power of an invincible faith ; in the assured conviction of the
truth of the Gospel ; in irrepressible joy and in fearless ardour
in the face of persecution and even death. Its reality is vouched
by a much earlier document than the Acts—the testimony of
Paul, who reminds the Thessalonians " how that our Gospel
came not unto you in word only, but also in *power*, and in the
Holy Ghost, and in much assurance." [12] The early community

[8] Acts i. 4-5.
[9] *Ibid.*, i. 8.
[10] *Ibid.*, viii. 14, etc.
[11] *Ibid.*, ii. 38 ; v. 32 ; *cf.* iv. 31.
[12] 1 Thess. i. 5.

is an inspired community. The gift of the Spirit is the gift of the Father,[13] as in the case of Jesus himself. Experimentally, it is also the Spirit of Jesus,[14] inspiring them with the heavenly power whereby he was enabled to carry on his own mission of healing and teaching, and perpetuating it in theirs.[15]

VIII. THE PRIMITIVE GOSPEL AND JUDAISM

Primitive Christianity is emphatically the religion of the Spirit on which Jesus had laid such stress against the current legalist one. It conforms, indeed, to the established religious usages. So little of a revolutionary subjectivism did the Pharisee, Gamaliel, see in it that he is found opposing the persecuting spirit of the high-priestly Sadducean hierarchy, on the ground that the movement may be of God, and advising its members to leave the issue to Him. Erelong, in fact, we hear of " certain of the sect of the Pharisees who believed," [1] and Ananias of Damascus, the early disciple who baptised Paul, is described as " a devout man according to the law, well reported of by all the Jews that dwelt there." [2] In this respect the primitive disciples, unlike their Master, whilst proclaiming and confessing Jesus, the Christ, were careful to avoid a collision with the pundits of the law. Among the Jewish Hellenist converts, on the other hand, the reaction from traditional Judaism in the spirit of Jesus himself erelong finds marked expression in the preaching of Stephen. Stephen stands out as the aggressive critic of the perverse religious spirit of his race, which lives in his persecutors. In the lengthy discourse before the Sanhedrin he reprobates its rebellious faithlessness, as evidenced by its history. Towards its conclusion he contrasts the Tabernacle or Tent of Meeting in the wilderness with the temple, as the true house of God, emphasises His spiritual worship, whose temple is the universe, and denounces Jewish obtuseness and perverseness in resisting the Holy Spirit and persecuting the prophets, the mouthpiece of the Spirit and the harbingers of the Christ. In so doing they have been untrue to the Law, as originally delivered,

---

[13] Acts ii. 33.
[14] Paul uses both designations—the Spirit of God, the Spirit of Christ.
[15] Acts iii. 4 f. ; iv. 30 ; v. 12 f.
[1] *Ibid.*, xv. 5.   [2] *Ibid.*, xxii. 12.

and have filled up the measure of their guilt by murdering the Righteous One who had fulfilled it.[3]   In his more spiritual apprehension of religion, his aggressive attitude towards historic Judaism and its representatives in the present, the speaker strikes the old prophetic note.   The difference of spirit and outlook comes into vivid relief in the concluding portion of the speech, and seems to presage the disruption between the old faith and the new.   The contrast is, indeed, rather between traditional and what is to Stephen true Judaism than between Judaism and Christianity.   For Stephen, the representative of the Hellenist-Christian section of the Church, as for the purely Hebrew believers, the primitive community is still a sect or party within Judaism, which is only distinguished by its faith in Christ as the actual Messiah. Both sections, so far, appear as members of an association of believers in Jesus as the Messiah within the Jewish religious fellowship.   The charge of speaking against Moses and changing the customs which Moses delivered is described as false.[4]   The speech, in fact, breathes a spirit of deep veneration for Moses and the Law as " the living Words " of God.[5]   At the same time, there is already discernible in the tendency represented by the speaker a certain reaction from traditional Judaism [6] in favour of a more spiritual religion, and this tendency might erelong lead to the emancipation of the primitive Gospel from its Jewish limitations.   As the result of his martyrdom the movement on behalf of this emancipation speedily takes shape in the preaching of the Gospel to the Greeks as well as to the Jews at Antioch.[7]   It is not without a poignant interest that the man who was to take a leading part in this movement was among the instigators of Stephen's martyrdom.   " And Saul was consenting unto his death." [8]   Did the clarion words of the doomed martyr, in testimony of the heavenly existence of the triumphant Son of Man, continue to ring in the ears of the young Pharisaic zealot from Tarsus ?

---

[3] Acts vii. 38 f., 46 f., 51 f.   The designation " The Righteous One " is probably a reference to Isa. liii. 11.

[4] *Ibid.*, vii. 11 f.   [5] *Ibid.*, vii. 38.

[6] M'Giffert discovers no trace of an incipient reaction from Judaism in Stephen's discourse, " History of Christianity in the Apostolic Age," 85 f. I think that there is such a trace.

[7] Acts xi. 20.   [8] *Ibid.*, viii. 1 ; *cf.* vii. 58.

IX. AN EXPERIENCED GOSPEL

The primitive Gospel thus breathes a distinctively Jewish atmosphere. It is a combination of Jewish religious thought with the definite recognition of the risen and exalted Christ and Lord, and the religious implications which this involves. The train of thought, the religious usage, and the outlook on life and history are Jewish. Jewish the idea of a Messianic deliverer, the doctrine of a resurrection, the apocalyptic view of history, the judgment, baptism, the common meal, etc. All this is familiar to the student of Hebrew religion. What was original in it was Jesus himself rather than the message about him. " Jesus," says Irenæus, " brought all that was new in bringing himself." [1] " The originality of Jesus," says Deissmann, " lies in his whole personality, in the peculiar energy of his experience of the living God. It is not his concepts that are original, but his power ; not his formulæ, but his confessions ; not his dogmas, but his faith ; not his system, but his personality. . . . The new, the epochmaking thing is himself." [2] And what is new in the Primitive Gospel is the centring of it all in a historic personality and the linking it up with the life and mind of the historic Jesus. It is based, as we have repeatedly pointed out, on what he claimed to be or had become. It is primarily an appeal to experience. It is personal testimony to Jesus the Christ and Lord. What the apostles proclaim is not doctrine in the ordinary sense of mere belief, though the writer of the Acts, looking back from a later standpoint, speaks of " the apostles' teaching." It is a conviction about Jesus, based not on the schools, but on personal contact with the Master in his life, and spiritual contact with the Lord through the resurrection experience. There is, indeed, the beginning of reflection about him in the apologetic attempt to explain and vindicate his death, resurrection, and exaltation by the appeal to the divine decree and to prophecy. But it is personal conviction about Jesus as he had been and become to them—as he lived amongst them and now lived in their hearts and thoughts—that forms its distinctive content and imparts to it the character of a living message. The Primitive Gospel perpetuates the power of Jesus' personality.

[1] " Adv. Haer.," iv. 34, 1.
[2] " The Religion of Jesus and the Faith of Paul," 149 (1923).

It is this that makes it the dynamic of a new movement which already bids fair to become a world movement. The Church owed the beginnings of its organised existence to the power emanating from Jesus as Master and Lord which, in spite of the antagonism of official Judaism and the apparent failure of the Master himself, enables his followers to continue and perpetuate his mission. This power is already becoming the most living religious influence in the ancient world. This potential miracle doubtless owed much to the leadership of the Twelve, especially of Peter. The real secret of it lies in the close association with the historic Jesus which had discovered to them the unique potency of the Master, whose personality had indelibly impressed itself on their hearts and minds.

To modern thought some of the ideas embodied in the primitive preaching may seem problematic. The appeal to prophecy is not always convincing. That King David foresaw the resurrection of the Christ, as Peter contends,[3] is rather crude. That the risen Jesus is seated at the right hand of God, as Peter proclaimed and Stephen envisaged, is an imaginative touch of Hebrew symbolism.[4] The divine decree of the death on the Cross has for us, as I have noted, its speculative difficulties.[5] The idea of a coming on the clouds of heaven is naïve. The Messianic belief, with which these childlike notions are bound up, has its drawbacks for the modern thinker. The apocalyptic element in the Primitive Gospel is, in this respect, a hindrance rather than a help to faith. But Jesus had undoubtedly spiritualised this element, and the grosser features of it have disappeared into the background in the faith of his disciples. After all, at the root of this apocalyptic lies the fact of a moral government of the world and the moral responsibility of the individual in a world so governed—the obligation to repent of sin, to turn to God, to live the higher life in the light of this fundamental fact. This is what really gave birth to Christianity, coupled with the fact that in Jesus of Nazareth there appeared

[3] Acts ii. 26 f.

[4] Sitting or standing on the right hand of the Lord can only be figuratively understood. It expresses the idea of the divine power exercised in the higher heavenly sphere, in contrast to the lower earthly sphere in which the left hand of God operates, Ps. cxviii. 16; Isa. xlviii. 3. See Strack and Billerbeck, " Kommentar," ii. 619.

[5] On the crude and barbarous idea of vicarious bloodshed for the expiation of sin, see the conclusion of Section V. of the following chapter.

one worthy to be its founder. To say that he, through his
disciples, was worthy to be the founder of the Christian Church,
as the corporate agent of God's purpose in the salvation of men,
is to explain the continuance and permanence of his mission.
He and they thought in the apocalyptic groove, and perhaps
without this Messianic belief, as embodied in a concrete
personality, the memory of his personality might have perished.
The Gospel might never have taken root and the movement
inaugurated by him might have been extinguished by his
death, though it is difficult to believe that, even minus this
belief, the new spiritual life which he had created in their
souls would have evaporated into blank silence.[6] It is at
least a measure of their estimate of the historic Jesus. Whether
we share this Jewish belief or not in the sense that these
primitive Christians shared it, it serves to convey to us a sense
of the surpassing greatness of the life and personality in which
they saw the embodiment of it. This at all events was a reality,
and this reality is the abiding thing. The nearer to him, the
nearer to this reality.

The fact of this new spiritual life needs no apology and
no critical readjustments. The faith in Jesus the Christ is,
on its practical side, the best vindication of itself and of
his claim to the religious supremacy of the world. Even as
reflected in the representation of the writer of the Acts at a
distance of more than half a century, we feel its inspiration and
its exaltation of heart and mind. " The day of the Lord "
is already there in all its " power." The kingdom of God
in this sense is already being established. The first years
of the Christian Church are one long day of Pentecost, a time
of " signs and wonders," a dynamic time, a time of irrepressible
gladness, of wonderful enthusiasm in well-doing, of self-denying
devotion and benevolence—the radiant spring morning of the
Church. It is an extraordinary transition from the hopelessness
of the Jewish spirit under the régime of the Roman conqueror,
and the heaviness of soul under the load of the Law to the
enthusiastic assurance, the dynamic experience of the new
religious faith in the exalted Messiah. This is a decided

---

[6] Harnack thinks that it probably would. " The Gospel would probably
have perished, if the forms of primitive Christianity had been scrupulously
maintained in the Church," " History of Dogma," i. 75 (Eng. trans., 1894).

advance on current Judaism, a new departure in the spirit of
Jesus himself, tending to reshape old beliefs and usages, to
enlarge the religious horizon in a more spiritual direction, to
transform the religious life. The " living oracles," the spiritual
temple, of which Stephen speaks, tend to displace alike the
legal verbalism of the scribes and the ritual worship of the
priests. It is this new Spirit-inspired life, not a Messianic
kingdom in the literal apocalyptic sense, that takes its rise
with the primitive community.

NOTE ON THE SOURCES

Besides the early chapters of the Acts of the Apostles,
which narrate the beginnings of the Christian mission, light
is thrown on the Primitive Gospel by other New Testament
writings. In certain passages of the Pauline Epistles—the
earliest Christian documents—and the First Epistle of Peter, in
which the primitive teaching is reflected, we are in closer touch
with the incipient Christianity than in the Acts. Even if we
assume that the first Epistle ascribed to Peter was not written
by him, it undoubtedly contains echoes of the early apostolic
preaching. In the Synoptic Gospels which, in their present
form, are of later composition than the Pauline Epistles, there
are also reflections of primitive thought about Jesus, as well as
a genuine record of what the Master taught and achieved.
The Synoptic tradition (especially as represented by Mark)
contains what was narrated and believed about Jesus in the
primitive community, and shows how his personality and
message appeared to the disciples before the more developed
conception of both supervened, even if it also shows traces of the
influence of this conception.   In Matthew we have the primitive
limitation of the Gospel to the Jews combined with the later
universalism, which is especially characteristic of Luke. The
emphasis on the observance of the Law, so characteristic of
Matthew, is another reflection of the early Jewish-Christian
standpoint. So also in the Epistle of James and the Book
of Revelation, which contain characteristic indications of
archaic Jewish-Christian ideas. Something may also be
gleaned from the other New Testament writings, including the
Fourth Gospel, in spite of its markedly subjective character.

The main source for the earliest Christian movement is, however, the first part of the Acts, which attempts to present this movement from the resurrection onwards. During the last thirty years the authorship, composition, and historicity of this source have been the subject of keen discussion, and this discussion has been reviewed with great fullness in Vol. II. of " The Beginnings of Christianity," edited by Foakes-Jackson and Lake (1922), in which a number of competent scholars have joined with the editors in focussing it and its results. This is the most valuable recent contribution to the subject, though it does not finally settle a number of the questions involved in the problem. It is generally agreed that the author of the Acts is the same person as the author of the Third Gospel, and tradition has assigned both to Luke, the companion of Paul. Critical opinion strongly differs, however, in its evaluation of this tradition, and this is strikingly brought out in this volume, in which different writers argue out the case for and against the tradition. On the whole, the arguments for, which were insistently put forward by Ramsay, Hawkins, and particularly by Harnack in the first decade of this century, are feasibly convincing. At the same time there is always the difficulty of surmounting the doubt whether a companion of Paul could have portrayed some things in the Acts as he has done, if, as we should naturally infer, he had an intimate knowledge of the Apostle and his writings. Harnack's works on the subject are all available in English translations. See " Luke the Physician " (1907), " The Acts of the Apostles " (1909), and " Neue Untersuchungen zur Apostelgeschichte " (1911), the translation of which I have not seen. See also Cadbury's criticism in *Harvard Theological Studies* (1919). In composing the Acts Luke made use of tradition, oral or written, which he wove into a consecutive narrative, and which, apart from traces of the author's later standpoint and colouring, reflect the main content of the incipient Christianity. Legendary elements have intruded themselves into the tradition (the account of the visible ascension, for instance, which is a later popular presentation of the exaltation of Jesus). Misinterpretation of facts are patent (the speaking in foreign languages for the Glossolalia). The gift of the Spirit is limited to the mediation of the Apostles, in accordance with their later enhanced ecclesiastical importance, though, from his own narrative, it is clear that it was originally not so. He is at times extremely credulous and also inexact. The discourses reported can hardly be the actual words of the speaker, and Luke himself may, in accordance with ancient historic method, have thrown the content of the preaching into the form of speeches (see on this point Foakes-Jackson, " Commentary on Acts," Introduction, 15 f. (1931)). Nevertheless, the narrative does in substance give a reliable account both of events and the primitive teaching, which is too archaic to be invented, though we may hesitate to adopt Mr Torrey's contention that chapters 1–15 are simply a Greek translation of an Aramaic original, written by an early Jerusalem Christian (" Composition and Date of the Acts," *Harvard Theological Studies* (1916)). (See also Cadbury, " The Making of Luke-Acts " (1927)).

There are numerous secondary works on primitive Christianity. I have found the following in German helpful, whilst demurring to the more or less pronounced tendency to deny or minimise, with critics like Wellhausen, the genetic connection between the teaching of Jesus and that of the apostles, and to ascribe the apocalyptic ideas, etc., in the Synoptic Gospels to them and the primitive community, rather than to Jesus himself. This tendency to derive the main ideas of primitive Christianity from the apologetic reflection of his followers on Jesus has certainly been overdone in some of these works. Weizsäcker, " The Apostolic Age," i. (English trans., 1894) ; Holtzmann, " Neutestamentliche Theologie," i. (2nd ed., 1911) ; Pfleiderer, " Das Urchistenthum," i. (2nd ed., 1902) ; Wernle, " Beginnings of Christianity," i. (English trans., 1903, brilliant, but rather one-sided) ; J. Weiss, " Das Urchristenthum," concluded by Knopf (1917, in many respects an excellent example of the Liberal school of thought) ; Schlatter, " Geschichte der ersten Christenheit " (4th ed., 1927, a rather slight outline). Feine, " Theologie des Neuen Testaments " (1910) represents the Conservative standpoint. Von Dobschütz, " Probleme des apostolischen Zeitalters " (1904), discusses a number of problems connected with the beginnings of Christianity, as these presented themselves about thirty years ago. It is still helpful. In English there are solid contributions

by M'Giffert, " History of Apostolic Christianity " (1897), and
Stevens, " The Christian Doctrine of Salvation " (1905), and
sketches by Bartlet, " The Apostolic Age " (1900), and Ropes,
" The Apostolic Age " (1906), which, however, do not specially
deal with doctrine. Among commentaries in English, that of
Rackham, with its exhaustive Introduction (4th ed., 1922), is
written from the orthodox standpoint. Those of Menzies in
Peake's " Commentary " (1920), Blunt in the " Clarendon
Bible " (1922), Foakes-Jackson (1931), Moffatt " Commentaries," and, in German, Knopf, in J. Weiss' " Schriften des
neuen Testaments," i. (2nd ed., 1907), represent more or less
the critical-historical standpoint.

CHAPTER II

THE PAULINE GOSPEL

I. Paul and the Gospel

In his Epistles Paul speaks of his message as " the Gospel,"
and of his preaching as " evangelising." What he preaches is
" the Gospel of God," or " of Christ," or simply " the Gospel."
Sometimes he substitutes " the word of the Lord," or " the
word of faith," or " the truth." [1] To judge from the sum-
maries of his mission preaching in the Epistles, this Gospel
is a reflection of the primitive proclamation. It is concerned
with the death, resurrection, exaltation, and return of Christ,
the Lord. " We preach not ourselves, but Christ Jesus as
Lord," he tells the Corinthians.[2] To the Romans he adduces
the primitive appeal to prophecy and the resurrection in proof
of the Messianic sonship of the historic Jesus. " Separated
unto the Gospel of God promised afore by the prophets
concerning his Son, who was born of the seed of David according to the flesh and declared to be the Son of God with power,
according to the spirit of holiness, by the resurrection from
the dead, even Jesus Christ our Lord." [3] He tells the
Corinthians that what he preached to them he had learned
from the primitive tradition of the death, burial, resurrection,
and appearances of Christ to the disciples.[4]

As in the primitive Gospel, confession of Jesus as Lord
and implicit belief in his resurrection is the indispensable
condition of salvation. " If thou shalt confess with thy mouth
Jesus as Lord, and shalt believe in thy heart that God raised
him from the dead, thou shalt be saved." [5] The same primitive

[1] 1 Thess. i. 6, 8 ; Rom. x. 8 ; ii. 8, etc. " The word of faith " is
the Gospel in the distinctively Pauline sense of saving faith in contrast to
works.

[2] 2 Cor. iv. 5.

[3] Rom. i. 1-4.

[4] 1 Cor. xv. 1 f.

[5] Rom. x. 9.

note appears in the preaching to the Thessalonians, who have turned from idols unto God.[6]

The Pauline Gospel is thus based on the primitive Gospel and, through it, on the teaching of Jesus himself on his passion, resurrection, and exaltation. It is in this sense the Gospel of Jesus as well as the Gospel about Jesus. In contrast to this acknowledged dependence on the primitive Gospel, there is, indeed, a marked tendency in other passages to emphasise his independence of the primitive tradition. He speaks of " my Gospel " or " our Gospel " in a markedly distinctive sense.[7] In the Epistle to the Galatians he asserts categorically that he neither received it from man, nor was taught it by man, but derived it by direct revelation from Christ.[8] This is certainly an excessive statement. In the fever of the controversy with the Judaisers and other opponents he was prone to over-statement. His dependence on the primitive preaching is patent from the samples which he gives in the Epistles of his own mission preaching. This preaching thus reproduces essentials of the Gospel in its primitive form, and in this respect may fairly be described as the Gospel of Jesus himself. It retains the thought of his self-sacrifice for the salvation of others. It emphasises his claim to be the revealer of God and the instrument of His will in achieving the promised redemption and the consummation of the new order or age. It enthrones him as the exalted Lord who, in virtue of the resurrection, takes the place of the earthly Master in the faith of his disciples. It perpetuates his spiritual view of religion and his ethical teaching. Even in its universalism it only gives explicit expression to the implications contained in Jesus' spiritual conception of God and the wider outlook of the closing period of his mission, which embraced Samaritan as well as Jew.

At the same time, the primitive Gospel undoubtedly under-went a development of a far-reaching character in the mould of Paul's religious thought and experience. There is substantial truth in his claim to independence of the other apostles, if he at times tends to exaggerate this independence. He does not merely reiterate or elaborate the primitive Gospel. He makes an original contribution to it out of his own thought

[6] 1 Thess. i. 9-10.
[7] Rom. ii. 16 ; xvi. 25 ; 2 Cor. iv. 3.   [8] Gal. i. 12.

and experience. In doing so he puts into it a good deal that it did not contain. He not only develops, he creates. He did more than any other man to free the nascent faith from its Jewish limitations by maintaining the right of the Gentile believer to freedom from Jewish legalism. In thus emancipating the Gospel from Jewish legalism, he enabled it to take root and expand in the Græco-Roman world. He transmuted it from a simple faith in Jesus as the approved Messiah and Lord into a redemptive religion independent of, and really incompatible with, Judaism. In so doing, he markedly heightened the person of Christ as well as greatly enlarged his redemptive function. He presented Christ to the Gentile mind as the divine redeemer, rather than the Jewish Messiah, and thus met the Gentile aspiration for a Saviour God and life eternal. He attributed to him a cosmic as well as a religious significance as the agent of the divine will and purpose in creation and its redemption. His death, resurrection, and exaltation constitute the supreme fact in the history of both the universe and man. The problem of redemption embraces the whole universe, and in Christ this problem finds its solution apart from any limitation of race or legal prescription. In relation to man, this solution is found in a distinctive theory of expiation by the blood of Christ, in an elaborately constructed doctrine of justification by faith apart from the works of the Law, and of the reconciliation between God and man thereby achieved by Christ. Moreover, in this theory the Cross becomes the means of the ethical renewal of the believer in mystic fellowship with Christ in his death and resurrection. It makes possible the ethical and spiritual life—the higher life—which is absolutely unattainable by way of the Law.

This, in brief, is the Gospel which Paul develops in the Epistles. It assuredly marks a development of the primitive faith, though the primitive faith might furnish the basis of the imposing structure which the original mind of Paul built on it. So much is this the case, that it is no exaggeration to see in its creator the second, if not, with Wrede and Wernle, the real founder of Christianity. It was Paul, more than any other man of the first generation of believers, that made possible the reception of the Gospel in the Græco-Roman world. Harnack even hazards the opinion that without this transformation the primitive Gospel would probably have perished.[9]   One wonders whether the influence of the life, teaching, and person of Jesus, as recorded in the Synoptic Gospels, would thus have flickered into extinction.   This influence was perpetuated and intensified by these Gospels, which took shape in the instruction of the Christian communities, and in view of this fact this assumption is extremely questionable.   Equally questionable, on the other hand, as we shall see later, is the assumption that the developed Pauline Gospel is, in all respects, substantially an exact, or at least a legitimate interpretation of that of Jesus.   It is rather a transmutation than a transmission.   Meanwhile, in order to account for this transmutation, it is necessary to examine its antecedents in the religious and intellectual influences that underlie it.

II. Antecedents of the Pauline Gospel

The main formative influence was undoubtedly the Hebrew one.   We are not left merely to conjecture.   We have his own testimony in the Epistles to the Galatians and Philippians. In speaking of his pre-Christian experience, he reminds the Galatians of the fact, well known to them, that he had advanced in the Jews' religion beyond many of his fellows, being exceedingly zealous for the traditions of the fathers.[1]   To the Philippians he emphasises his descent from the tribe of Benjamin, his ultra-racial and religious spirit as a Hebrew of the Hebrews, his devotion to the law as a Pharisee, which made him the bitter persecutor of the church.[2]   Equally conclusive is the high estimate of the privileges of Israel as the chosen people, which he continued to cherish long after he became a Christian.[3]

Even without this direct testimony we should infer from the general train of thought of his Epistles that he had grown up in an intensely Hebrew atmosphere.   He had a profound knowledge of the Hebrew scriptures, though he quotes from the Greek version of them.   As a child he learned not only to read, but to memorise " the Book of the law " in the original Hebrew [4] (Mishnah).   As a young man he passed through the

---

[9] " History of Dogma," i. 75.   [1] Gal. i. 13-14.
[2] Phil. iii. 4-6 ; cf. Rom. xi. 1 and 2 Cor. xi. 22.
[3] Rom. ix. 3-5.
[4] Smith, " Life and Letters of St Paul," 22 f. (1919).

school of the Rabbi or Rabban [5] Gamaliel at Jerusalem, who
instructed him "according to the strict manner of the law of
our fathers." [6] This instruction consisted of the interpretation
of the sacred writings (*Midrash*), and as the result of it he
obtained that mastery of Rabbinic exegesis and reasoning of
which his Epistles bear such ample trace. The Rabbinic exegesis
did not ignore the obvious or literal meaning of Scripture.
But it was concerned mainly with the additional meaning
supposed to underlie the plain text, which is to be extracted
by the allegoric method. Proficiency in this kind of interpretation was an essential of the office of Rabbi, and Paul's resource
in seeking to prove his Christian contentions from the Old
Testament shows that he possessed this qualification in a
high degree. He does not make a lavish use of the allegoric
method in his Epistles. But he handles the Scriptures in a very
free fashion, allegorises in the usual arbitrary fashion on
occasion, and is not much concerned with the exact historic
sense. For him, as for the earlier apostles, the appeal to
Scripture is the indispensable proof of the claim of the new
faith to be the true religion. It is sufficient to quote a text from
the law, the prophets, even the purely historical narratives, to
clinch the assertion or the argument in support of this claim,
apart from the historic meaning in the light of the context.
The supreme authority ascribed to the Old Testament, thus
arbitrarily handled, is of itself sufficient to show to what an
extent the Hebrew element entered into his Christianity.

In addition to the Rabbinic method, he evidently derived
from this source [7] many of the ideas to which he gave a Christian

---

[5] The higher title conferred on a distinguished Rabbi.

[6] Acts xxii. 3. " Brought up in this city " (Jerusalem) probably means
that he had been trained in the law there, not that he had spent his childhood
and youth there.

[7] Mr Montefiore questions whether Paul derived his ideas from the true
Rabbinic teaching of his time. He seeks to show that he was reared in
what he deems the inferior Rabbinic teaching of his Hellenist-Jewish environment. It is an acquaintance with this pseudo-Rabbinic teaching that
his Epistles reveal. In support of this thesis he rejects, with Loisy, as
unhistoric the tradition that Paul was a disciple of Gamaliel at Jerusalem,
and compares his Rabbinism with that revealed in the later Rabbinic writings,
say, A.D. 500. His argumentation is highly theoretic, and to me not convincing, in view of Paul's explicit testimony to his strict Pharisaic upbringing,
which I see no substantial reason to question. In the face of it, it is not easy
to maintain that he had imbibed what Mr Montefiore calls an inferior type
of Rabbinic teaching. See his interesting book, " Judaism and St Paul "
(1914).

adaptation. The function of the Rabbi was interpretation in accordance with the exegetical rules of the school, not the systematic elaboration of a theology. Even so, his teaching included certain characteristic conceptions with which his pupils were familiarised, and these Paul brought over into his Christian faith. Below his Christian teaching there is thus a substratum of Rabbinic doctrine which contributed to shape the content of his Christian Gospel. The emphasis on Jewish monotheism and the heinousness of Gentile idolatry, for instance, which forms so characteristic a feature of the presentation of the Gospel to the Gentile world, as in the first chapter of the Epistle to the Romans. With this is combined the doctrine of the Messiah in the form of the transcendental figure of Jewish Apocalyptic. A number of the apocalyptic writers belonged to the Pharisaic party, and we may assume from the story of his conversion that, as a Pharisee, he had a keen interest in this sublime figure, as depicted in " The Book of Enoch," though he evidently revolted against the Christian conception of a suffering Messiah. In spite of Isaiah liii., such a conception was unknown to the current apocalyptic in which Paul's mind appears to have been steeped. It was for him and the Jews generally the great stumbling-block, and his bitter persecution of the nascent Church seems to have been largely actuated by his revulsion from the monstrous idea that the crucified Jesus could be the promised and expected Messiah. But it may be taken as certain that he had some knowledge of the pre-existent Messiah as depicted in " The Book of Enoch," and also of the conception of the divine Word or Wisdom, as the grand intermediary between God and the world, characteristic of the Jewish Wisdom literature. We may safely assume that he did not discover for himself the pre-existent Christ after he became a Christian. He already as a Pharisee knew of the supernatural Christ waiting to be revealed, in God's good time, as the agent of the expected divine intervention in human history, the saviour of Israel, and the judge of the world.

Closely connected with this apocalyptic outlook was the belief in angelology and demonology, in the elemental spirits— the principalities and powers of the air—whose dominion over man and the world the Christ is to destroy. This belief was a relic of the primitive mythology which Persian influence on Hebrew religious thought had developed, and which the Epistles so realistically reflect. Along with this conception he inherits the current notion of the creation of man and the world, of the fall and the introduction of sin through the wiles of Satan, of the coming judgment which sin involves for man and the universe, and makes ample use of it in working out his doctrine of redemption. His Pharisaic heritage included, too, the profound sense of the holiness and righteousness of God and a corresponding sense of sin as transgression of God's revealed law, with its concomitant, death, physical and moral. He appears to have been a Pharisee with a very sensitive conscience, who took religion very seriously. He was, we may be sure, not one of those who thanked God that he was not as other men and made a merely ostentatious profession of devotion.

He seems, in fact, to have been haunted by the thought of God's righteousness and the impossibility of fulfilling the Law as the revelation of this righteousness. The Rabbis, indeed, whilst emphasising God's righteousness, taught that repentance could bring into operation God's mercy and forgiveness.[8] To Paul's sensitive conscience it was difficult, it would seem, to find appeasement in this aspect of the divine character, in the face of the sense of sin and the inexorable obligation to fulfil the whole Law. At all events, he tells us, in reference to an indelible religious crisis of his youth, of the overwhelming discovery of the fact of God's retributive righteousness and the sense of the awfulness of sin, which seem to have haunted him in the school of the Rabbis and throughout his own life as a Rabbi. "Apart from the law sin is dead. And I was alive apart from the law once ; but when the commandment came, sin revived, and I died, and the commandment which was unto life, this I found to be unto death. For sin, finding occasion, through the commandment beguiled me and through it slew me." [9] In religious psychology the effect of such an obsession of God's righteousness and the soul's impotence to

---

[8] Kohler, "Jewish Theology," 114 f., 246 f. (1918); Montefiore, "Judaism and St Paul," 37 f.

[9] Rom. vii. 7-11. There is no reason to doubt that this is autobiographical, or to infer that he is merely putting a supposed case, as Wrede (" Paulus," 83), Rawlinson ("New Test. Doct. of Christ," 88 f.), Machen ("Origin of Paul's Religion," 65 (1921)), and others do. The language is too tense, and clearly indicates a personal experience.

attain it is explicable enough, in the case of some temperaments. It does not necessarily rule out this experience by merely saying, with Loisy, that it could not have happened to a Pharisee and could not have entered Paul's consciousness as a Pharisee.[10] Such things do, nevertheless, happen in religious experience, even if they are contrary to the received system of the day.

In his Pharisaic period Paul was acquainted with the Rabbinic doctrine of vicarious merit. According to this doctrine the Jew is subject to the Law of an absolutely righteous God (the Torah), and is responsible for the observance of every jot and tittle of it. " To the Rabbis," says Kohler, " the root of faith is the recognition of a divine judge, to whom we owe an account of all our doings."[11] " The God of Judaism rules over mankind as guardian and vindicator of justice ; no wrong escapes his scrutinising gaze."[12] He keeps a meticulous account of a man's actions, and according to his record in the book of God will his destiny—his acquittal (justification) or his con- demnation—be on the day of judgment. The juridical conception of salvation is the principle underlying this doctrine —the balancing of the merits and demerits of the individual in the light of the Law at the final reckoning. God may, however, take account of the merits of the righteous for the unrighteous, in virtue of the validity of such merit in making good the lack of it in others, and thus securing their justification, or acquittal. The idea of the merit of vicarious doing or suffer- ing for others must have been familiar to Paul as a Pharisee. He could have learned it from the fifty-third chapter of Isaiah, in which the problem of sin and vicarious suffering had found its most sublime expression. It was involved in that of sacrifice, atonement for sin as embodied in the Jewish sacrificial cult, and though the Pharisees were more concerned with the legal and moral aspect of Judaism, as embodied in the Law, and with its exposition in the synagogue, they were keen to resent any attack on the temple worship. The martyrdom of Stephen, in which Paul took so active a part, was in truth

---

[10] " Revue d'Histoire et de Literature religieuses," iii. 573 (1912). On the reality and the effects of this discovery see Deissmann, " St Paul," 93 f. (1912).
[11] " Jewish Theology," 20.
[12] *Ibid.*, 119.

due to this attack, and the death of Jesus himself is, in part at least, ascribable to the same cause. He must, too, have been familiar with the idea of reckoning faith, in the sense at least of a good work, for righteousness and the supreme significance of faith (Emunah) in God's promises in the religious life of Israel.

With the belief in a judgment to come is associated that in a resurrection, which paved the way for Paul's characteristic doctrine of the risen Christ, as the grand guarantee of the divine power over death, as well as the symbol and the condition of the new spiritual life of the Christian believer. That he held the belief in the resurrection as a Pharisee we know from his own assertion before the Sanhedrin.[13] Kohler even traces his conception of the resurrection or renewal of the believer in baptism to the Pharisaic view of the rebirth of the Gentile proselyte to Judaism in the baptismal rite by which his former life was transformed.[13a] With another Pharisaic belief—that in predestination and election, which forms such a grim element of his Christian apologetic against his former co-religionists, he was also familiar.[14] The destiny of peoples and individuals alike depends on the sovereign will of God, the eternal divine decree. This belief provided him, too, with the key to the mystery of his own transformation from a blind Pharisee into a believing Christian, which he ascribes in the Epistle to the Galatians to " the good pleasure of God, who separated me from my mother's womb, and called me through his grace, to reveal his Son in me."[15] Whilst the Pharisees believed in predestination in the sense of a determining Providence controlling human destiny, they also emphasised the fact of free will, the power of the individual to mould his own character. As a Christian, Paul threw over this element of the Pharisaic doctrine, though he shared the belief in human responsibility, and even ascribes to the Gentiles the power " to do by nature the things of the law." For him the will is enslaved by sin and impotent to do the will of God apart from grace.

From Phariseeism he also carried over into his Christianity the intense zeal and intolerance which already characterised

---

[13] Acts xxiii. 6.   [13a] " Jewish Theology," 417.
[14] Rom. ix., x., xi. On the Pharisees and their beliefs see Josephus, " Antiq." xiii. 5, 9, etc.
[15] Gal. i. 15.

his pre-Christian career. His Christian proselytism is a reflex of the Pharisaic striving to win proselytes for the God of Israel in the Gentile world. The intolerance which appears in the persecuting spirit of the young zealot, who took a leading part in the death of Stephen, reappears in the uncompromising attitude of the Christian apostle towards both his Jewish-Christian and Gentile opponents. Temperament would, of course, count for something, apart from the system in which he had been reared. But the system itself was very intolerant, as Jesus and his disciples experienced in spite of their general conformity to the Law and its institutions.

The Hebrew element in Paul's Christianity is thus unmistakable. Jewish scholars are too disposed to minimise his Pharisaic inheritance, to question his claim to have been a product of Pharisaic teaching. To Mr Montefiore, as we have seen, he represents a degenerate type of Pharisaism, which is traceable to the influence of his Gentile environment. According to Dr Kohler what he represents as Rabbinic teaching is not in accordance with this teaching. We must, of course, make allowance for the influence of his conversion in not only transforming his previous convictions, but colouring his representation of them. He is the type of man who in religion must go from one extreme to the other. Even so, he works with the old ideas, though he transforms them and adds to them. In the main he evidently did bring into his Christian faith a train of thought largely derived from a Hebrew source. He learned much, indeed, in the school of Christ. Some things, and these very important things, he had to unlearn. But many things he had merely to modify and adapt in passing from the old train of thought to the new. His Christianity is the product of his experience as a Pharisee as well as a Christian. It would be to a considerable extent true to say that Paul's Christianity is Christianised Phariseeism. It is Phariseeism modified by the teaching of Jesus and his early disciples, which was itself to a large extent in accord with that of the Pharisees, if, as in the case of Jesus, it also shows, though in a greater degree, a reaction from Pharisaic legalism. " Phariseeism," in the striking words of Harnack,[16] " had

[16] " History of Dogma," i. 94.

fulfilled its mission for the world when it produced this man."

At the same time there was undoubtedly another school—that of his Hellenist environment—which contributed its quota to the making of the Christian thinker and apostle. In this sense the Hebrew critics of Paul have some justification for the contention that he was not the exclusive product of the conventional Rabbinic teaching. He was born at Tarsus, one of the chief centres of Greek culture.[17] He had a feeling of pride in his native place (" no mean city "), and seems to have spent his boyhood up to his fifteenth year in this city of schools and philosophers, rather than, as some have inferred, at Jerusalem, where his sister resided. He returned to Tarsus after the completion of his education as a Rabbi at the feet of Gamaliel. He seems to have spent another fifteen years there as a Rabbi of the local synagogue and in the prosecution of his trade as a tent-maker. As the son of a strict Jew (his parents, he tells us, were Pharisees),[18] he would attend the Hebrew school of his native place. He probably also attended the lectures of one or more of its Greek teachers. At all events, his Epistles reveal his mastery of the common or Hellenistic Greek, his habitual use of the Greek version of the Old Testament, as well as his familiarity with Aramaic, the marked influence of this version on his thought, his training in rhetoric in addition to his command of the Rabbinic dialectic, his working knowledge of the Stoic-Platonic philosophy, and of Græco-Roman Law. He knows, for instance, and makes use of the Stoic doctrines of the divine immanence, of a natural moral law, which is the Gentile equivalent of the Mosaic Law, of conscience as an innate witness to God and the good, of human brotherhood, of " contentment " or self-sufficiency.[19] He knows, too (probably

---

[17] On Tarsus see Böhlig, " Die Geisteskultur von Tarsus " (1913).

[18] Acts xxiii. 6.

[19] Böhlig argues with no little force that Paul derived his conception of conscience (συνείδησις), as the witness within to good and evil, from the Tarsus philosopher, Athenodorus (circa 74 B.C. to A.D. 7), who professed a syncretistic Stoicism, and whose ethical teaching has been preserved by Seneca in his " De Tranquilitate Animi." " Geisteskultur von Tarsus," 117 f. Böhlig's work contains a good deal of mere conjecture, whilst throwing light on the cultural influences with which, he assumes, Paul was brought into contact. On Paul's Hellenist culture see also Norden, " Agnostos Theos," 240 f. (1913) ; Wendland, " Hellinistisch-Römische Kultur," 140 f. (1912) ; J. Weiss, " Das Urchristenthum," 130 f. Deissmann

at second hand), the Platonic doctrine of the distinction between
the visible world and the eternal spiritual reality beyond it,
of which it is the reflection, and of the dualism in man and
the universe between spirit and matter. Common to him and
the current Platonism is the longing for redemption from this
material existence and its moral and spiritual limitations,
though the actual redemption is markedly different. The
Epistles also show traces of a knowledge of the Greek mystery
cults and bear ample evidence of his acquaintance with the
social and industrial features of Greek city life. Whether he
was also acquainted with the Hellenist teaching of Philo is
open to debate. Lightfoot [20] is of opinion that the use of
certain terms and ideas in the later letters suggests that he
was, whilst Harnack cannot discover in them any trace of this
influence.[21] This teaching was widely known in Jewish-
Hellenist circles, and it is not improbable that indirectly, if not
directly, he had some acquaintance with this train of thought.[22]
From the Epistle to the Colossians it is evident that he was
brought into contact with the movement later known as
Gnosticism, and he himself not only uses terms characteristic
of this form of thought, but claims to be in possession of the
true Gnosis, or higher religious philosophy. These influences
might be secondary, and it is advisable not to overemphasise
them. Bousset,[23] for instance, applying the religious-historical
method, derives the main content of Paul's thought from
Hellenist ideas and the Hellenist atmosphere of his time,
especially that of the mystery cults. His Christian mysticism
is largely the product of this atmosphere. This, as Wernle [24]

seems, in my opinion, unduly to minimise the culture of Paul. He thinks
that " Paul, although his native town was a seat of high Greek culture, did
not come from the literary upper class, but from the artisan, non-literary
classes, and that he remained with them," " St Paul," 50 f. A. Schweitzer
far too sweepingly rules out the Stoic influence on Paul, " Die Mystik des
Apostels Paulus," 5 f. (1930). See also his " Geschichte der Paulinischen
Forschung," 54 f. (1911).
    [20] " Commentary on Colossians," 141 f.
    [21] " History of Dogma," i. 113.
    [22] For examples, see Kennedy, " Philo's Contribution to Religion "
(1919). See also Windisch, " Die Frömmigkeit Philos," 104 f. (1909).
    [23] See " Kyrios Christos " (1913).
    [24] " Jesus und Paulus." " Zeitschrift f. Theol. u. Kirche " (1915), f.
Wernle is, however, inclined to go too far, in his " Beginnings of Christianity,"
in minimising the influence of education and environment on Paul's Christian
thought, i. 226. He is, moreover, not consistent, as he at times emphasises
this influence. See also Bacon's more recent book, " Jesus and Paul " (1921).

has shown, is a questionable thesis which takes too little account of his specific religious experience as a Jew and a Christian. Paul himself, it must be remembered, regards Greek thought and religion, as far as the central fact of Christ's death and resurrection is concerned, as innately antagonistic to the Gospel. If the Gospel is to the Jew a stumbling-block, to the Greek it is foolishness. How far this influence is reflected in his Christian thought, I shall consider more particularly in due course.

The Hellenist influence was, however, largely of secondary importance in his pre-Christian period at all events. Even on the eve of his conversion his bitter opposition to the Christian-Hellenist Stephen—a member of the Jewish-Hellenist synagogue, or one of these synagogues at Jerusalem, which Paul seems to have attended during his sojourn in the Holy City—shows that Saul, the Pharisee, Jew of the Diaspora though he was, was not inclined to tolerate any aberration from the traditions of the fathers. The Hellenist influence on his Pharisaic thought and training did not materially affect his Hebrew predilections. If the story in Acts v., which attributes to Gamaliel a tolerant attitude in religion, could be accepted as authentic, we might infer that even in the school of his great Pharisaic teacher he must have been brought into contact with liberal influences. In any case, his subsequent career as a Pharisee shows that he was nothing if not intolerant.

On the other hand, given the fundamental experience of his conversion, the Hellenist influence could not fail to assert itself in shaping his conception of the Gospel. Though a Pharisee, he was a Roman citizen,[25] and was familiar with Roman law and legal [26] procedure, and with the larger conception of humanity which the Roman Empire embodied. He was no ultra-patriot like the Zealots, but friendly to the Roman state, whose citizenship he accounted a privilege. Here, too, the Stoic

[25] Tarn contends that Paul was not actually, but only potentially, a Roman citizen. He or his father had been given an honorary citizenship, of which they had not actually made use, since it involved the worship of the city's gods. In an emergency a potential citizen might appeal to his citizenship, "Hellenistic Civilisation," 193 (2nd ed., 1930).
[26] On the influence of Roman law and practice on Paul, see Ball, " St Paul and the Roman Law " (1901). The latest treatise on the subject is the Ph.D. dissertation of Edinburgh University, by W. Phillips, " Influence of Roman Law on Early Christian History and Doctrine " (1931).

doctrine of human brotherhood would undoubtedly have some effect in widening his outlook, and in helping him to attain to the larger view of Christianity as a universal religion. The fact that he became intimately associated with the more liberal Gentile church at Antioch rather than with that at Jerusalem is, I think, an indirect evidence of the influence of his up-bringing in a Hellenist environment. It was no accident that it was a Jew of the Diaspora who became the great apostle of the Gentiles. In largeness of knowledge and outlook he was better fitted for this vocation than the simple disciples of Galilee or their converts of Judæa. To the Greek, he tells us, he became a Greek and all things to all men [27] in the prosecution of his Christian mission, and he could hardly have done so without the previous knowledge, experience, and insight of his Hellenist environment. His was the complex mind which belonged to both spheres—Jewish and Hellenist—though it is only in his activity as a Christian apostle that the influence of the latter makes itself distinctively and decisively felt.

At the same time it must not be forgotten that a man of genius like Paul cannot be explained as the mere product of external influences, of the complex religious currents of the age. His Christianity is, indeed, the product of Hebraism, supplemented by Hellenism. But it is also the product of the man himself—of his personal religious experience, especially the superlative experience of his conversion ; of the subtle and powerful intellect which, making use of inherited Jewish thought, gave this thought a new content ; of the ethical and spiritual intensity which transformed the zealous Pharisee into the apostle of a new faith, the prophet of a new spiritual life. The man of genius not only inherits ; he creates. Paul is a religious genius. His originality is writ large on his Epistles, even if his mind works with inherited ideas and is dependent on the primitive Gospel. He is certainly to be reckoned among the greatest creative minds in Christian history. His Epistles are assuredly those of a mind of strong grasp, subtle, resourceful, transforming. They are, too, those of a man with a wonderful passion for God, with a heart aflame with the highest idealism in the service of others. Moreover, he is no mere thinker. His thought is intensely wedded to action.

[27] I Cor. ix. 21-22.

He achieves what may justifiably be termed a revolution of Judaism and what is, at the same time, a far-reaching development of the Gospel in both its doctrinal and practical aspect— as a message and a movement. His intellect is dominated by a driving will power which carries the Gospel, in an aggressive campaign, from city to city—from Antioch to Rome. His creative mind is not that of the solitary thinker, but the born leader of men. In view of the results of his intense activity, there is truth in the assertion that his missionary journeys were a repetition of Alexander's conquests, only in the opposite direction.[28]

In the light of this achievement the personality of the man is a far more potent thing than the heritage of race, or school, or party, or environment. In any case, there is much that is subjective in Paul—much distinctively Pauline. Paulinism— if we may use this somewhat unpopular term is not a mere description of what he assimilated from external sources. He himself claimed to be independent of these. He confesses, indeed, that he is a debtor to both Greeks and barbarians, but only in the sense of the obligation he is under to preach the Gospel to all and sundry as the power of God unto salvation. This Gospel he claims to have received by revelation. He is independent of Jew and Greek, independent even of the other apostles. His Gospel is revealed, not borrowed from others, whether Jew or Christian. In this he tends to overemphasise, overstate his originality, and overemphasis is apt at times to become a habit in a man of his intense emotional temperament and genius, as his Epistles show. He is prone to think and speak and write in absolute terms, which fail at times to compel assent, especially when the absolute conclusions are the result of a train of rabbinic reasoning or exegesis, or reflect the influence of current beliefs concerning man and the world. The student of the Epistles cannot always take him at his own evaluation in this respect. And yet we cannot but feel the power and originality which, inspired by his faith in Christ as the revealer of God and the Redeemer from sin and death, he imparts to them. Out of inherited religious materials and his religious experience as a Pharisee and a Christian, he created the Christianity that was to make of the religion of Jesus a world

[28] Weinel, " St Paul " (Eng. trans., 1906).

religion. This creation is surely more than Judaism plus primitive Christianity. Judaism certainly could not have become a world religion, and it is debatable whether primitive Jewish Christianity could have done so without the constructive genius and the mission of Paul.

The cardinal fact in this religious experience was his conversion. This momentous experience came to him on the road near Damascus, whither he was travelling as the commissioned repressor of the Christians. But the initial stage of it may be traced to Jerusalem. It was at Jerusalem that he had become acquainted with the fact of Jesus' existence and his claim to be the Messiah. If he had not actually seen him there, he had heard a great deal about him. He had evidently listened to the proclamation by the apostles of the crucified, risen, and exalted Christ. He had actually taken part in the controversy over this question which resulted in the death of Stephen, of which he was one of the chief instigators. He had heard the words of Stephen, " Behold I see the heavens opened and the Son of man standing on the right hand of God," and these words probably kept ringing in his ears on the journey to Damascus. This knowledge was an essential preliminary of his conversion, for the subsequent vision shows that he recognised who the Jesus of Nazareth was that spoke to him from the sudden blaze of light which prostrated him on the road. The thought of Jesus as the exalted Christ must, in fact, have been in his mind before this visual appearance. At Jerusalem he had, indeed, spurned the idea of such a Messiah as the apostles proclaimed and had taken an active part in suppressing their preaching—" breathing threatening and slaughter against the disciples of the Lord." But he evidently was unable to shut his mind against the strange proclamation. It seems to have obsessed him as he toiled along the road in spite of his violent prejudice—obsessed him so persistently that the thought of this crucified man would not be shaken off.

At length, as he nears the end of his journey, he was suddenly enveloped by a dazzling light and fell to the ground. One thinks of a thunderstorm and a flash of lightning, which, as in the case of Luther, his great modern exponent, prostrated him to the ground and in a moment changed the whole course of his

career. There is, however, nothing in the record in Acts [29]
to indicate a thunderstorm. The experience seems to have
been a psychic, not a physical one, though the vision was so
vivid that it affected his eyesight for the time being. He was
naturally disposed to such visions, and on this occasion it took
the form of a visual projection before his mind of the thought of
Jesus on which it had been brooding on the journey Damascus-
wards. From the dazzling light came a voice which such
visionaries, with a strange realism unknown to less susceptible
natures, hear out of the eternal silence, upbraiding him for his
anti-Christian violence. The voice is his sensitive conscience
that at last decisively asserts itself as the conviction flashes into
his mind, in this visionary fashion, that the crucified Jesus, of
whom the apostles preached, was in verity the Christ of his
apocalyptic belief. " It pleased God to reveal his Son in me."
" God shined in our hearts to give the light of the knowledge
of the glory of God in the face of Jesus Christ." [30] So he
himself describes this experience. The vision is an inner
illumination—the great discovery that the Messianic expectation
of the ages had been fulfilled in the crucified, risen, and exalted
Jesus, in whom he sees the actual, the historic embodiment of
the Son of Man conception of Jewish Apocalyptic, with which
he was already familiar. This is the grand revelation. However we may conceive the vision, to which the high-strung,
ecstatic Paul was particularly liable,[31] this revelation was henceforth the absolute and dominating fact of his life. It is the
secret of that conception of the heavenly Christ which so
largely overshadows the historic Jesus in his Epistles,
though it is associated with him. It is, too, the secret
of the conviction which henceforth grips him that his past
religious life in the service of the Law had been a mistaken one, and of the radical reaction from it which is
the keynote of his Christian life and teaching. It is, farther,
the secret of that profound sense of the mercy and
love of God in Christ, of the love of Christ [32] which breathes

[29] Acts ix., xxii., xxvi.   The three accounts are in substantial agreement,
whilst differing in some of the details.   Of the three I prefer the first, which
shows that Paul alone had the vision, though his companions hear a voice
(apparently that of Paul) in converse with the speaker in the vision.

[30] Gal. i. 15 ; 2 Cor. iv. 6.

[31] 2 Cor. xii. 1 f.

[32] Rom. viii. 35 f.

in every one of the Epistles. That the Christ, whom he had
cursed and persecuted so fiercely in his disciples, should make
himself known to him and, in spite of himself, save him from
the doom which, but for this revelation, his blindness, his
mistaken zeal would have brought upon him—this is the
unspeakable mercy. From that moment Christ takes possession
of him. This Christ possession begetting the new man, with
his absolute faith in, and his passionate devotion to, the Lord
from heaven, which is also so characteristic a feature of the
Epistles, goes back to this experience. This is what his
conversion more immediately meant for Paul from the outset.

Much else that it meant only came to him in the solitude of
the Arabian desert, in the intercourse with Peter at Jerusalem
and other disciples (as far as the actual facts of Jesus' life and
teaching were concerned), and in the course of his activity
as the apostle of the Gentiles.[33] His Christianity was, like all
vital things, a growth. It is highly probable that he thought
out his mission to the Gentiles, for instance, after a considerable
period of reflection, and more especially in the liberal atmosphere of Antioch. A good many years, it must be remembered,
elapsed before the earliest of his Epistles were penned, when
he had already evangelised far and wide in the Græco-Roman
world. Even in those of the later period of his activity this
growth is still apparent. In his mission preaching he seems to
have confined himself to a simple proclamation of the Gospel,
which, to judge from the summary of it occasionally given in
the Epistles,[34] was similar to that of the early apostolic preaching,
adapted to his Gentile hearers. In these passages the note
of his mission preaching is the primitive and distinctively
eschatological one. The confession of Jesus as Lord, and faith
in him as risen from the dead, is the essential of his missionary
message. But this is only the elements of the Pauline Gospel,
and in his matured thought, as communicated to his converts,
in contrast to his simpler preaching to the unconverted, this
Gospel becomes a theory of redemption based on the person
and work of Christ, far more elaborate than that of the simpler
followers of Jesus in the early years at Jerusalem.

[33] For details see Anderson Scott's recent book, " Christianity According
to Paul," 12 f. (1927).
[34] 1 Thess. i. 9-10 ; 1 Cor. xv. 3 f. ; Rom. x. 9.

NOTE ON THE SOURCES FOR THE PAULINE GOSPEL

These are primarily the Epistles and, to a limited degree, the Acts of the Apostles. In regard to the Epistles there is general agreement (from which only the small ultra-radical school of Van Manen dissents) that 1st Thessalonians, Galatians, Romans, 1st and 2nd Corinthians, Philippians, and Philemon were written by him. There is doubt about Colossians, and especially about Ephesians, owing to their more advanced thought and more developed conception of the Church, which the defenders of their authenticity explain by a corresponding advance in the apostle's views, and to the existence of heresies which seem to the objectors to belong to a later period. A considerable number of even advanced critics now accept Colossians as Pauline, whilst regarding Ephesians and 2nd Thessalonians as post-Pauline. The Pastoral Epistles, in the opinion of a majority of critics, are of later date, though containing some Pauline sections. In the following sections on the Pauline Gospel I do not make use of Ephesians, 2nd Thessalonians, and the Pastorals by reason of their doubtful authenticity, which I subsequently discuss in the chapter on the Subapostolic Gospel. For reviews in English of the evidence in favour of the authenticity of the eight Epistles, see Moffatt, " Introduction to the Literature of the New Testament " (1911); Peake, " Critical Introduction " (1909); M. Jones, " The New Testament in the Twentieth Century " (1914); Blakeston, " The Bible of To-Day " (1914); " The Introductions to the Moffatt Commentaries " and other recent commentaries in English. For the Acts of the Apostles, see the first two volumes of " The Beginnings of Christianity," edited by Foakes-Jackson and Kirsopp Lake, in which the relative problems are discussed by them and other contributors. The literature on Paul is so extensive, that it is impossible in a note to give an account of even the more recent contributions, and the reader is referred to the footnotes.

The Epistles do not contain a systematic exposition of Paul's theological views. They are letters to communities and deal with specific situations, which moved the apostle to address them. Deissmann contends that they are of the nature of purely private and personal communications, and

are distinguishable from the more purely literary Epistle of
the age (" St Paul," 8 f.).   The distinction seems overwrought.
Paul undoubtedly seeks to communicate instruction to the
Churches which he addresses, though, in keeping with the
situations which called forth the letters, the instruction is not
systematic.   The Epistle to the Romans comes nearest to
being a treatise on a specific theme.   At the same time they are,
as Dean Inge points out (" Outspoken Essays," 207 (1919)),
real letters, not literary productions like the Epistles of Seneca.

III. The World and Man

Paul takes over the apocalyptic view of the world from the
primitive Gospel.   He shares with Jesus and his immediate
disciples the current belief in angels, the devil, and the demons,
and in the sway of these demonic spirits over the world and
man.   He adopts the primitive view of the coming of the exalted
Christ to execute judgment on the world, and inaugurate the
rule of God in the new age or æon.   At the same time, he
elaborates and adds to what he adopts.   He has a more articulate
and developed theory of the creation and its redemption from
evil.   If Christ is the agent of God's will in creating and
maintaining the universe, the universe is the arena of the
activity of a host of ethereal spirits—angelic or demonic—
which exercise a potent sway over it.   So great is their sway
that, as in the teaching of Jesus himself, the present æon is
subject to this demonic power.   This subjection extends over
the whole of created things.   Creation is consequently in
bondage to corruption, which is due to their malign power.[1]
" The whole creation groaneth and travaileth together in
pain until now."   In these tragic words he gives expression
to the prevailing conviction, in the ancient world, of being
in the grip of a malevolent power or fate, from which nature
and humanity are impotent to free themselves.   He knows
in considerable detail about these ethereal spirits and their
doings.   They are " the principalities and powers," " thrones

[1] Rom. viii. 20 f.   Jewish Pre-Christian Apocalyptic has much to tell
us of the régime of these nefarious spirits.   See especially " The First Book
of Enoch," Charles' edition (1912), and " Apocrypha and Pseudepigrapha of
the Old Testament," ii. (1913).

and dominions," " the rulers of this world " or æon, who have instigated and accomplished the death of the Christ.[2] They are the elemental or astral spirits which control, for their own nefarious purposes, the constitution or elements of the universe and the life of man.[3] At their head, for Paul as for Jesus, is Satan, the adversary in chief of God and the good in creation and man, the God of this world or age. He and these demonic powers are the Gods whom the Gentiles worship, and to take part in Gentile sacrificial feasts is to have fellowship with them and places the believer in bondage to them.[4] Satan and his demonic crew are as real figures in the Epistles of Paul as in the writings of Luther. They blind men to the truth of the Gospel. So clever is Satan that he can take on the guise of an angel of light. He hinders and thwarts the apostle in his mission plans. The thorn in his flesh—that ever-recurring malady—is " a messenger of Satan to buffet me." It is he that tempts the Corinthians into sensuality.[5]

With these demonic powers Paul ranges the angels, though he knows the distinction between good and bad angels. Ultimately, however, the angels, as intermediaries between God and the world and man, also exercise a sinister dominion over both. It is to them, as mediators of the Law at Sinai,[6] that is due the bondage of Jewish legalism, which the Law signifies for Paul. He appears to have based this singular conclusion on the tradition which inferred the mediation of angels from Deut. xxxii. 2 ; Ps. lxviii. 17, in which Yahweh is represented as coming to Sinai with a host of angels. Thus the angels have acquired a dominion over the unbelieving Jews similar to that exercised by the astral spirits, the false Gods over the Gentiles. They appear among the principalities and powers as seeking to separate the believer from the love of God in Christ. The return to the weak and beggarly elements, which he denounces

---

[2] Rom. viii. 38 ; Col. i. 16 ; ii. 10 ; iii. 15 ; 1 Cor. ii. 6.
[3] στοιχεῖα, Gal. iv. 3, 9 ; Col. ii. 8, 20. The idea was probably taken from a pagan source. See Dibelius, " Die Geisterwelt im Glauben des Paulus," 227 f. (1909). On the pessimism begotten of this belief, which is reflected in the speech of Stephen (Acts vii. 42), " the host of heaven," and the fear in the presence of the universe and death, see Bevan, " Hellenism and Christianity," 77 f. (1921).
[4] 2 Cor. iv. 4 ; Rom. iv. 9 f. ; 1 Cor. x. 20.
[5] Ibid., iv. 3 ; xi. 14 ; xii. 7 ; 1 Thess. ii. 18 ; 1 Cor. vii. 5.
[6] Gal. iii. 19 ; cf. Stephen's words, Acts vii. 53.

in the Epistle to the Galatians, evidently included angel worship and the bondage to these supernal powers, from which the Christ had delivered them.

Paul's conception of the universe is in this respect very pessimistic. In this mood he has a very vivid sense of the power of evil in creation, as embodied in these demonic spirits. He seems untouched by its marvellous order and grandeur. He sees only the agency of corrupting, diabolic forces. He seems to have no eye for the beauty and fertility of nature in the spring garb of its reviving life, for instance ; no appreciation of it as the revelation of an infinite, beneficent intelligence and will. He views it from the religious and ethical angle, not from that of the philosopher and the poet. He is, too, dominated by the apocalyptic conception of the present order of things, which reveals the presence of diabolic forces in conflict with the good. But this antagonism is not inherent in the creation. Evil is not omnipotent or independent of God, though its sway in the present order is so powerful in blighting the good. The cloud of his pessimism has its silver lining. In spite of the demons, " the earth is the Lord's and the fullness thereof." [7] Christ's cosmic function is not merely that of the agent of God's creative will ; it is also concerned with the ultimate realisation of the rule of God over that of the devil in the world. Through him the power of evil is being undermined in the creation as well as in man. From the cosmic point of view, redemption, reconciliation includes all things in heaven as well as on earth. Ultimately the cosmos will be transformed into a new heaven and a new earth. Christ will, in the final conflict with these cosmic powers, triumph over evil, and finally, with his triumph, all being will be raised to a higher plane, and God will be all in all.[8]

For Paul, as for Jesus, man is subject to these ethereal spirits. Sin and, with it, death entered into the human race

[7] 1 Cor. x. 26.
[8] Ibid., xv. 24 f. ; Phil. ii. 10-11 ; Col. i. 20. For the latest discussions on the subject, see M. Jones, " Lectures on the Epistle of St Paul to the Colossians " (1924) ; Radford, " Westminster Commentary on Colossians," 96 f., 224 f. (1931) ; A. Schweitzer, " Die Mystik des Apostels Paulus," 54 f. (1930). See also Reitzenstein, " Poimandres," 69 f. (1904) ; J. Weiss " Urchristenthum," 464 f.

through the fall of Adam. Paul does not mention the story of
the temptation and fall of man through Satan. But he implies
it. The origin of human sin is thus traceable to demonic
agency. Thereby man's originally good nature has been fatally
vitiated. The first man's sin has been transmitted to his
descendants. The sinful tendency is hereditary and, in virtue
of this hereditary influence, man as well as the creation is in
bondage to the demonic powers. Paul does not teach original
sin in the sense that all sinned in Adam,[9] but that all sin, and
cannot but sin, as the result of his sin. The fact of sin is thus
universal. " All have sinned and fall short of the glory of
God." [10] All are in bondage to sin,[11] and all are liable to the
judgment of God.[12] The dominion of sin is the teaching of
Scripture, which he quotes in proof of his contention, " The
Scripture hath shut up all things under sin." [13] " There is
none righteous, no, not one." [14] It is evidenced by the Law,
which was given not merely as the standard of the moral life,
in accordance with God's will, but to emphasise and even
augment the fact of sin.[15] To Paul this fact is not merely a
theological dogma, based on Old Testament mythology ; it
is a fact of history, observation, and experience. His outlook
is the pessimistic one of such late Jewish Apocalyptic books
as ii. (4) Ezra [16] and of his Greek environment. For him
history is largely the mirror of man's disobedience to the
will of a holy and righteous God, the persistent aberration,
under demonic influence and inherited depravity, from God and
the good. He finds the evidence of this in the moral declension
of the Gentile world, of which he gives so terrible a picture
in the first chapter of the Epistle to the Romans. He finds
it, too, in the widespread moral depravity of the Jews. In
spite of their superior enlightenment in virtue of their possession
of the Law, they are ever transgressing the Law and giving
the Gentiles occasion to blaspheme the name of God.[17] He

[9] The ἐφ' ᾧ of Rom. v. 12, does not mean " in whom," as Augustine
interpreted it, but " inasmuch as " all actually sinned.
[10] Rom. iii. 23.
[11] *Ibid.*, vi. 6.
[12] *Ibid.*, iii. 19.
[13] Gal. iii. 22.
[14] Rom. iii. 10 f.
[15] Gal. iii. 19 ; Rom. iii. 20.
[16] See Charles, " Apocrypha and Pseudepigrapha of the Old Testament,"
ii. 554 f.
[17] Rom. ii. 17 f.

doubtless overcolours the picture of the prevailing moral
depravity of Jews and Gentiles. He is apt to see everything
black in the blurred light of his theological theory, and his keen
sense of transgression, which his former Phariseeism nurtured.
In the case of the Gentiles, he ascribes their moral depravity
to their idolatry, which he is prone to equate with evildoing.
In consequence of their aberration from the true God, he " has
given them up to vile passions." For Paul the practical issue
inevitably follows from the theory. But the list of moral
enormities which he lays to their charge, and which he had
ample opportunity of observing in cities like Antioch and
Corinth, tends to substantiate the all too common existence of
these enormities, if not the sweeping generalisation which he
bases on it. He himself, in fact, corrects the generalisation of
the first chapter of Romans by his admission, in the second,
that the Gentiles, though deprived of the light of the Law,
do by nature the things of the Law in virtue of conscience,
the law written in their hearts. Alongside the fact of sin, he
thus also, perforce, acknowledges the fact of the good in human
nature and history.

Paul's own experience tended to confirm his inference from
history and observation of the universal and innate dominion
of sin. His personal sense of sin is very profound and realistic.
As already noted, it goes back to his early youth, to his discovery of the heinousness of transgression in the face of the
Law, with its inexorable " Thou shalt not." It was probably
intensified by his training in the school of Phariseeism, with
its meticulous anxiety over the minutiæ of legal observance.
Equally keen the sense of the righteousness of God, also
inherited from Phariseeism, which emphasised the Law, both
written and oral, as the revelation of His holy will and juridical
character. Temperament doubtless also contributed to deepen
this twofold sense of man's sin and God's righteousness.
Intense and high strung, his is not the objective, balanced
mind which can control its religious obsessions. He does
not belong to the all too rare type, in which life is tuned in a
harmony of soul and body, and God and goodness are the
atmosphere which it naturally seems to breathe. Tempera-
mentally he belongs to the intense nature, to which the higher
life is a life of conflict, all the more poignant in proportion to

the consciousness of the jar between the ideal and the real. In this respect he differs markedly from Jesus, the supreme exemplar of the former type, who exhibits a serene faith and a more balanced, optimistic outlook on nature and life, though he does not blink the darker side of both and shares the current apocalyptic mood. Jesus knows the weakness of the flesh, which hampers the higher life of the spirit. " The spirit indeed is willing, but the flesh is weak." [18] He knows from experience the temptations to which it is exposed. " Ye are they that have continued with me in my temptations." [19] But man is also possessed of the power to overcome the weakness of the flesh, and he calls men to seek the kingdom of God and his righteousness in the conviction that they can seek and find it. Jesus is the sublime, self-possessed master of his own soul and of the souls of men. In contrast to Jesus, Paul is an ecstatic and an extremist. He is obsessed by the impossibility of attaining righteousness by way of the Law—the Law in the moral as well as the ceremonial sense. In this respect he has experienced an utter revulsion from Phariseeism. To attain to righteousness in God's sight, in accordance with the divine standard as expressed in the Law, has become for him a sheer impossibility. The Law, as the expression of the holy will of God, not only condemns all achievement below this ideal standard, it renders such achievement impossible and only accentuates the fact of sin and its absolute dominion. Nay, the evil desires are only vitalised by the Law that condemns them. Like Luther, Paul gives vivid expression to their potency in his personal life, " O wretched man that I am ! who shall deliver me out of this body of death ? " In both cases it is not necessarily the conflict with the sensual self, as in that of Augustine, that finds expression in this agonised cry. It expresses rather the keen sense of sin overclouding the spiritual life and begetting that of impotence to realise true freedom from the bondage to sinful nature.

Such is Paul's personal experience as a believer in Christ, even if previously the experience had been less acute. For Paul, the Christian, there is, as the result of the dominion of sin, an inveterate antagonism between the higher and the lower elements in human nature. This antagonism is not

[18] Mark xiv. 38 ; Matt. xxvi. 41.   [19] Luke xxii. 28.

merely a personal experience, it is generalised into a universal feature of human nature. In consequence of sin, the flesh and the spirit in man are in diametrical opposition. So absolute is this opposition that man is for Paul an incompatible duality of flesh and spirit. The flesh, because of sin, has become inveterately evil and antagonistic to the good.[20] So much so that for Paul flesh and spirit represent a sort of double personality. The natural—the carnal, or the psychic in the sense of the natural—stands opposed to the spiritual, the rational, and moral element in man's being. These are in their nature radically different and are governed by radically different laws. He contrasts the mind of the spirit with the mind of the flesh, the law of my mind with the law of sin in my members.[21] In the evil that he inevitably does it is not he, but sin that does it. The words are not merely figurative. To Paul they express the double being residing within him in the flesh and the spirit. The conflict between them arises from the radical difference inherent in them. In the flesh, as vitiated by sin, inheres corruption, perishableness, death ; in the spirit the eternal, imperishable element which aspires to God and His righteousness. This double being is evidenced by the struggle of which he is conscious. It is no mere theory evolved in order to undermine the Law for the Gentile believer. It is a reality of experience. Paul is sin-possessed. " The flesh lusteth against the spirit and the spirit against the flesh, for these are contrary the one to the other."[22] " I am carnal, sold under sin. In me, that is, in my flesh dwelleth no good thing ; for to will is present with me, but to do that which is good is not."[23] " The mind of the flesh is enmity against God, for it is not subject to the law of God, neither indeed can it be. O wretched man that I am who shall deliver me out of the body of this death ? "[24] Deliverance is possible ; for the antithesis and the struggle are not hopeless. But it is only by the power of Christ and his Spirit that this dualism can be overcome, and Paul can thank God that, through the Lord Jesus Christ, the spiritual part of his being can serve the law of God in the

[20] For a contrary view see Bandas, " The Master Idea of St Paul's Epistles," 22 f. (1925). This writer represents the orthodox Roman Catholic view.
[21] Rom. viii. 6 ; vii. 23.
[22] Gal. v. 17.
[23] Rom. vii. 14 f.
[24] Ibid., vii. 24.

conflict with the law of sin in the flesh.[25] " In all things we are more than conquerors through him that loved us." [26]

This dualism has a resemblance to the current Greek dualism between good and evil, the flesh and the spirit. It reminds of Plato's conception of the body as the prison of the soul, of matter as in itself inherently evil. This conception Philo adopted and read into Old Testament passages which speak of man, in deprecatory terms, as flesh.[27] Some have seen a reflection of this conception in the Pauline antithesis between spirit and flesh which, it is assumed, was thus influenced by the anthropology of his Hellenist environment. The inference is doubtful, though it must be admitted that some of his extreme utterances lend colour to this assumption.[28] The source of this antithesis lies rather in the Old Testament emphasis on the weakness of the flesh, which he intensifies, and from which he developed his extreme doctrine of the antagonism of flesh and spirit, as he had experienced it in his own religious life. In this he was only following a tendency discernible in late Jewish Apocalyptic, particularly in the Fourth Book of Ezra.[29] In this, too, he diverged from the current Rabbinic Judaism which, while emphasising the sinful tendency in man, recognised his capacity to overcome this evil inclination (*Yetzer-ha-ra*). " Rabbinical Judaism," says Kohler, " never followed Philo so far in the footsteps of Plato as to consider the body or the flesh the source of impurity and sin or ' the prison house of the soul.' This view is fundamental in the Paulinian system." [30] At the same time, the flesh, though dominated in its fallen state by sin, is not for Paul,

---

[25] Rom. vii. 22, 25.
[26] *Ibid.*, viii. 37.
[27] Gen. vi. 3, 12 ; Isaiah xl. 6, etc. See the quotations from Philo given by Lietzmann, " Handbuch," 71 f. Also Bousset, " Religion des Judentums," 441 f. (3rd ed., 1926).
[28] On this point see E. F. Scott, " The Spirit in the New Testament," 133 f. Professor Scott thinks that he was to a certain extent influenced by the Hellenist conception of matter, as well as the Hebrew one, and that there is a certain inconsistency in his thought on the subject.
[29] See Charles, " Apocrypha and Pseudepigrapha," ii. 554 f. Kohler, " Jewish Theology," 222, finds it also in the " Apocalypse " of Baruch. " We cannot deny that these two books contain much that is near the Paulinian view of original sin." Charles, on the other hand, holds that the teaching of this apocalyptic writer on the fall and the total depravity of man " differs wholly from the Pauline doctrine." Man, according to Baruch, possesses free will and his moral nature remains unimpaired, ii. 477 f.
[30] " Jewish Theology," 215.

in itself, inherently evil in the Greek sense of the essential evil of matter. In this respect Kohler's judgment is misleading. It is capable of consecration to God as the temple of His Spirit.[31] "Nothing," he declares, "is unclean of itself." "All things have been created through Christ and unto Christ."[32] Matter as well as spirit is capable of redemption. The Greek doctrine of the inherent evil of matter would, in fact, have rendered impossible the Pauline doctrine of redemption operated by and attainable through Christ for both man and creation. Though there is antagonism, there is no essential dualism. The evil in man and the universe is capable of redemption and will be overcome. Paul's pessimism is streaked with optimism.

Paul's view of the world and man, which underlies his doctrine of redemption, makes a mixed impression on the modern mind. Apart from his crude cosmology and his anthropology, there is force in his emphasis on the presence of evil in nature and man. In nature what seems to us to be a demonic force bursts forth at times with desolating effects on this fair earth and its human life, and this force seems to operate in other parts of the universe. In the brutality of the lower creation there is also a revelation of something that we can only call diabolic. "Nature red in tooth and claw" is, to the sensitive mind, a revolting spectacle. On the other hand, there is discernible the ample operation of a beneficent power in the adaptability of nature to meet the needs of man and beast, and in the magnificent spectacle of an ordered universe. In the picture of the whole creation "in bondage to corruption," "groaning and travailling in pain until now,"[33] and dominated by evil astral spirits, whom Christ has come to destroy, he certainly takes a one-sided view of the economy of nature and of the heavenly luminaries as far as they affect the earth and its living organisms. Moreover, his cosmology is based on a mythology which is no longer valid for the modern reason. Modern reason does not assume the existence of astral spirits, demonic beings which were believed to dominate the creation and man. Paul naturally shared this mythical belief, and in imparting it to his doctrine of redemption, he has weakened its appeal for modern thought.

The fact of sin and its dominion over mankind is real

[31] 1 Cor. vi. 19.   [32] Col. i. 16.   [33] Rom. viii. 21-22.

5

enough. History and human experience sufficiently substantiate its terrible reality in defacing the image of God in man and hampering, weakening the aspiration and the progress of the spirit Godwards. In the individual and the race the diabolic is found throughout history in persistent and deadly antagonism to the divine in man. The history of both, with its tale of human superstition, aberration from the ideal of justice and humanity, the persistent predilection for a godless egotism, only too tragically exhibits the operation of this fatal tendency. Apart from evil in its grosser form, we are all conscious more or less in our personal experience of the conflict of flesh and spirit, good and evil, which vitiates our moral and religious life. It is true in our experience, as in Paul's, that the Law, as he proclaims in the wonderful eighth chapter of the Epistle to the Romans, is weak through the flesh. It is true that in the person, life, and death of God's Son we behold the condemnation of sin in the flesh, even if we may not share all the theological implications which he reads into such assertions. It is true also that they that are after the flesh do mind the things of the flesh, *i.e.*, give full scope to the lower impulses within them, and that, in so doing, they cannot please God and are at enmity with God. True, further, that only in seeking to live the life of the spirit by mortifying the deeds of the body, in the Spirit of Christ, do we realise its true life and come to the full consciousness of our Sonship of the Heavenly Father. Wholeheartedly can we respond to the emphasis on our need of the Spirit of God or of Christ to elevate us, in suffering and striving, to conformity to the image of God's Son, the first-born of many brethren.

At the same time, we cannot fully share his deprecatory conception of the flesh as so vitiated by sin that the spiritual element in our nature is completely impotent to will or to do the good. If human history reveals only too realistically the weakness of the will and the strength of the passions, it also reflects the perception of the good and the effort of the will to realise it in the subjection of the passions. Here, too, Paul's view of human nature and his reading of history are one-sided. The modern reason does not believe in the existence of astral spirits dominating and subjecting creation and man to evil. It does not believe in the assumption of a primitive perfect man, whose lapse brought absolute corruption as well as physical death on his race, but in the evolution of man and his gradual mental and moral progress. It does not regard death as the consequence of the sin of this primitive man, but as a physiological law, inherent in man's animal nature. Neither is it prepared to accept his all too deprecatory conception of the flesh, in view of the marvellous organism of the human body as the divine, if temporal, encasement of the immortal spirit, even if the fleshly impulse may tend to hamper its moral development. It is the worthy instrument of the intellect and the will, which tabernacle within it, and too often abused instead of reverencing and rightly using it.

IV. THE PAULINE CHRIST

As the result of his vision, Paul naturally emphasised the transcendental side of the Christ conception. In this respect he is in unison with the teaching of Jesus himself, as represented in the Synoptic Gospels, on the Son of man exalted, in spite of the cross, to the right hand of God and coming to judge the world. He does not, however, use the term Son of man, habitual in the later Synoptic teaching. For it he substitutes the term Son of God, as more intelligible to his Gentile hearers. Nor does he seem to base his conception on this teaching, but on the revelation of the heavenly Christ at his conversion. Under the profound impression of this revelation, he does not seem to have concerned himself with the latter-day utterances of Jesus about his Messiahship, as reflected in the Synoptists, though he may have consulted Peter on the subject. At all events the revelation of Christ to himself seems the decisive element in his conception of him. This conception includes, however, elements which are lacking in that of Jesus and the primitive disciples. From the teaching of Jesus himself in the Synoptic Gospels one would not conclude that he had preexisted with God before the creation and had been God's agent in creation. He is the Messiah who, by his death and exaltation, will effect God's purpose in the great climax when the Son of man shall come as the transcendental deliverer and judge. Whilst he is also, though more rarely, the Son of God in the unique, filial sense, his sonship does not seem to have a retrospective, pre-existent sense. Nor is the idea of pre-existence discernible in the early apostolic proclamation of Jesus as a man chosen or approved of God by his mighty works to be Lord and Christ. Paul himself shows a trace of this primitive adoptionist view in the assertion that " Jesus Christ was declared or marked out to be the Son of God with power," in the occasional emphasis on " the man " Jesus Christ, and in the confession of " Jesus as Lord " current in the Pauline churches.[1] But he goes beyond both Jesus and the primitive apostles in his more developed and distinctive Christology. He greatly enhanced the supernatural and divine element in the Messianic conception of Jesus himself and the early disciples. It is not so much the historic Jesus, who claimed and was proved to be the Messiah, as the heavenly Christ and Son of God that fills the developed thought of Paul.

On his own confession, he was not primarily concerned with " Christ after the flesh," *i.e.*, Christ as he actually lived on earth, the Christ of the primitive tradition, the man personally known to the early disciples. " Though we have known Christ after the flesh, yet now we know him so no more." [2] Whilst he knows this tradition, it is the Christ who has passed, through death and resurrection, to the heavenly sphere and has revealed himself to him that looms in his religious thought and experience. At the same time " the man Jesus Christ " is also there. Even in the designation, " The second man of or from heaven," [3] the manhood of Jesus is present to his mind. Some have seen in this designation Paul's equivalent for the Son of man of the Synoptic tradition. To others it stands for the ideal, pre-existent, archetypal man of Gnostic-Oriental mythology and of Philo, which Paul transferred to his conception of the heavenly Christ. Whilst the former inference is feasible, the context of the passage in which the designation

---

[1] Rom. i. 4 ; v. 15 ; Cor. xii. 3. Machen denies this inference point blank, " Origin of Paul's Religion," 118. Too positive.

[2] 2 Cor. v. 16.

[3] ὁ δεύτερος ἄνθρωπος ἐξ οὐρανοῦ, 1 Cor. xv. 47 ; *cf.* Rom. v. 12 f. There is uncertainty as to the exact meaning of the designation. It may be Paul's equivalent for the Son of man of the Synoptic Gospels and the Book of Enoch, though the identification is a disputed point among commentators and theologians. See " Expositor's Greek Testament," ii. 939, in the negative, and J. Weiss (" Urchristenthum," 374) and Feine (" Theologie des N.T.," 61) in the affirmative.

occurs does not tend to bear out the latter.[4] In this passage
he contrasts the first man Adam with Christ, the last or second
Adam. The contrast is concerned with two concrete, historic
figures. " The first man Adam became a living soul," the
historic representative of humanity on the lower " earthy "
or " natural " side, through whom " sin entered into the world
and death through sin." " The second or last Adam became
a life-giving spirit "—the historic representative of a new
humanity on its higher " spiritual " side, who, as man, exemplified this higher life and by his resurrection and exaltation
now belongs to the heavenly sphere. The heavenly man thus
seems not to stand for the archetypal, pre-existent man of
Philo, whose incarnation Paul finds in Christ, but for the
human Jesus, in whom the ideal spiritual life was realised
and who, through his resurrection and exaltation to heaven,
has become the life-giving spirit of a new humanity. His
representation of " the heavenly man " may thus not really
go beyond the Synoptic and primitive conception of the historic
Jesus as the Son of man who, by his resurrection, has been
exalted to God's right hand and now belongs to the heavenly
sphere.

On the other hand, in other passages he undoubtedly over-
steps the Synoptic and primitive conception of him as the
Christ, who lived on earth and has been exalted to heaven.
In these the Christ is the pre-existent Son of God, a primal
being, and in the representation of him in his pre-existent
state the influence of the Logos doctrine of Philo is unmistakable.
As in Philo, he is the first-born of all creation.[5] He is before
all things and creates all things in heaven and earth.[6] Through
him are all things, and in him all things consist.[7] He is the
medium between God and the universe, its vitalising, sustaining
force, and has been associated with the history of Israel as the

----

[4] On this subject see Feine, " Theologie," 353 f. ; Kennedy, " Philo's
Contribution to Religion," 76 f. (1919) ; " Creed," Article on " The Heavenly
Man " in *Journal of Theological Studies*, 1925. On the Urmensch of Philo
see Bousset, " Hauptprobleme der Gnosis," 194 f. (1907).

[5] πρωτότοκος, Col. i. 15. Philo, πρωτόγονος, and see Lightfoot,
" Commentary on Colossians," 141 f. Burney, on the other hand, thinks that
Paul could have taken the description of the pre-existent Son from the
Old Testament conception of Wisdom and the Rabbinic exegesis of
Gen. i. 1. This last inference seems fanciful. See his article in *Journal
of Theological Studies*, 1926.

[6] Col. i. 16-17.   [7] 1 Cor. viii. 6 ; Col. i. 17.

instrument of the divine will and purpose.[8] He is the image
of the invisible God [9] (as in Philo), *i.e.*, the manifestation or
reflection of God.   His face reflects " the light of the glory
of God." [10]   He was " in the form of God " before he became
man and took " the form of a servant." [11]   In him dwelleth all
the fullness of the godhead bodily,[12] and through him the
believer becomes a partaker of this fullness—all that God
confers in and through him.   He is the mediator of God's
grace and, in part at least, the source of it.   " Grace and
peace from God, the Father, and the Lord Jesus Christ." [13]
God and Christ are closely associated in Paul's thought of the
divine.   The Gospel is interchangeably the Gospel of God and
the Gospel of Christ.   He is invested with all authority and
dominion in the universe, for at his exaltation God gave him
the name that is above every name [14] (Lord, the Yahweh of the
Old Testament), and in Rom. x. 13, and other passages this
Old Testament title is understood as applying to him.   He is
superior to angels and demons, and has in all things the
pre-eminence.   He will overthrow the power of Satan and,
as in the Synoptic Gospels, he will be the agent of the transformation towards which history is rapidly tending.   To
him the believer owes subjection as well as devotion.   He is the
head of the Church and the object of worship.[15]   Praise and
prayer are offered to him,[16] though prayer is, as a rule, made to
God.   Religious rites—baptism and the eucharist—which have
a mystic significance, are a cardinal part of this cult.[17]   He
enters into the heart and dominates the life of the believer
in a mystic fashion, for the believer dies and rises with Christ,

[8] See, for instance, 1 Cor. x. 1-4.
[9] 1 Cor. iv. 4 ; Col. i. 15, εἰκών.
[10] 2 Cor. iv. 6.   [11] Phil. ii. 9.
[12] πλήρωμα, Col. ii. 9 ; *cf.* i. 19.
[13] Rom. i. 7, etc.
[14] Phil. ii. 9 f.; *cf.* Isa. xlv. 22-23.   On Rom. x. 13, see Dodd,
" Commentary on Romans," 167 f. (1932).   Morgan, following Bousset,
would ascribe the origin of the title to a Gentile source.   " Religion and
Theology of Paul," 46 f. (1917).   So also Böhlig, " Geisteskultur," 52 f.
The occurrence of the title in its Aramaic form in the primitive community, as I have pointed out in ch. i., and its use in this form by
Paul himself are strongly against this assumption.   Paul knows the term
" Lord " as applied to heathen gods (1 Cor. viii. 5).   But only to contrast it
with the Lord Christ.
[15] Col. i. 18 ; Phil. ii. 10.
[16] 2 Cor. xii. 8.
[17] Rom. vi. 3-4 ; Col. ii. 12 ; 1 Cor. x. and xi.

and lives in Christ, and Christ, or the Spirit of Christ, lives in him as an overmastering ethical and spiritual power.[18]

This is the sublime figure of the Christ as Paul conceives him—the transcendental Lord, the manifestation and the agent of God's will and purpose in creation and onwards in the history of the universe and man, till the final realisation of this purpose at the end of the ages.[19] Whence did he derive this sublime figure ? Hardly from the primitive tradition about the historic Jesus, as he actually lived and taught on earth. Rather from the revelation to himself on the Damascus road, which transformed him into the ardent believer in the heavenly Christ. To the risen and exalted Christ of the primitive tradition and his own experience he evidently transferred ideas derived from Jewish Apocalyptic and the Jewish-Hellenist Wisdom literature. It is, as we have seen, highly probable that, as a Pharisee, he knew the figure of the pre-existent Son of Man as depicted in the Book of Enoch.[20] He does not, indeed, make use of this designation in the Epistles. He prefers that of Son of God, which also, though rarely, occurs in Jewish Apocalyptic, as more suitable for the Greek world. But his conception of the pre-existent Christ or Son of God reflects in some respects the figure of the Enochian Son of Man. It reveals, too, familiarity with the doctrine of the pre-existent Logos or divine Word, as the medium of the creator-God, of the Wisdom literature and Philo ; and though he does not make use of the actual term in this connection, he speaks of Christ as " the wisdom of God." [21]

[18] See the characteristic passages in Rom. vi. 5 f. ; Gal. ii. 20 ; iii. 27 ; 2 Cor. xiii. 5 ; Col. ii. 10, 20 ; iii. 1.

[19] 1 Cor. xv. 22 f. I might have amplified the references in elucidation of Paul's conception of Christ from the Epistle to the Ephesians. It is, however, of doubtful authenticity, and does not materially add to the testimony of the generally accepted Epistles.

[20] On this figure see Charles' edition of the " First Book of Enoch " (1912) and " Apocrypha and Pseudepigrapha of the Old Testament," ii. (1913). On Paul's knowledge of the ideas and phraseology of this book see his " Introduction " to it, 99-100.

[21] 1 Cor. i. 24. He may also have drawn on the Targums, or Aramaic Paraphrases of the Old Testament, in which the hypostatised Word of God (Memra), like the Greek Logos, is conceived as the intermediary between God and man. It would appear, however, that this hypostatising of the Word of God was subsequent to the age of Paul. But the tendency to posit an intermediary between God and the world was already in Jewish theology. See Kohler, " Jewish Theology," 197 f. For the probable influence of Philo, see Lightfoot, " Commentary on Colossians," 141 f.

To the sublime figure of the Christ, who thus existed with
God before the creation and by his resurrection and exaltation
is enthroned in the heavenly sphere, Paul assigns a superlative
place in the religious thought and experience of the believer.
The Lord Jesus Christ seems in the Epistles at times to overshadow, if not displace, God as the object of faith. To some,
in fact, the Gospel of Paul is Christolatry pure and simple. It
certainly seems to go beyond the simpler relation of the disciples
to Jesus in his lifetime and in the primitive community at
Jerusalem. Jesus as the Christ was not to his early followers
all that he is to Paul, and he himself is silent on much on
which Paul expatiates in regard to his person and function.
At the same time, it is an exaggeration to say that Christ displaces God in the Epistles. Along with his pronounced and
developed Christolatry, Paul retains the monotheism which
he inherited from Judaism. In his mission preaching he
emphasises this monotheism and denounces Gentile idolatry.[22]
There is no God but one, he insistently proclaims to the
Corinthians, in contrast to the " many gods and lords " of the
Græco-Roman world. To the Thessalonians he speaks of
" the true and living God " in contrast to the idols from which
they have turned. This God is the supreme and ultimate source
of all, even of the heavenly Christ. " For of him and to him
and through him (God) are all things." [23] In this and similar
expressions of his monotheism he seems to borrow from the
Stoic philosophy as well as the Old Testament, though, in
contrast to Stoicism, God is no abstract idea, or first principle,
or all-pervading force of the universe, but is conceived in an
intensely personal sense. This " one God," this " true and
living God " is the Father, and in the classic passage in
1 Cor. viii. 4-6, in which he gives such pointed expression
to his monotheism, he reserves the title God to the Father
alone and differentiates between Him as God and Jesus Christ
as Lord. " There is no God but one . . . one God, the
Father, of whom are all things and we unto him ; and one
Lord, Jesus Christ, through whom are all things, and we
through him." To the Father-God Christ stands in distinct
and subordinate relation. Similarly in another classic passage

[22] Rom. i. 23 ; 1 Thess. i. 9 ; 1 Cor. viii. 4-5 ; Gal. iv. 8, etc.
[23] Rom. xi. 36.

in 1 Cor. xv. 24 f., his subordination and his final subjection to " God, even the Father," are unmistakably asserted. Paul, in fact, systematically distinguishes between God and Christ, though he often combines the two in the same sentence. He reserves for God the supreme place in his thought and assigns to Christ a distinct and dependent relation to Him. For him he is specifically the associate and instrument of God in the working out of the divine plan and purpose in the creation of the world and the redemption of man. If Christ is the head of the Church, God is the head of Christ.[24] If Christ is the image of God, so is man.[25] If the believer is Christ's, Christ is God's.[26] If he is the first-born of all creation, he is also the first-born of many brethren.[27] The repeated phrase " the God and Father of our Lord Jesus Christ " leaves no doubt that for Paul Christ stands not only in a filial, but a dependent relation to God. He is not God in the absolute sense ($\theta\epsilon\acute{o}s$),[28] or a second God, as in later theological speculation. As A. Schweitzer remarks, " he first became God in the later Greek theology." [29] The term God in Rom. ix. 5 (" God be blessed for ever ") is not applicable to Christ. The similar clause in 2 Cor. xi. 3 (" he who is blessed for ever ") is plainly referable to God, not to Christ, and the phrase " our great God and Saviour Jesus Christ " in Tit. ii. 13 is not

---

[24] 1 Cor. xi. 3.
[25] 1 Cor. xi. 7, $\epsilon\grave{\iota}\kappa\grave{\omega}\nu$ $\kappa\alpha\grave{\iota}$ $\delta\acute{o}\xi\alpha$ $\theta\epsilon o\hat{\upsilon}$.
[26] 1 Cor. iii. 23.
[27] Col. i. 15 ; Rom. viii. 29.
[28] There is much debate on this question. A large number of writers can be quoted for and against. Morgan, for instance, denies that for Paul Christ is God in the distinctive sense. So also Anderson Scott, " Christianity According to Paul," 273 f. ; H. A. A. Kennedy, " Theology of the Epistles," lxxxii. 86 (1919) ; Dodd, " Commentary on Romans," 152 (1932) ; J. Weiss, " Urchristenthum," 363-364. On the other side see A. T. Robertson, " Paul the Interpreter of Christ," 56 f. (1921) ; Radford, " Commentary on Colossians " (1931) ; M'Giffert, " The God of the Early Christians," 27 (1924), and " History of Christian Thought," i. 25 (1932) (with reservations in the sense, that while he regarded him as a divine being, a second God, he did not identify him with God) ; Clement, " Primitive Christianity and its Non-Jewish Sources," 337 (Eng. trans., 1912), but without adducing any proof. Rawlinson is convinced that he held " the idea of a co-essential, yet derivative Godhead ' of Christ,' " " New Testament Doctrine of Christ," 132-133 (1926). Dr Matthews is more cautious : " He is perhaps never explicitly spoken of by St Paul as God, but His relation with God is one of identity of function with respect to men," " God in Christian Thought and Experience," 71 (1930).
[29] " Geschichte der Paulinischen Forschung," 152 (1911).

genuinely Pauline.[30] Whilst in the speech to the elders
at Miletus, God is said to have purchased his church
with his own blood, in many MSS. " the Lord " is
substituted for God. Even if the traditional version is the
correct one, the meaning is probably " the blood of his own
(Son)." [31]   God is, indeed, said to have been in Christ reconciling the world unto himself,[32] but only as far as he was the
instrument of His redeeming purpose. He is invested with
full power as God's vicegerent in creation and redemption,[33]
and in this sense the fullness of the Godhead dwells in him in
order that he may carry out his divinely assigned function.
Before his appearance " in the form of a servant, the likeness
and fashion of a man," i.e., in his human life, he existed " in
the form of God." He belonged to the sphere of the divine.
But to belong to the sphere of the divine is not necessarily
to be God. He was not the equal of God. Instead of grasping
(presumably like Satan) at this equality,[34] he showed his
humility by emptying himself of his pre-existent being and
status, and taking those of a servant in order to carry out God's

[30] For the various interpretations of Rom. ix. 5, see " Expositor's Greek
Testament," ii. 658-659. See also Sanday and Headlam, " Commentary on
Romans," 233 f., who, " with some slight hesitation," refer the term God
to Christ. Lietzmann concludes for the negative, " Handbuch," iii. 86.
On Titus ii. 13, see Lietzmann, iii. 212 f. Even if the Pauline authenticity
of these words be granted, there is the alternative reading, " The Great God
and our Saviour Jesus Christ." In 1 Tim. iii. 16, ὅς must be read
for θεός.

[31] Acts xx. 28. τοῦ ἰδίου (υἱοῦ). See Blunt, " Commentary on
Acts," 232.

[32] 2 Cor. v. 19.   [33] Colossians i. 19 ; ii. 9.

[34] Phil. ii. 5 f. This seems to be the meaning of the words οὐχ ἁρπαγμὸν
ἡγήσατο τὸ εἶναι ἴσα θεῷ. This interpretation is also that adopted
by Deissmann, " St Paul," 169 ; Lohmeyer (Meyer's " Commentary,"
90 f., 8th ed., 1930) ; Dibelius (Lietzmann's " Handbuch," iii. 53, and
" Die Geisterwelt im Glauben des Paulus," 104 f.) ; Adeney in Peake's
" Commentary," 873. See also " Expositor's Greek Testament," iii. 435 ;
Michael, Commentary on Philippians," 85 f. (1928) ; Kennedy, " Theology
of the Epistles," 158 f. (1919). On the orthodox interpretation, which
holds that the clause means that he did not esteem it an usurpation to be
equal with God, see Lebreton, " Les Origines du Dogme de La Trinité,"
i. 320 f. (3rd ed., 1910). The clauses, " taking the form of a servant, being
made in the likeness of men, being found in fashion as a man," seem to
suggest a docetic view of Christ's humanity (man only in appearance). But
they must be interpreted in the light of Paul's unequivocal statement of his
real humanity in other passages of the Epistles. It is significant that he
refrains from saying outright " Being God " and only says " being in the form
of God." The same idea of Christ humbling himself to the level of humanity
is expressed in 2 Cor. viii. 9, in which it is said that though he was rich,
for your sakes he became poor.

redeeming purpose in a human life. On this account God has conferred on him a higher rank than he previously possessed—that of Lord—and invested him with supreme authority over the whole universe till His purpose shall be fulfilled. And as the heavenly Christ was before the creation not the equal of God, so, after the accomplishment of his redemptive function, he will resign his dignity as Lord of the kingdom and become subject to Him that invested him with this dignity. There will be a second act of renunciation at the final achievement through him of the divine will and purpose " in order that God may be all in all " [35]—remain the supreme and sole ruler.

However high he rates the Christ as the agent of the divine will and purpose from the beginning to the end of things, Paul's monotheism thus retains its sway in the thought of " the Father, even God," the " one God the Father." It does so, we might say, in view of the rather compromising terms in which he depicts him at times, in spite of himself. The application to him of the Old Testament name for God is, to say the least, misleading from the strict Jewish monotheistic point of view. Though Hellenist Judaism conceived the divine Wisdom or Logos as an intermediary between God and man and nature, it would hardly have identified him with the Old Testament Lord. So, too, such phrases as " in the form of God," " the fullness of God,' must have seemed questionable to a strict Jewish monotheist. But they must be understood in reference to the general Pauline conception of Christ in relation to God. In his pre-existent being and the creative and redemptive function with which he is invested, he belongs to the sphere of the divine. He is there as the first-born of all creation before any other being, whether ethereal or non-ethereal, existed. All being in heaven or on earth owes its existence to his creative activity, though God is the ultimate, transcendental, absolute source of all. This holds of the whole hierarchy of ethereal or supernatural being for which Judaism found room in the heavenly sphere, and Paul strenuously opposes the current Jewish or Jewish-Hellenist tendency within the Christian communities to supplement the cult of Christ by that of other ethereal beings. As the agent of creation, Christ is the supreme intermediary between God and the

[35] I Cor. xv. 24 f.

universe and man, the sole instrument of His redemptive will
and purpose.   To him alone of this ethereal hierarchy is worship
due as God's vicegerent.   Nevertheless, he is not God in the
absolute sense or the equal of God, the ultimate, the transcendental source of all things.   Whilst this transcendental God
becomes immanent in Christ [36] and reveals and works His will,
as the Father, through him, in creation and redemption, Christ
stands specifically in a distinct, subordinate, if unique relation
to Him.   He performs certain functions in connection with the
universe and man which no other ethereal being can fulfil.
He is invested with the divine fullness adequate to this end,
and after the consummation of his destiny, and with it that of
man and the universe, will resign his function and his supremacy
over both to God, who remains supreme.

V. His Cosmic Significance

Was Paul justified in ascribing to Christ not only pre-
existence, but a cosmic significance as the medium of God's
creative power ?   In other words, Was the historic Jesus, who
has been exalted to God's right hand, all that Paul predicated
of him ?   Did it follow from the fact of his resurrection and
his exaltation that he was the embodiment of a speculative
theory of creation current in Jewish and Jewish-Hellenist
thought, as represented by the Wisdom literature, by Philo,
and to a certain extent by Jewish Apocalyptic ? [1]   This theory
of a pre-existent agent of God's creative power—the Wisdom
or Word (Logos) of God—occupied in ancient thought the
place that is taken by the theory of evolution in modern

[36] As in Judaism, God is for Paul, apart from Christ, transcendental.
Even in Judaism, however, as well as in the old prophetic teaching and in
current Jewish Apocalyptic, God is in touch with the human spirit, and is
accessible to its aspiration Godwards, and Kohler rebuts the assumption
of Christian theologians that the God of Rabbinism was " an empty, transcendental abstraction," " Jewish Theology," 142 f.   Box also utters a caveat
against this assumption, article on " Jewish Apocalyptic in the Apostolic
Age," "Expositor" (1922).   For Paul the Pharisee, He was probably also
not such an abstraction.   At the same time, this aspect of Him was emphasised in Jewish thought, with its assumption of intermediary beings between
God and man, as Kohler admits.   *Ibid.*, 197 f.

[1] The Book of Proverbs, The Wisdom of Jesus Ben Sirach, for instance ;
the pre-existent Son of Man in 1st Enoch ; the Word as the medium of
creation in the " Sibylline Oracles," iii. 20 ; 2nd Enoch xxx. 8.   The belief
in the pre-existence of certain persons, or objects, or even institutions invested
with a religious significance (Moses, the Temple, the Sabbath, etc.), seems
to have been current in Rabbinic circles in Paul's time.

thought. In applying this theory to Christ, Paul made a cardinal contribution to the developing conception of the risen and exalted Lord. Is this contribution substantiated by the actual record of the life and teaching of Jesus, as reflected in the Synoptic tradition? Is it a necessary corollary of the conception of the exalted Christ?

Jesus himself had envisaged his transcendental function in the future æon or age, which should supervene on the present age or order of things. But in the authentic tradition of his life and teaching he does not seem to have claimed the exercise of such a function in the creation of the world or proclaimed his pre-existence. His future function in the imminent consummation is religious and ethical—that of the judge of the world.[2] He was probably acquainted with the personified pre-existent and creative Wisdom of the Book of Proverbs. He may further have known the Wisdom of Jesus Ben Sirach, in which the same conception appears. Some have seen an indication of this knowledge in the invitation of Matthew xi. 28 f. to the weary and heavy laden. There are certain verbal resemblances to this invitation in the passages of this book[3] cited in support of this contention. But that Jesus, in using a terminology current in Hebrew thought, was identifying himself with the pre-existent Wisdom of this book is rather a sanguine conclusion. Equally unconvincing the attempt to see such an identification in the use of the phrase " the Wisdom of God " in the saying of Jesus, as reported by Luke,[4] on the sending of prophets and apostles. In the Matthæan version of the saying, Jesus speaks in the first person, and this seems the more natural form of it.[5]

Even if, with Harnack,[6] we regard the Lukan form of it as a quotation from a book so entitled,[7] it does not involve any

[2] Mark xiii. 24 f.; xiv. 62, and parallels.
[3] xxiv. 19; li. 23 f. Charles, " Apocrypha and Pseudepigrapha," i. (" Sirach " edited by Box and Oesterly).
[4] Luke xi. 49. " The wisdom of God said," etc.
[5] Matt. xxiii. 34. " Therefore I send unto you," etc.
[6] " Sayings of Jesus," 111 (Eng. trans., 1908).
[7] Rendel Harris sees in it not a book, but a title which was applied to Jesus earlier than the Logos of the Fourth Gospel, with which it is practically identical. " Origin of the Prologue to St John's Gospel," 4 (1917), and " Origin of the Doctrine of the Trinity " (1919). Bacon also finds in the saying, " Wisdom is justified by her works " (Matt. xi. 19; cf. Luke vii. 35), a hint of the incarnation in Jesus of the eternal Wisdom of God, " Gospel of Mark," 227-228. Surely rather far-fetched.

personal application of the term Wisdom to the speaker. To me it seems that the implication that, in these passages, Jesus anticipated the Pauline teaching of his pre-existence and his creative function, rests on a very dubious foundation.

It might be said in support of this teaching—indeed it has often been said—that if Jesus could, by his resurrection and exaltation, become the Lord of Christian faith, he might well have pre-existed with God and exercised the cosmic function ascribed to him by Paul. It might be so, and one would wish that it were. But one would fain have more solid historic proof of it in his own teaching, as reflected in the authentic tradition. According to this tradition, Jesus realises himself as the One chosen by God to be the suffering and also the triumphant, transcendental Messiah. So also the disciples conceive him as the result of his teaching and their resurrection experience. They look for the coming of the risen Lord and Christ and proclaim salvation from judgment through faith in him. Paul shares and proclaims this conception as the result of his own experience of the risen Lord, supplemented by what he has learned from the immediate disciples of Jesus. So far we are warranted by history in going. In going beyond this into the region of apocalyptic and Jewish-Hellenist speculation and belief, and representing Jesus and the exalted Christ in the light of this speculation and belief, he goes beyond the actual evidence. What he gives is not evidence, but inference, and it is a real problem whether the inference is warranted in view of the silence of Jesus himself and the primitive tradition. Whilst the theologian may get over the problem by stressing the probability of the inference, the historian in search of actual proof is not so easily satisfied. Even the birth stories represent his coming into existence as the result of the generative act of the Holy Spirit in time. Nor is it sufficient to say that this developed conception of Christ does not seem to have met with opposition on the part of Paul's Jewish fellow-believers, as in the case of the controversy over the Law, and that it was, therefore, implicit in primitive Christian belief. That, under his influence, a conception of this kind became general does not prove that it was contained in the primitive tradition, or the primitive preaching. The pre-existent, cosmic Christ is not discernible in either. At most, it proves the disposition to accept such a conception as accordant with a prevailing speculation or belief in current Jewish religious thought. Whilst Paul ascribes his belief to revelation, to the witness of the indwelling Christ or the Spirit, it is obvious that it shows a distinct trace of current speculative thought. The appeal to revelation might be cogent in matters of purely moral or spiritual experience. It is not necessarily a proof of a certain speculation which dominated the intellectual and religious outlook of the time, and which Paul shared in his Pharisaic days. We cannot prove an opinion about the creation of the world, or the ethereal hierarchy, or the state of primitive man, etc., from the current dicta of pious belief. In this revelation, professedly received from the heavenly Christ, it is rather singular that there is a reflection of current Jewish or Jewish-Hellenist speculation. In this respect the revelation is markedly subjective and something more substantial in the way of evidence is necessary if modern thought is to be fully convinced. Mr Somerville, for instance, hardly meets the case when he claims that " experience of what Christ is to us decides what we believe to be true regarding Him." [8] There is a certain truth in this judgment. But it is surely precarious to see in our moral and religious experience in relation to Christ a guarantee of the truth of cosmic speculation about him, which bears the stamp of current subjective ideas on the universe and its creation. Why should we be asked to burden our faith with all that Paul, under the influence of contemporary thought, reads into his conception of the exalted Christ ? Why not be content with ascribing to him the Lordship in the religious sense which is his due ?

This Lordship is assuredly evidenced by the unique personality revealed in the authentic record of the life, supplemented by the resurrection appearances to the disciples and to Paul. Of the historical reality of these experiences there is, as I have pointed out in a previous section, no reason to doubt unless we adopt a purely dogmatic scepticism towards such psychic communications from the spirit world. Moreover, the unique personality revealed by the record tells powerfully

[8] " St Paul's Conception of Christ," 180 (1897).

not only in favour of its continued existence, but of the exalted place in the spirit world which Jesus undoubtedly held in his earthly existence among his fellow-men. Historically he stands on the highest moral and spiritual level—a level higher than we can attain in the mortal life which he shared with us. The transition of the historic Jesus to the rank of exalted Lord in the spirit world is the natural and fit consummation of his earthly life as the highest manifestation of the divine in the human. He had really won the Lordship in the consciousness of the disciples which they, with Paul, wholeheartedly assigned him. We may strip him of the theoretic pre-existence and the cosmic significance with which Paul invested him. We shall nevertheless respond to the evaluation of him as the highest concrete revelation of the divine known to us, the exalted Lord of our life, the chief medium of our approach to and communion with God. We shall feel that he passed by a natural transition from his rôle as the Master to that of the Lord of his disciples, even if we have had no such manifestations of his exalted being as were vouchsafed to them. If the earthly life was a reality, the heavenly Lordship is a natural, a cogent corollary of this reality. Jesus, we instinctively feel, was worthy of his exaltation in the faith of his disciples and in our faith as well, even if we must perforce walk by faith and not by sight.

But this Lordship did not necessarily involve for them, and does not necessarily involve for us, as it did for Paul, the attribute of pre-existence and a cosmic significance as the agent of creation. One need not *a priori* rule out his pre-existence. As a speculation, it is debatable whether the pre-existence of the soul is possible or not. It is possible that the rational, moral, and spiritual element, in which human personality consists, and which Jesus as a man shared with us, pre-existed before its incarnation in a human existence. That, at all events, it is of divine origin will be admitted by all but the confirmed materialist. Reason and conscience alike attest that man is, in this sense, made in the image of God—His handiwork. But they do not attest the pre-existence of our personality, which comes into conscious existence with the development of our organic being. Was it different in the case of Jesus ? His real identity with us in his human life, even if we make allowance for the uniqueness of his personality and life, would seem to preclude this inference. At all events it is not deducible from his earthly life and teaching. Jesus is silent on the subject. Nor is it involved in the primitive belief in the exalted Lord, begotten by the resurrection experience, backed by his expressed teaching on his future transcendental function. In going beyond this, Paul allowed himself to wander into the realm of current speculation and belief which Jesus himself refrained from entering. It is a subjective, not a historically founded evaluation.

From this point of view it is unfortunate that Paul, in his evaluation of the Christ, did not take more account of " the Christ after the flesh "—the Jesus of the authentic tradition, who is largely displaced in his consciousness by the heavenly Christ. Unfortunate, too, that he had not known Jesus as a disciple, and thus could not have a direct impression of him as he lived and taught. His fellowship is not really with the historic Jesus, but with the heavenly Christ. Equally unfortunate that, owing to the controversy with the Judaisers, he was led to emphasise his independence of those who had.[9] He knows, indeed, a number of facts bearing on his earthly career. His Epistles are the earliest written record of these facts, of which he made use in his mission preaching. But with the exception of the mention of his birth, they are confined to the close of his career—the institution of the Lord's Supper, his death, resurrection, and exaltation, on which, with the primitive tradition, he lays characteristic stress. He has something to say, incidentally, on his teaching and character. We may assume that he knew more than his Epistles, which are didactic or apologetic or practical, not historical missives, reveal. He speaks of the traditions or primitive record about Jesus which he had received (evidently from Peter and others), and about which he exhorts the Corinthians to hold fast.[10] He is acquainted with his character as manifested in his life among men, with his " meekness and gentleness," with the poverty which he endured for our sakes, with " the form of a servant," which he took as a man, with the life of service in which " he

[9] On his independent attitude towards the Twelve, see Wagenmann, " Die Stellng des Apostels Paulus Neben den Zwölf," 31 f. (1926).
[10] 1 Cor. xi. 2, 23 ; xv. 13.

6

pleased not himself." [11] He may actually have seen and
heard him " in the flesh," and his violent antipathy, as a
Pharisee, to his followers may indicate that he had witnessed
his encounters with his party at Jerusalem. He keeps before
him his example as the norm of his own life.[12] He speaks of
his preaching Jesus, in contrast to those who proclaim a different
Jesus from his.[13] The believer is thus brought into contact
not only with the heavenly Christ, but with the historic Jesus
in the practice of the Christian life. Though " the Christ in
you " is the heavenly Christ operating by his Spirit in the
believer's heart, the fruits of the Spirit, as manifested in the
believer's life, have their perfect counterpart in that of Jesus.
He is, indeed, very near to Jesus in his ethical teaching. He
quotes some of his sayings as absolutely authoritative for
Christian practice.[14] He reflects his teaching on the Fatherhood
of God and his followers as the children, the sons of God,
who invoke him as " Abba, Father." [15] He breathes the same
otherworldly atmosphere in his eschatological teaching.

On the other hand, there is a divergence, in some respects,
between the Jesus of the Synoptic record and the Christ of
Paul, and this divergence has given rise to the problem, so
much discussed in recent years, of Jesus and Paul.[16] Paul's
historic sense was weak, though he frequently appeals to history
to substantiate his arguments. His treatment of it is vitiated
by the rabbinic method of extracting from it data or doctrines
which are not strictly in accordance with obvious facts. The
method might easily lead to the mistaking of impressions for
facts under the influence of dogmatic prepossessions, as later in
the case of the author of the Fourth Gospel. It may be said
that a certain development of thought about Jesus was inevitable
in the light of his resurrection and exaltation and the spiritual

[11] 2 Cor. x. 1 ; viii. 9 ; Phil. ii. 7 ; Rom. xv. 3. According to some
modern theologians, these traits were derived from Old Testament passages
rather than from the primitive tradition. See Wrede, " Paulus," 84 f.
(1905) ; Brückner, " Entstehung der Paulinischen Christologie " ; Morgan,
" Religion and Theology of Paul," 32 f.
[12] 1 Cor. xi. 1.　　　　　　　　　[13] 2 Cor. xi. 4.
[14] 1 Cor. vii. 10 ; ix. 14 ; Gal. v. 14.
[15] Rom. viii. 15-17 ; Gal. iii. 26.
[16] See, for recent instances, Bacon, " Jesus and Paul," 120 f. (1920),
and McNeile, " New Testament Teaching in the Light of St Paul's,"
68 f. (1923). Machen, " Origin of Paul's Religion," 130 f. ; Porter, " The
Mind of Christ in Paul," 13 f. (1930).

experience of the believer, and that, in view of Paul's training and personality, his apprehension of Jesus would naturally differ from that of the simpler Galilean disciples. It is none the less questionable whether his conception of the pre-existent, cosmic Christ is warranted by the actual evidence. In the genuine tradition his function is religious and ethical, as the chosen instrument of God to lay the foundation of the kingdom in the present and bring about its full realisation in the near future. We need not, therefore, regret, with Lightfoot, that the Pauline conception of his pre-existence and cosmic activity is tending to recede into the background of the Christian consciousness [17] as a questionable inheritance from ancient mythology and speculation. We need not burden our faith with a literal interpretation of this speculation, as we need not with the literal interpretation of the story of the creation in the first two chapters of Genesis. The cosmic Christ is, after all, but an inference. Paul's grand preoccupation is the Cross of Christ, his significance and his achievement as the agent of man's redemption.

VI. The Spirit

As we have seen, Christ is for Paul the sole intermediary between God and man, and his supremacy does not admit of the recognition and worship, alongside him, of other ethereal beings. Whether he made an exception in the case of the Holy Spirit, and regarded it as an additional and personal medium of the divine will and purpose in redemption, depends on the view of the Spirit reflected in his Epistles.

Belief in the Spirit of God and its operation in man is characteristic of the Old Testament religion. There was no difficulty here for a Jewish monotheist in accepting this belief, inasmuch as the Spirit in the Old Testament generally appears as an enlightening and energising divine effluence or power operating on the spirit of man. "The Spirit of God is in itself only a wonderful power by which the life of man is regulated. . . . As the full inner life of reason and will is,

[17] Mr Carrington, in his Hulsean Essay on "The Christian Apologists of the Second Century" (1921), makes an eloquent effort to revive it. But not, it seems to me, with convincing result.

in the case of man, described as spirit, so too, in the case of
God, a similar fullness of strength, energy, life is thought of,
which is then also capable of proceeding forth from Him as an
active supramundane principle." [1]   There is discernible in the
Old Testament at most only the beginning of the later tendency
to hypostatise the Spirit.[2]   In the primitive preaching it is
also, as we have seen, impersonal.   Is it still so regarded by
Paul, or does he conceive of it in a personal sense as the third
member of a divine triad or trinity ?   To this question it is
difficult to give a definite answer.   In his teaching on the
Spirit he seems at times to be elusive and inconsistent.   Sometimes the phraseology suggests personality, distinct from that
of God or Christ.   Sometimes this personality is identical
with that of God or Christ.   Often it seems to be impersonal
—a divine effluence and power derived from God or Christ.

In Rom. viii., for instance, which has been called " the
chapter of the Holy Ghost," it is both the Spirit of God
dwelling in you, and the Spirit of Christ, of which believers
are in possession, or the Spirit of life in Christ Jesus which
has freed them from the law of sin and death.[3]   In other
passages of the same chapter, it takes on a more distinctive
personality.   It bears witness to us of our adoption as children
of God.   Our needs are known to " the mind of the Spirit,"
which makes intercession for the saints, though Christ also
performs this function.[4]   On the other hand, it appears as the
dynamic, but not necessarily personal, medium of the new
ethical life which accrues from justification through Christ,
and which God begets through the Spirit in believers.   Through
it the love of God is shed abroad in their hearts, the righteousness, peace, and joy befitting the kingdom of God is exemplified,
and believers abound in hope and in the power of the Spirit.[5]

---

[1] Schultz, " Old Testament Theology," iii ; cf. 184, 202 f. (Eng. trans.,
1892).
[2] Volz, " Der Geist Gottes," 145 f. (1910); Lietzmann, " Handbuch,"
iii. 78 (1913) ; Wheeler Robinson, " Christian Experience of the Holy
Spirit," 8 f. (1928).   Kirk would go farther than this, " There can be
little doubt that in certain cases the personification of the Spirit had gone a
long way."   See his very thorough essay in " Essays on the Trinity and the
Incarnation," 182 f. (ed. by Rawlinson, 1928).   See also Moore (" Judaism,"
i. 415 f.), who denies that the Spirit is a hypostasis in late Judaism.   Also
Strack and Billerbeck, " Kommentar," ii. 131 f. ; Asting, " Die Heiligkeit
im Urchristenthum," 89 f. (1930).
[3] Rom. viii. 2, 9 f.   [4] Ibid., viii. 14 f.
[5] Ibid., v. 5 ; xiv. 17 ; xv. 13 ; cf. 19.

In the First Epistle to the Corinthians it is, similarly, conceived in a personal and impersonal sense. In chapter ii.—another chapter of the Holy Spirit, as we may term it—it searches all things, even the deep things of God, which are known only to the Spirit of God, and reveals and teaches them to the spiritual man.[6] Whilst the phraseology thus seems to indicate distinct personality, it is clear that it is identical with God Himself. " For who among men knoweth the spirit of a man save the spirit of the man ? Even so the things of God none knoweth save the Spirit of God." In view of this identity, the Spirit of God dwelling in believers as His temple —" the Holy Spirit which is in you and which ye have from God "—is evidently an effluence from Him.[7] In one passage the three are distinguished and their functions defined. " Now there are diversities of gifts, but the same Spirit. And there are diversities of ministrations and the same Lord. And there are diversities of workings, but the same God who worketh all in all." [8] Whilst here also the apposition of the three seems to imply the distinctive personality of the Spirit, it subsequently appears to be identical with Christ who is described, in contrast to Adam, as " a life-giving spirit." [9] In other passages it is, as in Romans, equivalent to the divine power operating through the preaching of the Gospel and in the life of the believer. Paul's preaching is " in demonstration of the Spirit and of power . . . the power of God," which co-operates with Christ in the justification, sanctification, and inspiration of the believer.[10]

In 2 Cor., though Christ, God, and the Spirit again appear in conjunction, the Spirit is God's gift operating in us and is not necessarily more than the divine power, experienced by the believer.[11] In the apposition at the conclusion of the Epistle the distinction between the three reappears without any qualification. " The grace of the Lord Jesus Christ, and the love of God, and the communion of the Holy Ghost be with you all." [12] In other passages,[13] it is dynamically conceived. Whilst the identity of the Lord and the Spirit in iii. 17 seems to refer to Yahweh in the preceding quotation from Exodus

[6] 1 Cor. ii. 10 f.
[7] Ibid., iii. 16-17 ; vi. 19.
[8] Ibid., xii. 4-6 ; cf. Rom. xv. 16.
[9] Ibid., xv. 43.
[10] Ibid., vi. 11 ; xii. 3 ; cf. Rom. xv. 16, 30.
[11] 2 Cor. ii. 21-22.
[12] Ibid., xiii. 14.
[13] v. 5 ; vi. 6 ; xii. 18.

xxxiv. 34, not to Christ, it is undoubtedly identified with him in the Epistle to the Galatians. " And because ye are sons, God sent forth the Spirit of his Son unto your hearts, crying, ' Abba, Father.' " [14] Otherwise it appears here also, and in the first Thessalonian Epistle,[15] to be the dynamic of the Christian life. Similarly, in the Epistle to the Philippians,[16] he speaks of the Spirit of Jesus Christ, though he subsequently distinguishes between them.[17] Moreover, there is a number of passages throughout the Epistles in which the identification appears in the common phrase " in Christ," and " in the Spirit." These tend to show that the two are interchangeable in Paul's thought, and that what is thus ascribed to the Spirit is predicable of Christ.

It thus appears, in this brief review of the evidence, that, whilst there are passages in which the distinct personality of the Spirit is inferable, it is at times identical with that of God and Christ, and is preponderately a divine effluence or power operating in the thought and life of the believer. As the result of this review, I am inclined to agree with E. F. Scott's conclusion that, for Paul, it is not at bottom conceived in a personal sense, but as an effluence or power. " In not a few passages Paul appears to speak of the Spirit in terms that may be understood as personal. . . . None the less, it is clear that for Paul the Spirit is not a personality, but a power or a divine effluence." [18] It would, therefore, be hazardous to maintain that for him God, Christ, the Spirit form a personal triad or trinity, far less that he conceived of this Trinity in the later metaphysical sense of the equal divinity and the essential oneness of all three. If there is a Trinity at all, it is only in the experimental sense [19] — the association of Father, Son, and Spirit in the divine plan of redemption and its application in the religious experience of the believer. It is not speculative, as in the later form of the Creeds. It is based on the experience

---

[14] Gal. iv. 6.
[15] 1 Thess. i. 5-6 ; v. 19.
[16] Phil. i. 19.
[17] Ibid., ii. 1.
[18] " The Spirit in the New Testament," 192.
[19] What some theologians call " an economic Trinity." Feine, for instance, " Theologie des N.T.," 459. Swete, as the result of his examination of the New Testament teaching on the Spirit, concludes that what " it places before the mind is not a doctrine, but an experience." " The Holy Spirit in the New Testament," 359 (1909). He thinks, however, that it ascribes personality to the Spirit. Ibid., 293.

of what God, Christ, the Spirit stand for in the thought and life
of the believer. It is, however, very questionable whether,
at bottom, Paul's faith is not what has been called binitarian,
rather than trinitarian—the belief in a twofold rather than
in a threefold Deity. Even so, this belief has to be qualified
by the reservation that, for him, the Father alone is God in the
absolute sense, Christ the distinct, derived, and subordinate
agent of His supreme redemptive will and purpose. It is
highly significant that, in the introductions to his Epistles,
the grace and peace only of God, the Father, and the Lord
Jesus Christ are invoked on those to whom they are addressed.
In this invocation the Spirit is never combined with them.
Similarly, in the thanksgivings which usually follow the
invocation, only God, the Father, in association with Jesus
Christ, His Son, is mentioned ; the Spirit never.[20] Equally
significant the omission of the Spirit in the classic statement
of his monotheistic faith, as against the pagan gods in 1 Cor.
viii. 6. " To us there is one God, the Father, and one Lord,
Jesus Christ." The emphatic omission of the Spirit in all
these explicit expressions of his conception of Deity is in-
explicable, if Paul believed in a triune God. " We cannot,"
concludes Dr Kirk, " eliminate from his thought a very large
admixture of purely binitarian elements, in which the Spirit—
if distinguished from Christ at all—is distinguished as the thing
from the person, the gift from its giver, the influence from the
fount, and not as one hypostasis in the Godhead from
another." [21] Paul would evidently not have subscribed the
Nicene and later creeds.

VII. REDEMPTION—ITS JURIDICAL ASPECT

In its cosmic significance, redemption means the overthrow,
through Christ's death and his resurrection to his rôle as Lord,

[20] Lebreton, in his exposition of Paul's view, in the orthodox sense,
ignores these very significant facts. It is a serious defect. See " Origines du
Dogme de la Trinité," 325 f.
[21] " Essays on the Trinity and the Incarnation," 207. See also Matthews,
" God in Christian Thought and Experience," 185. Dr Matthews emphatically rebuts the assumption that Paul held the Trinity in the metaphysical
sense. " St Paul knew it not and would have been unable to understand
the meaning of the terms used in the theological formula on which the
Church ultimately agreed." Ibid., 180. He would probably have been
denounced as a heretic by the majority of the Nicene and later Fathers.

of the demonic powers. Thereby the rule of God over these powers has been guaranteed. The reigning Christ will ultimately, at his coming, triumph over them and over death itself.[1] The saints will ultimately sit in judgment on the world and the angels.[2] This triumph began on the Cross itself. On the Cross Christ not only annulled the condemnation inherent in the Law. He triumphed over the principalities and powers operating through the Law to man's undoing.[3] In crucifying the Lord of glory these infernal powers were unwittingly undoing themselves.[4] In the present age they still exercise their nefarious sway. But they are waging a losing battle, and Paul is persuaded that they will fail in their attempt to separate the believer from the love of God in Christ Jesus, the Lord.[5] His pessimism passes into a soaring optimism as he carries the mythological conception to its final issue in the defeat and destruction of the demons. Nay, in one passage in the Epistle to the Colossians, he can even contemplate their ultimate redemption in the final reconciliation, through Christ, of all things in heaven and earth, and the establishment of an eternal peace " through the blood of his cross." [6]

In respect of man, redemption has for Paul a juridical, an ethical, and a mystic aspect. The problem is a twofold one. Sin, being an offence against God, involves guilt, and the problem, from this point of view, is how man can be absolved from the guilt of sin and attain the righteousness which God requires. Man is in bondage to sin, which inheres in the flesh, and the problem, from this point of view, is how to find deliverance from the dominion of sin, and, thus delivered, realise in the higher life of the spirit the righteousness which, in consequence of this bondage, he cannot achieve. The answers to those two problems Paul finds in the redemption effected by Christ.

In dealing with the juridical aspect of redemption, he emphasises the retributive righteousness of God, which requires him to punish sin. Though in bondage to sin, Jew and Gentile

---

[1] 1 Cor. xv. 23 f.
[2] *Ibid.*, vi. 2-3.
[3] Col. ii. 14-15.
[4] 1 Cor. ii. 8.
[5] Rom. viii. 38-39.
[6] Col. i. 19-20. On this subject see Morgan, " Religion and Theology of Paul," 69 f. ; Anderson Scott, " Christianity According to St Paul," 28 f. (1927).

are alike accountable to God for their transgression of the Law
—the Jew under the revealed Law, the Gentile under the
natural Law of conscience.[7]   God's righteousness, which is an
essential of His nature, must take account of transgression
whether of the revealed or the natural Law. Transgression
incurs the wrath of God.[8]   Hence the emphasis on God's
wrath " revealed against all ungodliness and unrighteousness
of men," which, in the case of the Gentiles, are luridly described
in Rom. i. 18 f.   This unrighteousness is likewise manifest
in the case of the Jew, who, in spite of his possession of the
Law, is equally culpable,[9] equally exposed to the exercise of
God's retributive righteousness. Both, by despising His goodness, forbearance, and longsuffering in refraining from punishing their sin, which should lead to repentance, have to reckon
with the divine retribution " in the day of wrath and revelation
of the righteous judgment of God, who will render unto every
man according to his works."[10]   Both will be judged at the
great assize in accordance with the retributive righteousness
which " visiteth with wrath."[11]   Both are enemies of God, and
God, in one passage at least (Rom. ii. 28), is the declared enemy
of the sinner, though it is distinctively God's enmity to sin,
which is the moving cause of His wrath, that is emphasised.
Since all have incurred this wrath, it is obvious that none
can escape this retribution unless by a redemption, by which
God can be just or righteous, and still justify or acquit the
transgressor.

This redemption Paul finds in " the Gospel," which " is the
power of God unto salvation to every one that believeth,"
Jew and Gentile alike.[12]   In the Gospel there is revealed to
faith a righteousness of God, apart from or outwith the Law.[13]
Under the Law the sinner, who cannot possibly be justified in
His sight by the works of the Law, is inevitably exposed to His
judgment. This revealed righteousness is more particularly
described as " the righteousness of God through faith in Jesus
Christ unto all them that believe "[14]—" the righteousness which

---

[7] Rom. ii. 12 f.
[8] *Ibid.*, i. 18 ; ii. 8 ; iv. 15 ; v. 9 ; 1 Thess. i. 10 ; Col. iii. 6.
[9] *Ibid.*, ii. 17 ; iii. 9 f.
[10] *Ibid.*, ii. 4 f.   [12] *Ibid.*, i. 16.
[11] *Ibid.*, iii. 5.   [13] *Ibid.*, i. 17 ; iii. 19 f.
[14] *Ibid.*, iii. 21 ; *cf.* ix. 30 f. ; x. 3 f.

is of faith." In contrast to His retributive righteousness under the Law, it is a saving righteousness revealed to and available to faith in Christ and operating the salvation of the believer through him. The revelation and the operation of it, in and through Christ to the salvation of the believer, is what constitutes the Gospel. In the Gospel the means of justification or acquittal from the transgression of the Law, which God must otherwise needs punish, has been provided through a righteousness available to faith in Christ. The Gospel is thus the fulfilment of God's redemptive purpose and promise of justification by faith, which was " preached beforehand to Abraham," through whom all the nations were to be blessed,[15] and is now freely operative for salvation to all believers in Christ. " Through the redemption that is in Christ Jesus," believers are " justified freely by God's grace."[16]

This redemption has become possible inasmuch as God " purposed or set forth Christ to be a propitiation through faith, by his blood."[17] The object of this propitiation, which God Himself provides, is both to vindicate His righteousness in the retributive sense in hitherto forbearingly passing over sins done aforetime, and, at the same time, to make possible the operation of his saving righteousness in the justification through Christ of the believer. " It enables God to be alike just (righteous) and to justify (in the sense of pronouncing righteous)

[15] Gal. iii. 8-9.
[16] Rom. iii. 24.
[17] *Ibid.*, iii. 25. ἱλαστήριον. On its meaning, which is the subject of dispute among commentators and theologians, see " Expositor's Greek New Testament," ii. 611, iii. 169; Deissmann, " Bibelstudien," 121 (1895); Feine, " Theologie des N.T.," 394; Weinel, " St Paul," 304 f. (Eng. trans., 1906); Lietzmann, " Handbuch," iii. 47 f.; Anderson Scott, " Christianity According to St Paul," 68 f.; Dodd, " Commentary on Romans," 54 f. (1932); Denney, " Christian Doctrine of Reconciliation," 154 f. (1917); Somerville, " St Paul's Conception of Christ," 83 f. (1897). Deissmann, Somerville, Anderson Scott, and Dodd attempt to soften or explain away the propitiatory character of the death of Christ. Denney, Lietzmann, Weinel, and Feine regard it as a blood offering necessitated by God's essential righteousness. Personally, I think that for Paul Christ's death was necessary to expiate sin in God's sight and vindicate His righteousness or justice as against sin, though it is by no means the only aspect of it. Schweitzer finds the doctrine of the forgiveness of sin, in virtue of the expiatory death of Christ, in Paul's teaching, but thinks that it is subordinate to that of forgiveness in virtue of the death and resurrection of Christ, by which sin has been destroyed, so that those who have died and risen with Christ appear in God's sight as actually sinless. This, he judges, is the specifically Pauline doctrine, which springs from his mysticism, " Mystik des Apostels Paulus," 217 f.

him that hath faith in Christ." [18] It is an act of expiation
vicariously and voluntarily performed by Christ as the head
and representative of humanity.[19] He has taken upon him
the curse pronounced by the Law on every one who does not
fulfil it and has redeemed us from this curse.[20] " He who
knew no sin he made to be sin in our behalf." " While we
were still weak, Christ died in due season for the ungodly."
" When the fullness of the time came, God sent forth his
Son that he might redeem them that were under the Law." [21]
By his expiatory death he pays the price for man's redemption,[22]
just as the slave pays to his god out of his savings, through the
priest in the pagan temple, the price of his redemption or
emancipation.[23] This is, indeed, not the only aspect of Christ's
death, as we shall see. But it is a fundamental, not a merely
incidental one, as the frequent reference in the Epistles to
" the blood of Christ " tends to show. The sense of sin, the
guilt of sin, judgment for sin are realities for Paul. Without
the expiation offered on the Cross in the sinner's behalf, God's
free grace cannot operate for his justification. To excise or
minimise this aspect of his redemptive teaching is to evade
an essential element of it. " Delivered up for our trespasses."
" Being justified by his blood, we shall be saved from the
wrath of God through him." " God sending his own Son
in the likeness of sinful flesh and (as an offering for) sin,
condemned sin in the flesh.[24] Such statements are not mere
parerga.

Paul thus develops the primitive teaching of the Suffering
Servant into a doctrine of expiation required for the exercise

[18] Rom. iii. 25-26. On the meaning of δικαιοῦν, see Sanday and
Headlam, " Commentary on Romans," 28 f. ; Feine, " Theologie des
N.T.," 408 f.
[19] Rom. v. 12 f. ; 2 Cor. v. 14.
[20] Gal. iii. 10 f., ἐξηγόρασεν. It has the same meaning as ἀπολύτρωσις.
See " Expositor's Greek Testament," iii. 169. Schweitzer thinks that
the words, as quoted by Paul, do not refer to the atoning death of Christ,
but to the destruction of the Law by his crucifixion, " Die Mystik des
Apostels Paulus," 64 (1930). This does not seem conclusive. It is the
curse of the Law on those who do not fulfil it, not the Law itself that, for
Paul, Christ's death has removed.
[21] 2 Cor. v. 21 ; Rom. v. 6 ; Gal. iv. 4-5.
[22] 1 Cor. vi. 20 ; vii. 23.
[23] On the metaphor, as applied to the redemption of man, see Deissmann,
" St Paul," 149 f.
[24] Rom. iv. 25 ; v. 9 ; viii. 3.

of God's saving righteousness. From the frequency with which he uses the phrase "the blood of Christ," he evidently had in mind the Jewish idea of blood sacrifice for sin.[25] He appears also to have had in view the fifty-third chapter of Isaiah, from which he infers not only the vicarious, but the expiatory suffering of the Servant. He only quotes the first verse of this chapter, incidentally,[26] as a proof of Israel's perversity in not believing the Gospel as he preached it. But we may safely place this sublime prophetic utterance, among others, in the background of his theory of redemption by expiatory suffering. It is, in fact, implied in his representation of Jesus taking the form of a servant and bearing the reproaches of men for their salvation.[27] "The language which Paul often uses in connection with the death of Christ reflects the terminology of Isaiah liii."[28] He evidently also had in mind the words of Jesus in instituting the Eucharist, which had for Paul a supreme significance in this connection.[29] He may, further, have been familiar with the idea of the death of the martyred Eleazar and his sons under Antiochus Epiphanes as a ransom, a propitiation for sin.[30] For Paul the Cross is no "stumbling-block," as it is to the Jews of his time (1 Cor. i. 23). As a propitiation for sin, it is an essential of the Jewish religion itself.

This propitiation becomes operative in virtue of the Jewish conception of the non-reckoning or non-imputation of sin,[31] as in Ps. 32, which he quotes, and the imputation or reckoning of the merit of the righteous for the unrighteous, as in current Rabbinic teaching.[32] It enables God both to impute man's sin to Christ and Christ's righteousness to man. On man's part it is made available in virtue of another Jewish conception

---

[25] Anderson Scott argues against this inference, but not conclusively. "Christianity According to St Paul," 86 f. Dodd admits that Paul, in using the phrase "blood of Christ," is thinking in sacrificial terms, but holds that he means only the self-dedication of his life to God, the blood being conceived as the life, "Commentary on Romans," 55-56. E. F. Scott thinks that it means merely a violent death, "Commentary on Colossians and Ephesians," xxvi.143 (1930).

[26] Rom. x. 16.   [27] Phil. ii. 7; Rom. xv. 3.
    [28] Kennedy, "Theology of The Epistles," 128 (1919).
    [29] 1 Cor. x. 16; xi. 23 f.
    [30] IV. Maccabees, vi. 28; xvii. 22. Charles, "Apocrypha and Pseud-epigrapha," ii. 654.
    [31] λογίζεσθαι, Rom. iv. 6 f.; 2 Cor. v. 19.
    [32] On the Rabbinic view see Kohler, "Jewish Theology," 304—that of Hillel, for instance.

—that of reckoning faith for righteousness, as in the case of Abraham, whose faith in God's promise was reckoned for righteousness.[33] It is with these ideas in his mind, supplemented by the concepts and terminology of Græco-Roman law, with which, as a Roman citizen, he was familiar, that Paul works out his fundamental doctrine of justification by faith.

Faith in Christ is fundamental for salvation. " Knowing that a man is not justified by the works of the law, but only through faith in Christ, even we believed in Jesus Christ, that we might be justified by faith in Christ, and not by the works of the law, because by the works of the law shall no flesh be justified." [34] By faith the sinner appropriates the benefit of the non-imputation of sin and the imputation of righteousness, which Christ's expiatory death has made possible. He is thereby acquitted, justified, and assured of redemption from the guilt of sin, which is impossible by the works of the Law. Faith is not intellectual assent, but wholehearted acceptance of, and reliance on the redeeming grace of God in Christ. Redemption, which is a thing of this free grace, has, in fact, always been by faith, not by works. This is proved not only by the case of Abraham, whose faith was reckoned for righteousness, but by other Old Testament passages, particularly Habakkuk ii. 4. " The just shall live by faith." The promise to Abraham that in his seed all the nations of the earth should be blessed, and Abraham's faith in this promise are assumed to imply the conscious forecast of the Pauline scheme of redemption through Christ—" the Gospel beforehand preached unto Abraham." [35] Christ's redeeming efficacy is thus carried back to the period before the Law, and the reckoning of faith for righteousness in Abraham's case applies to all of whom he is, by promise, the father—Gentiles as well as Jews.[36] Faith is thus an essential of God's redemptive purpose whether in the past or the present. In the past it has been operative in trust in God's promise to Abraham of redemption through Christ. It is now operative in trust in its actual fulfilment in him. Thereby a reconciliation [37] has been effected between God and man. Man, the enemy of God by reason of sin, has by

[33] Rom. iv. 1 f. ; Gal. iii. 6 f.
[34] Gal. ii. 16.
[35] Ibid., iii. 8.
[36] Rom. iv. 9 f.
[37] καταλλαγή, Rom. v. 10-11 ; 2 Cor. v. 18-19.

adoption [38] entered into a filial relation to Him. Fellowship with God has displaced alienation from God. " There is, therefore, now no condemnation to them that are in Christ Jesus." Justification is a present experience, though it will only be completed at the last judgment.[39]

This is the juridical aspect of redemption which Paul worked out in the Epistles to the Galatians and Romans in conflict with his Judaising opponents. In this conflict, he strove to invalidate the Law as a means of salvation and substitute for it the Gospel of Justification by faith alone, in virtue of the expiatory death of Christ.

Waiving meanwhile the detailed consideration of his argumentation in proof of man's impotence to attain salvation by the works of the Law, his theory of justification solely by the grace of God in Christ receives a certain measure of support in Old Testament thought. At the root of the theory is the conviction that man is dependent for salvation, not on his own merits or works, but on the mercy of God. It is one that makes, or ought to make, a universal appeal, and it finds frequent expression in both prophet and psalmist. Both emphasise the fact of sin and the need of the sinner to throw himself on God's merciful acceptance.[40] In the prophets the failure of Israel to keep the Law, and its inveterate tendency to moral and religious lapse is the refrain of many a denunciation of the prevailing degeneration of the people. Israel's history is, in fact, from the prophetic ideal, largely a history of this failure. In view of this fact, its salvation is ascribable to the mercy or grace of God, not to its own merits. In Paul's own time the writer of Ezra iv. emphatically voices the thought of man's impotence to keep the Law, to work out his salvation by its means,[41] in opposition to the current idea of justification by works.[42] Similarly, the idea of faith as a means of attaining

---

[38] υἱοθεσία, Rom. viii. 15 ; Gal. iv. 5. A legal term, borrowed from Græco-Roman law and referring to the investing of a slave with the rights and privileges of a son. The practice is Græco-Roman, not Jewish.

[39] Rom. v. 1, 9 ; viii. 1 ; 1 Cor. vi. 11.

[40] See, for instance, Isa. lix. and lxiv. ; Ps. cxliii. 2.

[41] vii. 116 f. ; ix. 32 f. Charles, " Apocrypha and Pseudepigrapha," ii. 591, 602.

[42] As expressed in " II. Baruch," li. 3, 7, etc., and, though not so strongly, in the " Assumption of Moses," written in the early part of the first Christian century.

righteousness in God's sight finds expression in Abraham's reliance on His promise. " And Abraham believed in the Lord and he counted it to him for righteousness." [43] Moreover, sacrifice, bloodshed in atonement for sin is an integral part of the Old Testament cultus, with its various sin offerings, which " expressed the desire to propitiate an offended Deity." [44] The justification of the sinner by vicarious suffering is also an Old Testament conception, as in Isaiah liii., in which Israel, as the Suffering Servant, vicariously suffers for " the justification of many."

Paul's theory of justification is thus, to this extent, in unison with Old Testament thought. At the same time, he shows a tendency to interpret this thought in the light of his own religious experience and reflection, and it is questionable whether his interpretation is, in all respects, historically valid. Questionable, further, whether his doctrine of justification from the juridical point of view is altogether in harmony with the teaching of Jesus himself.

It is, for instance, only by a Rabbinical quibble that the word " seed " in the promise to Abraham is made to refer to Christ, and the Gospel is thus arbitrarily preached beforehand to Abraham [45] and Christ's redeeming efficacy is carried back to the period before the Law. Similarly, one is by no means sure that, in the reckoning of faith for righteousness, in the case of Abraham, faith had the significance which Paul reads into it.[46] Faith in Gen. xv. 6 seems to have been reckoned in the sense of a meritorious work, rather than as the substitute for such a work.[47] In the other classic passage, " The just shall live by faith " (Hab. ii. 4), which he quotes [48] in support of his thesis that faith, not works, justifies, he only succeeds in proving his point by a mistranslation of the original, which bears that the just shall live by his " faithfulness " (to God and His will).

Moreover, in his view of the propitiatory death of Christ as a

[43] Gen. xv. 6.   [45] Gal. iii. 8, 16.
[44] Kohler, " Jewish Theology," 263.   [46] Rom. iv. 3 f.
[47] It is possible by reading into the word " faith " trustful fidelity, which some hold that the context warrants, to get something like Paul's meaning out of it. Normally, the word means fidelity or faithfulness. Deut. xxxii. 20. On the Jewish conception of faith as a meritorious work, see Feine, " Theologie des Neuen Testaments," 404-405.
[48] Gal. iii. 12.

condition of justification, he overlooks the fact that in the Old
Testament, in spite of its blood sacrifices, God exercises His forgiving grace in return for repentance alone.   In the prophetic
writings and the Psalms He is often represented as antagonistic
to the priestly idea of blood sacrifice for sin, which had become
subversive of true piety and real well doing.   Justice, righteousness, not sacrifice is what God desires, insists Amos.[49]   " I
desire mercy and not sacrifice, and the knowledge of God
rather than burnt offerings," reiterates Hosea.[50]   The same note
appears in Isaiah.   " To what purpose is the multitude of your
sacrifice unto me ? . . . I delight not in the blood of bullocks
or of lambs or of he-goats." [51]   " For I spake not unto your
fathers nor commanded them in the day that I brought them
out of the land of Egypt concerning burnt offerings and
sacrifices, but this thing I commanded them, saying, Hearken
unto my voice and I will be your God and ye shall be my
people ; and walk ye in all the way that I commanded you,
that it may be well with you." [52]   " Sacrifice and meat offerings
thou hast no delight in," cries the Psalmist, " burnt offering
and sin offering hast thou not required." [53]   God is represented
as ready abundantly to pardon the repentant, to save those who
seek His mercy without money and without price,[54] " pardoning
iniquity and passing over the transgression of the remnant of
his heritage, because he delighteth in mercy." [55]   The teaching
of the prophets, in their revulsion from the sacrificial cult,
seems, in fact, to run counter to Paul's assumption of the
necessity of a blood atonement for sin as the condition of
acceptance with God.   His saving mercy operates freely and
directly in return for repentance, which leads to the restoration
of the people to His favour and obedience to His righteous
will.   The prophets do not, indeed, minimise the fact of
sin, and in Isaiah liii. the need of vicarious suffering on behalf
of the sinner finds sublime expression.   It is, however, disputable whether the sin-bearing Servant offers himself as an
expiation for sin in the Pauline sense.[56]   In Israel's suffering

[49] v. 21 f.   [52] Jer. vii. 22, 23.
[50] vi. 6.   [53] Ps. xl. 6.
[51] Isa. i. 11.   [54] Isa. lv. 1 f.   [55] Micah vii. 18 f.
[56] Morgan, for instance, holds that the idea of God requiring an atonement for sin is not expressed in the Suffering Servant of Isaiah.   " Religion
and Theology of Paul," 77 f.   Feine maintains that it is.   " Theologie des
Neuen Testaments," 128.

the idea of service, rather than expiation, for others seems to be the main thought.[57]   On the other hand, it is hardly disputable that the idea of expiation is the one that Paul read into it.[58] He holds not only that man can do nothing to satisfy God's righteousness and attain salvation by way of the Law, but that God's righteousness, as revealed in the Law, requires the vicarious propitiation of sin in order to save the sinner.   He does not seem to have been troubled by the question, which occurs to the modern reader, of the equity from the point of strict justice, of annulling the real guilt of one because of the assumed guilt of another.   Nor does he seem to have concerned himself with the farther question how this assumption accords with such Old Testament passages as Proverbs xvii. 15.   " He that justifieth the wicked and he that condemneth the just, even they both are an abomination to the Lord."   For him justification in virtue of the expiatory death of Christ is the only way out of the impasse created by his keen consciousness of sin and its consequences of condemnation and death.   How this subjective conviction accords with the prophetic proclamation of the abounding mercy of God towards the repentant sinner, apart from a blood equivalent for sin, he does not explain. From the point of view of the prophetic teaching, his doctrine of the propitiatory death of Christ, as an indispensable condition of justification, is, to say the least, one-sided.   It is not only difficult to reconcile it with this teaching considered in the broad sense.   It is questionable whether it truly reflects that of Jesus himself.

Was Paul justified in reading this interpretation of it into the words of Jesus at the Last Supper ? [59]   As we have seen,

[57] See Section V. of previous chapter.

[58] Morgan contends that Paul does not really hold the view that God's forgiveness is conditioned by the satisfaction of his retributive justice. " Religion and Theology," 88 f.   Bacon appears to agree with him.   " Jesus and Paul," 91 f. (1921).   So also Anderson Scott, " Christianity According to St Paul," 75 f.   Stevens, on the other hand, argues forcibly that Paul does teach the necessity of a satisfaction to God's justice.   " Christian Doctrine of Salvation," 61 f.   So also Weinel, " St Paul," 306 f. ; Denney, " Christian Doctrine of Reconciliation," 155 f. ; and Cone, " Paul," 260 f. (1898).

[59] Feine insists that the words of Jesus at the Last Supper, " My blood shed for you," have an expiatory significance, mainly on the ground that they betray a reference to Isa. liii., which, he holds, rather dogmatically, is to be understood in an expiatory sense. See " Theologie des Neuen Testaments," 142 f. ; cf. 145-146.

7

Jesus, in this and several other passages, did regard his death as a vicarious sacrifice for man. But it is difficult to read into these passages, especially in view of his distinctive teaching of the Fatherhood of God and the ethical character of the kingdom, the Pauline doctrine of justification in virtue of his expiatory death. Taking these passages by themselves, one does not necessarily find in them what Paul seeks to establish. It is the ethical, rather than the juridical element in redemption that Jesus emphasises. Though he has also in mind the juridical element in the coming judgment at the establishment of the kingdom, salvation from judgment is not conceived in the Pauline sense of justification through his expiatory death. His death is a necessity demanded by the antagonism of his enemies, his overmastering love of man, and his fidelity to the will of God. It will be of the greatest efficacy in leading many into the kingdom and thus realising their salvation in the life of suffering—the losing of this life which is the condition of life eternal. The sacrificial idea in the teaching on the kingdom is that of the utmost self-denial for him and his disciples for its sake. If, in the closing period of his mission, the sacrifice for others is connected with his death, it is only by surrendering himself to the Cross that he can attain the end that God has appointed for him in bringing the kingdom to its final fruition. Was it, in addition, a blood offering to God in order that He might acquit, justify the sinner in the Pauline sense? There is no indication of this in his characteristic conception of God as the Father and of men as His children in virtue of their innate faith in Him, the consciousness of their filial relation to Him, and their obedience to the Father's will. He calls them to do His will on the supposition that, as His children, they can do it, not, as in Paul, that, as the slaves of sin, they cannot do it at all. He summons them to repent and seek the kingdom of God and His righteousness on the assumption that they are capable of doing both. Whilst waging, like Paul, a polemic against the current legalism and criticising even the Mosaic Law, he respects the Law and bids men do its commandments and live. " This do and thou shalt live." He does, indeed, in the parables of the publican and sinner and of the servant who does the duty enjoined on him by his lord, emphasise the dependence of the sinner on God's mercy. " God be merciful to me, a sinner," is the true attitude in His presence. But he does not seem to have shared Paul's view either of sin or of the sinner, and certainly did not elaborate a juridical theory of justification from sin in the Pauline sense. The publican in the parable is " justified " in virtue of his repentance and God's mercy in accepting it.[60]

Paul works out his doctrine of redemption in the juridical sense in terms of the rabbinic theology. This element of rabbinic thought in it lends it a certain scholastic technicality which does not appeal to our modern mentality. What was to a man of his rabbinic training convincing reasoning is not necessarily so to us. Similarly, the theory of expiatory bloodshed is not attractive to modern thought and feeling, and the tendency in recent times has been to eliminate it from his thought and discard expiation in the sense at least of the propitiation of an angry deity. Whilst it is possible to tone down the theory by emphasising the divine love and grace working behind and through it, which, as we shall see, Paul himself does, it really seems that he saw in the death of Christ a satisfaction of the divine justice, if not of the divine wrath. In any case, the theory of vicarious blood sacrifice in the expiatory sense, for religious ends, now appears to many to be out of place in the higher forms of religion. In practice the slaughter even of animals, on the assumption that their offered blood has an efficacy in taking away moral guilt, reflects a crude and barbarous conception of religion, in spite of its prevalence even among otherwise highly civilised peoples in the ancient world. Still more so the shedding of human blood to this end. To seek atonement by substituting the blood of an innocent victim for one's own not only grates on our sense of humanity, it is difficult to reconcile with a truly spiritual conception of God and with man's sense of responsibility. Our moral sense witnesses emphatically that we ourselves, not another for us, must bear the consequences of our own wrongdoing, and impels us to seek acceptance with a righteous God in repentance and amendment, in reliance on His mercy and gracious aid. This teaching has the sanction of Jesus as well as the prophets, and modern thought, whilst recognising that

[60] I am not convinced by Professor Dodd's reasoning that Paul's teaching on justification is built on that of Jesus. " Commentary on Romans," 58.

the moral character of God, in His government of the universe, involves the condemnation of sin, prefers to emphasise, in their spirit, His readiness freely to pardon the repentant sinner in virtue of repentance and return to the Father. But for the practice of blood sacrifice in the ancient world and the natural tendency to explain the offence of the Cross under the influence of this practice, " the blood theology," as it has been called, would hardly have secured a hold in Christian teaching. The Cross was there as a tragic fact. The Jews had crucified the greatest and noblest of their race in an access of hatred and passion. Had the tragedy another cause and significance ? This was the problem for Paul, as for the early disciples. With them, he held that it had, and he solved it (in part at least) by reading into the martyrdom of Jesus an expiatory significance in accordance with the dominant idea of blood sacrifice.[61] In so doing he seems to have gone beyond the more primitive view as well as that of Jesus himself. In this respect it is difficult for modern thought to follow him or to appreciate his reasoning in working out his doctrine in terms of rabbinic juristic theory.

Happily the martyrdom of Jesus is capable of an interpretation more in accord with the conscience and reason of our modern world. This interpretation, which comes home to us with an appealing force, is to be found in the self-sacrifice that faces death for the sake of a great ideal and the good of humanity. This we can understand and appreciate, and this we can read without violence into the self-sacrifice of Jesus, who believed that only by it could he bring about the establishment of the kingdom and lead many into it. Vicarious suffering—suffering of the one for the many—is, indeed, a law of human life, which Jesus exemplified in the highest degree. His suffering, by contributing to draw the sinner from his sin to God, had, and has, a redemptive value. From this point of view, in spite of the crass form it too often assumed in theological thinking, his death has had a mighty redeeming and ennobling influence in Christian history. Moreover, it was the fitting, if tragic finale of his life, and the life as well as the death is of infinite redemptive importance. Paul

[61] The prevailing idea is reflected in Heb. ix. 22, as well as in the Pauline Epistles. " Apart from shedding of blood, there is no remission."

concentrated too exclusively on the latter in relation to man's salvation. He deliberately sets himself to " forget the things that are behind " in this sense. In the recurring emphasis on the blood of Christ, he obscures, if he does not entirely ignore, the unique significance of the life and teaching of the Master and their redemptive influence as a revelation of the nature and will of God, and as an overmastering incentive to self-sacrifice in His service. In this respect, by bringing man into a living and inspiring relation to God, the life has potently tended to their salvation. The Gospel of Jesus is not all contained in the Cross. The Cross is, indeed, the grand confirmation of the life, and to us its compelling moral and religious appeal lies in this direction rather than in the problematic reasoning on it in the light of the crude and repellent sacrificial cultus and juristic conceptions of the age.

VIII. Redemption—Its Ethical Aspect

The juridical aspect of redemption thus appears as an integral part of Paul's teaching. It is a mistake unduly to minimise it and try to explain it away. It is not merely set forth in the early chapters of Romans and in chapter iii. of the Galatian Epistle, it is reflected in the references to " the blood of Christ " throughout the Epistles. It is, however, not the only one, and it is equally a mistake to minimise the ethical aspect which is intermingled with it in Paul's thought. This aspect is, in fact, for Paul the most distinctive, if not the exclusive one. The grand and all significant fact is that the redemption available through Christ not only absolves the believer from the guilt of sin, but delivers him from its dominion in the flesh. From being a bondman to sin, he thereby becomes a free man and a victor over the corruption and death inherent in sinful flesh.

In redeeming man through the expiatory death of Christ, God is not merely the judge. He does not act purely on the retributive principle. If Christ's death is required by his retributive righteousness, as revealed in the Law, it also shows forth His infinite mercy and love. His purpose is not to punish, but to save. " God has appointed us not unto wrath, but unto the obtaining of salvation through our Lord Jesus Christ

who died for us that we should live together with him." [1]   The
Gospel is "the power of God unto salvation to every one that
believeth." [2]   It reveals not only his saving righteousness, but
the desire freely to impart it to the sinner.   In Christ's sacrifice
God shows His love in the self-sacrificing love of Christ.
The Cross is the channel in which this love flows out to the
sinner.   Paul has struck a note that rings true to the reality
in placing at the centre of Christianity the love of Christ and
the love of God in him.   Man, by reason of sin, is God's
enemy, and in the death of Christ He reveals His longing
for reconciliation with rebellious man.   " God commendeth His
love towards us in that, while we were yet enemies, Christ
died for us. . . . Whilst we were enemies we were reconciled
to God through the death of his Son." [3]   " God was in Christ
reconciling the world unto himself, not reckoning unto them
their transgressions." [4]   " For it was the good pleasure (of the
Father) . . . through him to reconcile all things unto himself,
having made peace through the blood of his Cross. . . . And
you being in time past alienated and enemies in your mind in
your evil works, yet now hath he (Christ) reconciled in the body
of his flesh, through death, to present you holy and without
blemish and unreprovable before him." [5]   God seeking to
effect a reconciliation with sinners ; Christ freely giving himself
as the medium of this reconciliation—this lends to Christ's
sacrifice an element in which the juridical aspect, if not
superseded, recedes into the background.   The obedience of
Christ in submitting even to the death on the Cross, in his
self-imposed mission for man's sake, is emphasised as a cardinal
feature of his sacrifice in God's sight.[6]   The wonderful thing
in this aspect of redemption is the fact that, viewed in this
light, not retribution, but a matchless self-sacrifice for the
benefit of the undeserving sinner is at the bottom of it.   The

---

[1] 1 Thess. v. 9-10, σωτηρία.   [2] Rom. i. 16.
[3] Rom. v. 8, 10 ; cf. xi. 28 ; cf. Gal. ii. 20. Stevens contends that ἐχθροί
in these passages imply that God was the enemy of the sinner. " Christian
Doctrine of Salvation," 59. So also Sanday and Headlam, " Commentary
on Romans," 129-130. It is more natural to interpret in v. 10 at least the
enmity of man. On this subject see the detailed discussion by Anderson
Scott, " Christianity According to St Paul," 75 f. He shows a tendency
to explain away passages like Rom. xi. 28, which does seem to imply God's
enmity against the wilful sinner.
[4] 2 Cor. v. 19.
[5] Col. i. 19-22.   [6] Phil. ii. 8-9.

ethical quality of this self-surrender of the righteous for the unrighteous could not be higher. " For while we were yet weak, in due season Christ died for the ungodly. For scarcely for a righteous man will one die ; though peradventure for the good man some one would even dare to die." [7]

The purpose of this redeeming sacrifice is that man might be ethically benefited as well as juridically acquitted. If the righteousness of God in making Christ sin for us is accentuated, its purpose is that we might become the righteousness of God in him.[8] If he sent His Son to condemn sin in the flesh, it was that " the ordinance of the Law might be fulfilled in us who walk not after the flesh, but after the spirit," and that " through the obedience of the one man shall many be made righteous." [9] It makes possible the realisation of a righteousness " not mine own, but the righteousness which is of God by faith," and which impels the apostle to gain Christ and be found in him.[10]

Its ethical effects are manifest in the experience of the believer. Justification brings him into a new ethical relation to God—the relation of a son to his heavenly Father by means of spiritual adoption.[11] The idea of adoption is derived from Græco-Roman law—the adoption of a slave as a son by his lord. From being a slave the believer has become a son and an heir. He belongs to God as His property.[12]

In keeping with this relation, faith works in him a positive righteousness, not merely lends him an assumed righteousness. It delivers him from the power as well as the guilt of sin. For faith, Christ is not merely there as an objective sacrifice. He is there to be assimilated in character as well as accepted as a shield from the wrath of God. It initiates a new ethical life, which is maintained by the Spirit of God or of Christ working within him. Redemption in the ethical sense is already being experienced, though it is only gradually being achieved and awaits its completion at the last judgment. " The word of the

[7] Rom. v. 6, 7.
[8] 2 Cor. v. 21.
[9] Rom. viii. 3-4 ; v. 19. " If," says Stevens, " to Paul's mind he (Christ) died to vindicate justice and satisfy law, it is also true for him that he died for men that they should no longer live unto themselves." " Christian Doctrine of Salvation," 66.
[10] Phil. iii. 9.
[11] Rom. viii. 14-17 ; Gal. iv. 5-7.　　　　[12] Gal. iv. 8.

Cross . . ., unto us that are being saved, is the power of God." [13] Through the Cross " the world has been crucified unto me and I unto the world." [14] The indwelling Christ or Spirit of Christ evinces this power in the crucifying of the flesh—the lower nature—and the making alive of the spirit—the higher nature of the believer.[15] Christ is being formed in him.[16] He has died to the Law in order to live unto God, or rather Christ lives in him in the life of faith, which has transformed the life of the flesh.[17] Christ's death means for the believer not only death for sin, but his own death to sin in and with him. Death in the ethical sense has a redeeming value for the believer. " He that hath died with Christ is justified from sin," [18] not merely in the sense of acquittal, but in that of being done with sin as a motive force in his life. Not only the death, but the risen life of Christ has a saving value for those who have been reconciled to God.[19] Paul can speak of Christ being raised for our justification and making intercession for us to this end at God's right hand.[20] In such passages, in fact, the saving value of the resurrection takes precedence of that of the death, inasmuch, apparently, as it is the proof that what God has purposed in the redemption and the ethical renewal of the believer, through Christ, has been triumphantly accomplished.

Justification is thus the initial act of a far-reaching ethical transformation of the life of the believer and is indissolubly bound up with this transformation. The believer dies with Christ and is raised with him to new life.[21] " If any man is in Christ he is a new creature ; the old things have passed away, behold they are become new." [22] Paul speaks from his own experience of redemption in thus depicting the transformation from the life of sinful flesh to the new life of the Spirit, from bondage to the law of sin and death to the freedom of the spirit of life in Christ Jesus.[23] He still, indeed, knows the power of the old man, of sin in the flesh, the old weakness of will, and the disharmony between the real and the ideal.

[13] 1 Cor. i. 18 ; cf. 2 Cor. ii. 14 f.
[14] Gal. vi. 14.
[15] Rom. viii. 1 f. ; Gal. iv. 24 f.
[16] Gal. iv. 19.
[17] Ibid., ii. 19 f.
[18] Rom. vi. 7.
[19] Ibid., v. 10.
[20] Ibid., iv. 24-25 ; viii. 34.
[21] Ibid., vi. 1-11.
[22] 2 Cor. v. 11 ; cf. Gal. vi. 15.
[23] Rom. viii. 2 f.

In his own experience as well as, more grossly, in that of the Christian communities—Corinth, for example—the real is far from corresponding to the ideal.   Nevertheless, it does represent something concrete, if imperfect.   Paul and his converts did experience the transforming power emanating from the Cross and working in them through the risen Christ and his spirit dwelling in them.

Moreover, whilst Paul has generally in view the power of the indwelling Christ or Spirit of Christ, he does not altogether ignore the historic Christ as the inspiration and norm of the Christian life.   The indwelling Christ is also the Christ who was without sin and lived on earth the ideal life, which is for the believer the standard of his own.   " Have this mind in you which was also in Christ Jesus." [24]   " Be ye imitators of me even as I also am of Christ." [25]   He can speak of the law of Christ as the imperative of the Christian life.   " Bear ye one another's burdens and so fulfil the law of Christ." [26]   He can even recognise and adduce the Mosaic Law as a force in the trans-formed life of the believer.   Faith working by love is indeed opposed to the law in the legalist sense.[27]   But in the ethical sense it is the fulfilling of the whole law.   Paul is at one with Jesus in stressing love as the fulfilment of the Law.   " For the whole law is fulfilled in one word, even in this, Thou shalt love thy neighbour as thyself." [28]

Whilst the believer is thus to some extent brought into touch with the historic Jesus as Master and example, the distinctive feature of his view of redemption, on its practical side, is the new ethical life originating in Christ and maintained by him as the risen Lord, who is also the ideal spiritual man in heaven.   He finds the demonstration of this in his own experience of the risen Lord, and with it the demonstration of all that he ascribes to this Lord.   Whilst we have found reason to criticise the speculative element in his Christ concep-tion and the juridical view of his sacrificial death, there is an appealing force in his presentation of the risen, living Christ in relation to the believer.   The Christ of his religious experience is, indeed, a personal apprehension.   It is the product of the faith engendered in him by the revelation of

[24] Phil. ii. 5.   [26] Gal. vi. 2.   [28] Ibid., v. 14.
[25] 1 Cor. xi. 1.   [27] Ibid., v. 5-6.

the risen Christ on the Damascus road. But, as we have seen, there is no compelling reason for rebutting this initial experience as unreal and therefore unhistoric, just as there is no compelling reason for rejecting the appearances to the disciples as purely visionary fancies. In the one case, as in the others, we can point to the marvellous practical effects of these experiences in begetting a new spiritual and ethical life of incalculable range and potency. Pious hallucinations may produce, and have indeed produced extraordinary effects, bad as well as good. But given the fundamental reality of the unique personality and life of Jesus, as revealed in the authentic record, backed by the evidence of the resurrection experiences, the faith in him as risen Lord, and the inspirer of a new ethical life in men's souls, as Paul represents it in his own personal experience, cannot be reasonably dismissed as the fruit of a visionary imagination. It cannot be denied that it did produce in him and his converts, in spite of lapse or failure, in some cases, an unexampled moral transformation in an environment very unfavourable to this transformation. That the spirit of Jesus was actually operative in fostering it, who will doubt that has come, and strives to live under the spell of this unique personality in his personal religious life. In it we are, or may be, conscious of a spiritual presence and power operating in us, as from spirit to spirit, in our fellowship with him and through him, as the highest embodiment of the spiritual life, with God. The Christ of religious experience has thus for us in our religious life, as for Paul, a place alongside the Jesus of history, and his right to that place is vindicated by the ethical effects which his " lifegiving spirit " produces in the soul of the believer. With this Christ we are assuredly in the realm of reality, the reality of the highest moral and spiritual life, a life worthy of the Master and the living Lord. To those who cannot, or will not accept any reality beyond the purely phenomenal, spiritual reality is, of course, purely imaginary. But even the scientific reason has been moving towards the conviction of the spiritual as the ultimate and necessary reality in and behind the phenomenal, and of the relation of the rational and moral element in man's nature to this reality, and its capability of contact with it. The confirmed materialist may deny and reject anything of the nature of religious faith

as unreal. For him Paul is a pure visionary ; his belief in
the risen Lord and Christ a will o' the wisp ; his religious
experience based on nothing more substantial than a legend,
on which he constructed a purely subjective cult. Surely
a superficial, inadequate, and highly subjective method of
dealing with spiritual phenomena exemplified in the solid
actualities of character and life.

Our apprehension of the Christ may differ in some respects
from that of Paul.[29] The mystic element in his religious
experience which, as we shall see in the next section, is such
a distinctive feature of it, may also be peculiar to himself,
and only those endowed with the mystic temperament may fully
appreciate it. The expression of the ethical and religious
life takes varying forms, and Christian mysticism is only
one of these forms. It is the reality of this life as expressed
in conduct that is the great thing, and this reality is for Paul
an essential of the redeeming purpose of God. Christ is for
him not merely a propitiation for sin in his death. In communion with his spirit he is the Creator, the inspirer in the
believer of a new life. In the triumphant consciousness of
this new ethical and spiritual life in and through him, a grand
optimism has taken the place of the pessimism begotten of
the sense of sin in the flesh. New life has displaced the death
and corruption inherent in the old ; a new freedom has sprung
out of the old bondage. This triumphant note breaks out
again and again in the Epistles and finds its sustained " Heroica "
in the eighth chapter of Romans.

IX. REDEMPTION—ITS MYSTIC ASPECT

The mystic aspect of redemption appears in the teaching
of Paul on the indwelling Christ and the experienced power
of his death and resurrection. The indwelling Christ expresses
the closest personal fellowship with him. God has called

---

[29] The revelation of God to our souls can only be expressed in terms of
the mentality of the age in which we live. This may be a defect of it,
inseparable from human limitation, and the gradual and progressive development of our knowledge which this limitation involves. In his apprehension
of Christ, Paul was no exception to this law, though in some essential respects
he was in front of his time ; for example, in his contending for the spirituality
and universality of Christianity against Jewish legalism and particularism.

the believer " into the fellowship of his Son Jesus Christ, our Lord." [1]   For Paul this fellowship means more than spiritual communion with the heavenly Christ, who revealed himself to him on the Damascus road.   It means the possession by Christ of his whole being, so that Christ seems literally to live in him and he in Christ.   This Christ-possession becomes an obsession which has taken captive his heart and imagination. " I live, yet no longer I, but Christ liveth in me." [2]   " To me to live is Christ." [3]   His experience of the inner Christ is also assumed to be the common experience, though it seems to be really a reflection of that of Paul himself.   He repeatedly speaks of " Christ in you " [4] and of the Spirit of Christ dwelling in you.[5]   So close is this personal connection that the baptised believer shares in a real sense in Christ's death and resurrection to new life,[6] though the process is a continuous one till the final issue in life eternal.[7]

Death and Resurrection are fundamental features of Paul's conception of redemption in the mystic sense.   The ethical aspect merges into the mystic in the dying of the believer with Christ and his rising with him in his resurrection, and in the complete union thereby realised, though the ethical element in this mystic experience is ever present to Paul's mind.   Both are repeated in the experience of the believer in his death to sin and his resurrection to a new spiritual life —the higher life which the resurrection connotes.   Both have thus a mystic efficacy.   Christ's death is not merely juridically significant and ethically conditioned and motived. It not merely achieved something *for* the believer.   It is something in which the believer participates in his mystic experience of its significance and effects.   Paul has been " crucified with Christ." [8]   He can identify his sufferings with those of Christ—" always bearing about in the body the dying of Jesus "; " as death working in us "; " knowing the fellow-ship of his sufferings, becoming conformed unto his death." [9] Similarly believers " have died with Christ," " have been baptised into his death," " buried with him through baptism

---

[1] 1 Cor. i. 9, κοινωνία.   [2] Gal. ii. 20.   [3] Phil. i. 21.
[4] 2 Cor. xiii. 5 ; Rom. viii. 10 ; Col. i. 27.
[5] Rom. viii. 11.
[6] *Ibid.*, vi. 1 f.   [7] Phil. iii. 10.   [8] Gal. ii. 20.
[9] 2 Cor. iv. 10, 12 ; Phil. iii. 10.

into death," "are united with him by the likeness of his
death." Their "old man was crucified with him." [10] This
dying with Christ means the actual dying to sin, the sinful
self, the sin-ridden side of our nature. Even in this respect
believers participate in the death of Christ, who is said to have
died to sin once for all.[11] This does not, of course, mean
that Christ died to actual sin in himself, but only to sin as it
affected his activity as the Redeemer from sin and brought
about his death. Paul emphatically believes in the personal
sinlessness of Jesus. "Him who knew no sin, he made to
be sin in our behalf." [12]   Only in the sense that by his death he
was done with sin once for all do believers die with him. In
baptism, in which the old man within dies and is buried, they
too have done with sin in the sense of dying to the sin-enslaved
self. In this respect they share in and even repeat the death of
the crucified Lord in a real, if mystic sense. Their death
with him is a complete and a real wrench with their past life,
mystically conceived and operated in baptism. At the same
time, in other passages, this mystic, ethical process is described
in concrete terms. "They that are of Christ Jesus have
crucified the flesh with the lusts and passions thereof." [13]
This crucifixion of the flesh is ascribed to the Spirit operating
in the believer. "If by the Spirit ye mortify the deeds of
the body, ye shall live." [14]   Similarly, it is through the Cross
that "the world hath been crucified unto me and I unto the
world." [15]

The believer not only dies, he rises with Christ. The
resurrection is also invested with a mystic significance. For
Paul it was not only a guarantee of Christ's immortality and
ours ; [16] not only a revelation of his divine nature and power
as Son of God,[17] a liberation from the limitations which his
human life imposed on him.[18] It is the means whereby this
fullness of the spiritual life—" the life unto God "—is realised
in us, as in him, and we are restored, redeemed from the
dominion, the slavery of sin. The believer has, in baptism,

[10] Rom. vi. 2 f. ; Col. ii. 20 ; iii. 3.
[11] *Ibid.*, vi. 10.
[12] 2 Cor. v. 21.
[13] Gal. v. 24.
[14] Rom. viii. 13.
[15] Gal. vi. 14.
[16] 1 Cor. xv. 12 f. ; *cf.* Rom. viii. 11 ; 2 Cor. iv. 14 ; Col. i. 18.
[17] Rom. i. 4.
[18] *Ibid.*, vi. 9-10.

died to sin with him only to rise with him in newness of life. United with him in the likeness of his death, he shall also be united in the likeness of his resurrection. Dead with him to sin, he is alive unto God in Jesus Christ.[19] From his union with him in death a new life has sprung up. He has become " a new creature." " Wherefore if any one be in Christ, he is a new creature ; the old things have passed away ; behold they have become new." [20] The purpose of his death and resurrection is that " they who live should no longer live unto themselves, but unto him who for their sakes died and rose again." [21] The believer's risen life is centred not in the Christ after the flesh, but in the risen Christ, in whose life he shares.[22] " Delivered unto death for Jesus' sake, that the life also of Jesus may be manifested in our mortal flesh, . . . knowing that he who raised up the Lord Jesus shall raise us up also with Jesus, and shall present us with you." [23] The power which raised Jesus is at work raising up Paul and his converts to a life eternal. Thus, though the outward man is decaying, the inward man is being renewed day by day until the visible gives place to the invisible, the temporal to the eternal.[24] The resurrection of the believer with Christ in this new life, the participation in his larger resurrection life is not for Paul purely metaphorical. It represents a real transformation of his moral self, of character by a mystic assimilation of the risen life of Christ, whose fullness is being gradually transferred to the believing soul. The believer is a redeemed person who, in dying and rising with Christ to new life, already lives a supernatural life in fellowship with him. Its mystic feature consists in the idea, so congenial to the mystic soul, of the gradual assimilation by the ordinary self of a superself, completely penetrating it and taking possession of it. For this experience the mystic temperament, which Paul possessed in a high degree, is essential. It is a distinctively Pauline conception and contribution. He is an ecstatic who sees and hears strange things,[25] even if he also evinces the practical sense. Deissmann thinks that he brought from

[19] Rom. vi. 4 f.
[20] 2 Cor. v. 17 ; *cf.* Gal. vi. 15.
[21] *Ibid.*, v. 15.   [22] *Ibid.*, v. 16.   [23] *Ibid.*, iv. 10 f.
[24] *Ibid.*, iv. 16 f. ; *cf.* Col. iii. 10.
[25] *Ibid.*, xii. 1 f.

Phariseeism this mystic temperament and tendency.[26]   Though
Rabbinic Phariseeism can hardly be described as mystic, some
of the Apocalyptic writers were Pharisees, and in the Apocalyptic
writings, as in those of the prophets, the visionary and ecstatic
strain is patent enough.   Paul evidently belonged to this type
of Pharisee, and, on his own confession, had his transcendental
experiences, of which that on the road to Damascus was
probably not the first, and certainly not the only one.   Hence
the mystic indwelling of Christ in the believer, and the mystic
power of his death and resurrection in his Christian experience.

His doctrine of a mystic oneness with the indwelling
Christ, and the mystic dying and rising with him, has an affinity
to the mystic striving to attain deification, the divine life by the
absorption of the human personality in God, whether in its
pagan or later Christian form.   Paul is, however, not a mystic
in the sense of seeking to merge his personality in that of God.
He shares the Jewish conception of the distinct personality of
God and man.[27]   His mysticism is a Christ mysticism.   It
consists not in the absorption of the human personality in
God, but of the appropriation of the indwelling Christ, whereby,
as the result of dying and rising with him, he becomes a new
creature, and attains a new relation to God—the relation of a
son to his heavenly Father.

This Christ mysticism, like much in Paul's Christian
thought, is lacking in the teaching of Jesus and the primitive
teaching about him.   Jesus was no mystic in the Pauline sense.
His life was, indeed, a life in God in the sense of the closest
personal fellowship with the Father.   There is a deep mystery
in his unique consciousness of God and his God-appointed
function.   But there is no mysticism in his conception of
God in relation to himself or his communion with Him.   It
is that of Son and Father, closely related, but distinct, and
the inspiration and power of his teaching and his healing
ministry are ascribed to the Spirit of God operating through
him.   Nor is there anything like the Christ mysticism of
Paul in his converse with his disciples, which is that of the
revealer of the Father and the exponent of the kingdom, and his

[26] " The Religion of Jesus and the Faith of Paul," 186 f., 192.
[27] The reference to Stoic Pantheism in the discourse at Athens in Acts
xvii. is of doubtful authenticity, and, in any case, Paul would understand
it only in the Jewish theistic sense.

part and theirs, in its realisation. In order to enter the kingdom the disciple must, like him, be capable of the utmost self-surrender—must die in order to live. But this dying in order to live is purely ethical. It means the utter renunciation of self in order to find and foster its true life. Whilst in the primitive apostolic preaching he is spiritually present in the operation of the Spirit of God in the hearts of believers, it is not in the Pauline sense of the indwelling Christ. Nor do his death and resurrection suggest to them the Pauline mystic dying to sin and rising with him to new life.

Whence, then, did Paul derive the Christ mysticism which he engrafted on the Gospel ? It is undeniable that there is a certain affinity between his mystic thought and that of his Hellenist religious environment, as expressed in the Greek mystery cults, in which the initiate, by participating in the death of the mystery god and rising again to new life, attains to deification. Possession by spirits, good or evil, was also a current belief in the world of Paul, and has a striking affinity to his doctrine of the possession of the believer by the in-dwelling Christ. Was his Christ mysticism derived from this pagan mysticism ? J. Weiss and other recent writers on the subject see in it the reflex of this influence,[28] direct or indirect. A. Schweitzer, Deissmann, Kennedy reject it.[29] Schweitzer, who one-sidedly regards early Christianity from the eschatological point of view, finds the clue in Jewish eschatology. But while there were elements in this ecstatic, apocalyptic tendency which might foster the mystic temperament, it does not seem to account for the distinctive Pauline

---

[28] J. Weiss, " Urchristenthum," 403 f. ; Böhlig, " Geisteskultur," 81 ; Morgan, " Religion and Theology of Paul," 124 f. ; Wilson, " St Paul and Paganism," 110, 116-117, 177 (1927); Emmet, " Commentary on Galatians," 25 f. (1912); " Dieterich, Eine Mithrasliturgie," 176 f. (1910); Inge, " Outspoken Essays," 226, who thinks that, whilst Paul resisted the Judaising of Christianity, he took the first step, and a long one, towards the Paganising of it. In regard to the influence of the Oriental mystery religions, in addition to that of the Greek mysteries, our knowledge of the early spread of these religions in the Græco-Roman world is too indefinite to warrant dogmatic conclusions on the subject. Böhlig assumes the existence of Mithraism at Tarsus in Paul's time, but adduces no real evidence in support of this assumption.

[29] Schweitzer, " Die Mystik des Apostels Paulus " (1930); Deissmann, " St Paul," 131 ; Kennedy, " St Paul and the Mystery Religions," 221 f. (1913). M. Jones thinks that it is not proved, though he concludes that it is discernible as far as terminology is concerned. " New Testament in the Twentieth Century," 158 f. (1914).

mystic conception of the Gospel. Deissmann finds the source in Paul's conversion. Whilst it is clear that his mysticism grew out of his Christian experience, it does not necessarily follow that its origin lies in the initial act of this experience. As has been noted, Paul was endowed with the mystic temperament, and so endowed he might well have developed his Christian mysticism by his own meditation on the death and resurrection of Christ. At the same time he was probably familiar with the Greek mystic conception of the regeneration and deification of the soul, and this mysticism may have, directly or indirectly, contributed something to his mystic conception of the crucified and risen Christ in relation to the inner life of the believer, and provided him with the terminology wherewith to make it intelligible to his Hellenist converts. On the other hand, it is a mistake to overlook the extraordinary originality of his mind and what appears to be his innate mystic tendency, and, with the extreme votaries of the comparative religious-historical method, to regard his Christ mysticism purely as Christianised Hellenist mysticism. We are probably nearer the truth in seeing in it substantially the product of his own religious experience expressing itself in terms of Hellenist religious thought and ritual.

Whether, under this influence, he infused Greek mysticism into his conception of the rites of baptism and the Lord's Supper, and thus transformed Christianity into a sacramental mystery religion, has also been the subject of keen debate. Both sacraments are professedly based on Christian practice. Baptism he took over from the primitive community, whilst he himself derives the Eucharist directly from the institution of Christ.[30] Baptism in itself he does not evaluate highly, compared with the preaching of the Gospel. He thanks God that, with some exceptions, he baptised none of the Corinthians lest they should contentiously misinterpret the rite at his hands. " For Christ sent me not to baptise, but to preach the Gospel." [31] " The word of the Cross " is the all-important thing. At the same time he does, in the sixth chapter of Romans, assign to baptism a mystical redemptive efficacy, to which Jesus, who did not baptise his followers, was quite alien, and which does not appear in the primitive preaching. In one

[30] 1 Cor. xi. 23.   [31] Ibid., i. 14 f.

8

version of this preaching baptism in the name, following repentance and faith, is emphasised in connection with the remission of sin and the gift of the Spirit.[32] In another version [33] repentance alone is emphasised, though baptism may be assumed. Whilst in the First Epistle to the Corinthians Paul seems to hold it of little importance, in those to the Romans and Colossians it is stressed as an initiation into the death to sin and the new life of the believer. By it the believer enters into a real union with Christ in his death and resurrection, whereby the old man is crucified, the body of sin done away, and he is no longer in bondage to sin.[34]

Is the mystical efficacy thus ascribed to baptism magically conceived? Has baptism an *ex opere operato* effect? Deissmann, Kennedy, Morgan, Deissner, Feine, and others rebut this interpretation.[35] Schweitzer, Lake, Heitmüller, Bousset, and others maintain it.[36] J. Weiss hesitates to say so, and whilst finding the magical sacramental conception in certain passages, lays stress also on its ethical significance, and thinks that it is not the decisive element in his redemptive teaching.[37] Certain it is that, while conceiving the rite as a real dying and rising in the mystical sense, Paul systematically stresses the operation of the Spirit of God or of Christ in the believer as the grand power in the Christian life, apart from baptismal ritual. Nor does he lose sight of the efficacy of faith in living the crucified life in this most intimate fellowship with Christ. "The life which I now live in the flesh I live by faith, faith in the Son of God, who loved me, and gave himself up for me." [38] Personal faith is always asserted or assumed to be the fundamental, the all-important thing in the religious

[32] Acts ii. 38.
[33] *Ibid.*, iii. 19.
[34] Rom. vi. 1 f. ; Col. ii. 12 f. ; iii. 3. The baptism into Moses of 1 Cor. x. 1-2 is allegorically understood. In 1 Cor. xii. 13 the reference is to baptism by the Spirit.
[35] Deissmann, "St Paul," 130 f. ; Kennedy, "St Paul and the Mystery Religions," 232 f. ; Morgan, "Religion and Theology of Paul," 203 f. ; Deissner, "Paulus und die Mystik," 122 f. (1921); "Feine," "Theologie," 528 f.
[36] Schweitzer, "Mystik des Apostels Paulus," 18 f. ; Lake, "Earlier Epistles of St Paul," 385 f. (1911) ; Heitmüller, "Taufe und Abendmahl bei Paulus," 14 (1903) ; Bousset, "Kyrios Christos," 163 f.
[37] "Urchristenthum," 497 f.
[38] Gal. ii. 20.

life. The real magic of the renewal [39] of the believer, if one
may so describe it, is not for Paul the sacramental element,
but the ethical-mystical working of faith and the Spirit—faith
in appropriating Christ, the Spirit as the dynamic of the
Christian life. Whilst the experience of the believer in baptism
is realistically conceived in terms of death and resurrection,
the element of individual faith is presupposed and, with it,
the operation of the Spirit in the heart of the believer. This
it is that constitutes the real dynamic of his life.

Nor does there seem to be a material and magical element
in the teaching on the Lord's Supper. It is a memorial of
Christ's sacrifice and a mystic communion with him in his
death. It is not a sacrament in the sense of the mystery
religions—a participation in the life of the deity. Here
the language is evidently symbolic. The celebration is
a spiritual, not a material or magical experience. There
is no transubstantiation in the double formula, in the First
Epistle to the Corinthians,[40] of the body and blood,
which Christ offers for his disciples. That it is for Paul
spiritual food and drink is shown by the reference in the
preceding chapter to the Israelites typically partaking in the
wilderness of the manna and the water flowing from the rock.[41]
In so doing they partook in a spiritual sense of the heavenly
Christ who, by an allegoric exegesis, is represented as the
rock that followed them.[42] The further reference [43] to the

[39] Paul explicitly inculcates the renewal by death and resurrection
rather than the regeneration of the soul. Regeneration is a distinctive
Johannine idea in keeping with Greek religious thought. But the new
creation that results from this process has a resemblance to the regenerated
soul of the Fourth Gospel. Schweitzer contends that there is a real difference
between the two conceptions. He holds that the dying and rising with
Christ has nothing to do with regeneration, but signifies that the believer
belongs to a new world or order of things, "Mystik," 15. He is too inclined to
judge Paul and his teaching exclusively from the eschatological point of view.

[40] 1 Cor. xi. 23 f.   [41] Ibid., x. 1 f.
[42] Lietzmann, on the other hand, thinks it "probable" that Paul is
here adopting the Hellenist mystic conception of the sacrament as a realistic
partaking of the body and blood. "Handbuch," iii. 110. He translates
πνευματικόν as "supernatural," not "spiritual," in its ordinary meaning.
J. Weiss hesitates to accept this advanced sacramentalism, and stresses the
religious significance of the rite. "Urchristenthum," 508 f. Kennedy
(261 f.) and Morgan (221 f.) decisively reject it. Schweitzer, whilst also
rejecting the sacramentalism of the mystery religions, regards the rite as
embodying a real mystic union of the believer with Christ, "Mystik," 257 f.,
and producing a material effect on the soul, "Forschung," 128 f. "The
rite effects what it represents," Ibid., 166.
[43] 1 Cor. x. 16 f.

sacramental eating and drinking of the Gentiles in communion with their demonic gods does not connote the transference of the ideas, associated by them with their sacrificial feasts, to the Christian rite. It is not the identity, but the analogy that Paul has in mind. He betrays a marked revulsion from this pagan sacramentalism.

Paul's mysticism is the expression of his personal apprehension and experience of redemption in Christ. It is a distinctive contribution accruing from his mystic temperament and train of thought. It has made a powerful appeal throughout the centuries to similarly constituted minds. The appeal is less forcible for those whose faith is more tempered by reason and have no experience of the Pauline indwelling Christ and of this mystic process of dying and rising with him. They prefer the teaching of Jesus of dying to self in order to live to God under the inspiration of his spirit and example.[44] Jesus would probably have been as mystified as we are by this Pauline mystic adaptation of his teaching, which seems to ascribe to his death and resurrection a real, if not a magical, transformation of the body as well as the soul of the believer. The Pauline mysticism cannot be acquired. It must be an experience, and for this experience one must have the predisposing temperament of the apostle. It can never be to those not thus predisposed more than a symbolic representation of the power of the crucified and risen Christ to transform the believer's character in following him in his self-surrender, as the pathway to the fuller spiritual life.

X. Paul and the Law.

In working out his doctrine of justification by faith, Paul strives to invalidate the Law for the Christian believer. In so doing he made a further advance on the primitive Gospel,

[44] Schweitzer strives to make out that Jesus taught, though indirectly and furtively, a mystic relation to his disciples to him as Son of Man, and that a number of his sayings have a distinctively mystic meaning. Those he quotes seem to me to have no such meaning, and Schweitzer merely reads it into them, " Mystik," 106 f. He discovers even in the baptism of John a mystical-sacramental significance which Paul took over from him and the primitive community, " Paulinische Forschung," 189. He seems at times to let his imagination go.

which combined the observance of the Jewish cult and legal system with the faith in the risen and exalted Christ. He broke up this combination for the Gentile believer at least, and thus made of Christianity a distinct and independent religion. Hence the importance of his conception of the Law and his negative attitude towards it.

His thesis is that redemption being possible only through Christ, it is not attainable by means of the Law. It is dependent solely on the grace of God in Christ, not on the doing of the Law. Hence the radical antithesis of the Law and the Gospel, of faith and works. The Law, he maintains, is an inferior expression of the will of God, and God is not really to be regarded as its author. It was given not directly by God, but through the mediation of angels, who belong to the demonic powers which dominate the world and man. It has to do with this material, demon-ridden existence, with " the weak and beggarly elements " of the demonic régime, with which it is bound up, to which man and the world are in bondage, and from which Christ has delivered them.[1] He, indeed, recognises the moral element in the Law as valid and obligatory for all time, and in so far corrects the sweeping representation of its inferiority. From this point of view, it is holy, righteous, and good, and is differentiated from the law of sin in the flesh. It is " spiritual " and has to do with the spiritual in contrast to " the carnal " element in man, which is enslaved by sin.[2] He can even speak of establishing, not making void the law through faith in Christ.[3] But as it is concerned with this lower, sinful existence, it can do nothing, apart from faith in Christ, to effect deliverance from it. It is in reality a hindrance, not a help to redemption, since it is impossible for the sinner to fulfil it. It sets forth an ideal, a standard of righteousness too high for his moral capacity. His will is not equal to his responsibility by reason of the power of the flesh. He fails, and cannot but fail to observe it.[4] From the redemptive point of view it is a case of the whole Law or nothing. Redemption would be possible by way of the Law if the sinner could keep it perfectly. " If there had

---

[1] Gal. iii. 19 ; ii. 4 ; v. 1 f. ; cf. Col. ii. 14-15.
[2] Rom. vii. 12 f.
[3] Ibid., iii. 31.
[4] Gal. iii. 10 ; v. 3.

been a law given which could make alive, verily righteousness would have been of the law." [5]

This being the case, its function is purely negative. It can only condemn, not justify. It pronounces a curse on the sinner.[6] It arouses and intensifies the knowledge of sin. "Through the law cometh the knowledge of sin." [7] "I had not known sin except through the law." [8] "Apart from the law sin is dead." [9] "Where there is no law there is no transgression." The Law, if not in itself sinful, breeds the sense of sin. It was, in fact, enacted to increase sin. "It was added because of transgressions," [10] i.e., not to check, but to deepen the consciousness of sin.[11] It "came in beside that the transgression might abound and grace might abound more exceedingly." [12] Under its régime the sinful passions have free scope. "When we were in the flesh the sinful passions, which were through the law, wrought in our members to bring forth fruit unto death." [13] It holds us in captivity to sin,[14] and even incites to sin. "Sin, finding occasion through the commandment, beguiled me, and through it slew me." [15] It is, therefore, the minister of God's wrath and tends to death. The law worketh wrath." [16] It is due to it that "sin reigned in death." [17]

Its only positive redemptive significance lies in forcing the sinner to turn to Christ for deliverance. "The law hath been our tutor to bring us to Christ, that we might be justified by faith." [18] Christ's redemptive function is to destroy the régime of the Law and with it the bondage to sin. The whole point of this anti-legal argumentation is to prove that only by the grace of God operative in Christ, not by legal works, is redemption possible and available. Hence the accentuated antagonism between Law and grace, faith and works. Paul could only vindicate the freedom of his Gentile converts and universalise the Gospel by invalidating the Law as he understood it. To bind on the Gentile believer circumcision and other Jewish legal practices, as the Judaisers insisted on doing, was

---

[5] Gal. iii. 21.
[6] Ibid., iii. 10.
[7] Rom. iii. 20.
[8] Ibid., vii. 7.
[9] Ibid., vii. 8.
[10] Gal. iii. 19.
[11] Emmet, " St Paul's Epistle to the Galatians," 34 (1912).
[12] Rom. v. 20.
[13] Ibid., vii. 5.
[14] Ibid., vii. 6.
[15] Ibid., vii. 11.
[16] Ibid., iv. 15.
[17] Ibid., v. 21.
[18] Gal. iii. 23.

to sever him from Christ and fall away from grace.[19] For Paul his whole doctrine of redemption through faith in Christ was at stake.

Logically, if his view of the Law and of the impossibility of redemption by the works of the Law is sound, his contention has no little force. The principle of the Law was, as he contends, based on the legalist idea of recompense for keeping the commandments and penalty for not keeping them. " To him that worketh the reward is not reckoned as of grace, but as of debt." [20] But unless the whole law is inviolably observed, the penalty cancels the recompense and salvation is impossible. This the Law itself explicitly asserts in pronouncing a curse on every one who fails to do so. " Cursed be he that confirmeth not all the words of this law to do them." [21] The whole Law, both ceremonial and ethical, must be observed if the curse is to be obviated. This is the note of Old Testament legalism, or, as Paul would have expressed it, the system of salvation by " works." Under such a system salvation, he holds, is impossible. In virtue of man's moral impotence by reason of his bondage to sin, it is impossible thus to keep the Law and thereby ensure salvation.

From the legalist point of view there is force in this reasoning. The ceremonial element in the Law, which, to the Pharisaic temperament, counted equally with the ethical element, was both complicated and exacting. It greatly augmented the occasion and the consciousness of sin, in the case at least of a highly sensitive conscience like that of Paul. Moreover, the moral element in it, which demanded the absolute love of God and one's neighbour,[22] was equally exacting, if not so complicated, and might well seem beyond the capacity of frail human nature. In the face of this high imperative, even the best of us cannot stand erect or evade the sense of shortcoming and guilt. To a highly sensitive conscience the Law might well seem alike an impossible ideal and a terrible torment, begetting the sense of bondage to sin, without offering the means of deliverance from it. If God is purely the Lawgiver, as he appears to have been to Paul in his pre-Christian days; if religion consists in the

[19] Gal. v. 3 f.
[20] Rom. iv. 4.
[21] Deut. xxvii. 26.
[22] Ibid., vi. 5 ; Lev. xix. 18.

perfect observance of a set of rules, no other conclusion is possible. Salvation cannot be by way of the Law.

On the other hand, the legalist conception of God and religion is not the only one in the Old Testament. In the prophets God is represented not merely as the Lawgiver, but as a merciful God, who not only delights in the sincere effort to observe the Law, but graciously forgives its transgression, if coupled with repentance. Moreover, unlike Paul, the prophets believed in man's relative capacity at least to observe the Law. "He hath shown thee, O man, what is good; and what doth the Lord require of thee, but to do justly and love mercy, and walk humbly with thy God." [23] For them man is a moral agent, and his striving to attain to righteousness by keeping the Law, even if imperfectly, has, relatively, an ethical and religious value in God's sight. For them the law was not given merely to foster the sense of sin, though doubtless it might do so. It was given to foster the life of righteousness. They do not share Paul's purely negative attitude towards it.

Historically, therefore, salvation at the hands of a gracious God was not impossible under the régime of the Law. Nor does it seem to have been conditioned by his elaborately reasoned theory of the redemptive work of Christ, which completely rules out salvation by " works," *i.e.*, the observance of the Law in the sincere effort to serve God in reliance on His mercy in accepting this service, in spite of its imperfection. Nor was the life of the pious Jew under this régime necessarily a life of bondage to sin and absolute impotence thus to serve God. Nor, further, was the Law itself inherently an incentive to sin, or purely the nurse of the sense of the divine wrath and condemnation.

It is hardly surprising, therefore, that his Judaising opponents should not have been convinced by his diagnosis of the Law, especially on its ethical side. To represent not only the ceremonial Law, but the Law in the ethical sense, as a hindrance to salvation must have seemed to them not only paradoxical, but irreligious. For to Paul it is not merely a question of disputing the validity of the ceremonial Law for salvation, though this is the main issue in dispute in the Epistle to the Galatians. In this contention he would have found no little support from

[23] Micah vi. 8.

the prophets. It is a question even of the ethical content of
the Law—the whole Law (the Torah) [24]—which, in the Epistle
to the Romans, is also represented as the agent of sin and
death, not as an incentive to righteousness and well-doing.
Paul explains the failure of the Jews to recognise his view of
it by saying that, like the veil over the face of Moses at Sinai,
their minds have been veiled from the truth. " For until
this very day, at the reading of the Old Covenant, the same
veil remaineth unlifted ; which veil is done away in Christ.
But until this day, whensoever Moses is read, a veil lieth upon
their heart." [25] A more natural explanation is that Paul's
one-sided conception of the Law is not an exact reflection of
what the Old Testament Law was in itself or its effects. He
would have been much more effective had he, like the prophets
and Jesus himself, directed his attack against the legalist spirit
in religion, instead of striving to prove the incompatibility
of the Law itself with faith in the exercise of God's grace,
as he understood it. Historically, Rabbinic piety of the better
type did not find in the Law what it had become for Paul,
though, on the principle of strict recompense, his contention
might be logically forcible. He forgot that logic and religion
do not necessarily harmonise, and he would have been more
convincing had he questioned the right of the old Hebrew
lawgiver, or rather the code ascribed to him, to curse people [26]
in the name of God for failing to observe the whole minutiæ
of an intricate legalism.

Paul further attempted to invalidate the Law for salvation
by a Rabbinic survey of Old Testament history. Here, too,
his argumentation is open to question. God has planned the
redemption of man through Christ, and the Old Testament
history is rather arbitrarily interpreted in the light of this
redemptive purpose. Christ, who, as the second Adam, the
representative of a new humanity, was to take the place of the
first Adam, the representative of fallen humanity, is, in his
pre-existent state, visible to Paul in the history of Israel. He
is already performing part of his redemptive function in this

[24] In Galatians it is the ritual side of the Law that is in the foreground ;
in Romans the ethical. See Grafe, " Die Paulinische Lehre vom Gesetz
(2nd ed., 1893), and Schweitzer, " Geschichte der Paulinischen Forschung,"
34 f. (1911).
[25] 2 Cor. iii. 13 f. [26] Deut. xxvii. 26.

history throughout the Old Testament. He figures in the promise to Abraham that in his seed should all the nations of the earth be blessed, the word " seed " being forcedly referred to him.[27] By a similar forced exegesis, he is the spiritual rock which, according to Rabbinic legend, followed the Israelites, the spiritual manna of which they partook.[28] Redemption by faith in the promise precedes the Law, and is a proof that salvation cannot, in God's plan, be by the works of the Law. The promise to Abraham is assumed to imply the forecast of the Pauline scheme of redemption through faith in Christ : " Now it was not written for his sake alone, that it was reckoned unto him, but for our sake also who believe," etc.[29] The Law and its bondage are fancifully typified by Hagar, the bondwoman, and her son Ishmael ; the Gospel of freedom from its bondage by Sarah, the freewoman, and her son Isaac, the offspring of the promise.[30] Equally question-able the notion that, though Adam brought his descendants into the state of sin and death, no real guilt in the sense of transgression can be ascribed to them before the age of Moses and the promulgation of the Law. Adam alone transgressed the positive command not to eat, and it was not till the Law came that sin involved the consciousness and the consequences of guilt. The Law first brings the sense of guilt, along with the incapacity to realise righteousness. " Sin is not imputed where there is no law." [31] Nevertheless he emphasises the fact of conscience, in the case of the Gentiles, as a testimony to man's guilt, apart from the Law, and runs straight in the teeth of the evidence, in the pre-Mosaic record, of the sense of transgression before the giving of the Law. The story of Cain and Abel, for instance. Very dubious, too, the argument that because Abraham's faith in the promise preceded the institution of circumcision, the righteousness of faith is, therefore, avail-able for all that believe—uncircumcised as well as circumcised —and that, consequently, circumcision is not essential for salvation ; makes, in fact, the promise void.[32] From the story of the institution of circumcision, it is evident that the benefits of the covenant between God and Abraham, of which it was

[27] Gal. iii. 1 f.
[28] 1 Cor. x. 3-4.
[29] Rom. iv. 23-24.
[30] Gal. iv. 21 f.
[31] Rom. v. 13.
[32] Ibid., iv. 9 ; cf. Gal. iii. 17 f.

the seal, were limited to the circumcised,[33] though it was subsequently added that in his seed all the nations of the earth shall be blessed.[34] It is this saying, and not the argument based on the precedence of faith over circumcision, that would lend force to his contention that circumcision is not necessary to salvation.

This arbitrary method of treating the Old Testament history is thus by no means convincing. Rabbinic logomachy is not the Gospel of Jesus and does not appeal to us like the Sermon on the Mount and the parables. It stands in glaring contrast to the method of Jesus who, in his conflict with the Scribes and Pharisees, does not attempt to invalidate the Law as a means of salvation by the use of Rabbinic subtleties, though he does not hesitate to criticise even the Mosaic legislation from his elevated moral and spiritual standpoint. He attacks, not the law, but the lawyers. He is a reformer of the Law, not, like Paul, its destroyer. His polemic is against the tradition of the elders, which he denounced as a perversion of the Law. According to Matthew he came not to destroy, but to fulfil the Law. If this saying expresses the view of the Jewish-Christian editor of the First Gospel, Jesus, at all events in the Sermon on the Mount, unreservedly inculcates the practical value of the Law, and emphasises the doing of the will of his Father in heaven and the practice of his own ethical teaching.[35] It is very significant that, in working out his theory of the Law and its function, Paul does not appeal to the teaching of Jesus. It is the Christian Rabbi, not the prophet of Nazareth, that speaks to us in this laboured argumentation.[36]

At the same time Jesus, too, goes beyond the Law and requires a new righteousness superior to the old legalism. He denounces the bondage to this legalism and strikes a new note of freedom from at least the ceremonial Law, from the religion of the letter in behalf of the religion of the spirit.

[33] Gen. xvii.
[34] Ibid., xxii. 18.
[35] Matt. vii. 21 f. Deissmann surely exaggerates when he says, " There is no contrast between Paul and Jesus," " St Paul," 160.
[36] H. Lohmeyer, in his puzzling book, "Grundlagen Paulinischer Theologie " (1929), makes of Paul a metaphysician rather than a rabbinic reasoner. In his reasonings on the Law, at all events, it is the rabbinic exegete, not the metaphysician that speaks.

In this respect he anticipates Paul, and Paul only carries farther the conflict which he waged with the Scribes and Pharisees. If, in so doing, his conclusions would be stronger without the proofs, the conclusions themselves in behalf of the universality and freedom of the Gospel, reflect the spirit of Jesus, and were of momentous importance for the perpetuation of the movement which Jesus started. In this respect he may be regarded as the interpreter and successor of Jesus, whilst advancing beyond him as an apostle of freedom and achieving the actual separation of Christianity from Judaism. For him the Gospel is not a mere modification of Judaism. It is a new interpretation of religion in the spirit of the prophets and Jesus, for which he finds, all too arbitrarily indeed, the preparation and the proof in the Old Testament. Moreover, in his contention that the religion of faith preceded the religion of works, he hit on a historic verity—the verity that the spiritual and ethical tendency of the prophets did precede the developed legalism of the priests and the scribes. Faith in God and freedom from legalism are the characteristic features of the earlier and the higher type of Jewish piety and teaching. In this sense the religion of faith is before the religion of works, and Paul, in insisting on this aspect of religion, did an immense service to Christianity. He made of it a universal religion in unison with the nature of God and the spiritual nature of man—the religion of the spirit, not of the letter, as religion, even the Christian religion, tends to become. At the same time he imparted to it, in spite of his extreme antilegalism, a surpassing ethical force. If he swept away " the works of the Law," it was only to put in their place " the fruits of faith," " faith working by love." The Christian ethic which he built on his superlative principle of faith may be justly described as a replica of that of Jesus.

XI. Universalism

By his antagonism to the Law and his insistence on the Gospel of God's free grace in Christ, Paul universalised Christianity and emancipated it from the legalism and religious racialism which would have made its conquest of the ancient world impossible. Redemption is available for Gentile as well as Jew without any legalist or racial restriction. Possibly

his universalist conception of the Gospel was influenced by
his larger outlook as a Hellenist-Jew and his Roman citizenship.
He himself had experience of the working of the liberal policy
which conferred the privilege of the imperial citizenship,
without regard to race or nationality. But apart from this
possible influence, his conception of the Gospel involved its
independence of race or nationality. The Gospel is, for him,
concerned with faith, not with " works," with grace, not with
law, with the spirit, not with the flesh, which are radically
antithetical. The redemption wrought by Christ is spiritual.
It means " deliverance from the bondage of corruption "
which infects man and the universe, and is available for " the
whole creation." Through this redemption the believer is
under the régime of grace, not of law, and God's grace in Christ
is free and unfettered.[1] In place of the Jewish nation he sets
the Church as an association freed from all political and racial
limitations. Moreover, Paul apprehended the great truth that,
if God is one, humanity must be one. " Is God the God of
the Jews only ? Is he not the God of the Gentiles also, if so
be that God is one ? "[2]

In thus universalising God and redemption, in emphasising
the unity of humanity in accordance with the unity of God,
he was following a tendency discernible in some of the prophets,
notably in the Second Isaiah and Jonah, and in the Psalms
and the Wisdom literature. God is not merely the God of
the chosen people. He is the God of the whole earth, and it
is the mission of Israel to make Him known among the nations
and win their allegiance to Him.[3] Jewish proselytism was an
attempt to Judaise the Gentiles in the universalist spirit of the
later prophets and the Psalms. In their zeal to spread the
knowledge and worship of the true God, its more liberal-minded
emissaries were even prepared to relax the prescriptions of the
Law in favour of the semi-proselytes. To secure participation
in the full privileges of the chosen people, the acceptance of
the whole Law was, however, essential, and herein lies the
radical difference between Jewish universalism and that of
Paul. His universalism is unconditional. He went the length
of abrogating the Law for his Gentile converts, whilst willing

[1] See Rom. v.-viii. [2] Rom. iii. 29-30.
[3] See Kohler, " Jewish Theology," 332 f.

to retain it in the case of the Jewish Christians, on condition that they recognised his principle of salvation by faith, not by the works of the Law. The spiritual fellowship of believers in Christ, whether Jew or Gentile, was wholly freed from religious as well as racial limitation. " Actually and historically and, in the fullest sense, theoretically and verbally, universalism was never preached and practised up till St Paul's day as it was preached and practised by him." [4]

Whilst he thus universalises faith in the spirit of Jesus and the larger-minded prophets, his universalism is conditioned by the doctrines of predestination and election, which he carried over from Phariseeism into his Christianity. According to Josephus, the Pharisees ascribed all that happens to fate [5] and to God. At the same time they held that it lies in man's power to choose right or wrong, though fate co-operates in his every action.[6] They thus recognised the relative freedom of the will, and in this respect they differed from the Sadducees, who taught its absolute freedom. This Pharisaic doctrine seems to have been the prevailing one in the Rabbinic schools, as reflected in " The Sayings of the Fathers." " All is foreseen and free will is given." [7] Paul, on the other hand, seems to have adopted the Pharisaic doctrines of predestination and election without any reservation. In his Christian Apologetic, at all events, he maintains these doctrines in the absolute sense. His teaching is rather that of the Essenes, who asserted that all human action is predetermined by God, and roundly denied the freedom of the will.[8] " Whom he foreknew he also foreordained, and whom he foreordained he also called, and whom he called he also justified, and whom he justified he also glorified." [9] Predestination and election being thus absolute, free will is for Paul a misnomer. Man being enslaved by sin cannot will or do the good unless his will is redeemed from the power of sin by Christ. At the same time, he does not consistently adhere to these extreme doctrines. On occasion he combines predestination with human responsi-

[4] Montefiore, " Judaism and St Paul," 144.   [5] εἱμαρμένη.
[6] " Bell. Jud.," ii. 8, 14 ; " Ant.," xiii. 5, 9 ; xviii. 1, 3.
[7] " Pirké Aboth," iii. 19, ed. and trans. by Herford, " Apocrypha and Pseudepigrapha " (Charles), ii. ; cf. " Psalms of Solomon," ix. 5 f., Ibid.
[8] Josephus, " Ant.," xiii. 5, 9 ; xviii. 1, 5.
[9] Rom. viii. 29-30.

bility and, consequently, with the freedom of the will, in the
spirit of his Pharisaic teachers. He seems to recognise the
exercise of free will in the case of the Gentiles, who " do by
nature the things of the law." God, he categorically asserts,
will render to every man according to his works.[10]

Predestination and election involve, on God's part, a purpose
in relation to man and his destiny, which is being worked out
in human history.[11] " The purpose of God according to
election " is clearly discernible in history. In pursuance of
his redemptive purpose, He elected Israel as the instrument of
His will. Hence its religious privileges and mission, as
displayed in Old Testament history. Through Israel God
determined to work out His redemptive purpose. Theirs
" the adoption, and the glory, and the covenants, and the giving
of the law, and the service of God, and the promises, and of
whom is Christ concerning the flesh." [12] With the prophets
and his Rabbinic teachers, Paul sees in Israel's history the
evidence of their divine election. Israel has been chosen to
be the witness of God to the nations and to render them
service even in its sufferings, as the Suffering Servant passages
in Second Isaiah show. It is a noble idea and it is in keeping
with the indubitable religious genius of the Hebrew people,
which marked it out from the other peoples of the ancient
world. In its elevated ethical monotheism it was, in truth,
an elect, a peculiar people. Historically, and apart altogether
from theological theory, this small Semitic people did play a
distinctive and invaluable part in the religious and moral
development of mankind. The world would have been much
poorer without the lofty religious and ethical ideal which
found expression in the Hebrew prophets from Moses onwards.
Israel, the religious teacher of the nations, their servant in
suffering in behalf of their enlightenment and uplifting—in this
respect, in spite of its shortcomings, its frequent moral lapse
and failure, was a truly elect race. " The election of Israel,"
justly remarks Kohler, " presupposes an inner calling, a special
capacity of soul and tendency of intellect which fit it for the
divine task. The people which has given mankind its greatest
prophets and psalmists, its boldest thinkers and its noblest

[10] Rom. ii. 14 ; v. 6.
[11] *Ibid.*, viii. 28 ; ix. 11, 17.   [12] *Ibid.*, ix. 4-5.

martyrs, which has brought to fruition the three great world religions, the Church, the Mosque, and—mother of them both—the Synagogue, must be the religious people *par excellence*. It must have within itself enough of the heavenly spark of truth and of the impetus of the religious genius as to be able and eager, whenever and wherever the opportunity is favourable, to direct the spiritual flight of humanity toward the highest and holiest." [13]

On the other hand, the election of Israel only holds in the sphere of religion and ethics, and in the Old Testament the divine purpose in history is generally conceived in an exclusive and narrowly national spirit. With the exception of the larger-minded prophets, God's providential working is confined to the interest and the destiny of a comparatively insignificant people. After all, the Hebrew mind is by no means the measure of the mind of God in relation to man. His purpose is equally discernible in the history of other peoples who, according to their several capacities, have rendered high service to human progress in the contributions which they have made to civilisation. With the larger minds among the Hebrew religious teachers, Paul takes a wider view of the divine purpose in history. Though he has little appreciation for what lay beyond the religious sphere, he at least deserves the credit of outstepping the narrow national aspect of election, and broadening the divine purpose so as to include the Gentiles within its scope. In this respect his contention that God has been working out a universalist purpose in this development is a forcible one. The development of Judaism into a universal religion, as embodied in the Church, is a truly sublime phenomenon. Even if we regard it as the result of the working of purely historical forces, it does seem to reveal an over-ruling will—the divinity that shapes our ends, rough hew them as we will.

How, in the face of the divine election of Israel, explain the fact that God's redemptive purpose seems to have miscarried in Israel's failure to acknowledge the Christ? Has not the word of God come to nought? [14] How explain the stumbling of the Jews " at the stone of stumbling, the rock of offence " (*i.e.*, their rejection of Christ), if God had chosen

[13] " Jewish Theology," 326-327.   [14] Rom. ix. 6.

them to be the instruments of His redeeming purpose ?   God having chosen Israel, is it not unjust, queries the Jew, to reject Israel and substitute the Gentiles as the objects of his mercy and compassion ? [15]   Paul was faced with a real difficulty from the standpoint of Jewish faith, and strives to answer the querulous Jew on his own ground.   He adduces the Jewish belief in predestination and election, and appeals to Jewish history in proof of its limited application even in the case of Israel itself.   Predestination and election rest entirely in God's sovereign right to will what He wills.   This principle, he maintains, is clearly discernible in God's dealings with Israel.   He reminds his opponent that " they are not all Israel which are of Israel."   Not all who claim descent from Abraham are children of Abraham.[16]   In the exercise of his sovereign will, God discriminated not only between the seed of Abraham, but between the two sons of Isaac and Rebecca, choosing Jacob and rejecting Esau.   And this even before they were born and they had done anything good or bad, and solely " that the purpose of God according to election might stand, not of works, but of him that calleth." [17]   Moreover, throughout the history of Israel it is only a remnant that has formed the elect of God—" the election of grace "—as the case of Elijah and the 7,000 who had not bowed the knee to Baal, proves, and the prophet Isaiah testifies.[18]   Human destiny, Israel's election, thus depends wholly on God's determining will, not on the will of nations or individuals.   " So that it is not of him that willeth, nor of him that runneth, but of God that hath mercy." [19]   In the ultimate resort, salvation depends not on faith, which Paul elsewhere magnifies, but on the divine will and decree.   God uses nations and individuals like Pharaoh to show his power and make known his name, hardening their hearts or showing mercy as He wills.   Being possessed of absolute sway over his creation, His will cannot be subject to any restriction or limitation.   He is entitled to exercise it as He pleases.   Nor can He be charged with unrighteousness in the use He makes of it.   It is not for man to remonstrate or ask why God should find fault with him for doing what

[15] Rom. ix. 14 f.   [18] Ibid., ix. 27 f. ; xi. 2 f.
[16] Ibid., ix. 6-7.   [19] Ibid., ix. 16.
[17] Ibid., ix. 11.

He wills. God is the potter who makes out of the same lump of clay one vessel to honour and another to dishonour, as it pleases Him. It is within His province to devote some to destruction as vessels of His wrath, and to prepare aforehand others unto glory as vessels of His mercy. It may be a grim doctrine. But granting the conception of God as absolute, unconditioned will, as Paul conceives Him in the ninth chapter of Romans, the conclusion logically follows. The election of the Gentiles as the agents of His purpose is both in accordance with the prerogative of God to do what He wills, and is confirmed by the history of Israel itself, which shows His preference for some, his rejection of others of the Hebrew race. It has, moreover, been foretold by the prophet Hosea and by Isaiah, who foresaw " the stone of stumbling and the rock of offence " which brought to pass for the Jews their foreordained doom. In refusing to believe in Christ, whom the Gentiles have accepted, in spurning the righteousness which is of faith and adhering to the righteousness of works, they have stumbled into their predestined destiny.

The solution of the problem is, to say the least, one-sided. In his one-sided conception of God as sovereign will, Paul ascribes an arbitrariness to Him which grates on the moral sense. As in the case of his doctrine of inherent sin, it tends to compromise God and undermine man's moral responsibility. He does not really succeed in answering the question, Is there unrighteousness in God? He accentuates rather than solves the problem. He overbears. He does not convince. The reason appears to lie in his faculty of isolating one aspect of the subject—God's absolute, sovereign will— and concentrating exclusively on it in this ninth chapter of Romans. Theoretically, God, as absolute Sovereign, can do what He wills, since there is no other will to limit His. Paul does not pause to ask whether there are not other elements in the nature of God which tend to counterbalance the conception of sovereign will in the arbitrary sense.

Happily, he has also the faculty of concentrating on the other aspect of the subject in the following two chapters, in which he largely ignores the theoretic conclusions of the ninth. Having overwhelmed the unbelieving Jew with the logic of the absolute sovereign will of God, he proceeds virtually to cancel his own dialectic. In these chapters he practically ignores the divine decree and plainly assumes human freedom and responsibility and the universality of God's redemptive purpose. The Jews have made a fatal mistake in rejecting Christ and seeking to establish their own righteousness. They are chargeable with disobedience,[20] and disobedience implies the power to obey. Their unbelief is the real cause of their rejection.[21] The Gentiles are reminded that, though they have displaced the Jews as God's elect, they are liable to forfeit their election by their conduct.[22] In spite of the divine decree and his own dialectic, Paul offers salvation to all. His Gospel is a universalist Gospel. If it is " God's elect " that are justified, all may be included in the number.[23] In giving His own Son up *for us all*, God has shown that He is ready freely to give us all things.[24] If the Jews have been fatally mistaken in seeking to establish their own righteousness, they are free to participate in the righteousness which is of faith in Christ. " For Christ is the end of the law to *every one* that believeth." [25] Salvation here depends not so much on the divine decree as on faith in Christ, which is available for all. " If thou shalt confess with thy mouth Jesus as Lord, and shalt believe in thy heart that God raised him from the dead, thou shalt be saved. For with the heart man believeth unto righteousness, and with the mouth confession is made unto salvation." [26] Faith ignores all distinction of race or legal observance. " Whosoever believeth shall not be put to shame. For there is no distinction between Jew and Greek ; for the same Lord is Lord of all and is rich unto all that call upon him. For whosoever shall call on the name of the Lord shall be saved." [27] " There cannot be Greek and Jew, circumcision and uncircumcision, barbarian, Scythian, bondman, freedman, but Christ is all, and in all." [28] God's sovereignty is counterbalanced by His mercy. Even a remnant of Israel, of whom Paul himself is an example, is being saved. As in the days of Elijah, " even so at this present time there is a remnant according to the election of grace," [29] if God has meanwhile caused a spirit

---

[20] Rom. x. 21.
[21] *Ibid.*, xi. 20.
[22] *Ibid.*, xi. 21-22.
[23] *Ibid.*, viii. 33-34.
[24] *Ibid.*, viii. 32.
[25] *Ibid.*, x. 4.
[26] *Ibid.*, x. 9-10.
[27] *Ibid.*, x. 11-13.
[28] Col. iii. 11.
[29] Rom. xi. 5.

of stupor to come over the others that they should neither see nor hear.[30] His purpose in so doing is not their damnation, but " to provoke them to jealousy." [31] He is only biding His time for the realisation of their salvation. If the whole business of salvation is God's business, His sovereignty will in the end accomplish His saving purpose for Jew as well as Greek. If he has shown His mercy to the Greek, who was formerly disobedient, He will also show it to the Jew, who is now disobedient. If both have been shut up unto disobedience, it is only that He might have mercy on all.[32] " When the fullness of the Gentiles shall be come in, all Israel shall be saved." [33] Paul believes that Judaism will finally capitulate to Christianity. Though his sanguine belief has not been realised, it shows at least that the divine purpose is not the reprobation of any, but the salvation of all. With a magisterial inconsistency, Paul can defy his own one-sided logic. His heart is better than his head.

In the doctrine of election he reflects the teaching of Jesus, though Jesus' distinctive conception of God is rather that of the heavenly Father who cares for all—the righteous and the unrighteous alike. " Many are called, but few are chosen." Jesus, too, had contemplated the admission of the Gentiles into the kingdom in preference to the children of Abraham, and had included in his healing ministry Gentiles as well as Jews. Paul's universalism is only the practical exemplification of his ideal.

XII. Freedom

Universalism presupposes freedom from legalism. It was not merely a question of the right to preach the Gospel to the Gentiles. Others before Paul had done this, and his Judaising opponents admitted what had become a recognised practice. It was a question of what the Gospel itself is. For Paul it is a gospel of freedom—freedom from legal ordinance and prescription. These tend to obscure and pervert the Gospel of redemption by faith in Christ. Consequently Paul resisted the demand for the circumcision of his Gentile converts and the imposition on them of the restrictions which circumcision involved. He set his face firmly against the Judaising

[30] Rom. xi. 8.
[31] Ibid., xi. 11.
[32] Ibid., xi. 30-32 ; cf. Gal. iii. 22.
[33] Ibid., xi. 26.

reaction at Antioch, and sternly rebuked Peter for refusing to eat with Gentiles (apparently at the Agape or common meal) unless they conformed to Jewish practice.[1] He passionately denounced the recourse of his Galatian converts to Jewish-Gnostic observances as a betrayal of the Gospel, a falling away from Christ, a return to the old legalist bondage.[2] Circumcision, etc., is wholly null for the Gentile believer. It is, in fact, in itself a thing indifferent, even for the Jew, though he does not go the length of forbidding this and other legalist observances in his case. " For neither is circumcision anything, nor uncircumcision, but a new creature."[3] " Circumcision is nothing, and uncircumcision is nothing, but the keeping of the commandments of God."[4]

Hence the uncompromising spirit in which he took up the challenge of the Judaisers in his Galatian churches. His Gospel of faith and freedom was at stake. To grant their demand was to betray the Gospel and sap the vital force of its appeal to the Gentile world. It would certainly have paralysed the Gentile mission. " With freedom did Christ set us free. Stand fast, therefore, and be not entangled again in a yoke of bondage. Behold I, Paul, say unto you that, if ye receive circumcision, Christ will profit you nothing. Ye are severed from Christ, . . . ye are fallen away from grace."[5] " Judaism," says Montefiore, " could not be a universal religion together with its inviolable Law."[6]

His principle of freedom granted, he was ready to bear with the susceptibilities and prejudices of his Jewish brethren. In the Epistle to the Romans he seems, in fact, to retract somewhat the intransigent attitude of the Epistle to the Galatians, written in the fever heat of the early stage of the controversy. He entreats the Romans to respect the scruples about meats and other observances of their fellow Jewish Christians. He deprecates judging these weak brethren and quarrelling over such things. To him nothing is unclean in itself. Nevertheless, he will do nothing to cause scrupulous consciences to stumble. He will follow the example of Christ, who pleased not himself, and will bear the infirmities of the

---

[1] Gal. ii. 11 f.
[2] *Ibid.*, iii., iv., v.
[3] *Ibid.*, vi. 15.
[4] 1 Cor. vii. 19.
[5] Gal. v. 1 f.
[6] " Jud. and St Paul," 145.

weak. " It is good not to eat flesh nor to drink wine nor to do anything whereby thy brother stumbleth." [7]   In the case of eating meats sacrificed to idols, whilst owning the right of his Gentile communities to eat, or not eat, he applies the same self-denying principle. " Meat will not commend us to God, neither if we eat not, are we the worse, nor if we eat are we the better." [8]   He tells them, if they are invited to a pagan feast, to eat, asking no question for conscience's sake. " For the earth is the Lord's and the fullness thereof." [9]   But if such eating is a cause of stumbling to a weak brother, then it is a duty to abstain.   He will curb the liberty of his own conscience for the sake of his weak brother's conscience. " Wherefore, if meat maketh my brother to stumble, I will eat no flesh for ever-more, that I make not my brother to stumble." [10]   " All things are lawful, but all things are not expedient. All things are lawful, but all things edify not. Let no man seek his own, but each his neighbour's good." [11]

Whilst the liberty of the believer is thus limited by ex-pediency, the inspiration of the Spirit, which is common to Jews and Greeks,[12] bond and free, emancipates him from the old servitude.   The new spiritual life, which it inspires and which was to be the distinctive feature of the Messianic age,[13] is incompatible with the old legal bondage—" the works of the law " or " the flesh." " This only would I learn of you (the Galatian Judaisers), Was it as a result of works of the law that ye received the Spirit, or by the hearing of faith ?   Are ye so foolish ?   Having begun in the Spirit, are ye now perfected in the flesh ? " [14]   " If ye are led by the Spirit, ye are no longer under the law." [15]   Through the witness of the Spirit in his heart the believer is thus no longer a bondservant, but a son and an heir.[16]   The Spirit in this sense is practically the in-dwelling Christ, and means for Paul complete liberation from his former life of subjection to the law of sin and death.[17]   Hence the great saying, " Now the Lord is the Spirit, and where the Spirit of the Lord is, there is liberty." [18]   And that other

[7] Rom. xiv. 1 f. ; xv. 1 f.
[8] 1 Cor. viii. 8.
[9] Ibid., x. 26.
[10] Ibid., viii. 13.
[11] Ibid., x. 23-24.
[12] Ibid., xii. 13.
[13] Joel ii. 28 ; cf. Acts i. and ii. ; x. 44, etc.
[14] Gal. iii. 2-4.
[15] Ibid., v. 18.
[16] Ibid., iv. 6-7 ; cf. Rom. viii. 14 f.
[17] Rom. viii. 2.
[18] 2 Cor. iii. 17.

great saying about the new covenant, not of the letter, but of the spirit, not in tables of stone, but in tables that are hearts of flesh, on which the Spirit of the living God operates. " For the letter killeth, but the spirit giveth life." [19] Here, too, liberty has its limits. It is not liberty to sin, as some of Paul's converts in the corrupt environment of imperial cities, like Corinth, were only too apt to assume. In spite of his antagonism to the Law, Paul is no antinomian. The inspiration of the Spirit means the crucifixion of the flesh, as " contrary the one to the other," and the exemplification of the fruits of the Spirit.[20] Body as well as soul is being spiritualised in an ethical process, if it will only be brought to full fruition in the life to come. " Ye are not in the flesh, but in the spirit, if so be that the Spirit of God dwelleth in you. But if the Spirit of him that raised up Jesus from the dead dwelleth in you, he that raised up Christ Jesus from the dead shall quicken also your mortal bodies through the Spirit that dwelleth in you." [21]

Nor is it liberty in the political and social sense. Like Jesus, Paul teaches submission to the Roman Government, without concerning himself with the question of national or individual liberty. He is proud of his status as a Roman citizen and accepts Roman rule as a divine ordinance, which no one may resist and every one must obey.[22] Persecution by the Roman Government had not yet made itself felt. Otherwise Paul would at least have added a caveat that, where allegiance to constituted authority clashes with allegiance to God, the Christian is even at the risk of his life to refuse obedience. He reasons on the assumption that the Government " is a minister to thee for good," and that " they are the ministers of God's service." It does not occur to him to inquire into its right to conquer and dominate other peoples, or into the moral basis of its power. He shares, moreover, the common view of the institution of slavery, assumes the right of one man to hold another in bondage, though he seeks to Christianise it. Christian brotherhood demands the recognition of all as God's children, apart from social as well as racial distinctions. The slave is the brother of his Christian master, if he still remains a slave, and the master is reminded that, morally and religiously,

---

[19] 2 Cor. iii. 6.
[20] Gal. v. 16.
[21] Rom. viii. 9 f.
[22] *Ibid.*, xiii. 1 f.

there is no respect of persons, and that he also has a Master in heaven.[23] " Likewise he that was called (to Christ), being free, is Christ's bondservant." [24] At the same time the slave is to abide in that vocation in which he was called. But if a bondservant, he is the Lord's freedman.[25] Similarly, the subordination of women is emphasised. " Let them be in subjection, as also saith the law." [26] With the modern emancipation of women he would have had no sympathy, though the relations of husband and wife and all other social relations are to be leavened by the Christian spirit. The mutual dependence of one on another is ever to be kept in mind.

In this respect the eschatological view of the world and man, which dominates his redemptive theory, is not altogether salutary. To be in Christ and be made fit to participate in the new order which is impending—this is the supreme concern of the believer. All else is by comparison a matter of indifference. Early Christianity, as Troeltsch contends, was a religious, not a distinctively social movement. It was concerned with the salvation of the soul, the realisation of a kingdom which was not of this world. For Paul, as for Jesus, the kingdom of God is purely spiritual.[27] Both contemplated the supersession of the present age or order by a new and spiritual order of things. The present age is vitiated by sin as the result of the fall. It is under the régime of Satan and the demons. It will speedily be destroyed and replaced by the rule of God. Jesus and his early followers did not, therefore, set out to reform the inequitable social order prevailing in a world so constituted. Their aim was to save the soul from the consequences of sin, the power of evil which vitiated human society.[28] In the main the contention is correct, though in view of Jesus' healing and benevolent ministry and the philanthropic teaching and practice of Paul and the early Church, one is disposed to query the too absolute assertion of it. The dogmatic and eschatological teaching of a Paul long hampered the influence of the Church in grappling with the problem of the social and political betterment of human society. It was deemed

[23] Col. iii. 25 ; iv. 1 ; Philemon, 16.
[24] 1 Cor. vii. 23.
[25] *Ibid.*, vii. 20.
[26] *Ibid.*, xiv. 34.
[27] Rom. xiv. 17 ; 1 Cor. vi. 6 ; xv. 50 ; Gal. v. 21.
[28] Troeltsch, " Social Teaching of the Christian Churches," i. 43 f. (Eng. trans., 1931).

no part of its business actively to oppose political oppression
and wrongdoing. Nor was the early Church in a position to
attempt any direct reform of political and social institutions
in the face of a hostile empire.

Nevertheless, it is an exaggeration to say, with A. Schweitzer,
that both Jesus and Paul were concerned exclusively with
eschatology and had no message bearing on the life of the
believer in the actual world. Jesus was engaged in actively
founding the kingdom of God in the present, and applying the
principles which should govern the conduct of its members,
if, in the later part of his mission, the kingdom is distinctively
envisaged from the transcendental point of view. Paul, in
founding his Gentile Churches was concerned with concrete,
not purely visionary institutions, and constantly inculcated the
practical virtues which his converts were to exemplify in
their relations with one another and with the world. The
Christian life is not for Paul a thing of the future, even if true
life—the higher life of the spirit—will only be fully realised with
the emancipation of the spirit from the body. Just as for Jesus
the kingdom was already in growth, working like the leaven,
so for Paul " life eternal " is being realised in the present
experience of the believer. As Professor Anderson Scott
aptly remarks, " What had been (in Judaism) eschatological,
in fact, the great hope of the future, had now become experimental, a hope which had been realised." [29] Paul, in fact,
seems in his more mature thought to have laid less stress on
the traditional eschatology and to have contemplated the
immediate union of the departed spirit, in a spiritual body,
with Christ as the completion of the mystic fellowship with him
in this life.[30] Whilst the believer thus awaits, and is being
already transformed for the higher heavenly life with Christ,
he is to give himself with fidelity to the duties of his earthly
calling. He is not to confine his interest or his goodwill to
his fellow believers, but to love and minister to even his
enemies in the spirit of the Sermon on the Mount.[31] The
expectation of the speedy coming of the Lord is not to degenerate
into visionary imaginings or be an excuse for idleness. He is

[29] " Christianity According to St Paul," 140.
[30] See 2 Cor. v. 6 f. ; Phil. i. 23.
[31] Rom. xii. 14 f.

to abound more and more in love of the brethren, to study
to be quiet, to attend to the practical side of life, and to work
with his own hands.[32] Of this obligation Paul himself is
the striking example. " For ye remember, brethren, our labour
and travail, working night and day that we might not burden
any of you." [33] He worked as a tentmaker for his living all
his life and disdained to live on charity, though he claimed the
right of support as a missionary. He dictated his letters,
apparently, because his toil-stiffened hands made writing
irksome to him.[34] He is a marvellous combination of the
idealist and the practical man of affairs, who spends himself
in the task of evangelising the world, founding and supervising
numerous communities of believers, and concerning himself
with their material as well as moral welfare.

In his conflict with the Judaisers, Paul may be regarded
as the champion of freedom of thought in the religious sphere.
Like Jesus, he claims the right to think for himself as against
the traditionists. He does not hesitate to attack the old
and substitute for it a new order of things, in accordance with
his own intuition. Against the old, he sets the supreme
authority of personal conviction, which he claims to have
received by revelation from Christ. He places the God-inspired
soul high above the traditional institution as the norm of
belief. Another of his great sayings is very significant from
this point of view. " Quench not the Spirit ; despise not
prophesyings ; prove all things ; hold fast to that which is
good." [35] He is not, of course, the champion of freedom of
thought in our large modern sense. There is an intolerant
strain in him imported from Phariseeism and Judaism in
general. There is always such a strain in him who would
transform his age and carry his age over to a new order. Such
a man must be intensely convinced himself and regard his own
convictions as the absolute truth. Jesus himself, in his conflict
with the Scribes and Pharisees, is as intense and insistent and
absolute as Paul in his conflict with the Judaisers. Without
this conviction what of truth there is in a movement could not
prevail. It is only thus that man is prepared to die for his
cause. Intolerance is, in this sense, an essential in the progress

[32] 1 Thes. iv. 9 f.
[33] *Ibid.*, ii. 9 ; *cf.* 1 Cor. iv. 12.
[34] Gal. vi. 11.
[35] 1 Thes. v. 19.

of enlightenment. At the same time, unlike Jesus, who appeals to moral and spiritual verities, Paul, who resorts to Rabbinic argument to enforce his convictions, is not at times convincing. He is prone to antitheses, and the antitheses are absolute. He sees man and the world in opposites, and the opposites are apt to be exaggerated. He judges from the watershed of his experience and his intense personality, and this watershed separates for him truth from error, light from darkness, life from death. It is hardly surprising that his Judaising opponents were not convinced, though they were better fitted to appreciate his arguments than we are. It is evident that he himself retained not a little of rabbinic thought, to which Jesus was alien, and entangled the original Gospel in a train of ideas which, to many nowadays, appear merely the old religion in a new form, though for him the operation of the Spirit in the heart and life of the believer, not mere belief, is the great thing. Apart from the issue in itself, which was of vital importance for Christianity, there was room for difference and dissent in these Rabbinic bouts, and some ground for accusing Paul of inconsistency.[36] The diatribe against the Apostles at Jerusalem and their agents as emissaries of Satan, as " dogs," is hardly a fair description of his opponents.[37] Happily, in his more reflective mood he can be less dogmatic and vituperative, and modify both his judgment and his standpoint.[38]

XIII. PAUL AND PHILOSOPHY

Paul has a profound contempt for Philosophy, or " the wisdom of this world," " the wisdom of men," as he calls it.[1] He depreciates reason and the exercise of reason, as exemplified by the philosophers, in the search for God and the good. If he urges his converts to prove all things and himself reasons vigorously and too often rabbinically, he does not believe that

[36] Gal. v. 11.   [37] Ibid., v. 10 ; 2 Cor. xi. 13-14 ; Phil. iii. 2.
[38] Special monographs on the subject : J. Weiss, " Die Christliche Freiheit nach der Verkündigung des Apostels Paulus " (1902) ; W. M. MacGregor, " Christian Freedom " (1914). H. Jonas gives an exposition of Paul's conception of the freedom of the will, as compared with that of Augustine, in " Augustin und das Paulinische Freiheitsproblem " (1930).
[1] 1 Cor. i. 20 f. ; ii. 5.

reason can carry man within reach of religious truth. He
recognises a natural knowledge of God and the good. But this
knowledge man has disfigured by the vain reasonings, the
senseless, darkened understanding which has led him into
idolatry.[2] So far as philosophy allied itself with the current
mythology, his criticism is justifiable. But he overlooks the fact
that the tendency of philosophy was to explain away the mythology, to resolve it into a symbolic representation of the divine
in nature, and thus really to undermine the polytheism which
outraged Paul's Jewish monotheism. Saving knowledge in his
sense, knowledge of God in Christ—the only knowledge that
matters—is a thing solely of revelation. Of this knowledge
he claims a monopoly against even the apostles, let alone the
philosophers. It came to him not from man, but through
revelation of Jesus Christ.[3] The Christ he has in view is not
so much the historic Jesus, as the heavenly Christ of his
experience, who appeared to him and has exercised his redemptive function in Old Testament history before he entered on his
earthly life. From the point of view of this revelation, " the
Gentiles know not God." [4] God's wisdom is pure foolishness
to their wisdom.[5] Unfortunately, his knowledge of Greek
philosophy, in the sense of at least an attempted reasoned
knowledge of God and man's relation to him, was only a
second-hand knowledge. He knew something of the Platonic-
Stoic thought of his Hellenist environment. He could not
adequately judge it on its own merits as a legitimate attempt
of the mind to attain to a reasoned conception of God and
the universe. He had not the philosophic mind or temperament. He retains in this respect the characteristic outlook of
Judaism, and Judaism did not foster the philosophic spirit.
Its distinctive function was, on the one hand, prophecy or
inspiration by the divine Spirit ; on the other, didactic instruction in the contents of the revelation thus inspired. Paul
has most affinity with the former tendency, though he also
shows his expert training in the latter. Inspiration and didactic
teaching on the strength of it are the distinctive features of his
thought. There is, indeed, an echo of Plato here and there
in the distinction between the visible and the invisible world,

[2] Rom. i. 19 f.   [4] 1 Thes. iv. 6.
[3] Gal. i. 11 f.   [5] 1 Cor. i. 23.

between the temporal and the eternal, between the spiritual
and the carnal or psychic constituents of human nature.[6]
In his mission preaching, as at Lystra and Athens, he seems
to have appealed on occasion to the natural evidence for the
existence of God, and emphasised the affinity of the soul with
God.[7]   But there is otherwise no attempt to evolve a reasoned
philosophy of mind and matter, to reason from the rational
and moral nature of man to the divine in and above nature.
He never thinks of setting forth the arguments for immortality
apart from the resurrection, or in confirmation of the resurrection.   There is at most only a glance at the Greek argument for
the immortality of the soul in the discourse to the philosophers
at Athens, of dubious authenticity.   He cannot wing his way
from Jewish traditional conceptions into the realm of pure
thought, which might have enabled him to reinforce his
arguments for the resurrection of Jesus by a larger view of
the rational nature, the innate moral capacity of man.

Mitigation of his rather obscurantist attitude may be found
in the type of philosophy with which he was familiar.   It was
evidently mainly of the Gnostic type.   Gnosticism was partly
a speculative, partly an ethical and religious movement.   In
its more developed form, which belongs to the post-Pauline
period, it strove to attain a solution of the problem of God in
His relation to other being ; of the creation or genesis of the
material world, in which evil is inherent and which is thus
antagonistic to God ; of the emancipation or redemption from
evil of the spiritual or higher nature of man who, in his mortal
existence, is subject to the power of evil.   In his search for
the solution of this complex problem, the Gnostic, in the
syncretistic spirit of the age, drew on Greek philosophy and
oriental thought and religion, particularly the mystery cults [8]
which professed, by means of a symbolic ritual, to initiate their
votaries into this higher or esoteric knowledge and enable them
to attain thereby the emancipation, the deification of the spirit

---

[6] Rom. i. 20 ; 2 Cor. iv. 18 ; 1 Cor. ix. 11 ; cf. ii. 13 ; iii. 5.

[7] Acts xiv. 15 f. ; xvii. 23 f. (assuming the authenticity of the discourse
at Athens).

[8] For a general review of the main features of Gnostic thought, see
Bousset, " Hauptprobleme der Gnosis," 319 f. (1907).   On the connection
between the Gnostics and the mystery religions, see Angus, " The Mystery
Religions and Christianity," 52 f. (1925) ;   Morgan, " Religion and Theology
of Paul," 135 f. ;   Kennedy, " St Paul and the Mystery Religions," 25 f.

and its union with God. "Gnosticism," tersely remarks
Mr Legge, "may be defined as the belief that man's place
in the next world is determined by the knowledge of it he
acquires in this." [9]

Hence the supreme importance of Gnosis, knowledge,
wisdom from the ethical and religious as well as the speculative
point of view. Hence the distinction between the Gnostic
or spiritually superior class, which is capable of the higher
knowledge and the higher spiritual life—the pneumatic or
spiritual superman [10]—and the inferior psychic or natural
class,[11] which either cannot rise to this higher knowledge and
life, or can only do so very imperfectly. Hence the doctrine of
the emanation of a series of divine or semi-divine beings, on a
descending and deteriorating scale, as intermediaries between
a perfect God and an imperfect world, in order to account
for the ultimate presence of evil in it. Hence the tendency
either to asceticism or to licentiousness, according as evil is
regarded as a thing to be repressed, or as a thing of no account
to the emancipated spirit in the pursuit of the higher life.
Hence, further, the assumption that the God of the Old
Testament, as the creator of the material, inherently evil,
world (the Demiourgos), must be distinct from the highest
God, the Lord of the spiritual world. The God of the Old
Testament appeared, in fact, to a Marcion, "very nearly the
Devil of the New." [12] Hence, finally, in its lower popular
form, the resort to magic in order to frustrate the demonic
power of evil.[13]

The germs of this developed Gnostic philosophy are
discernible in the pre-Christian Gnostic sects which are
represented, in Palestine, by the Essenes and the Simonians
(the followers of Simon Magus in Samaria [14]), and in the
Hellenist world by the Orphics. "All these fundamental
characteristics" (of Gnosticism), says Mr Legge, "find their

---

[9] "Pistis Sophia," Introd. 3 (Eng. trans. by Horner, 1924).
[10] πνευματικοί.   [11] ψυχικοί or σαρκικοί.
[12] Burkitt, "Church and Gnosis," 25 (1932).
[13] On the magical element in Gnosticism, see Legge, "Forerunners
and Rivals of Christianity," i. 97 f. (1915) ; Burkitt, "Church and Gnosis,"
35 f.
[14] Acts viii. 9 f. On the Simonians and other pre-Christian Gnostic
sects, see Legge, "Forerunners," i. 121 ; King, "Gnostics and their
Remains," 58 f. (1887, 2nd ed.).

origin in the beliefs of the pre-Christian religions and religious associations described above, and doubtless owed much to their influence." [15]

The Gnostic movement had adherents among the Jews of the Diaspora as well as among the Gentiles. Though independent of and anterior to Christianity, it made its influence felt in the Pauline Christian communities through Jewish or Gentile converts, who had evidently been Gnostics before they became Christians, and combined Gnostic with Christian ideas. In Galatia, at Colosse, and Corinth, for instance. In the Galatian churches the tendency of the Gentile converts is not only to put themselves under the régime of the Law, but to combine with it superstitious observances connected with the worship of the astral powers—the rudiments of this world.[16] At Corinth there is a coterie of intellectuals who pride themselves on the wisdom which " the Greeks seek after." [17] These superior persons are disposed to take offence at the foolishness of the ordinary preaching of the Gospel, and apparently prefer the more rhetorical and speculative preaching of the Alexandrian Apollos. They look askance at the uneducated members, " the weak," " the foolish," " the despised " brethren—chiefly of the slave class. Here, too, there is a glance at the profession of a wisdom which is concerned with the Gnostic belief in the principalities or rulers of the material world,[18] and there is some force in the contention that " the Christ party " [19] consisted of those who, like Cerinthus, held the Gnostic distinction between the man Jesus and the heavenly Christ who descended into him, but left him before the crucifixion. They are prone to party strife in their predilection for their vain reasonings.[20] Such belief is absolutely incompatible with fidelity to Jesus Christ, the only foundation of the faith. " For other foundation can no man lay than that which is laid, which is Christ Jesus." [21] To

---

[15] " Forerunners," ii, 14 ; cf, i. 121 ; ii. 5-7, 361. Prof. Burkitt, on the other hand, thinks that Gnosticism, as we know it, was a purely Christian product, specifically connected with Christian eschatology, " Church and Gnosis," 9 f. Rather dubious. On the attraction of Orphism, for certain early Christian circles, as expressed in early Christian art, see Eisler, " Orpheus the Fisher," 53 f. (1921).

[16] Gal. iv. 3, 8 f.
[17] 1 Cor. i. 22.
[18] Ibid., ii. 8.

[19] Ibid., i. 12, 13.
[20] Ibid., iii. 20.
[21] Ibid., iii. 11.

build on this foundation an amalgam of alien beliefs and practices is to court the fire of the last judgment, when every man's work will be tested. " Let no man deceive himself. If any man thinketh that he is wise among you in this world, let him become a fool, that he may become wise ; for the wisdom of this world is foolishness with God." [22] At Colosse, in addition to the danger in the Gnostic belief in and worship of the principalities and powers to the sole supremacy of Christ,[23] there is a marked tendency to asceticism.[24] Against this ascetic conception of the Christian life and its teachers, Paul reminds the Colossians that they have died with Christ to the (demonic) rudiments of this world, and that, being raised with him, the body is Christ's.[25]

The influence of " the philosophy," which Paul thus opposes, is discernible in his own thought. There is undoubtedly in it a Gnostic strain. His theory of the pre-existent Christ and his creative and redemptive function belongs to the Gnostic train of thought, though, as Paul develops it, it is free from the fantastic mythology which the Gnostics wove into their speculations. Like the Gnostics, he has a philosophy of history which, in spite of its speculative side, professes to have an actual historical basis. This philosophy is centred in Christ. It begins beyond history in the eternal purpose of God, of which creation and history are the unfolding, the realisation. It starts with the pre-existent, creative Christ as the predetermined and superhuman agent of God's purpose.[26] Evil enters into the creation through Satan and the spiritual

[22] 1 Cor. iii. 18-19.   [23] Col. ii. 8 f.   [24] *Ibid.*, ii. 10 f.
[25] Col. ii. 16 f. ; iii. 1 f. The Epistle seems to have been directed to Gentile Christians (i. 21, 27), who were being influenced by their Hellenist environment in combining the recognition of the demonic powers (angel worship) with their faith in Christ. Lightfoot contends that the " philosophy " which Paul attacks was a Jewish-Gnostic speculation and cult akin to Palestinian Essenism, " Commentary on Colossians," 96 f. The influence of the Essenes beyond Palestine is not proved. But there is no substantial reason for denying the Gnostic character of this philosophy, since early Gnosticism seems to have already been current in the Hellenist world. Hort, on the other hand, thinks that it was specifically Jewish, and that it was not speculative or Gnostic at all, but merely a theory of angelology, " Judaistic Christianity," 116 f. This conclusion is not warranted by the contents of the Epistle. It was certainly speculative, whatever its exact origin. On its character, see Dibelius in Lietzmann's " Handbuch," iii., 2, 78 f. See also the most recent and elaborate discussion by Radford, " Commentary on Colossians," 66 f. (1931).
[26] See especially Col. i. 16 f.

astral powers, which are supposed to dominate the universe
and man, and of which Satan is the supreme head.[27]   It takes
possession of humanity in the fall of Adam, through whom sin
and death enter into human history.   It is Christ's predetermined mission to redeem the universe and man from the
power of evil.   He is the second Adam, the sinless embodiment
in his human life of all that the first Adam, who is the type
of him to come, should have been, but failed to be.   He is
the medium whereby God's abounding and free grace operates
unto justification from sin, death, condemnation.[28]   He already
exercises his redeeming function throughout the Old Testament
history, inasmuch as he is spiritually active in the history of
Israel from Abraham onwards.   Abraham is already the
exemplar of the believer whose faith in the promised redemption by Christ is reckoned for righteousness.   Moses also
performs a supremely important, though negative part in the
realisation of God's redemptive purpose in Christ.   The
giving of the Law as the revelation of God's holy will deepened
the sense of sin and begat the sense of guilt, and leads the
sinner to seek the grace of God and the righteousness available
in Christ.   It is the schoolmaster to bring men to Christ.
From Moses onwards God's redeeming purpose and activity
in Christ are writ large in the prophets and in the history of
Israel, as shown in the numerous passages which Paul quotes
in his Epistles in proof of Christ's pre-Christian redemptive
mission.   There is thus traceable in history, from Adam
onwards, a gradual development in the sphere of religion and
ethics towards the grand climax of history—the advent of
the Christ.   At length, in his earthly life, the second Adam
appears in person to achieve the predetermined redemptive
purpose of God.   In his sinless life he exemplified the divine
ideal from which the first Adam had fallen.   In his death
and resurrection he conquered sin and death for mankind
and made eternal life available for the believer.   At the same
time, he destroyed the power of evil, the domination of Satan,
and the maleficent spiritual powers over the universe and
man.   Finally, with his exaltation to heaven he attained the
full emancipation from the limitations of the life in the flesh,

[27] 2 Cor. iv. 4.   " The God of this world or age " ;   *cf*. Col. ii. 15.
[28] Rom. v. 12 f.

entered on the full exercise of his powers as the heavenly, the ideal spiritual man,[29] and of his function as the agent of the divine purpose in creation and history " that God may be all in all." [30]

This, in brief, is Paul's philosophy of history. It is the Christian mystery of which he claims to be in possession. It is " the mystery of God," " the wisdom of God in a mystery," " the wisdom that hath been hidden from all ages and generations," " the mystery that hath been kept in silence throughout eternal ages." [31] It is the purpose " which God foreordained before the ages unto our glory." [32] It is, however, not a mystery in the sense of the mystery religions—something that is kept secret and dare not be divulged by the initiated. Not only is it discernible in the prophetic scriptures. It is now fully manifested. It has been committed to Paul and his fellow-preachers to be made known to the nations to bring them to the obedience of faith.[33] Its content is the Gospel, " the preaching of Jesus Christ " ; " Christ, and him crucified " ; " Christ crucified, the power of God and the wisdom of God " ; " Christ in you " ; " Christ in whom are all the treasures of wisdom and knowledge hidden." [34] Paul and his fellow-apostles are " stewards of the mysteries of God." [35] It is still hidden from the rulers of this world or age (the spiritual powers), who would not otherwise have crucified the Lord of Glory [36]—him who was destined to redeem the creation and man, and in whom the purpose of God has been and is being fulfilled. Hidden, too, from the wise of this world—the Greek philosopher who seeks after wisdom, the Jewish scribe who asks for signs.[37] To the Greek the wisdom of God is foolishness, to the Jew a stumbling-block. Greek superior wisdom, Jewish lack of spiritual discernment have alike failed to realise that " the foolishness of God is wiser than men, and the weakness of God is stronger than men." [38] Those who have discerned God's redeeming purpose in Christ belong not to the wise after the flesh, not to the mighty, the

[29] 1 Cor. xv. 47.   [30] *Ibid.*, xv. 20 f.
[31] *Ibid.*, ii. 1, 7 ; Rom. xvi. 25 ; Col. i. 26 ; ii. 2.
[32] *Ibid.*, ii. 7.
[33] Rom. xvi. 26 ; Col. i. 26-27.
[34] *Ibid.*, xvi. 26 ; 1 Cor. ii. 2 ; i. 22 ; Col. i. 27 ; ii. 3.
[35] 1 Cor. iv. 1.   [37] 1 Cor. i. 21 f.
[36] *Ibid.*, ii. 8.   [38] *Ibid.*, i. 25.

intellectual nobility, but to the weak, the base, the ignorant, the despised in the sight of men, " that no flesh should glory before God." Only these has God called to be partakers of His wisdom—" the righteousness, sanctification, redemption in Christ Jesus." [39] " If any man thinketh that he is wise among you in this world, let him become a fool, that he may become wise." [40]

In developing his philosophy of history and at the same time combating Gnostic ideas, Paul is himself, to a certain extent, influenced by Gnostic as well as Jewish apocalyptic ideas. As we have seen, he might have taken his cosmic Christ from the first Book of Enoch, with which he seems to have been familiar. But he makes use of Gnostic terminology, such as " wisdom," " mystery," " pleroma," " the spiritual " in contrast to " the psychic " or " natural " man, " the perfect," etc.[41] This terminology shows that his mind also worked in the groove of Gnostic thought, which, in its own mythological fashion, likewise sought to set forth the divine purpose of redemption from evil for the universe and man. At the same time, his philosophy has a distinctive character which differentiates it, in important respects, from that of the pre-Christian Gnostics. In opposition to the current Gnostic tendency to amalgamate the faith in Christ with the cult of other supernal beings, he emphatically asserts the sole supremacy of Christ in the spirit world, in subordination only to God. Christ alone is the heavenly agent of God's purpose in creation and redemption. He has abolished the dominion of the elemental, demonic powers. In him alone, as the historic manifestation of this purpose, is the true knowledge, gnosis, wisdom available. He alone is the object of Christian faith and worship. Moreover, Paul differs from these early Gnostics in discarding their fantastic mythological imaginings about a multitude of æons as media of God's redeeming purpose, and finds the medium in a historic person. If there is also in his philosophy a certain mythological element, its redeemer is a concrete figure—the man Christ Jesus, the ideal, spiritual man now in heaven, who once in the body walked and worked on earth. It is this real man, not the fictitious phantom of the Gnostic

---

[39] 1 Cor. i. 26 f.　　　　　[40] *Ibid.*, iii. 18.
[41] σοφία, μυστήριον, πλήρωμα, πνευματικοί, ψυχικοί, σαρκικοί, τέλειοι.

imagination, that is the embodiment, in his earthly life, of the redemptive idea and purpose of God. In the third place, he rebuts the Gnostic distinction between the spiritual and the natural man. Christ is the object of faith for all, the Saviour of all, Gnostic and simple believer alike. In this respect there is no essential distinction among believers, and those who profess such a distinction know not the wisdom of the Cross. There is no respect of persons with God in regard to those who are in Christ.

On the other hand, in investing Christ with a pre-existent, cosmic significance after the Gnostic manner, he introduced into his Christian philosophy a speculative element from which Jesus himself was far removed. In this respect, his theory may fairly be described as Pauline Gnosticism. The introduction of this speculative Gnostic element was, as we have seen, a questionable contribution to the faith of the nascent Church. In combating the Gnostic tendency to amalgamate the faith in Christ with the cult of other supernal beings, he would have been on surer ground had he rested his case solely on the unique personality of Jesus and his unquestionable supremacy in the moral and spiritual sphere, apart from his assumed pre-existence and creative activity. Jesus believed, indeed, with his age in demonology, in the ethereal powers which reign over the world and take maleficent possession of mankind. He, too, was in possession of a mystery—the mystery of the kingdom, which he reveals indirectly to the multitude in his parables and sayings, and communicates more directly to his disciples. In this respect, he teaches an esoteric knowledge. But it does not seem to have included any speculative theory about his pre-existence and his creative function. His philosophy of history is that of the prophets and the apocalyptists, who are concerned with the realisation of the divine will in the transformation of the present order of things into the coming order. It is not the developed Gnostic one by which Paul explains to himself the whole drama of existence from the creation onwards, and in which " the depth of the riches both of the wisdom and knowledge of God " is sounded.[42] It is his mission to overthrow the power of Satan, whose rule is reflected in the kingdoms of this world.

[42] Rom. xi. 33 f.

To this end he grapples with the sin and misery around him, and strives, in his teaching and healing ministry, to bring the sinner and the lost to repentance and alleviate human suffering. His mission, on its practical side, is concerned with the establishment of God's rule in place of that of Satan ; on its eschatological side with its ultimate and final consummation. He is the Messiah chosen by God for this purpose, and in his exalted, transcendental state he has a cosmic function to perform in the future æon or age. Farther than this the authentic record does not appear to go, and Paul in going beyond this into the realm of speculation goes farther than we can follow with assurance.

Again, whilst he rightly emphasises the historic personality of the man Christ Jesus as against Gnostic mythology, the elusive terms in which he refers on occasion to his human existence—" made in the likeness of men," " formed in fashion as a man," " in the likeness of sinful flesh "—might easily lead to Docetism. Paul is partly, if unwittingly, responsible for the later Gnostic tendency to explain, or rather explain away the humanity of Jesus in a Docetic sense—to invest the pre-existent, divine Christ with a merely seeming body, or to differentiate between this Christ and the man Jesus.[43] Moreover, whilst, in opposition to the Gnostic profession of a higher knowledge, salvation is available for all alike, he retains the Gnostic distinction between the spiritual and the psychic or natural man.[44] The knowledge available in Christ is not attainable by all in the same degree. He differentiates between these two classes of believers, in respect at least of the degree of higher knowledge and experience. He appears to have preached a twofold Gospel [45] in this sense—a simple and a

[43] On the Docetic element in this respect in Paul, see J. Weiss, " Urchristenthum," 337 f.

[44] Reitzenstein holds that for Paul the spiritual man is really no longer a man, but a supernatural man, with a distinctive or double personality which differs from that of the natural or fleshly man within him, " Die Hellenistischen Mysterien-Religionen," 168 (1910). Deissner seeks to refute this conception and to show that the spiritual man is the man gifted in an especial degree by the Spirit of God. The concept is to be ethically, not psychologically understood. " Paulus und die Mystik," 21 f. It appears to be the case that the distinction between the spiritual man and the man less advanced in the knowledge of Christ, the babe in Christ, (1 Cor. iii. 1 f.) is only relative.

[45] Deissner denies this twofold Gospel, and holds that the preaching of the Cross is the higher wisdom of which Paul speaks, and which the

more advanced one, according to the capacity of his hearers and the stage of their Christian life, though otherwise the ordinary believer may attain to the latter.   He himself claims to possess this knowledge, which has specially come to him from the Spirit of God or of Christ, which is higher than ordinary faith, and only " the perfect," the specially initiated believer, to whom he communicates it, is capable of receiving.[46] Though rude in speech, he is not lacking in this higher knowledge.[47]   It has been received by him through the Spirit. " For the Spirit searcheth all things, yea, the deep things of God." [48]   This revelation or higher knowledge concerns the mystery of which Paul, through the Spirit, possesses the key, especially that aspect of it which relates to the future " glory " of the believer.[49]   It is specifically the knowledge of the things which eye hath not seen, nor ear heard, nor the heart of man conceived—the things which God hath prepared for them that love Him.[50]   Paul was an ecstatic and seems to be referring to the revelations acquired in the visionary experiences to which he lays claim.   These revelations of the spiritual realm are apprehended only by the spiritual believer, who " judgeth all things," and are incomprehensible to the natural man.   With this higher knowledge he claims a spiritual discernment for himself in a special degree.   It is, he unhesitatingly asserts, the mind of the Lord.   " We have the mind of Christ." [51]

At the same time, Paul knows the limits of his own speculations and revelations.   The mystery is not even for the spiritual Christian fully revealed.   " Not that I have already obtained, or am already made perfect ; but I press on if so be that I may apprehend that for which also I was apprehended.   Brethren, I count not myself yet to have apprehended.   But one thing I do, forgetting the things that

---

world cannot understand ("Paulus und die Mystik," 45 (1921)).   This seems, however, to contradict the explicit statement in 1 Cor. iii. 1 f., where he distinguishes between the spiritual and the carnal Christian, and speaks of the difference in his teaching in each case.

[46] 1 Cor. ii. 6 f.   [48] 1 Cor. ii. 10.
[47] 2 Cor. xi. 6.   [49] Ibid., ii. 7.
[50] Ibid., ii. 9.   He quotes this beautiful saying as scripture.   It is apparently taken from Isa. lxiv. 4, though the source is not certain.
[51] Ibid., ii. 13 f.   See also the other references to the spiritual or perfect Christian (1 Cor. iii. 1 ; xiv. 37 ; Gal. vi. 1 ; Col. i. 28), in which the distinction appears as a recognised fact.

are behind and stretching forth to the things that are before,
I press on toward the goal unto the prize of the high calling
of God in Christ Jesus. Let us, therefore, as many as be
perfect, be thus minded." [52] The higher knowledge is to
be professed with humility in contrast to Gnostic presumption
and vanity. His Gnosticism is a thing of his Christian
experience, not a mere speculation, even if it burdens faith
with an alien speculative element. His faith centres in a real,
not a purely mythological figure. Knowledge of Christ is
the inspiration of the highest spiritual and moral life.[53]

[52] Phil. iii. 12 f.

[53] Feine, who is a strenuous critic of the tendency to explain Paul's thought
in the light of current Jewish and Hellenist ideas, is fain to admit this influence
on the apostle's mind. *Ya Paulus hat sein christusbild mit den Farben
seiner zeit dargestellt*, "Theologie des Neuen Testaments," 381 ; *cf.* 245 f.
His treatment of the subject from the traditional point of view against
Gunkel, Wrede, Brückner is able and interesting, but to me not always
convincing. Kennedy attempts to prove Paul's independence of Gnostic
ideas, "St Paul and the Mystery Religions" (1913), in opposition to
Reitzenstein, Dieterich, and others. This influence is accepted by
Holtzmann, "Neutestamentliche Theologie," i. 553 (ed. 1911); Bousset,
"Kyrios Christos," 222 f. (1913) ; Wernle, "Beginnings of Christianity,"
I., xvii., and II. ix.

CHAPTER III

THE SUBAPOSTOLIC GOSPEL

I. The Pauline Influence

PAUL's teaching made a deep impression on the Churches which were founded by him and in which his authority was supreme, despite the trouble in such communities as that of Corinth and those of Galatia. The anti-Pauline movement in these churches, which manifested itself especially in the controversy over the Law, was only spasmodic, and the Pauline view of the abrogation of the Law for the Christian believer erelong became general outside of Palestine,[1] despite some lingering traces of it towards the end of his career.[1] But Paul was only one, though the most effective, of many founders of churches. Contemporary with him were many missionary preachers—" apostles," in the wider sense, who were carrying the Gospel over a large area of the Græco-Roman world. Their preaching was not necessarily an echo of his, which was too individualistic to be the normal. The essential and simple facts about Jesus as the crucified, risen, and exalted Redeemer were the common theme of all missionary preaching. Beyond this it was more or less coloured by the experience and culture of the preacher, as we can see from the New Testament writings that emanated, or purported to emanate, from some of these preachers.

His influence is, indeed, more or less traceable in these, and in other early, non-canonical writings. His letters came to be known in churches not founded by him. Some of them were even directed to such churches, and his work and teaching must have been widely known even in his own day. Even

---

[1] See Phil. iii. 2-3.

so, there was, along with the more elementary common faith, such a thing, from the earliest period, as an individual Gospel, which depended on individual experience and culture. This individual Gospel varies in content, ranging from the more practical teaching of the Catholic Epistles and the Synoptic Gospels to the more theological type of the Epistle to the Hebrews and the Fourth Gospel, the apocalyptic message of the seer of Patmos, and the Gnostic speculations, of which we have no actual literary specimen, but to which some of these writings generally refer. In all of them, however, the Pauline influence is more or less apparent. They reflect in varying degree his enhanced conception of Christ, his doctrine of an expiatory redemption, his universalism, his gospel of freedom from the Law. The developing church permanently assimilated this teaching.

At the same time these writings reveal divergence from this teaching. His presentation of the Gospel was too individualistic, too subtle to be easily grasped or assimilated, and while the Pauline phraseology may be reproduced, it does not necessarily display a grasp of its specific significance. Faith in Christ as an emancipation from the life of the flesh, the mystic indwelling of Christ in the soul as the dynamic of the new life, the spiritual resurrection from the spiritual death wrought by sin, the joyful sense of reconciliation with God over against the Law, the abounding operation of the Spirit in the heart of the believer as against the more legal or ethical conception of the inner life—this side of the Pauline teaching was little understood or not at all. It was displaced by a more sober, less enthusiastic, less intense, less dominating type, as represented by the experience and faith of the ordinary believer. Generally speaking, salvation is more a thing of promise than a reality of the present, dominating, absorbing, directing the life of the believer. Divergence from, as well as conformity to, the Pauline type is the striking feature of the subapostolic period, when early Catholic Christianity was in the first stage of its making. These points of contrast and dissimilarity are plainly reflected in the New Testament and the non-canonical literature which belongs to the post-Pauline period. In particular, its conception of the Gospel as a new Law—usually described as " moralist "—is nearer

that of Jesus than that of Paul, though, as a rule, there may
be no conscious antagonism to his teaching.[2]

There has recently been rather a reaction from the overemphasis of the Pauline influence on the other New Testament
writings (particularly the First Epistle of Peter and the Epistle
to the Hebrews).   There is, in fact, a tendency to minimise
it and lay more stress on the common element in the primitive
tradition from which these writers drew.[3]   This tradition,
it is held, was not so meagre or so simple as is usually assumed.
It included ideas which are generally regarded as the fruit of
later development under Pauline influence.   Whilst this contention is debatable, there is force in it as far as it combats
the exaggeration of the Pauline influence (in the case of the
Gospel of Mark, for instance) and takes account of the individual
apprehension of the Gospel in accordance with personal
experience, or environment.   At the same time, it is clear
that the thought of Paul does, more or less, condition that of
the subapostolic period.   It is only a question of degree.
The fact is indisputable.

II. The Contested Epistles

The critics have long been, and still are, at variance over
the genuineness of the Epistle to the Ephesians, the Second
Epistle to the Thessalonians, and those to Timothy and
Titus.   One section contends that they were written by Paul,
with, at most, in the case of Ephesians and the Pastoral Epistles,
some later editorial revision.   The other holds that they were
written by disciples of Paul, and while containing matter that
might have been written by Paul himself, show the influence
of post-Pauline thought and ecclesiastical development.   It
is generally admitted, in the case of the Pastoral Epistles, that
the writer has incorporated genuine Pauline fragments.   In
view of this divergence of opinion, and also my own impression
that, in their actual form at all events, they were not written

[2] For a general review of the divergence from Paul in the post-apostolic
period, see M'Giffert, " Christianity in the Apostolic Age," 440 f.   On
his influence on the development of doctrine, see Krüger, " Das Dogma
der Dreieinigkeit und Gottmenschheit," 85 f. (1905).

[3] See, for instance, Kennedy, " The Theology of the Epistles," 166 f.
(1919) ; E. F. Scott, " The Epistle to the Hebrews," 49 f. ; 58 f. (1922).

by the apostle, I have refrained from using them as authoritative
sources for the Pauline Gospel.   On the whole, it is safer for
the historian to treat them as subapostolic productions, whilst
premising that, if not genuinely Pauline, they do in some
respects represent his distinctive teaching.

So strongly is the Pauline influence impressed on the
so-called Epistle to the Ephesians, that, at first sight, one
seems to be reading a genuine Pauline letter.   That the
Epistle " to the saints which are at Ephesus " was not addressed
by Paul to the Ephesian Church may be regarded as certain,
inasmuch as the writer appears in several passages to be
personally unknown to those to whom he writes.[4]   If the
writer was Paul, he could not possibly have professed to be
unknown to a community among which he had laboured for
wellnigh three years.[5]   The phrase " at Ephesus " is, in fact,
lacking in two of the oldest manuscripts, and some critics
would substitute for it " at Laodicea."   This is only a guess,
based on Colossians iv. 16, to get over a real difficulty.   More
plausible is the assumption that it was a circular letter to the
churches of the province of Asia, containing a blank to be
filled in by the bearer.   In this way the phrase " at Ephesus,"
which is present in all the other ancient MSS., might have
come to be inserted in an epistle not specially meant for the
Ephesian community.   This is also merely a guess to preserve
the Pauline authorship.   The Epistle does, indeed, in content
bear the character of an encyclical, rather than a missive to
a particular community, as in the case of all the genuine
Pauline Epistles, in spite of the restricted personal passages,
some of which are borrowed from that to the Colossians.[6]
It is plainly directed to the general body of Christians, Jewish
and Gentile alike ; to the Church at large, not to a section
of it.

Its authenticity is disputed on a variety of grounds besides
the impossibility that Paul could have addressed it to the
Ephesians as an unknown community.   The style is in part
very laboured.   It may be, as the upholders of its genuineness
contend, that it is the style of a worn-out old man,[7] whose

---

[4] Eph. i. 15 ; iii. 2 ; iv. 21.   [5] Acts xix. 8 f.
[6] Col. i. 1-2 ; iv. 7 ; Eph. i. 1-2 ; vi. 21-22.
[7] So Milligan, for instance, " New Testament Documents," 98 f. (1913).

mind was no longer so nimble or original as in the earlier
Epistles, in which, indeed, involved passages are not infrequent.
There is also a trace of the same tendency in the late Epistle
to the Colossians, the genuineness of which is generally
accepted. Even so, the recurring laboured passages suggest
the summariser and the adapter of the master's teaching to
a later generation. There are marked features in the situation
and the train of thought which tend to strengthen this suggestion. The situation seems to be that of the post-apostolic
Church—the general body of believers organised under its
recognised officials—whilst the train of thought is hardly in
all respects that of the apostle. At the same time the writer,
if not the apostle himself, has caught and presents much of the
apostle's teaching. He skilfully adapts Paul's thought to his
own time and to his purpose of inculcating the unity of the
growing Catholic or universal Church. He is a thinker as
well as a summariser.

As in Colossians and certain passages of earlier Pauline
Epistles, the Gospel is " the mystery of Christ that hath been
hidden from all the ages and is now revealed or manifested." [8]
Christ has accomplished the determinate will of God, who
purposed to sum up, or comprise,[9] all things in heaven and
earth in him as their head, in the fullness of the times. This
is the divine " economy " or dispensation, or ordering of
things—the writer's way of expressing the " reconciliation "
of all things (Col. i. 20), the " subjection " of all things, to
God as supreme sovereign (1 Cor. xv. 24 f.).[10] To this end
the exalted Christ is also here invested with the sole and
supreme authority in the spirit world—over the principalities
and powers, including Satan, the prince of the air.[11] Similarly,
whilst he is the exalted Lord,[12] he is subordinate to the Father
(" the God of our Lord Jesus Christ "), who, in Stoic phraseology, is " over all and through all and in all," [13] as in Romans
xi. 36. Salvation is due to the grace and love of God. It

---

[8] Eph. i. 9 ; iii. 3 f. ; v. 32 ; vi. 19.

[9] i. 10, ἀνακεφαλαιώσασθαι.

[10] See the illuminating note on its meaning in E. F. Scott, " Commentary," 145 (1930). He translates it " gather up again " what has been
disturbed by the jar introduced into the universe and human life by sin.
In this sense the word may also be translated " to reunite."

[11] i. 20-22 ; ii. 2 ; iii. 10-11 ; cf. vi. 11-12.

[12] i. 15 f.   [13] iv. 6 ; cf. 1 Cor. viii. 6.

is God's free gift in Christ Jesus ; is available by faith, not by works, though nothing is explicitly said of justification ; and is a present experience.[14] Again, Christ has abolished the Law and reconciled both Jew and Gentile unto God through the Cross.[15] By his death and resurrection the believer, who aforetime was dead in transgression and sin, has been quickened, raised up from the life of the flesh to partake in his heavenly life.[16] Through him believers have received the foreordained adoption as sons [17] and have been sealed (in baptism) with the Holy Spirit, the pledge or guarantee of their heavenly inheritance, as God's own redeemed possession.[18] Here, too, the indwelling of the Spirit or of Christ in the believer makes itself felt in the putting away of the old man and the putting on of the new [19] in the practical Christian life. Along with this we have the specific Pauline emphasis on the surpassing love of Christ and on the love to Christ as the fullness of God, the unsearchable riches in which the believer participates. In all this the train of thought is specifically Pauline.

On the other hand, it appears, on closer inspection, to be mingled with ideas that are, to say the least, doubtfully Pauline, and seem to reflect a development, in which the ecclesiastical element in the conception of the Church is very marked. In Col. i. 26 the mystery is manifested to the saints of God, the designation of the general body of believers in the Pauline Epistles. In Ephesians it is revealed to " Christ's holy apostles and prophets." [20] The revelation does not necessarily exclude a wider circle, and " apostles " may well include other missionaries besides the Twelve and Paul. At the same time, there is a distinct tendency to magnify the eminence of these and other functionaries—evangelists, pastors, teachers [21]—in the Catholic or universal Church, which is the conception exclusively present to the writer's mind. A development has evidently taken place compared with 1 Cor. xii. 28-29, where Paul enumerates only apostles, prophets, teachers. Moreover, in contrast to 1 Cor. iii. 11, where Jesus Christ is the foundation whereon Paul, the master builder, builds, the foundation in Ephesians is the apostles and

---

[14] i. 6-7 ; ii. 4 f. [17] i. 5. [20] iii. 5.
[15] ii. 14 f. [18] i. 13-14 ; cf. iv. 30. [21] iv. 11-12.
[16] ii. 1 f. [19] iii. 16-17 ; ii. 22 ; iv. 21 f. ; v. 18.

prophets.[22]   Christ is, indeed, assigned a cardinal importance in this connection as " the chief corner stone," [23] and the apostles and prophets might well be conceived as the actual founders of the Church in virtue of their mission work.   But the writer seems to imply more than this in transferring to them the function emphatically applied to Christ in the First Corinthian Epistle.   " For other foundation can no man lay than that which is laid, which is Jesus Christ."

Again the purport of the mystery thus revealed to the apostles and prophets is, in Ephesians, strikingly different from that in Colossians.   In chapter i. it is, indeed, generally the realisation of God's redemptive purpose in Christ, as in Colossians and other Epistles.   But in chapters ii. and iii., as revealed to the apostles and prophets, it is specifically stated to be the equal standing and rights of the Gentiles—" ye that once were far off, but now made nigh in the blood of Christ " —with the Jews in the one body or universal Church.   On this theme the writer lays the utmost stress.   It is the distinctive object of the Epistle to set this forth in the interest of the unity of the Church.[24]   To this end Christ has abolished the Law, and thus removed the partition, the alienation, the enmity existing between Jew and Gentile.   This is a different version from the characteristic Pauline one of the work of Christ in relation to the Law.   According to Paul, it consists in making possible to Jew and Gentile alike salvation from sin and condemnation, to which the Law testified and from which it could not emancipate the sinner.   According to this Epistle it consists in bringing about the union of Jew and Gentile in one body or household of God.   This union in the one body is " the economy " or dispensation, by which the manifold wisdom of God is made known through the Church to the heavenly principalities and powers.[25]

To the writer it is of the utmost moment that this unity on an equal footing should be maintained.   " There is one body, and one Spirit, even as also ye were called in one hope of your calling ; one Lord, one faith, one baptism, one God and Father of all." [26]   Hence the farther emphasis on the Church as the body of Christ, or the body of which Christ is the head.   Both

[22] ii. 20.   [24] ii. 11 f. ; iii. 21.   [26] iv. 3 f.
[23] ii. 20.   [25] iii. 10 f.

aspects of the Church are specifically Pauline. In Romans
and 1st Corinthians the former is emphasised.[27]   In Colossians [28]
the latter as well as the former. Similarly in Ephesians.[29]   As
far as these passages on the Church in both Epistles are concerned, Paul could have written both. In Colossians and the
earlier Epistles the Church is, indeed, conceived as the body
of Christ only in the metaphorical sense. In Ephesians it is,
in addition, conceived in the mystical sense of the union of
the Christian community—the new humanity—with Christ,
as in the case of the union of husband and wife. But this
more developed conception might well accord with the Pauline
mystical train of thought, and is, therefore, not necessarily
un-Pauline. There is, however, one glaring variation which
tells against the unity of authorship. In Colossians (ii. 10)
Christ is " the head of all principality and power," *i.e.*, head
in the cosmic sense, and in ii. 19 the Colossians, in their angel
worship, are denounced for not holding fast the head in this
sense. In Ephesians (iv. 16) the writer largely reproduces
the passage in Col. ii. 19, but transforms it so as to make
Christ the head of the Church, not of the cosmos. There is
no little force in the inference that, in so doing, he is manipulat-
ing the language of Paul to suit his own purpose, and is,
therefore, a different person from the apostle. In other words,
there is here, as in the use of the term " mystery," an evident
attempt to modify a Pauline utterance in the interest of the
unity of the Church, which is the main interest of the writer
of the Epistle. In this respect, there is also a striking
resemblance between it and those of Ignatius, of which the
stress on unity is the salient feature. In his insistence on unity,
Ignatius combats a heresy which was Docetic in character.
In the case of the writer of Ephesians no such heresy is definitely
discernible. His great object is to unite Jew and Gentile in
one universal Church—to obviate the disunion which race and
religious training tended to foster. At the same time, there
is a strain of heretical teaching in the Church at large, whatever
its exact character. Hence the distinct tendency to emphasise
the Gospel " as the word of truth "[30] against the wiles of
error, which is being craftily disseminated, and in opposition

[27] Rom. xii. 4, 5 ; 1 Cor. xii. 12.   [29] Eph. i. 22-23 ; iv. 15-16.
[28] Col. i. 18, 24 ; iii. 15.   [30] i. 13.

to which the writer stresses the truth and the need for a stable faith.[31] There is, too, an approximation to the Johannine conception of the Gospel as the light, in contrast to the darkness of the heathen world.[32] Similarly, the marked emphasis on the Gospel as revelation, as knowledge of, and insight into God's saving will and purpose suggests the predominant Hellenist conception of it, characteristic of the post-apostolic period. The eschatological outlook seems also to be that of this later period. Paul, who had recently written to the Philippians that "the Lord is at hand,"[33] is hardly likely to have relegated the coming to the indefinite future—"the ages to come."[34]

We need not rule out the possibility that, towards the end of his life, his thought may have advanced in the direction of that of the Epistle. It is not necessary to assume that he attained all at once, or at an early period, to the distinctive Gospel elaborated in the Epistles. On the other hand, it is hardly likely that the distinctive ideas of this Epistle, as compared with Colossians, were worked out in the short interval between them which, on the assumption of its genuineness, elapsed before its composition. On the whole, the Epistle, whilst deeply imbued with the Pauline spirit and teaching, is hardly a first-hand presentation of the Pauline Gospel. It is rather the Pauline Gospel as envisaged from the standpoint of the next generation, and moulded in the mind of an ardent disciple, who had an intimate knowledge of the Pauline Epistles and made special use of that to the Colossians. It may fairly be described as Catholicised Pauline.[35]

Whether Paul himself speaks in 2nd Thessalonians, or a later substitute speaks for him, is not easy to decide. In both the first and the second Epistles the coming is a distinctive theme, and the writer of the second evidently modelled it on

---

[31] iv. 14 ; cf. iv. 25 ; v. 6 ; vi. 14.   [33] Phil. iv. 5.
[32] i. 18 ; iv. 17-18 ; v. 8 f.   [34] ii. 7 ; cf. i. 21.
[35] Its authenticity is upheld by M'Giffert, "Apostolic Age," 377 f. ; Peake, "Critical Introduction," 53 f. (rather hesitatingly) ; Abbot, "International Crit. Com." (1897) ; E. F. Scott, "Commentary on Colossians, Philemon, Ephesians," 119 f. (1930) ; Duncan also accepts its genuineness, without discussing the question, "St Paul's Ephesian Ministry," 8 (1929). It is rejected by Dibelius, "Lietzmann's Handbuch," iii. (1913) ; Moffatt, "Introduction," 388 ; and by Lueken, "Schriften des N.T.," ii. (1908). Despite the large body of English critical opinion in favour of its Pauline authorship, I am of opinion that at best it is uncertain.

the first, with the exception of the distinctive apocalyptic section in chapter ii. 1-12. In the first Paul believes that he will himself live to experience it.[36] This belief he continued to cherish till the end when, in what appears to be an authentic passage in 2nd Timothy, he is facing death and looks only for the crown of righteousness which the Lord will bestow on him and on all who have loved his appearing, whenever it may take place.[37] The object of the second, on the other hand, is to discourage an undue and unsettling tendency to anticipate it, and to explain that it is not to be looked for immediately, as a number of the Thessalonian Christians have too readily assumed. The situation, the writer points out, is not yet ripe for the great consummation. It will be preceded by certain indications which have not yet materialised. These he proceeds to detail in the section of chapter ii. 1-12, which imparts to the second Epistle its distinctive content, as compared with the first. He finds them in the Book of Daniel, especially in the prognostication of the desecration of the temple by the Anti-God, or Antichrist, whose lawless régime is meanwhile being restrained by the Roman power. Not till this power shall have disappeared will the Antichrist have full sway and a general apostasy take place. Only then will Christ appear to put an end to his Satanic, lawless régime and achieve his destruction and that of those whom he has deceived by his lying signs and wonders.

The question which has divided the critics is whether Paul, unquestionably the author of the first Epistle, which reveals his expectation of the coming within his lifetime, could have written the second, which appears to postpone it to a rather indefinite future. That he was acquainted with the Daniel Apocalypse and with the apocalyptic discourse of Jesus preserved in the Synoptic tradition, which contains a reference to it, is probable enough. Probable, too, that he should have found it necessary to intervene with a caveat against the undue and unsettling expectation of an immediate coming, which had led to grave disorder in the Thessalonian community. In the first Epistle the coming, while sudden, is not necessarily immediate, though Paul expects to experience it. In the second it is the belief in its immediacy, and the questionable effect

[36] iv. 15, 17. [37] 2 Tim. iv. 6 f.

11

of this belief in the immediate coming that the writer is concerned to counteract. In these circumstances it is not in itself improbable that Paul should have attempted to do so by pointing out that, if sudden, the coming is not necessarily imminent. In this respect there is no real divergence between the two Epistles, and in the Epistle to the Romans he also seems to delay the coming so as to allow for the ultimate conversion of Israel, which is to follow on that of the Gentiles.[38]

On the other hand, it is singular that in none of his other writings outside 2nd Thessalonians does he appear to have envisaged the reign of Antichrist and the consequent widespread apostasy from God, which would herald the second coming. Possibly this is assumed in the eschatological passage in 1 Cor. xv. 24 f., in which Christ comes finally to abolish all rule, authority, and power, and to put all his enemies under his feet. At the same time, it is rather strange that, if he held the apocalyptic belief of the Second Epistle to the Thessalonians, there is no indication of it in this relevant passage which tells, not of the destruction of the Antichrist, but generally of that of the ethereal enemies of the Christ. Similarly, towards the close of his career, he reminds the Philippians that the Lord is at hand,[39] without any premonition of the preceding rule of Antichrist.

In view of such considerations, there is some reason for doubting or discarding the authenticity of the Epistle. It is a fair question whether it does not represent the attempt of a somewhat later writer to explain why Paul's expectation of the coming in his own lifetime was not realised and, at the same time, counteract the consequent tendency to question the validity of this unfulfilled belief, which, we know from the Second Epistle of Peter and other sources, was in vogue at a later time.[40] In this case it must have been written within five years of Paul's death, since the temple was evidently not yet destroyed. The unusual asseveration that the concluding salutation in Paul's own handwriting is a token of the genuineness of the Epistle, combined with the previous warning [41]

[38] Rom. xi. 25-26.
[39] Phil. iv. 5. On the Antichrist conception, see Bousset, "The Antichrist Legend," 19 f. (Eng. trans. 1896).
[40] 2 Peter iii. 3 f.
[41] ii. 2.

against a forged letter, tends to suggest the attempt to invest it with a Pauline authorship.[42]

The case against the genuineness of the Pastoral Epistles in their present form is, on linguistic grounds, very strong, as Mr Harrison has recently shown in detail.[43] They contain a large proportion of words not used by Paul in the other Epistles and characteristic of Christian and other writers of the second century. They are mainly concerned with the organisation of the Church and with the maintenance of the true apostolic teaching against its Jewish-Gnostic subverters. This is no new phenomenon, as the Epistle to the Colossians shows. But these false teachers are very active and aggressive. Their influence is not confined to a single community here and there, as at Corinth and Colosse in Paul's time. It is evidently widespread in the churches of the province of Asia and in Crete, and has become a serious menace to the Pauline Gospel. These Epistles contain genuine Pauline matter, partly didactic, partly autobiographical in character. This is most apparent in 2nd Timothy, professedly written from Rome at the close of the apostle's career and generally regarded as the earliest of the three. Compared with the other two, it also shows a comprehension of certain aspects of the Pauline Gospel, though coloured by the later development which the writer represents. God's redeeming purpose, which goes back into eternity, has been realised in Christ Jesus, who has abolished death and brought life and incorruption to light through the Gospel.[44] Salvation is dependent on the will and grace of God, who has called, elected those who are to be saved.[45] It is not according to our works, but according to His grace and mercy.[46] Justification, and, with it, the inheritance of life eternal, is due to grace, though faith is not mentioned in

[42] M'Giffert, "Apostolic Christ.," 250 f.; Peake, "Introduction," 12 f.; J. Weiss, "Urchristenthum," 217 f., conclude in favour of the authenticity—the first two rather doubtfully, J. Weiss, who thinks that the second Epistle was written first, decisively. Lueken, "Schriften des N.T.," ii. 20 f., is dubious, though inclining to accept. Schweitzer, "Die Mystik des Apostels Paulus," rejects. So also Holtzmann, "N.T. Theologie," ii. 213 f. Moffatt, "Introd.," 76 f., is on the whole favourable.

[43] "The Problem of the Pastoral Epistles" (1921).

[44] 2 Tim. i. 9-10. In 2 Cor. iv. 6, Paul speaks of the light shining out of the darkness . . . to give the light of the knowledge of the glory of God in the face of Jesus Christ.

[45] 2 Tim. i. 9; ii. 10; Tit. i. 1.   [46] 2 Tim. i. 9; Tit. iii. 5.

this connection.[47]   There is also an echo of Paul's view of the
Law as made for the lawless and as good in itself.[48]   There
is at least a passing reference to the Pauline conception of
dying with Christ in order to live with him.[49]   Regeneration
and renewing by the Holy Spirit are experienced in baptism,[50]
though Paul does not actually use the term regeneration, and
the use of it here suggests rather the influence of the Fourth
Gospel.

There is also a passing reference in 1st Timothy and
Titus to the voluntary death of Christ as a ransom for sin.[51]
The standpoint is universalist.   Christ gave himself a ransom
for all.   God willeth that all men should be saved.   God is
the Saviour of all men.   The grace of God has appeared
bringing salvation to all men.[52]   Christ is not only the Saviour.
He is to be the judge of both the quick and the dead at his
appearing, though Paul, who is now face to face with death,
will not witness it.[53]

This is the sum of the distinctively Pauline doctrine.   It
is not complete, and what there is, is assumed, not demonstrated
in the characteristic Pauline fashion.   This need not surprise
us, inasmuch as the object of these Epistles is practical, rather
than doctrinal.   They are concerned with the life and
organisation of the Christian communities, and these are in
possession of the deposit [54] of the apostle's teaching, which
he has committed to Timothy and Titus and they are to
maintain against the false teachers.   At the same time, it is
ensphered in a strain of thought which, though partly Pauline
in phraseology, contains an un-Pauline tincture.   The writer
clearly makes use of the apostle's name to convey his own
message to the Church of his time—the developing Catholic
Church of the late first century—and the voice of the messenger
is hardly that of Paul.   He is not consciously dishonest,
according to the literary standard of the time.   He would
probably only mean, " This is what Paul would say," and this
passes, by a device generally practised in the ancient world,
into, " Thus saith Paul."   The modern critic, whilst differing

[47] Tit. iii. 7.
[48] 1 Tim. i. 8 ; cf. Rom. vii. 12.
[51] 1 Tim. ii. 6 ; Tit. ii. 14.
[52] 1 Tim. ii. 6 ; ii. 4 ; Tit. ii. 11 ; 1 Tim. iv. 10.
[53] 2 Tim. iv. 1 f.
[49] 2 Tim. ii. 11.
[50] Tit. iii. 5, παλιγγενεσία.
[54] παραθήκη.

in toto from this lax literary morality, will in the circumstances
charitably bring in a verdict of falsification under extenuating
circumstances.

The " deposit " committed to and by Paul is described as
the Gospel of the glory of the blessed God.[55] Generally, it
is sound doctrine, in accordance with Paul's teaching, in
opposition to that of the Jewish-Gnostic teachers.[56] It is
" the good doctrine " ; " the knowledge of the truth " ; " the
doctrine according to godliness " ; " the sound words of
our Lord Jesus Christ," in contrast to such error.[57]
Particularly, it is " the mystery of the faith " ; [58] " the mystery
of godliness," in the sense of the secret disclosed by Christ's
manifestation in the flesh, his resurrection, his transition to the
spirit sphere, and the proclamation and acceptance of the
Christian message throughout the ancient world.[59] Its aim
is the salvation of the sinner by the abolition of death, the
revelation of life and incorruption.[60] God is characteristically
the Saviour-God, and Christ, to whom the epithet is also
applied, is the agent of His saving purpose.[61] The conception
reminds of the Saviour-Gods of the current polytheism,
especially the mystery religions and the imperial cult, which
celebrated the Emperor (Augustus) as the saviour of mankind.[62]
As the agent of God's saving purpose, Christ is the one mediator
between God and man, apparently in contrast to the multiple
Gnostic æons or emanations from God, and is markedly
differentiated from the one and only God of these Epistles.
" For there is one God, one mediator also between God and
man, the man Christ Jesus." [63] Whilst his humanity and his
distinction from God are thus emphasised, he is recognised
as Lord.[64]

[55] 1 Tim. i. 11.   [56] 1 Tim. i. 6 f. ; Tit. i. 9 ; ii. 1.
[57] *Ibid.*, ii. 4 ; iv. 6 ; vi. 3 ; Tit. i. 1.
[58] 1 Tim. iii. 9.
[59] *Ibid.*, iii. 16.   The passage appears to be a current rudimentary creed,
or a quotation from an early hymn.   It has a liturgical form and flavour.
[60] 1 Tim. i. 15 ; 2 Tim. i. 9-10.
[61] 1 Tim. i. 1 ; ii. 3, 4 ; iv. 10 ; Tit. i. 3, 4 ; iii. 4, 7.   The term Saviour
is rare in Paul (Phil. iii. 20), and is applied exclusively to Christ.
[62] See Dibelius, " Lietzmann's Handbuch," iii. 184 f.
[63] 1 Tim. ii. 5 ($\mu\epsilon\sigma\iota\tau\eta\varsigma$), an approximation to the characteristic thought
of the Epistle to the Hebrews.
[64] The term God in 1 Tim. iii. 16 is an intrusion for ὅς.   Tit. ii. 13
ought to be translated " the great God and our Saviour Christ Jesus," not
" our great God and Saviour Christ Jesus," if it is not to contradict the

Salvation is a thing of hope, of promise, rather than a present reality.[65]   It is largely conceived in the eschatological sense, and, while the expectation of the appearing of Christ is still ardent, it is left in God's hands to determine when it shall take place.[66]   It is attainable " through faith which is in Christ Jesus." [67]   Whilst the term faith is characteristic of the Pastorals, as of the genuine Pauline Epistles, it has hardly the characteristic Pauline significance.   For the writer it is distinctively right belief, enlightenment (as in the Fourth Gospel), the content of salvation.   It is markedly intellectual and ethical.   It is both equivalent to the knowledge of the truth, discrimination between truth and error, and to faithfulness in living and maintaining the Christian profession " in faith and love," [68] though the Pauline personal conviction, unquestioning persuasion, is incidentally there.

Hence the marked emphasis on " good works," which quite overshadows the passing disclaimer of salvation by works.   For the writer " godliness " [69] and " good works " stand in the forefront all through.[70]   Righteousness is a good life rather than the righteous relation in which the believer, in virtue of faith, stands to God.[71]   Whilst Paul does not minimise works as the concomitant of faith, the stress, in the Pauline Epistles, is on the vitalising principle, the spiritual dynamic, which produces the fruits of faith ; on the conception of the crucifixion of the flesh with Christ and in Christ.   In the Pastorals the great thing is the formation of character, the

distinction between God and Christ, otherwise characteristic of the Pastorals. M'Giffert, who accepts the traditional reading of this and similar passages in the subapostolic literature, has a theory that the Gentile Christians really worshipped the Lord Jesus as their only God, without reference to the Father-God of the Jewish Scriptures, and that it was only later that they added the worship of the Father-God to that of Christ, " The God of the Early Christians," 41 f.   But surely in the mission preaching, as reflected in early Christian literature, they were made acquainted with the supreme Father-God of Judaism.

[65] 1 Tim. i. 1 ; iv. 10 ; 2 Tim. i. 1 ; Tit. i. 2.

[66] 1 Tim. vi. 14-15 ; cf. 2 Tim. iii. 1 ; Tit. ii. 12-13.   It is another indication of Hellenist influence that the word for the appearing of the Saviour is ἐπιφάνεια — the Hellenist technical term for the appearing of a god.

[67] 2 Tim. iv. 15.

[68] 1 Tim. i. 14 ; ii. 15 ; iv. 12 ; 2 Tim. ii. 1, 13 ; Tit. ii. 2.

[69] εὐσέβεια.

[70] 1 Tim. ii. 10 ; v. 10, 25 ; vi. 18 ; 2 Tim. ii. 21 ; iii. 17 ; Tit. ii. 7, 14 ; iii. 14.

[71] 1 Tim. vi. 11 ; 2 Tim. ii. 22 ; iii. 16 ; Tit. ii. 12.

cultivation of godliness, piety in the regulated life of the community. " Piety," it has been aptly said, " may almost be called the watchword of the Pastoral Epistles." [72]   I should add, piety in connection with, and resulting from, sound doctrine. The conception of the good life in the Pastorals is that of the Stoic wise man rather than the new creature of Paul. The terminology in which the pattern of the good Christian is set forth might have been taken from the Stoic moral philosopher and preacher of the period. The religion of the Spirit, as Paul understood it, of faith and the mystical indwelling of Christ in the believer, as the source and power of the new life, is almost entirely absent from these documents. In its stead we have the religion of " good works," in accordance with a common standard, which leaves little scope for the individual inspiration of the earlier period. Except for a couple of phrases, the Holy Spirit seems to have disappeared. Doctrine and conduct are being standardised. The scripture and the apostolic teaching largely take the place of the Spirit,[73] though Timothy is not to neglect his gift, or charisma of teaching, which was conveyed by the laying on of the hands of the presbytery, or the apostle, and is now apparently construed in an official sense.[74] The Christian prophet seems to be non-existent in these documents, though we know of his continued existence from other sources. Christianity, in becoming staid, conventional, disciplined, respectable, is becoming less dynamic, and by its respectability strives to attract the better elements of pagan society.[75] The quiet and tranquil life in all godliness and gravity, in strict subordination to the constituted authority in the state and the Christian community, is the ideal.[76] We are in the atmosphere of Old Testament Law and commandment,[77] combined with Stoic precept. The more independent members of the community, who are disposed to think and act for themselves, are necessarily false teachers, though, with the exception of two whom Paul excommunicated,[78] they are still inside the Church. They are also to the writer *ipso facto* men of bad character. At the same time laxity of life and thought might well constitute

---

[72] Kennedy, " The Theology of the Epistles," 263.
[73] 2 Tim. iii. 14 f.   [75] Tit. ii. 7-8.   [77] παραγγελία.
[74] 1 Tim. iv. 14.   [76] 1 Tim. ii. 2.   [78] 1 Tim. i. 20.

a serious menace to the expanding Church in the midst of the lax environment, the speculative licence of the pagan world. In these circumstances the regulation of the individual and communal life had to be undertaken, the danger of alien speculation had to be met, if the individual and communal life was to be preserved from serious deformation. Paul himself had had to shoulder this double duty in the supervision of the newly founded communities. But these Epistles clearly reveal a later stage in the process of organisation and consolidation in accordance with the growing development, the altering situation of the communities as reflected in them. We miss in them the originality, the dynamic force of the Pauline genius. The writer is not a creative genius. He is only a skilful adapter, if in this adaptation a distinctive phase of early Christianity is clearly taking shape.[79]

III. FIRST PETER, HEBREWS, JAMES

It is not easy to decide whether the first Epistle ascribed to Peter was actually written by him. If not, it has, at all events, preserved characteristic features of the primitive Gospel, as contained in the discourses in Acts. The main difficulty in the way of accepting its Petrine authorship arises from the situation of the communities in Asia Minor, to which it was addressed, rather than from the contents of the Epistle. These communities seem to be exposed to persecution " because of the name " of Christ.[1] On the assumption of its Petrine authorship, such persecution could hardly be later than the closing

---

[79] There is a large literature on the Pastoral Epistles, beginning with the important work of H. J. Holtzmann, " Die Pastoralbriefe " (1880). See the exhaustive bibliography in Harrison, " The Problem of the Pastoral Epistles " (1921). This is a most important contribution, which states the case against their authenticity very forcibly on linguistic grounds. See also Peake, " Critical Introduction," 60 f. Another recent book in English by Parry, " The Pastoral Epistles " (1920), which urges their authenticity with equal conviction, is not convincing. The most recent in English is that of Lock in the " International Critical Commentary " (1924), who hesitates on the question of authorship, but nevertheless decides to treat these letters " as coming direct from St Paul's hand." He has, however, been shaken by Harrison's weighty contribution. In German, F. Koehler states the case against their authenticity forcibly, " Schriften des N.T.," ii. 390 f. Feine treats in detail of their theology in his " Theologie des N.T."

[1] iv. 14 f.

years of the reign of Nero, when the Roman Christians, as the
reputed authors of the burning of Rome, were subjected to
the terrible ordeal to which Peter is believed to have fallen a
victim.   This sudden outburst of revolting violence seems to
have been confined to the capital, whereas the communities
to which the Epistle is directed are located in the provinces
of Asia Minor.   Possibly the governers of these provinces
followed the example set by the emperor in the capital, though
we have otherwise no evidence that they did.   The outlook
for Christians everywhere was certainly a very threatening
one, and the author, who, on the assumption that " Babylon " [2]
is a veiled reference to Rome, writes from the capital, might
well have dispatched a letter of warning and exhortation to
steadfastness in the midst of trial.   At the same time, these
Christians were evidently exposed to actual persecution, and
the situation described seems to point to a later period, when
the mere profession of Christianity was accounted a crime,
and such persecution was becoming habitual.   Moreover,
by the time of its composition the Christians are specifically,
in the eye of the Roman Government, as well as the writer,
a distinct body.   Christianity is differentiated from Judaism,
and its adherents are a new people,[3] the object of the contempt
as well as the hostility of men, if elect in the sight of God.   This
might possibly be predicated of them from the Neronian
persecution onwards.   But this persecution was only a spasmodic outburst.   It does not seem to have recurred in the
reigns of Vespasian and Titus,[4] and the differentiation of the
Epistle rather indicates the more general antagonism of
the period from Domitian onwards, when the mere profession
of Christianity, involving allegiance to a rival authority, was
accounted disloyalty to the state.

Many critics have accordingly relegated it to the last years
of the reign of Domitian, i.e., towards the end of the first
century, or to that of Trajan in the early years of the second.[5]

---

[2] v. 13.   [3] ii. 4.

[4] Ramsay's attempt to make out that it did (" The Church in the
Roman Empire ") is not convincing.

[5] On the question of its authorship, see Pfleiderer, " Das Urchristenthum "; Zahn, " Introduction to the New Testament," ii. 150 ;
Moffatt, " Introduction," 318 f. ; Gunkel, " Die Schriften des N.T.,"
ii. 529 f. ; Peake, " Critical Introduction," 90 f.   Moffatt, in his Introduction
to his " Commentary on the Epistle " (1928), accepts its Petrine authorship.

In this case, it could not have been written by Peter, who, according to what seems a reliable tradition, was martyred at Rome towards the end of the reign of Nero. It was known to Polycarp, who quotes from it in his Epistle to the Philippians, written soon after the martyrdom of Ignatius in the early second century. But he does not ascribe it to Peter, and it was not so ascribed till towards the end of the second century. Linguistic and other considerations have given rise to the suggestion that it was written by Silvanus, or some later writer, and the postscript states that Silvanus was the actual scribe, writing to Peter's dictation.

Whilst the contents seem to point to a post-Petrine date and warrant dubiety of a direct Petrine authorship, it is clear that the writer was familiar with the primitive Petrine Gospel. There is the same pointed appeal to the testimony of the prophets to the suffering Christ ; [6] the same stress on his resurrection and exaltation to the right hand of God,[7] as the proof of this prophecy ; the characteristic reference to Christ as Lord [8] and the Pentecostal outpouring of the Holy Spirit, identifiable with the Spirit of Christ and manifested in the preaching of the Gospel ; [9] the same conception of salvation by faith as a future deliverance from judgment at his " revelation " or coming, which is at hand ; [10] the same combination of baptism with faith as the outward expression of the acceptance of this salvation.[11] The Christ of the Epistle is pre-eminently the suffering and exalted Christ as an example and an inspiration to his suffering disciples in these provinces. There is hardly any speculation about his person. " Foreknown before the foundation of the world," " manifested at the end of the times for your sake," [12] does not necessarily imply more than God's foreknowledge in Acts ii. 23, etc. It hardly warrants the developed belief in his pre-existence. Neither the designation Son of Man nor Son of God is applied to him. It is the suffering and the exalted Christ who, in virtue of his resurrec-

Bacon rejects it. " Few scholars would attempt to maintain Petrine authorship in any real sense," " Jesus and Paul," 15 (1921). See also his strong statement of the case against in " The Gospel of Mark," 279 f. " Modern criticism dares not classify the work as more than deutero-Petrine."

[6] i. 10 f.   [9] i. 11-12.   [11] iii. 21.
[7] i. 3, 21 ; iii. 21-22.   [10] i. 5 ; iv. 7.   [12] i. 20.
[8] iii. 15.

tion and exaltation is now invested with dominion and glory, and to whom the supernal powers are subject, that is portrayed. This conception is partnered with a vivid impression of the historic Jesus as he lived and suffered on earth, and with the supreme obligation of following his example in his life and death. The writer is decidedly closer to the historic Jesus than Paul. The Epistle is, in fact, primarily concerned with practical life, as modelled on Christ's example, and reflects reminiscences of his ethical teaching.[13]

On the other hand, the Pauline is blended with the Petrine conception of the Gospel, and this conception is sufficiently discernible to show the advance made, under the Pauline influence, on the primitive preaching as recorded in the Acts.[14] The direction of the Epistle " to the sojourners of the Dispersion " in Asia Minor, reminds us that the Gospel has completely burst the bonds of Judaism and has developed into the unrestricted, non-differentiated, universal faith of the Gentile Church. The phrase is equivalent to the new Israel or people of God, the elect race, the spiritual habitation, the royal priesthood, the holy nation,[15] which has displaced the old Israel as God's chosen people, apart from racial distinctions. It means the Church of the Græco-Roman world, as the result of the Gentile mission and the emancipating spirit of Paul. The distinction between circumcision and uncircumcision, the twofold mission represented by Peter and Paul, has evidently long ceased to exist. These Christians of Asia Minor, who constitute the Dispersion in the Christian sense, are Gentiles, not Jews by race. As believers in Christ, they have inherited the promise of salvation, proclaimed by the prophets, to whom the Spirit of Christ revealed the future grace of God available in him. Christian liberty is limited only by subjection as bondservants of God, which precludes the exercise of it as a pretext for evil-doing.[16] Nothing is, in fact, specifically said about the Law, which is replaced by

---

[13] iii. 14, for instance.
[14] Professor Kennedy, whilst minimising this influence, thinks that the writer had a knowledge of some of Paul's Epistles. " Theology of the Epistles," 166 f. ; M'Neile (" New Testament Teaching in the Light of St Paul's," 137 f. (1923)) and Moffatt (" Commentary on the Epistle," 85) also think that it is practically independent of Paul.
[15] i. 1 ; ii. 5, 9.   [16] ii. 16.

the Christian ethic, based on the example and teaching of Christ. The expiatory death of Christ—" the righteous for the unrighteous "—the redemptive significance of the Cross is apprehended in the Pauline sense.[17] Moreover, the Cross means for the believer death unto sin as well as for sin, the power of which Christ, by his suffering, has broken, whilst the life of the spirit is pointedly contrasted with that of the flesh.[18] We have, too, the Pauline combination of God the Father, Jesus Christ the Redeemer, and the Spirit as Sanctifier, in the realisation of the divine plan of redemption,[19] though the supreme place, in the author's thought, is assigned to God, whose will and purpose Christ and the Spirit carry out, which, to the writer, include the mission of Christ to the dead in Hades.[20] As in Paul, Christ is invested with the supremacy over the angels and ethereal powers which are made subject to him.[21]

At the same time, Paul's personal mysticism, his specific conception of faith are not discernible. Faith is belief in God who raised Christ from the dead and glorified him,[22] whilst his doctrine of justification by faith is lacking. The object of the Epistle is not instruction in doctrine, but rather the nurturing of the spirit of hope, patience, endurance in the midst of persecution, after the example of Christ, whose suffering was the prelude to his heavenly glory, and whose revelation from heaven is at hand, and, with it, the exceeding joy in which their fellow-suffering with him is to eventuate. With this the writer combines the further practical purpose to foster in these communities the high standard of life befitting the Christian name, for the profession of which they are suffering persecution. " The Gospel of God " which he propounds is thus a combination of primitive and Pauline ideas with the practical, ethically conceived type of Christianity of the Church at large.

The Epistle to the Hebrews is anonymous, and even the title, " To the Hebrews," is not original. It is largely a theological exposition, such as the writer might have spoken to the definite community to which he addresses it.[23] Nothing is definitely known of the author, except the little that can be

---

[17] i. 19 ; ii. 24 ; iii. 18.   [19] i. 1-2, etc.   [21] iii. 22.
[18] ii. 11 ; iii. 18 f. ; iv. 1 f.   [20] iii. 19.   [22] i. 21.
[23] See, for instance, vi. 9 f. ; x. 33 f. ; xiii. 17 f.

gathered from the Epistle itself. He was a friend of Timothy,[24] the companion and fellow-labourer of Paul, was a highly cultured teacher of the community addressed, and, like the community itself, whose members have been converted for a considerable period, belonged to the second generation of Christians.[25] The work is thus a post-apostolic production, and since it is quoted by Clement of Rome, it must have been written some time before the close of the first century. The belief which grew up in the Eastern Church, but which was for long not shared by the Western Church, that Paul was the writer, is untenable on internal grounds, though the writer was evidently influenced by Paul's teaching. The style is decidedly not that of Paul, and the contents equally tell against this assumption. Tertullian, following apparently an earlier tradition, is the first to ascribe it to Barnabas, the companion of Paul. This assumption, which is advocated by the latest English writer [26] on the question, seems also to be ruled out by the internal evidence. Barnabas would hardly have written in the tone of one who, like the community, belonged to the post-apostolic period. Modern critics have suggested other possible authors, including Apollos, also an associate of Paul and " a learned man, mighty in the scriptures," [27] to whom Luther was inclined to ascribe it. The writer was certainly strongly influenced by the Jewish-Hellenist thought represented by Philo of Alexandria, and the Alexandrian Apollos would very well suit the part of author, if we could reconcile his authorship with the post-apostolic character of the work. Authorship not definitely known is, therefore, the only verdict warranted by the evidence.

There is more substantial ground for concluding that the writer was a Christian Jew of the Dispersion, and that he wrote to a community of his fellow-Jewish Christians with which he was intimately connected. The argumentation of the Epistle assumes an intimate knowledge of Jewish religion and history on the part of the community. Though Gentile Christians read the Old Testament in the Septuagint Version and might be assumed to be familiar with its contents, the

---

[24] xiii. 23.   [25] ii. 3; v. 12; x. 32.
[26] Monsignor Barnes in the *Hibbert Journal*, October 1931.
[27] Acts xviii. 24.

impression is that the writer was a Christian Jew writing as an expert to Greek-speaking Christian Jews, for whom, as Jews, the Old Testament is a national as well as a religious book, and is invested with a supreme and unassailable authority as the Word of God. The reference to " the fathers " in chapter i., and " the elders " in chapter xi., *i.e.*, the great figures of the Old Testament history, seems to indicate that the writer is addressing those who are of their kith and kin, and not merely related to them in the religious sense.[28]

To what particular community was it addressed ? The most probable suggestion is that it was sent to a Jewish-Christian community at Rome by its experienced and watchful teacher, who was temporarily separated from it. The use of the Epistle by the Roman Clement points to its early circulation in the capital of the Empire, and the salutation from " those of Italy " is most naturally explained as a greeting from Roman Christians who, like the writer, were sojourning abroad.[29] It is not necessary to assume that it was addressed to the Roman Church as a whole, since, towards the end of the first century, this Church very probably consisted of several sections or congregations. This Jewish section evidently consisted of cultured members who had advanced beyond " the rudiments of the faith."[30] It was exposed to the increasing obloquy attached to the Christian name and to the suffering incidental to the Christian profession. It was, too, evidently menaced by an outburst of persecution. This threatened persecution could not be the Neronic one, since the Christians to whom the Epistle is addressed " have not yet resisted unto blood,"[31] though it is possible that the community, being confined to Jewish Christians, might have escaped the terrible ordeal under Nero, on the supposition that they might

[28] The critics differ on this point, and Professor E. F. Scott argues, not conclusively, in my opinion, that it was addressed to Christians in general, to the new Israel in the Christian sense, without reference to racial distinction. " Epistle to the Hebrews," 14 f. Windisch inclines, though not so decidedly, to the same conclusion. " Hebraeerbrief," 6 f., 115. Peake, " Commentary on the Bible," 887, questions this contention in a note to Scott's " Introduction to the Epistle."

[29] Numerous critics accept its Roman destination. See, for instance, M'Giffert, " Apostolic Age," 463 f. ; Moffatt, " Literature of the New Testament," 446 f. ; Peake, " Critical Introduction," 72 f. ; Scott, 10 f. ; Windisch is doubtful, " Hebraeerbrief," 115.

[30] v. 11 f.   [31] xii. 4.

have been regarded as Jews, not as Christians.   It is, however,
far more likely that the situation depicted is that of the Roman
Church under the Emperor Domitian who, towards the end
(A.D. 95-96) of his reign, revived the persecuting policy of
Nero.   In this case the date of the Epistle would be approxi-
mately round about A.D. 90.

We are impressed by the literary elegance and the resourceful
thought of the Epistle as an individual presentation of the
Gospel, even if we are far from being convinced by its allegorical
exegesis.   It is written in excellent common Greek and contains
passages of moving eloquence and human sympathy.   In the
practical sections the writer maintains the high level of the
New Testament ethic, though the first generation of teachers
has passed away and " divers and strange teachings " [32] (apparently Jewish-Gnostic) are perceptible in the Church.   If the
primitive ethical and spiritual enthusiasm is lacking in the
community, the writer himself reflects the primitive attitude
towards the world, in which the Christian is but a sojourner,[33]
and which is sharply distinguished from the spiritual, heavenly
commonwealth, of which he is a member.[34]   In the more
didactic sections he sets forth the supreme value of suffering
as a means of accomplishing the will and purpose of God
towards sinful humanity, and developing the highest qualities
of the soul.   Though he does not grapple with or solve the
problem of suffering in a world enshadowed by trial and
sorrow, he does bring out, in his own subjective fashion,
the effective part it has played in the moral and religious
sphere, and particularly the supreme significance and power
of the Cross in this sphere.   Himself a man of strong faith,
he strives to instil it into wavering or lukewarm members,
whilst unfolding to them his distinctive view of the Gospel—
" the good tidings preached unto us " [35]—viz., the sole and
eternal priesthood of Christ in his work of redemption and
intercession.   The other more rudimentary aspects of the
Gospel, as proclaimed in the primitive preaching—repentance
and faith in God, baptism and the laying on of hands, whereby
the new spiritual life is imparted, resurrection and judgment—
are assumed.   These elements presupposed, he seeks to unfold

[32] xiii. 7 f.
[33] xi. 13.
[34] xiii. 14 ; cf. xi. 10.
[35] iv. 2, ἐσμὲν εὐαγγελλισμένοι.

to the community, which is stagnant in thought, if not in welldoing, a more developed conception of the Gospel, viewed in the light of the old sacrificial cultus. In the face of its flagging faith and the possibility of a declension from the Gospel, under the stress of threatened persecution, and the suffering incidental to its profession,[36] he strives to convince its members that it is typified in the Old Testament. It is, therefore, necessarily the organic, divinely ordained development of the Old Testament religion. To renounce it (which, however, he does not believe possible in their case) would be to incur the guilt of apostasy from the true faith, as foreshadowed in the Old Testament and fulfilled in Christ, and to forsake the God-appointed way of salvation. In case of such apostasy, a second repentance would be of no avail. The writer is the forerunner of the later rigorist party in the Church, which denied to those who lapsed under persecution the possibility of salvation, even if they should repent.

He shares Paul's exalted conception of the pre-existent, cosmic Christ. Christ is the inheritor, the instrument, the upholder of the creation and the manifestation of the divine nature. As he sets it forth, the conception is evidently derived from Philo and the Wisdom literature as well as Paul.[37] He knows, directly or indirectly, the Logos idea of the Alexandrian philosopher and makes use of it (though not the actual term), as well as of Old Testament passages, in introducing Christ to his readers. It is substantially the Pauline conception with the addition of Philonic terms in the expression of it. His indebtedness to Philo is farther apparent in the conception of the Logos as the supreme High Priest, the mediator between God and man.[38]

[36] See ii. 1 ; iii. 12, and other passages, though the danger of a relapse to Judaism is contested by Windisch, Scott, and others.

[37] For his dependence on Philo, see Siegfried, " Philo von Alexandrien," 321 f. (1875) ; Kennedy, " Philo's Contribution to Religion," 120, 162, 170 (1919) ; and Scott, " Epistle to the Hebrews," 51 f. (1922). Windisch thinks that his indebtedness was only indirect, and suggests his acquaintance with the Jewish Wisdom literature, " Hebraeerbrief," 14 (1913). It is, I think, evident that, while he had a knowledge of the " Book of Wisdom," vii., viii., he also knew the works of Philo. Both writers use the words ἀπαύγασμα and χαρακτήρ, effulgence and image, as descriptive of the Son of God. The author uses the expression, ὁ λόγος τοῦ θεοῦ in iv. 121, and this seems another echo of Philo. But this is not the Logos as applied to Christ but the written word.

[38] Siegfried, 321 f. ; Scott, 163 f.

The difference in both cases lies in the fact that the Logos, as the instrument of creation and as supreme High Priest, is identified with the historic Jesus, with one who was " a partaker in flesh and blood " and shared the sufferings inherent in a real human life. In emphasising the humanity of Christ, along with his divinity, he anticipates the Fourth Gospel.

As in the Fourth Gospel, the Logos idea serves as an introduction to the main theme of the work. This theme is specifically the high-priestly function of Christ in his offering of himself as a propitiatory sacrifice for sin, and in his intercession for sinners in heaven as the intermediary between God and man. For him, as for Paul, Old Testament usages " are a shadow of things to come." [39] Of these usages, his special concern, in working out this theme, is with the sacrificial cultus of the Old Testament ; not, like Paul, with the Law in relation to the Gospel, though he incidentally shows the bearing of Christ's priestly function in abrogating the Law. His conception of the Gospel is dominated by the Jewish sacrificial idea of the vicarious offering of blood to God in expiation of sin. " Apart from the shedding of blood there is no remission." [40] As high priest, Christ offered his own blood to God for man's redemption.[41] Though he thus shares the crass notion of the necessity of bloodshed in expiation of sin, he at least deserves the credit of abolishing this barbarous practice in the self-sacrifice of Christ. By his sacrifice of himself as our high priest, he has once for all done away with the shedding of blood for " the putting away of sin." [42]

To the performance of his high priestly function, Christ's humanity is essential. Hence the emphasis at the outset on the real human life with its experience of suffering and death. God's plan of salvation could only be achieved through such a life. Only thus could Christ fitly become the leader of the way to salvation for mankind (" perfect through suffering " [43]). Without his death he could neither have brought to nought the power of death over humanity, nor could he cherish the fellow-feeling with suffering humanity in his function as intercessor.[44] As the heavenly High Priest, Christ is thus capable of being " touched with the feeling of

[39] Col. ii. 17 ; cf. Heb. x. 1.   [41] ix. 11 f.   [43] ii. 10.
[40] ix. 22.   [42] ix. 26.   [44] ii. 10 f.

12

our infirmities, having in all points been tempted like as we are, yet without sin." [45]

By his perfect obedience in suffering, as well as by his divine nature as Son, his priestly function is infinitely superior to that of the Aaronic priesthood, under which the people received the Law. He belongs to the higher order of priesthood typified by Melchizedek. This priesthood was independent of race and time and of the old imperfect legal system, which conditioned the relation between God and man, and which he has superseded in favour of a new spiritual relation to God. By offering himself once for all, he has both abrogated the old legal and sacrificial system and replaced the imperfect intercession of the Aaronite priesthood by his abiding intercession in heaven. Christ is at once the propitiatory victim, offered by himself for the sins of the people, and the eternal intercessor for sinners in heaven.[46] The medium of man's salvation has been transferred from earth to heaven, where Jesus continues to exercise his saving priestly ministry. He thus brings to fruition the new, inward, spiritual covenant— " the law written in the mind and heart," of which Jeremiah speaks, and which was to supersede the old defective legal covenant.

How Christ has operated this radical transformation by his propitiatory death, and continues to operate it by his heavenly intercession, the writer shows in detail, in allegorising fashion, in reference to the old sacrificial cultus.[47] His ultimate function—that of judge and bringer of salvation to those that wait for his reappearance—Christ will perform at his second coming.[48] Meanwhile, the old legal and sacrificial Judaism has been superseded by Christianity, the Gospel. Christianity has become the final and absolute religion.

It is thus that he expounds the religious significance of Christ and makes the Old Testament cultus attain its higher development in him and his work of propitiation and intercession. His theory is alike an apologetic and an interpretation in the light of this cultus, and is adapted to the position of those to whom he writes and who are exposed to suffering and menaced with martyrdom. As an apologetic, it serves to answer the question why Judaism has been superseded,

[45] iv. 15.   [46] v.-vii.   [47] ix.-x.   [48] ix. 27-28.

and must be superseded, in the development of the divine
plan of salvation, and why they are exposed to suffering and
persecution for the sake of Christ. As an interpretation, it
seeks to explain this plan in the light of this fact. In this respect
the theory claims to be a higher knowledge, compared with the
more rudimentary Christianity.[49] Like the apologetic and
interpretation of Paul, it is highly individualistic, and its
elaboration shows the same tendency to a subjective, unhistoric
exegesis of Old Testament passages in accordance with the
Rabbinic and Philonic method.[50] Whilst emphasising the
human life of Jesus, he shows the Pauline tendency to view
him in the light of his own thoughts about him, rather than
in that of the primitive record. He may have taken his idea
of Christ's priesthood from the words of the institution of
the Supper, in which he spoke of the covenant of his blood
shed for the remission of sin. But he was evidently keenly
interested in the sacrificial cultus and brings this special interest
to bear on the interpretation of the Gospel, just as Paul brought
his special interest in the law to bear upon his interpretation.
He thus transforms the historic Jesus into the supreme priest
and intercessor without specifically concerning himself with
the question whether this fits the actual facts of his earthly life
and mission. It is a subjective, theological interpretation and
representation of the Christ in the light of the Old Testament
cultus, in accordance with the current allegoric method, rather
than of the historic record of his life, that he lays before his
readers. In associating Jesus with the sacrificial cultus and
making him the fulfilment of it, he does what Jesus himself
did not do. This cultus did not figure in his thought or his
teaching. He does not seem to have shaped either with
reference to it. He belonged to the synagogue rather than
the temple, though he observed the ritual usages of the time.
In offering himself to God for man, he appears to have had
in mind the fifty-third chapter of Isaiah and the thirty-first
chapter of Jeremiah, rather than the sacrificial cultus. His
mind moved in the sphere of the prophets, not that of the
priests.

[49] vi. 1 f.
[50] Scott finds a shade of difference between the allegorising method of
the writer and that of Philo. It is, he thinks, more akin to that of the
Rabbis. "Epistle," 53-54.

The writer's conception of the high priestly Christ leads him to agree with Paul in emphasising his propitiatory sacrifice. He is also at one with Paul in his proof that in Christianity the old has given place to the new, though the line of argument is different. There is not, indeed, the radical Pauline antithesis between the old and the new. The Law was imperfect and could not produce perfection, and its abrogation was inevitable as the result of the radical difference between the spiritual priesthood of Christ and the old legal priesthood. " For the priesthood being changed, there is made of necessity a change of the law." [51] But it does not seem to have been for the writer, as for Paul, radically antagonistic in itself to the Gospel. Nor is the new covenant, of which Christ is the fulfilment, placed in absolute antithesis to the old. Whilst the new covenant is better than the old, which, like the Law, was also imperfect, the old was not inherently evil. It was only the practice of it that was at fault.[52] The contrast is more measured in Hebrews than in Romans and Galatians. But the result is the same for both Paul and the writer, though the point of view and the reasoning are different. The Jewish legal and sacrificial system, which, for the writer, was already tried and found wanting in Jeremiah's time (" becoming old and waxing aged and nigh unto vanishing away " [53]), is now defunct with the fulfilment of the new covenant in Christ. Judaism has been superseded by Christianity. The old controversy over the Law has subsided in the Gentile world. Paul's abrogation of the Law, with its resulting equality of Jew and Gentile, has triumphed.

The writer is not otherwise the exponent of the distinctive Pauline theory of salvation and the Pauline faith mysticism. His definition of faith, as alike the assurance of things hoped for—the unseen realities—and the proof of these realities,[54] reminds of Paul's assured faith in the things not seen, in contrast to the things seen—the eternal in contrast to the temporal.[55] The distinction is familiar to both, and in both it derives from Plato by way of current Hellenist thought. To both, too, faith is not only an assured apprehension of the invisible, eternal realities. It is the secret power of the

---

[51] vii. 12 f. [53] viii. 13. [55] 2 Cor. iv. 18.
[52] viii. 6 f. [54] xi. 1.

practical religious life, as the writer seeks to demonstrate in
the retrospect of the great figures of Hebrew history in
chapter xi. But he does not share Paul's specific doctrine of
faith as the means by which the mystic, divine life is engendered
and nurtured in the soul of the believer, and the life of freedom
from the Law and the flesh is realised. For him it is rather the
secret of the faithfulness, the endurance which culminates in
salvation, the reward of unflinching suffering. We miss, too,
the distinctive doctrine of justification by faith in the Pauline
sense, though he incidentally quotes the saying from Hab. ii. 4
that the just shall live by his faith.[56] He speaks of
sanctification,[57] not of justification as the result of Christ's
death. The object of the redemption effected on the Cross is
to cleanse rather than to justify from sin—the spiritual purify-
ing, of which the old sacrificial cultus was the emblem.[58]

In the superscription the Epistle of James assumes the
form of a letter. In the sequel it is rather an address or
exhortation couched in the terse, aphoristic style, of which
the writer was a master. The Twelve tribes of the Dispersion,
to which it is addressed, are not the Jews scattered over the
world, or the Jewish Christians among them, but Greek-speaking
Christians in general, conceived as the New Israel or people
of God. In the superscription the writer describes himself
as "James, servant of God and the Lord Jesus Christ," and
ultimately, from Origen onwards, though not without dis-
sentients, he was assumed to be James, the Lord's brother,
and one of the three pillar apostles. Among English critics
Mayor [59] and, more recently, Moulton [60] and Rendall,[61] adopt
this assumption, and regard the Epistle as the earliest New
Testament writing (circ. A.D. 50). Moffatt [62] and Ropes,[63]
following Harnack, Pfleiderer, von Soden, and many other
German critics, question this assumption, and assign its origin
to the end of the first or the first half of the second century.

---

[56] x. 38.   [57] ἁγιάζειν instead of δικαιοῦν, ii. 11 ; x. 10 ; xiii. 12.
[58] ix. 11 f.   [59] " Epistle of James " (1892).
[60] Peake's " Commentary " (1920).
[61] " Epistle of James and Judaic Christianity " (1927).
[62] " Introduction to the Literature of the New Testament," 463 f.,
and the Introduction to his " Commentary on the Epistle " (1928). M'Giffert,
" Christianity in the Apostolic Age," 579 f., also decides against the
authorship of the Apostle. See also Pfleiderer, " Urchristenthum," ii. 539.
[63] " Commentary on the Epistle " (1916).

There is no substantial reason for regarding the superscription, with Harnack,[64] as a later addition by a writer who thus sought to invest the Epistle with the authority of the Apostle James. The name James or Jacob was common enough, and the James of the superscription does not claim to be the Lord's brother. He was evidently not an apostle, but a teacher in some Jewish-Christian community. On the other hand, in view of the prominence of the Lord's brother as a leader of the Jerusalem Church after the disappearance of Peter, one would naturally infer his authorship, if the internal evidence were in keeping with this inference. The external evidence in its favour is very late and only begins with the belief of Origen in the first half of the third century. The critics differ greatly in their reading of the internal evidence. Spitta, for instance, unconvincingly inferred that the Epistle was a Jewish homily, to which a later editor gave a Christian colouring by interpolating a couple of passages.[65] Moulton hazardously thinks that it was written to unconverted Jews by the Apostle James, who avoided a more explicit statement of the Messianic claim of Jesus in order the better to commend it to them.[66] Rendall maintains that it was addressed by the Lord's brother to Jews as well as Christians, and rather subjectively finds in it a reflection of the religious, political, and social conditions of Palestine during his lifetime.[67] Ropes, on the contrary, finds that the conditions point to the period after the destruction of Jerusalem in A.D. 70, and before the disturbance which culminated in the rebellion of Barcochba in the reign of Hadrian (A.D. 132-135),[68] whilst also concluding that the writer has more particularly in view Jewish Christians residing in Palestine, at this period, under the social conditions reflected in the Epistle.[69]

The archaic character of the Epistle seems at first sight to favour an early, even a pre-Pauline date. On the other hand, there are weighty reasons, suggested by the contents, for postponing it to the subapostolic period and questioning the authorship of the Apostle James. All the critics, favourable and unfavourable to this authorship, pronounce the Greek

[64] " Chronologie," i. 485 f.
[65] " Der Brief des Jacobus " (1896).
[66] Peake's " Commentary," 903.
[67] " Epistle of James," 30 f., 47 f.
[68] " Commentary," 49.
[69] 40 f.

of the Epistle to be superior to that of the other New Testament writings, except Hebrews.[70] " The language," says Ropes, " is that of a writer of the Koiné, who uses Greek fluently and accurately, though his style has a certain Biblical tinge. . . . Greek was probably his mother tongue." [71] All agree that he made large use of the Greek translation of the Scriptures, and it is hardly likely that the brother of Jesus would be capable of writing so forcibly in the common Greek, or have preferred the Septuagint to the vernacular. Mere generalisations on the use of the Greek language in Galilee and the Decapolis are not convincing proofs to the contrary. If written by the Apostle James, within, say, twenty or twenty-five years after the crucifixion, we should expect some reflection of the primitive Gospel as preached by Peter. On the contrary, this feature is conspicuously lacking. The Gospel is vaguely referred to as " the word of truth," " the truth," " the implanted word," " the faith of our Lord Jesus Christ." The inspiration of the community by the Holy Spirit,[72] the appeal to prophecy in proof of the Messianic claim of Jesus and his resurrection, and in explanation of his death on the Cross, the dynamic, charismatic life of the community are ignored. The absence of these primitive features militates against a pre-Pauline date. The degenerate character of the communities to which he writes may not be conclusive against an early date, in view of the strife and lax morality of the Corinthian and other Pauline churches. But the impression is that of the relaxed moral and spiritual life which the lapse of time tends to produce.

The absence of any reference to the controversy with the Judaisers over the Law, which seems to have burned itself out, is singular if it was written by the Lord's brother during the active career of Paul. Even granting that James, according to the account of the Jerusalem conference in Acts, was ready to compromise, it is certain, on the testimony of Paul, that he was conscientiously attached to the old usages, and, as the representative of " the circumcision," opposed Paul's liberal attitude.[73] To the writer of the Epistle, on the other hand,

[70] See Mayor, for instance, Introduction to " Commentary on Epistle," 179.
[71] " Commentary," 24.
[72] The spirit in iv. 5 is not the Holy Spirit, but the rational faculty in man.
[73] Gal. ii. 11 f.

as for Jesus, the ethical element in the Law is the thing that
matters. The doing of the word is the essential in religion.
The ceremonial Law is entirely ignored. Nay, for him, as
for Jesus, the Law is " the law of liberty " [74]—the Law freely
accepted and willingly obeyed in the pursuit and practice
of the higher life, not the observance of imposed rules in the
spirit of bondage. This conception of the Law might include
the current legalism. But the stress is exclusively on the
moral content of the Law, especially " the royal or sovereign
law of love," and it is entirely alien to that of the Judaisers
on the ceremonial Law as the imperative of an external code.
Clearly, in this matter the writer represents the free and
independent spirit of Jesus, if not of Paul, and it is hardly
that of James who, in opposition to Paul, insisted on conserv-
ing the customs of " the circumcision " in antagonism to the
Gentiles. The address to the Twelve Tribes, in the sense of
the Church as the new people of God, shows that the old
Jewish separatist spirit has vanished from the writer's horizon.

Moreover, the traces of Pauline influence on the thought of
the writer point to a post- not a pre-Pauline date. With
Paul he emphasises the inveterate tendency of evil desire (lust) [75]
in the soul, which breeds sin and death, and speaks in terms that
remind of Paul, of " the warring in the members," produced
by the pursuit of pleasure, the gratification of the passions. [76]
He knows, too, the Pauline contention that failure to keep the
Law, even in one point, involves guilt in one bound to observe
the Law as a whole. These ideas may, indeed, be derived
from the common stock of Hebrew religious thought, without
necessarily involving a knowledge of Pauline teaching. But
this can hardly be maintained in the case of the doctrine of
justification by faith, which forms a distinctive doctrinal
feature of the Epistle. [77] Those who, in the interest of an
early date, maintain that the polemic against the abuse of
this doctrine has no reference to that of Paul, seem to me
to ignore the express reference to the Pauline formula of
justification by faith alone contained in ii. 24, " Ye see that
by works a man is justified and not by faith only." Here
the writer has undoubtedly in mind the profession of the
Pauline doctrine. He does not deny that faith has its part

[74] i. 25 ; ii. 12.   [75] ἐπιθυμία, i. 14, 15.   [76] iv. 1 f.   [77] ii. 14 f.

in justification. He does deny that mere faith, apart from works, can justify. " If a man say he hath faith, but have not works, can that faith save him ? " [78]   It is the contention that man, being justified by faith, need not concern himself with works that he seeks to combat.   This contention he meets with a decided negative.   Such a faith, he insists, is not a saving, but a dead, a barren faith.[79]   Paul, too, would have answered in the negative, seeing that for him faith necessarily involved the works, or as he would have preferred to say, " the fruits " of faith.   But he would have joined issue with the further inference, which the writer goes on to draw, that because works must ensue from saving faith, a man is, therefore, justified or saved by works as well as faith, as in the case of Abraham and Rahab.   In this contention he shows that he has not truly apprehended the Pauline doctrine, and that he is lacking not only in understanding, but in logic.   In ii. 10 he has previously maintained that if a man, who is bound to keep the whole Law, fails in one point, he is guilty of all. He confesses that " in many things we all stumble." [80]   Logic-ally he ought to have concluded with Paul that salvation cannot, therefore, be by way of the Law, or works, which man cannot perfectly perform.   Guilt would still remain and the guilt would be equivalent to that of the transgression of the whole Law.   Paul, assuming the same premises, more logically attributed salvation solely to God's mercy appropriated by faith, and, from the point of view of justification, absolutely ruled out works.   James has missed the distinctive point of Paul's logic and, therefore, his conclusion from the case of Abraham that " by works a man is justified and not by faith only " is non-Pauline, if not perhaps consciously anti-Pauline.   His con-ception of faith is the rabbinic one of a good or meritorious work, counting for salvation in God's sight ; not the Pauline one of the sole means of attaining justification, forgiveness by relying on the grace of God in Christ.

For this doctrine, as developed by Paul, James has neither understanding nor appreciation.   In this respect he belongs to the pre-Pauline period.   His master is not Paul, but Jesus, whose ethical teaching he has absorbed and seeks to enforce, if, like Paul, he shows no interest in his earthly life—not even

[78] ii. 14.　　　　[79] ii. 17, 20.　　　　[80] iii. 2.

in his death and resurrection and their saving significance
which, for Paul, had become the all-important elements of
the Gospel. So limited is his interest in the historic life
that he seeks in the Prophets, Elijah, and Job, not, like the
writer of Hebrews, in Jesus himself, " the example of suffering and patience." [81] The only point which he stresses, in
addition to the ethical teaching of Jesus, is the second coming,
which is at hand.[82] " The coming of the Lord is at hand."
Neither baptism nor the Eucharist is mentioned. The only
rite is the anointing of the sick in the name of the Lord, with
prayer for healing.[83] He represents the tendency to find the
Gospel in the Sermon on the Mount, in the implanted word
which is able to save the soul,[84] the word of truth by which
God, in fulfilment of his deliberate purpose, has effected
(" brought forth "), a new spiritual and ethical creation.[85]
He belongs to the type of Christian who, as in the first Gospel,
sees in Jesus and his teaching (the Logia) the lawgiver of a
new spiritual life, in reaction from the old legalism, if, unlike
him, he ignores the historic life and, strangely enough, seeks the
exemplification of it in Old Testament figures like Job and
Elijah. The teaching, if not the figure of Jesus himself, is
the norm of his Christianity, and in this respect he evidently
represents a distinctive tendency in the Church of his time.
This Christianity consists in the living of a Christian life in
faith in a fatherly God, and love of our fellows, according
to the teaching and spirit of Jesus—" the faith of our Lord
Jesus Christ." This teaching is supplemented by the Wisdom
literature, with which he was evidently familiar.[86] He has no
interest in the current speculation about him and his death
as developed by Paul or the early Gnostics.[87] His Christology
is of the simple primitive type, which recognised Jesus as the
Messiah, and the exalted Lord,[88] without speculating on his

---

[81] v. 10-11, 17.   [82] v. 7-8.
[83] v. 14-15. " The honourable name by which ye were called " (ii. 7)
does not seem to refer to baptism.
[84] i. 21.   [85] i. 18.   [86] iii. 13 f.
[87] The wisdom of iii. 13 f. is ethical, not speculative.
[88] In ii. 1, " Have not the faith of our Lord Jesus Christ (the lord) of
glory " the genitive " of glory " seems most probably to denote Christ
in his glorified state. To hold with Mayor, Rendall, and others that it
represents Christ as the Shekinah, the embodiment of the divine presence
and being, is not convincing. For the various interpretations of this difficult
phrase, see Mayor, 74 f.; Ropes, 187-188. It is not probable that the

person. Christian ethics, practical Christianity, not theology, is what interests this Christian " teacher." " The Epistle," forcibly remarks Dr Rendall, " is a revaluation of Judaism in terms of the thought and teaching of Jesus." [89]

IV. CHRISTIAN APOCALYPTIC

The writer of 2nd Thessalonians does not tell us who the Antichrist is, while making it clear that he is not the Roman Emperor. The Roman Empire is, for him, the restraining power that meanwhile prevents his appearance. The prophet John, who wrote the Apocalypse in the last decade of the first century, has discovered him. He finds him where the author of 2nd Thessalonians did not look for him—on the imperial throne itself. He is clearly the Emperor Domitian, " the beast," who insists on his divinity as head of the state, which was duly expressed in the imperial cult.[1] Here at last is the Antichrist who challenges the allegiance of the faithful to Christ, and determines to destroy them in consequence of their refusal to recognise his imperial divinity.

In the interval between 2nd Thessalonians and the Johannine revelation, the indications of the presence of Antichrist have thus become unmistakable. The prophet's purpose is " to show the things which must speedily come to pass." [2] The time is at last at hand,[3] and he has been commissioned by Christ to reveal these things. He is not concerned with what Christ has accomplished in the past, to which he refers only incidentally. His message is a message for his own time. It unfolds what Christ is about to accomplish as the deliverer of the faithful. It accordingly deals with the present, not with the future, or only with the future in as far as it is affected by his present-day message, which concludes with

condemning and killing of " the righteous one " in v. 6 refers to the primitive designation of the Messiah as " the holy and righteous one." It seems to refer to the oppression of the righteous in general by the rich, which the writer denounces in v. 1-6.

[89] " The Epistle of James and Judaic Christianity," 57.

[1] Dominus et Deus noster, " Suetonius, Domitian," 13. The persecution under Domitian may not have assumed the dimensions that the author has in view. But the beginning is there, in the imperial cult, of antagonism between the Church and the State, and the author sees in this antagonism the harbinger of a universal persecution.

[2] i. 1.   [3] i. 3.

the announcement of the millennial reign of Christ and the final judgment by God. Obviously these events, which are to supervene on the Second Coming, have a future bearing.

To judge from his Greek diction and style, which are Hebraic in a striking degree, the writer was a Palestinian Jew, who had resided for a time in the province of Asia, and was very imperfectly acquainted with the current idiomatic Greek. He thinks in Hebrew or Aramaic and writes throughout in very ungrammatical Greek. This feature by itself reveals the fact that his book is a unity,[4] since it bears the stamp of his own personality in thought, diction, and style from beginning to end, though he has incorporated older apocalyptic sources [5] and was familiar with the Old Testament, Jewish Apocalyptic, and a number of the New Testament writings. He is clearly influenced by Paul's teaching, and knows the train of thought

---

[4] The late Archdeacon Charles, in the Introduction to his " Commentary " (1920, International Critical Series), has made a thorough study of the style and diction of the book, and has shown that linguistically, up to chapter xx., it is the composition of a single writer, who has used older apocalyptic sources of varying dates in a Hebrew or Greek form, and also traditions or lore derived from Babylonian, Egyptian, or Greek sources. In chapter xi., for instance, in which the Temple is still standing, he has used a source or sources written before A.D. 70. There are some interpolations in the text by an editor who has revised the work, and this editor has added chapters xx.-xxii. in a bungling fashion from material left by the author. The writer shows familiarity with some of Paul's Epistles and other New Testament writings, as well as the Old Testament scriptures and Jewish Apocalyptic. Charles thinks that the prophet wrote the seven letters to the Churches under Vespasian, when the Church had no expectation of a general persecution, and that he revised them to bring them into line with the later outbreak of persecution in the reign of Domitian. Despite the use of sources, the book is a unity and an independent work, stamped by the author's individuality, style, and diction. Charles' masterly study of the grammar and diction of the writer places its unity beyond doubt. Its unity is now generally recognised, though critics like Joh. Weiss (" Die Offenbarung des Johannes," 3 f. (1904)—Ein organismus von eigentümlichen Sonderleben—) and Peake (" Critical Introduction," 159 f.), for instance, owing to their lack of Charles' special grammatical knowledge of the book, share in this recognition less emphatically than he. It is no longer regarded as the work of a mere compiler. For an account and a refutation of this discredited view, see M. Jones, " New Testament in the Twentieth Century," 436 f. There is a large amount of unanimity in ascribing the book to the late reign of the Emperor Domitian rather than to that of Nero or Vespasian (The Tübingen school, Lightfoot, Westcott, Hort, etc.). The authorship of the writer of the Fourth Gospel being linguistically impossible, a large number of critics assign it to a distinct writer, and Dr Charles argues forcibly that this writer was not John the Elder of the Johannine Epistles, to whom he credits the Fourth Gospel, but an influential Jewish-Christian prophet of this name, connected with the province of Asia. On the problems connected with the book see also Charles' " Schweich Lectures on the Apocalypse " (1922).

[5] Charles, " Commentary," Introduction, 62 f.

which found distinctive expression in the Fourth Gospel, if
he does not seem to have used the Gospel itself. Needless
to say, he is not identical with the author of this Gospel, since
this author could not have written the Greek of the prophet
John. He is neither the Apostle John nor the presbyter
John of the Johannine Epistles. He is what he designates
himself—a Jewish-Christian prophet, who bore the name of
John.

His thesis is that God will speedily intervene, through
Christ, to end the present order of things and inaugurate a
new one. This thesis he develops in a series of symbolic
visions, partly his own, partly adopted from previous seers,
in which the weird drama of the last things gradually unfolds
itself. It is to the modern reader largely enigmatic, though
its figurative allusions were doubtless intelligible to his fellow-
believers. He is a thoroughgoing visionary with a fixed belief
in the immediate catastrophic intervention by God, through
Christ, in the history of his time. This intervention is fantastic-
ally pictured and, as in the case of all such apocalyptic forecasts,
it proved illusory. As far as the actual coming and its sequel
are concerned, this apocalyptic belief led to a false reading
of history, which has often been repeated by those who have
since been influenced by it. Despite the imperial cult, the
Roman Empire was not the unmitigated incarnation of wicked-
ness which he depicts in his fantastic apocalyptic fashion.
For better or worse it was destined to endure for several
centuries as the supreme political power in the ancient world.
But apart from its visionary aspect, it makes a powerful impression from the moral and religious point of view. It is a
passionate protest against the oppression of conscience by a
persecuting state, against the usurpation by the state, as
embodied in the emperor, of the attributes of deity and the
enforced recognition of this deity in formal worship. This
usurpation the writer meets with the most uncompromising
antagonism, and strives to inspire his own passionate resistance
into his readers. If his reading of history is illusory, the
heroic faith that underlay it served a providential purpose in
sustaining the believer under the dire persecution, the deadly
enmity of a hostile government and a hostile world. His
call to endurance in the midst of this testing experience

contributed, by inspiring the heroic martyr spirit, to save Christianity from destruction. His Revelation may be a strange medley of apocalyptic fancies. But it is shot through with a red-hot moral and religious purpose, and it succeeded in achieving this purpose. Moreover, it contains passages of great power and beauty which are for all time. It reflects in moving language the power of Christian faith in surmounting the tragedy and suffering of mortal life, in reliance on God's presence and purpose in history, even if, under the influence of a realistic fantasy, it mistakes the manifestation of this presence and purpose. That Christ did ultimately prevail in the heroic faith of his followers is an unquestionable fact. The prophet had not prophesied in vain. Though the apocalyptic element in his prophecy was illusory, the principle of self-sacrificing fidelity to conscience and the kingdom of God, to which it gave expression, is of eternal validity. This principle was no mere illusion. Its powerful operation is writ large in Christian history from that day to this.

The Christology of the writer is akin to that of Paul, with some of whose Epistles he was evidently familiar.[6] Like Paul, he is mainly concerned with the exalted Christ, though he rivets attention on the drama of his coming and its effects on the present order of things, rather than on the heavenly Christ in relation to the life of the believer. Like Paul, too, he only refers to a few outstanding facts of his earthly career—to his natural birth and his descent from David ;[7] his crucifixion ;[8] his resurrection :[9] and his ascension.[10] At the same time, his predilection for the personal name "Jesus" seems to show that he knew and cherished the record of his earthly life, though nothing could be more unlike the historic Jesus than the Logos-Messiah of this fantasy. In this respect the warrior king reflects the bellicose spirit of the writer.[11] With Paul, he has a high conception of the exalted Christ. He equates him with the apocalyptic Son of Man—the ethereal, pre-existent figure of "The Book of Enoch."[12] He is "the

[6] See Charles, "Commentary," i., Introduction, 83 f., and the "Commentary" itself, *passim*.
[7] v. 5 ; xii. 1-2 ; xxii. 16.   [8] xi. 8.   [9] i. 5, 18.   [10] xii. 5.
[11] Charles points out his knowledge of the Gospels of Matthew and Luke. Introduction, 84 f.
[12] i. 13 f. ; xiv. 14.

beginning of the creation of God "[13]—the one through whom
all things came into existence, as in Paul. He is the Logos
or Word of God, as in the Fourth Gospel.[14] With the Fourth
Evangelist, he evidently adopted the Logos theory of his
Ephesian environment. As in the New Testament literature
generally, he is the Son of God and stands in a special relation
to the Father.[15] With Paul the writer applies to him titles
which are used of God.[16] He sits with God on His throne,[17]
and worship is offered to him as divine equally with God.[18]
He ascribes to him eternal glory and dominion,[19] and herein
goes beyond Paul, according to whom the Christ ultimately
delivers up the kingdom to God and returns to subjection
to Him. He is the conqueror of death, the ever-living One
who alone possesses the power to deliver from death and
Hades.[20] He is the supreme authority in the Church and
ruler over the kingdoms of the earth—the King of kings
and Lord of lords.[21]

Whilst thus emphasising the unique rank and vocation of
the exalted Christ, he follows Paul, in preference to the Fourth
Evangelist, in representing his subordination to God. He
does not, like the latter, call him God. God alone is absolute
and self-existent, who is and was and is to come,[22] the Lord
God Almighty.[23] He alone holds the last Judgment over all
the dead,[24] and His will alone is the source of creation.[25] The
Christ speaks of Him as his God,[26] and though closely associated,
they are strictly differentiated. There is no distinctive doctrine
of the Spirit in relation to God and Christ. The Spirit that
speaks in the letters to the seven churches and in other similar
passages is the Spirit of Christ.[27] The attempt of the editor
of i. 4 to interpolate the Spirit into the duality of Father and
Son is utterly fantastic.

The redemptive work of Christ is not enlarged on except
in the eschatological sense. It is not the redemption wrought
by Christ on the Cross, but the deliverance which he is about

[13] iii. 14.
[14] xix. 13.
[15] ii. 18, 27 ; iii. 5, 21 ; xiv. 1.
[16] i. 17 ; xxi. 6.
[17] iii. 21.
[18] v. 12-13 ; cf. iv. 10 ; vii. 10.
[19] i. 6.
[20] i. 18.
[21] i. 5, 13 f. ; ii. 1 ; xvii. 14 ; xix. 16.
[22] i. 4.
[23] iv. 8.
[24] xx. 11-15.
[25] iv. 11 ; xiv. 7.
[26] iii. 2.
[27] See Charles, Introduction, 114, 115.

to accomplish that engrosses the seer's mind. It is only incidentally generalised in certain retrospective passages in which his redeeming sacrifice, in the Pauline and Johannine sense, is accentuated. In his redemptive capacity Christ is the Lamb—a characteristic designation which is applied to him twenty-eight times by the writer. He is the victim who has " loosed us from our sins by his blood," [28] has " purchased unto God with his blood " the redeemed of every tribe, and tongue, and people, and nation.[29] As the Lamb, Christ is the suffering Messiah on earth, by whose self-sacrifice on the Cross man has been redeemed from sin, as in the Fourth Gospel and in Paul.[30] But, with his exaltation and his coming, he becomes the triumphant Messiah, is transformed from the slain victim into the leader of the faithful and, as Lord of lords and King of kings, wages war with the antichristian Roman power and overcomes it.[31] How his redemptive work is appropriated by the faithful, we are not told. There is no explicit statement of the Pauline doctrine of justification by faith. It is presumably assumed, if not explicitly developed.[32] At the same time, for the writer faith is distinctively fidelity to Christ in the stress of persecution. The emphasis is on faith in the sense of faithfulness, and on " works " in the practical sense of " love, faith, service, endurance," [33] as manifested in the life of Jesus himself.[34] Whilst emphasis is laid on " the keeping of the commandments of God and the faith of Jesus," [35] the writer ignores the Mosaic Law and, with it, the Pauline reasoning on faith versus works in the legalist sense. His absorbing, if not his exclusive interest is in the ethical aspect of faith, as the power to endure and conquer.

Though a Jewish Christian, the writer, under the influence of Paul, has emancipated himself from Jewish legalism. Whilst not so liberal as Paul in the matter of eating meat sacrificed to idols, which, evidently in accordance with the apostolic ordinance of Acts xv., he denounces in the letters to the

---

[28] i. 5.

[29] v. 9 f. ; cf. xiii. 8.

[30] John i. 29 ; 1 Cor. vi. 20 ; vii. 23.

[31] xvii. 14.

[32] As in vii. 14, for instance (cf. xxii. 14), in which the redeemed have washed their robes and made them white in the blood of the Lamb, i.e., obtained forgiveness of sin through faith in the death of Christ. See Charles, " Commentary," i. 214.

[33] ii. 19, etc.

[34] ii. 26.

[35] xiv. 4.

churches of Pergamum and Thyatira,[36] he has wholeheartedly
discarded Jewish particularism. The Church has become a
world-wide community or kingdom,[37] consisting of " the called
and chosen and faithful," [38] who include all nations and
peoples, apart from racial distinction. As in 1st Peter, the old
priestly caste has been superseded by the universal spiritual
priesthood of the followers of Jesus.[39] Universalism has
triumphed. Christianity has severed itself from Judaism,
whilst the controversy between Jewish and Gentile believers
over the Law, in relation to it, has become a thing of the past
in the Church of the Græco-Roman world. Its place has
been taken by the conflict between Christians and Jews, which
is still very active. The Jews are evidently instigating the
persecution of the Christians, and are, for the writer, " a
synagogue of Satan." [40]

Peculiar to the author, among the New Testament writers,
is the conception of the binding of Satan and of a first resurrection and judgment of all the martyred Christians to reign with
Christ in the new heavenly Jerusalem for a thousand years,
and to evangelise the world. Thereafter Satan is unloosed
and, at the head of the nations of the earth, wages an un-
successful warfare against the saints and is doomed, with his
dupes, to everlasting torment in the lake of fire and brimstone.
Finally come the general resurrection of all the dead and the
last judgment by God Himself, the destruction of death and
Hades, the consignment of the wicked to the lake of fire, and
the advent of the new heaven and earth.[41]

V. THE SYNOPTIC TRADITION

The Synoptic Gospels, so named from their common
presentation of the life and teaching of Jesus, are primarily
a record of the primitive tradition in which his deeds and his
sayings were preserved. All three Synoptists describe the
preaching of Jesus as the Gospel,[1] and though the term came to

---

[36] ii. 14, 20.   [37] i. 6 ; v. 10.   [38] xvii. 14.   [39] i. 6 ; v. 10.   [40] ii. 19.
[41] xx.-xxii. According to Charles, these chapters have been added by
an editor, from material collected by the writer, in a bungling fashion. As
a result, he has mixed up and dislocated the sequence of events. " Introduction," i. 50 f.
[1] Mark i. 15 ; Matt. iv. 23 ; Luke ix. 6.

13

be applied to their writings and to the teaching of the apostles,[2] it originally meant the message of Jesus as he delivered it in Galilee and elsewhere, and as the apostles imparted it in their mission preaching and in the instruction of their converts. It was their evident intention to relate what Jesus actually taught and did, as this was preserved in the primitive tradition, whether written or oral.

The Synoptic tradition represents the tendency to rivet the developing Christianity to the historic Jesus. It shows clearly that, in spite of the more speculative tendency to which Paul gave so marked an impulse, there existed a keen interest in the Jesus who lived and taught and suffered on earth. In this respect it is a counteractive to Paul's insistence on the spiritual Jesus in contrast to Jesus " after the flesh." The writers appear to have shared the more developed view of the Christ. But they did not share Paul's slight estimation of the earthly life of Jesus, whilst, like him, stressing his death, resurrection, and exaltation. A large part of their narratives is, in fact, concerned with these supreme events, and this feature shows that in the Gentile-Christian communities, to which they belonged, these events counted most. At the same time, the primitive tradition recounting the life and teaching of Jesus was accorded a far more important place in the thought of the community than appears from the Epistles of Paul. The early preaching of Peter, as recorded in the Acts, makes this clear enough. The Gospel of Jesus as well as the Gospel about Jesus was cherished as a precious inheritance. It is this Gospel that the Synoptists profess to hand down in written form, and to the interest of the community in it we owe the fact of its preservation.

This interest was religious rather than historical. The writers are not historians in the modern scientific sense. The tradition survived in the community because of its religious importance and value. It formed an essential part of the mission preaching of the apostles and of the instruction of converts, and in the meetings for worship and edification. It was put into written form as thus utilised, and the writers chose the historic incidents and the didactic sayings which had a special value for the life of the community. It is not history for its

[2] Paul, for instance, speaks of " my Gospel," Rom. ii. 16 ; xvi. 25.

own sake, but for its pragmatic utility that they record. They envisage the Gospel, to a certain extent, from the angle of its development in their own time, and have, more or less, left the imprint of this development on their narratives. An apologetic purpose lies also, to a certain extent, behind it. It is intended to vindicate Christian belief about Jesus from the objections of its Jewish opponents, to invalidate the offence of the Cross, to beget and confirm the conviction that the Messianic claim of Jesus is an assured fact, and that Christianity is the true development of Judaism and the God-appointed way of salvation. The didactic and apologetic element is indirectly discoverable in the narratives, and it appears explicitly in the preface to the third Gospel. Luke writes his Gospel not merely to furnish Theophilus with an accurate account of the tradition, but to confirm his confidence in the instruction which he has received from the teachers of the Church.[3]

Despite the pragmatic motive behind these Gospels, the writers have, on the whole, given a wonderfully realistic view of the person, life, and teaching of Jesus. The tradition which they narrate is substantially true to fact, if it has to be critically sifted.[4] Criticism has been busy with the work of sifting for a hundred years, and the more extreme critics between them have left very little of the narrative as authentic. Wellhausen, for instance, carved away portions of it very freely as later additions of the Christian community. Wrede rejected outright the Messianic portions as unhistoric. Recent adepts " in form history," as they call it, like Bultmann, have similarly excised very liberally. In the face of this extreme use of the critical pruning knife, one may well ask, Is there such a thing as the Synoptic tradition? Happily the evidence which the Synoptists furnish, when judicially examined, enables us to reply in an emphatic affirmative. Whilst didactic and apologetic elements are discernible, the negative tendency of the extreme critics has been vastly overdone. It is largely hypercritical, though it may, to a certain extent, be suggestive and stimulating. Subtracting the later and ulterior influence discernible on its transmission, the Synoptic tradition remains substantially

---

[3] Luke i. 4.
[4] See, in detail, my " Historic Jesus " (1931), and the recent concise work of Easton, " The Gospel Before the Gospels " (1929).

intact in its presentation of the life and teaching of Jesus. At all events, the writers have furnished us with the means of judging for ourselves.

It is a real human figure that acts and speaks in these Gospels. The birth stories seem to endanger its real humanity. A supernatural generation is incompatible with the full human life and suggests the demigod rather than the brother man. But these stories do not belong to the primitive tradition which, in the primitive preaching and in Mark, begins with the baptism by John. They are later apologetic additions to counteract Jewish calumny and strengthen the enhanced evaluation of the exalted Christ. In the primitive tradition, as recorded by Mark, the human Jesus is less idealised than in the later narratives of his fellow-evangelists, who appear more under the influence of later speculation or belief. In spite of this more marked influence, the human origin of Jesus appears in the course of the first and third Gospels as well as in Mark. In Mark, the oldest of the three and also the nearest to the actual Jesus, the human traits are very marked. Jesus gives full scope to the emotions of ordinary humanity. He adopts a stern tone towards the leper whom he heals.[5] He is angry with his Pharisaic opponents.[6] He gives vent to his indignation with the disciples for seeking to prevent the children being brought to him and shows his tenderness by taking them in his arms[7] human touches which Matthew and Luke omit.[8] Mark alone tells the very human story of his mother's and brethren's impression that he was beside himself, and their efforts to save him from himself, which the other two evangelists also ignore. At the same time, while omitting such traits, the human figure is otherwise also depicted in their narratives. All three show him taking part in the social life of the time as a man among men. He eats with publicans and sinners and does not practise fasting, to the chagrin of the scribes and Pharisees.[9] All three reveal the straining effect of his strenuous activity on mind and nerves, and the need for retirement to pray and seek strength and guidance in communion with God. This is especially noticeable in Luke, who, in emphasising his

[5] Mark i. 43.   [6] Ibid., iii. 5.   [7] Ibid., x. 16.
[8] Matt. xix. 13 f.; Luke xviii. 15 f.
[9] Mark ii. 13 f.; Matt. ix. 10 f.; Luke v. 29 f.

recourse to prayer, emphasises his dependence on God. From him, too, we learn more particularly of his interest in, and attraction for women.

On the other hand, he is no mere sentimentalist. He requires of his followers the utmost self-renunciation in the practice of the new righteousness, the demands of the ethical Law.[10] Even Luke outdoes Matthew in stressing not only the inexorable note of self-sacrifice which he demands in his followers,[11] but the inflexible sternness with which he pronounces doom on unrepentant sinners. " Except ye repent, ye shall all likewise perish." [12] A man of overpowering strength of character and conviction, who fearlessly encounters opposition and ultimately carries the conflict with his opponents to a life-and-death issue. In the later stage of his mission—on the way to Jerusalem and in Gethsemane—he wrestles with inexorable doom in obedience to the will of God, and never falters in his tragic determination to fulfil it. The figure of Jesus is thus that of a real man. He is no creation of the religious fantasy, a God, the object of a cult invested with an artificial history, as the mythologists would have us believe. A real personality is present throughout these narratives.

On the other hand, there is an element of strangeness, mystery in this personality, which strikes us as, in some respects, alien to our modern thought. Jesus moves in an apocalyptic atmosphere which we find really difficult to assimilate, and which does not really appeal to the Western mind. We would gladly eliminate it, in its literal sense at least, from the narrative, if it did not form so integral a part of it. Jewish Messianism, with its fantastic reading of the riddle of human destiny, the divine ordering of the universe, its crude philosophy of history, is an encumbrance, not an enrichment of the Gospel. It is there, however, and if Jesus largely spiritualised it, he retained the catastrophic intervention in the near future, the supernatural transformation from the old order to the new. He is, in this respect, an otherworldly figure ; human, indeed, but obsessed with this otherworldly train of thought. He is Messiah as well as man, the man whom God has chosen and commissioned to inaugurate His reign in a new order of things. This conception, though

[10] Matt. v. 21 f.   [11] Luke xiv. 26 f.   [12] *Ibid.*, xiii. 5.

natural to a Jew, is alien to us, and the Jesus who embodied it is, and cannot but be, somewhat of an enigma. We might explain away the apocalyptic element in his teaching, or eliminate it, as some have attempted to do. But this would be to do violence to the record, of which the apocalyptic element is an essential. All three evangelists represent him as the Messiah, and it may, I think, be taken as certain that he did regard himself as invested with a Messianic function and mission. The keynote of Mark's Gospel is his Messianic Sonship.[13] Matthew with his Jewish predilections, emphasises, in addition, his descent from David, and there is no convincing reason to question this descent, though Jesus himself does not seem to have attached undue importance to it, and the first evangelist, as a member of the Gentile Church does not, ultimately at least, regard the Messiah in the narrow national sense. For the Gentile Luke the Messiah is from the outset the universal Saviour.

According to all three, the consciousness of his Messianic vocation came to him at his baptism. Such an illumination at a time of tense religious feeling—the prophetic preaching of the Baptist—is psychologically explicable, and scepticism as to the historicity of the incident is unwarranted. Jesus most probably did not forsee all that this vocation implied. He had attained the conviction that God had chosen him as the instrument in bringing to pass His rule or kingdom on earth. What this ultimately involved—a cross, not a crown—he does not seem to have divined. This revelation came only with the march of events. Mark has a theory which his fellow-evangelists adopt—that at first Jesus kept his Messiahship a secret, which only the demons, assumed to be gifted with supernatural insight, knew. He is generally recognised as a new prophet and adopts the prophetic rôle in preparing the people for the ultimate development. Mark's theory may be a later apologetic, intended to show the blindness of the Jews in failing to recognise the Messiah. At the same time, such demoniacs may, in their deranged fashion, and under the influence of the Messianic excitement of the time, have seen in Jesus the embodiment of their own fantasy. In any case, it was obviously advisable to discourage the danger of a popular

[13] Mark i. 1.

commotion, which a premature announcement of his vocation might easily provoke. Hence the prominence of the preparatory prophetic mission in the Synoptists. It was only the growing antagonism of the religious leaders, who, in contrast to the people, adopted a critical and, erelong, a hostile attitude, that convinced Jesus that his Messianic vocation must erelong lead to the Cross. Then it was that, in the face of the deadly antagonism of the legalists—the local scribes and Pharisees and the representatives of the religious authorities at Jerusalem —it became clear that this vocation was that of the Suffering Servant of Isaiah liii.[14] Then, too, that the conception of the Son of Man, hitherto only vaguely mentioned, came into the foreground of his consciousness. The combination of these two conceptions—Suffering Servant, Son of Man—is the ultimate evolution of Jesus' thought of his Messianic vocation and function. He foresees his death. But he believes in his resurrection and exaltation and his future destiny as Son of Man ; the speedy return to judge the world and establish the final reign of God in the new order or age. He believes, too, that his sacrifice will effect the deliverance or redemption from sin which the Messianic idea connotes, and gives his life a ransom for many.

All this, say the extreme critics, is merely a reading of history after the event. It is the reflection of the apologetic explanation of the death of Jesus, the offence of the Cross, and the failure of his mission, which we have seen in the primitive and Pauline preaching. Surely a hazardous, suppositious handling of history. Instead of being a later invention, this record of the later stage of Jesus' conception of his Messianic vocation and function seems to me to be in accordance with the actual situation. Making allowance for later colouring, this development alone explains the heroic persistence and self-sacrifice that carried Jesus onwards to his doom. Only one who was inspired by the apocalyptic conviction reflected in this record could have faced this doom, and only one who really held himself to be the divinely commissioned Son of Man, as he declared to the High Priest, could have incurred the charge of blasphemy and determined his enemies to destroy him. His belief in the resurrection he shared with his Pharisaic

[14] Mark viii. 31 f. ; ix. 12 and parallels.

opponents, and this belief is, therefore, no anachronism. It, too, is necessary to explain the conviction that death was but the transmutation to a higher life. To him whose mind was steeped in the prophecy of Israel's vicarious suffering, it was assuredly no impossible conception that his vicarious sacrifice was essential for the realisation of God's plan and purpose in the redemption of man.

In the Synoptic record Jesus is the Son of God in the filial as well as the Messianic sense. His vocation as Messiah came to him, we may fairly assume, through his profound sense of his filial relation to the Father-God. In all three Synoptics this Sonship appears,[15] and in a distinctive utterance, preserved by Matthew and Luke,[16] it finds special expression. In this utterance Jesus claims to be the revealer of the Father in contrast to " the wise and understanding "—the Rabbis of his day. In the Gospel of Jesus the Fatherhood is a distinctive theme, and he claims to know and make known the Father in a deeper and more personal sense than in the current Rabbinic teaching. It is the outflow of his own spiritual experience, not of the current scholastic theology. His personal Sonship is a fact of experience, learned in profound communion with the Father-God, and, in a less degree, Sonship is predicable of all His children, who are also sons of God. His special relation as Son is, however, not that of the Logos-Christ of the Fourth Gospel. The language of these passages reminds, indeed, of the Fourth Gospel, and the more conservative critics see in them an anticipation of the Johannine conception of the Son of God, the germ of the more developed conception elaborated in this Gospel. Others find in them a reflection backwards into the Synoptic narrative of the Johannine conception. Neither contention, it seems to me, is necessarily involved in this saying. The Jesus of the Synoptists is untouched by philosophy. The Synoptic tendency is rather to show Jesus in the light of Old Testament prophecy than of Hellenist philosophy, as in the Fourth Gospel. In the Synoptics his Sonship does not involve pre-existence. It

[15] Mark viii. 38 ; xiii. 32 and parallels. On this subject, in more detail, see my " Historic Jesus " ; Harnack, " The Sayings of Jesus," 245 f. ; Moffatt, " Theology of the Gospels," 130 f. (1912).
[16] Matt. xi. 25 f. ; Luke x. 21 f.

does not express oneness with the Father in the Johannine sense. There is no pre-existence in the record, though it might be in the minds of the writers of it. Even the birth stories of the first and third evangelists, though meant to enhance his supernatural being, bring him into existence in time and know nothing of an eternal origin in God. He appropriates the Son of Man title, and in Jewish Apocalyptic (" Book of Enoch ") this Messianic title is that of a pre-existent being. But this does not necessarily imply a belief in his previous existence. As used by Jesus, the title points forwards, not backwards, though ultimately, under the influence of Paul, the Christian community interpreted it in a pre-existent sense. But the community did not attempt to intrude it into the primitive tradition. Had it done so the Synoptists would assuredly have revealed the intrusion. Instead, the tradition as reported by Mark, who is copied by Luke, pointedly rebuts any assumption of a timeless existence in union with God. " Why callest thou me good ? None is good save one, even God," [17] which Matthew significantly modifies to " Why askest thou me concerning the good ; one there is who is good." [18]

All three evangelists depict the power of Jesus to work miracles. The healing ministry is a succession of miracles, and Jesus is besides invested with a supernatural power over nature. He can not only heal a variety of bodily ailments. He can raise the dead, still a storm by a word, multiply loaves and fishes indefinitely, walk on the water. This is in keeping with his vocation as a prophet and as the Messianic Son of God, and the intention of the writers evidently is to convey to their readers the impression of a sovereign command over natural law, exercised by Jesus as an essential of his Messianic vocation. Not only his superior authority as a Teacher to that of the Rabbis, but his unique power to counteract by his healing ministry the demoniac effects of evil, the régime of Satan, and dominate nature is emphasised throughout. In their striving to deepen the impression of the story on their readers, the writers tend to overcolour the picture of his supernatural mission. At the same time, they have so depicted the mission that they enable us to control their own impression

[17] Mark x. 18.   [18] Matt. xxi. 17.

and the impression they seek to impart. The primitive tradition is there to speak for itself. From what it tells us, we can see that the cures effected by Jesus are the result of psychotherapy, in which the faith and insight of the healer and the faith of the patient contribute to the result. Modern medical science has no difficulty in accepting the recorded cases as examples of the effect of spiritual power over bodily disease.[19] From the primitive tradition we further learn that his power as a healer is ascribed to the Spirit of God acting through him and using the appropriate means, spiritual and material. If, as indirectly appears, the writers regard these and other " mighty works " (δυνάμεις) as signs of Jesus' supernatural power, their narratives prove conclusively that Jesus did these works not to prove his divinity, as explicitly in the Fourth Gospel, but from an intense sympathy with the sufferers. To heal disease and alleviate human suffering is an integral part of his mission. It is an attack on the kingdom of Satan in preparation for the kingdom of God. He positively refused to grant the Pharisees the signs they demanded, and in doing so he gave vent to his impatience of this miracle-mongering craze. " He groaned in spirit," we read in Mark,[20] over such demands as evidence of the lack of true religious insight and understanding.

Unfortunately this lack is apparent in the later Christian community as well as among the Pharisees. Hence the accretion of tales of the marvellous, of works of a magical character. Such tales intruded themselves into the tradition, as the result of the inventive imagination working on incidents which it magnifies into miracles. This tendency is observable in the first and third evangelists who attempt to heighten the miraculous power of Jesus as depicted by Mark,[21] as well as to tone down or minimise the human element in Jesus.

---

[19] On this and other aspects of the miraculous element in the Synoptic narratives, see the chapter on " The Healer " in my " Historic Jesus."

[20] Mark viii. 12, ἀναστενάξας τῷ πνεύματι αὐτοῦ.

[21] Cf. Mark i. 32 f. with Matt. viii. 16, Luke iv. 40, for instance ; or, Mark vi. 5-6, describing the failure at Nazareth, " He could do no mighty works there," because of their unbelief, which Matt. xiv. 58 modifies to " not many mighty works." In the account of the Gerasene miracle in Mark v. 19, Jesus ascribes it to the Lord (God). Matthew omits the saying. He omits, too, Jesus' lack of knowledge in the case of the cure of the woman with an issue of blood, Mark v. 30 f. ; Matt. viii. 45 f.

Matthew, in particular, shows a predilection for this legendary matter, as in the account of the walking on the water, which, in contrast to Mark, he regards as a sign of his divinity and, in consequence, makes the disciples worship him as the Son of God.[22]

Equally noticeable is the attempt to handle the primitive tradition in the light of prophecy. The apologetic appeal to prophecy already, as we have seen, appears in the primitive preaching in proof of the thesis that Jesus must needs suffer, and that his life, death, resurrection, and exaltation are in accordance with the divine will as revealed by the prophets. It was further developed in the early Church as a proof that Christianity is the divinely ordained consummation of Judaism, the culmination of God's redemptive plan in Christ. It was read into the primitive tradition and colours the Synoptic record, especially in its Matthæan form, which systematically attempts to show that the acts and words of Jesus, from beginning to end, are the fulfilment of prophecy. It is also markedly present in Luke's concluding chapter and in certain passages in Mark, repeated by his fellow-evangelists. In these Jesus himself appeals to the prophets in confirmation of his Messianic claim and in explanation of the tragic trend of events. There is no reason to question the fact that Jesus did find in prophecy guidance and strength in carrying out his mission.[23] It may be taken as certain that he applied to himself the prophetic conception of the Suffering Servant and the Son of Man, which he adapted in a personal sense.

The appeal to prophecy is thus an integral part of the primitive tradition. It goes back to the example of Jesus himself. At the same time the tendency of the Synoptists to view present events in the light of the past is undoubtedly largely a later accretion. We may be certain that Jesus did not speak in parables in order to mystify rather than enlighten

[22] Matt. xiv. 27 f.

[23] Mark gives four of these appeals, which he makes in the closing period of his life (xii. 10 = Ps. cxviii. 22 f.; xii. 36 = Ps. cx. 1; xiv. 27 = Zech. xiii. 7; xiv. 62 = Dan. vii. 13), and there is one indirect reference by Jesus to Isa. liii. as the suffering Messiah (ix. 12). Mark xii. 10 is regarded by the critics as a later apologetic intrusion. The others are reasonably assignable to Jesus himself. The four are also given by Matthew, and two of them by Luke. Luke (xxii. 37) gives a direct quotation from Isa. liii. by Jesus as about to be fulfilled in his death.

his hearers, as the evangelists assert in a prophetic saying ascribed to him in the early period of the ministry.[24] This is evidently a reflection of later apologetic to explain why the Jews refused to accept the Messiah and his teaching. The same apologetic aim is observable in Luke's account of Jesus' exposition of prophecy to the two disciples on the way to Emmaus.[25] In this respect the Synoptic Gospel is a Gospel adapted to the times, and whether we accept its elaborate application of prophecy to Jesus as historically justifiable or not, it is plain enough that it did not bulk in Jesus' own teaching to the extent that it appears in the First and Second Gospels. The appeal is undoubtedly traceable to him and, once made, it was apt to lead to a systematic attempt to elaborate it for apologetic purposes. It gave ample room for the play of fancy as well as argument, as we see in the lavish use of it by Matthew and by Luke at the close of his Gospel. Unlike them, Mark was content to keep more closely to the primitive tradition.

The universalist note appears in all three Synoptics, and here again the critics have seen a modification of the primitive tradition under Pauline influence. This raises the question whether Jesus was a particularist or a universalist ? It seems to me that the tradition shows that he was both, whilst Matthew and Luke, and, less directly, Mark, tended to impute the later universalism of the Gentile Church to him. This note and this tendency are least observable in Mark. He knows only of one, or possibly two instances in which Jesus directly extends his healing mission to Gentiles—in the case of the Syro-Phœnician woman and, if the Gerasene maniac was a Gentile, in his case also. Even to the Syro-Phœnician woman Jesus emphasises his exclusive mission to the Jews.[26] Unlike Luke, he and Matthew do not take Jesus into Samaria in the course of his progress southwards to Jerusalem. At the close of the mission—in the episodes of the anointing at Bethany, and the cleansing of the temple, and in the apocalyptic discourse— he appears frankly universalist. " Wheresoever this Gospel shall be preached throughout the whole world." [27] " My

[24] Mark iv. 11-12 ; Matt. xiii. 13 f. ; Luke viii. 10.   [25] Luke xxiv. 25 f.
[26] Mark vii. 27. The word " first " (" Let the children first be filled ") may seem to imply the ultimate Gentile mission. But the granting of the request of the woman is treated in verse 29 as an exception.
[27] Mark xiv. 9.

house shall be called a house of prayer for all nations." [28]
" The Gospel must first be preached to all nations." [29] The
first and third passages look like a later reflection of the Gentile
mission, and as the apocalyptic discourse bears marks of later
manipulation even in Mark, the third saying, at all events, is
somewhat doubtful. It is significantly absent from Luke,
who would certainly have included it had he found it in his
version. Apart from these closing sayings, the primitive
tradition in Mark is generally non-universalist. But it may
well be that the lack of the larger spirit in the sayings recorded
by the other two evangelists, at an early stage of the mission,
is due to the writer's concentration on the deeds rather than
the sayings of Jesus.

In Matthew universalism alternates with exclusiveness,
till at the conclusion of the Gospel he, like Mark, becomes
wholly universalist. In addition to the Syro-Phœnician episode,
he gives that of the centurion, to whose request for help Jesus
instantly responds, and whose faith he emphasises as the
great thing, apart from race or privilege. In the teaching,
of which Matthew gives large blocks, both features appear.
On the one hand, the Twelve are to confine their mission to
the lost sheep of the house of Israel. They are not to go in
the way of the Gentiles, or into any Samaritan city.[30] On
the other, in connection with the centurion episode, Jesus
fervently accentuates the inclusion of the Gentiles in the
kingdom and the casting forth of the Jews, and at the conclusion
of the parable of the vineyard unconditionally proclaims that
the kingdom of God shall be taken away from them and given
to another nation.[31] In Matthew, accordingly, we see the
note of exclusion gradually disappearing as the mission pro-
gresses, and the larger universal spirit and outlook taking its
place. This is probably true to the actual development which
the antagonism of the representatives of Jewish legalism and
exclusion tended to beget in the mind of Jesus. One who
emphasised the Fatherhood of God and sought to spiritualise

---

[28] Mark xi. 17, a quotation from Isa. lvi. 7.   [29] Ibid., xiii. 10.
[30] Matt. x. 6.
[31] Ibid., xxi. 43. He brings the wise men of the East to do homage
to the newborn Saviour King, though this is only an indication of the
universalism of the writer, not of the mind of Jesus himself. The same
is the case with the reference to the Gentiles in iv. 14 and xi. 21.

the current Judaism could hardly have conceived of his
Messianic vocation in the exclusive, as he certainly did not in
the Jewish nationalist sense. At the same time, the writer of
the First Gospel, who also gives the three late universalist
sayings in Mark, appears in the post-resurrection command, to
teach and baptise all nations,[32] to be ascribing to the risen
Christ an utterance that expresses the mind of the Gentile
Church rather than the actual injunction of Jesus. Though
a Jewish Christian, he belongs to the universal Church and
makes no secret of his universalism in bringing, in the birth
story, the wise men of the East to do homage to the Saviour
King of the Jews. Similarly, in the case of the reference to
the Gentiles in iv. 14 and x. 18, in which the Gospel is to be
offered to the Gentiles as well as the Jews.

In contrast to both Mark and Matthew, Luke is consistently
universalist. He not only, like Matthew, introduces his own
universalism into the birth story ; not only preserves the story
of the centurion, whilst significantly omitting the Syro-
Phœnician incident and certain narrow-minded sayings recorded
by Matthew, such as vii. 6 and x. 5-6. He has a predilection
for the teaching in which the universalist note predominates.
He makes Jesus extend his mission to the Samaritans [33] and heal
a Samaritan leper.[34] Jesus chooses a Samaritan, in contrast
to a priest and a Levite, as an illustration of the supreme law
of love.[35] Similarly, in the discourse at Nazareth, Jesus reminds
his Jewish opponents of the mission of Elijah and Elisha to
non-Jews.[36] In the parable of the prodigal it is the lost son
that is the object of the father's joy, to the chagrin of the
elder.[37] In that of the great supper it is parabolically the
Gentile outcasts that take the seats which the invited guests
have declined to occupy. Like Matthew, he closes with a
reference to the mission to all nations. But, unlike him, the
reference is consistent with the universal note which runs
through his account of the life and teaching of the Master.
As a Gentile he has doubtless seen in Jesus the anticipator
of Paul, the apostle of the Gentiles. Substantially, his interpretation of the spirit of Jesus was justified by the larger

[32] Matt. xxviii. 19.
[33] Luke ix. 53 f.
[34] Ibid., xvii. 17.
[35] Ibid., x. 33.
[36] Ibid., iv. 24.
[37] Ibid., xv. 11 f.

outlook which the Third Gospel reveals in the friend of publicans and sinners.

The critics have found in Mark as well as Luke a large intrusion of Pauline teaching into the primitive tradition. From Cæsarea Philippi onwards the story of the suffering Messiah is a reflection of the beliefs of the later community, as influenced especially by Paul. Though, according to later tradition (Papias), Mark was the mouthpiece of Peter's reminiscences, he was doubtless an adherent of Pauline Christianity. We have a strong hint of this in vii. 20, " This he said making all meats clean," which echoes Paul's teaching in 1 Cor. viii. and x. Similarly, the description of Jewish legalism in chapter vii. may be overcoloured in the interest of the later conflict between the Church and the Jews, and the parabolic theory of iv. 10 f. points in the direction of Paul's hardening of the heart of Israel. But such Pauline touches are only incidental and do not warrant the rash contention that Mark and, with him, the other two Synoptists, who largely copy his narrative, is virtually writing the history of Jesus in the light of Paulinism. It is certainly an exaggeration to maintain that his Gospel " in its whole structure employs Petrine material in the interest of a Pauline Gospel," and that " the whole conception and object of the Gospel of Mark is Pauline." [38] There is no reason to suppose, for instance, that the conflict of Jesus with the legalists is not faithfully depicted and that it is influenced by that of Paul with the Judaisers. Equally far-fetched to see in the Markan depreciation of the Twelve, especially Peter, a veiled apologia for that of Paul towards the other apostles. Nor does a mere resemblance in the Markan terminology of certain of Jesus' sayings to that of Paul necessarily betoken Pauline influence. " The mystery of the kingdom " is hardly a reflection backwards of Pauline mysticism and the mystery religions. What " mystery " meant to Jesus—his apocalyptic secret—is not what it meant to Paul. In view of the difference between Jesus' world of

[38] Bacon, " Jesus and Paul," 143-144. Among English-speaking critics Bacon has persistently maintained this extensive Pauline influence on the Second Gospel. See also his " Gospel of Mark," 242 f. (1925). On the other side, see Wernle, " Die Synoptische Frage," 199 f.; Menzies, " The Earliest Gospel," 39; Moffatt, " Theology of the Gospels," 22 f.; Werner, " Der Einfluss Paulinischer Theologie im Markus-Evangelium " (1923).

thought and that of Paul, the identity is by no means apparent. Nor has the term " ransom " on the lips of Jesus the developed meaning which Paul puts into it. The conception of vicarious suffering which it implies for Jesus is not that of an expiatory sacrifice as propounded by Paul. That the Son of Man in the second part of the Markan record thinks and speaks in terms of Paul is a pure assumption. As I have noted, Jesus thinks and speaks in accordance with the historical situation, which had burned into his soul the tragic outlook and convictions of which the record tells. Presupposing this situation and the Messianic consciousness of Jesus—presuppositions which are substantially true to fact—the figure of the Son of Man in this record is not a fictitious figure, invented by the Church and depicted by the writer under this influence. The impression made by the narrative is not that of fiction, but of the grim reality which unfolds itself in this story, even if there is some *post-eventum* colouring in it.

Nor is the emphasis of Jesus on the resurrection necessarily a Pauline product. That Jesus held fast to the belief in a resurrection appears in his controversy with the Sadducees, which there is no adequate reason to question. That it should appear in the later stage of the narrative is in the highest degree probable. Only as Jesus clung to the conviction of a life beyond the grave and to a higher destiny, could he have continued steadfast in his resolution to die for the kingdom of God. And only as the disciples, in turn, grasped the fact of the resurrection, as the result of the appearances of the risen Jesus to them, is it possible to explain the triumphant revival of their faith in him and the rise of Christianity. The only question is whether the bodily resurrection, of which all three narratives tell, is historic. The primitive evidence as related by Paul, which knows only of the appearances of the risen Jesus and the spiritual body, tends to show that the story of the empty tomb is a later apologetic addition. Further, the belief in the coming again is cogently ascribable to Jesus himself, and is not an afterthought of the community. The early community did not invent it. It took it over from Jesus, of whose faith there is the strongest reason for inferring that it formed an integral part. Why, we may ask in conclusion, if the inventive tendency was so active in modifying the tradition, did not

Mark and his fellow-evangelists intrude into it Paul's view of the pre-existent Christ ? In these writers it is the adoptionist view of the Messiah—the Jesus who at his baptism becomes conscious of his vocation as the Beloved Son—that comes on the stage and occupies the stage to the end. His exaltation to a higher destiny lies in the future. It does not begin, as in Paul, in eternity. The tendency to read into the text, or between its lines, one assumption after another thus reveals, it seems to me, the inventive fancy, rather than the historic sense of the extreme critic.

The traces of Pauline influence are naturally evident in the companion and fellow-worker of Paul, though it is remarkable how comparatively little of this influence there is even in the Third Gospel. Luke incorporates a large part of Mark's narrative without materially modifying it. At the same time his frank universalism is stamped on his Gospel. He has borrowed from Paul in his account of the institution of the Eucharist. The parable of the Pharisee and the publican is Pauline in spirit, and there is an echo of his cardinal doctrine in " the justification " of the sinner. God's grace and love, if also his retributive righteousness, shimmers throughout the Gospel. " The tone of the Gospel is Pauline," rightly says Plummer, " It exhibits the liberal and spiritual nature of Christianity. It advocates faith and repentance apart from the works of the Law, and tells abundantly of God's grace and mercy, and the work of the Holy Spirit." [39]

In Matthew, on the other hand, there is an apparent reaction from Paul, or at all events from the extreme anti-legal tendency under his influence. The writer is a Jewish Christian of the Diaspora who has retained his love for the Law, if not for Jewish legalism as represented by the scribes and Pharisees, whom he denounces more liberally than his fellow-evangelists. He accepts wholeheartedly Jesus' liberal and critical attitude towards this legalism. Unlike Paul, and, it would seem, in antagonism to Paulinism, he emphasises the passages in Jesus' teaching which assert the permanence of the ethical Law as

---

[39] Introduction to " Commentary on Luke," 43. Vincent Taylor, on the other hand, too hastily (following Harnack ("Luke, the Physician," 142 f.)) concludes that " there is no Paulinism in Luke," " The Gospels," 80 (1930). Harnack does admit that in a sense he was a Paulinist.

a revelation of God's will. " Think not that I came to destroy the law or the prophets. I came not to destroy, but to fulfil. For verily I say unto you, Till heaven and earth pass away one jot or one tittle shall in no wise pass away from the law till all things be accomplished." [40] The following verse, 19, " Whosoever, therefore, shall break one of these least commandments," seems not to be in accord with the liberal attitude of Jesus towards the ceremonial law, and it, as well as 17 and 18, is rejected by a number of critics as a later addition. Similarly, the saying about the Pharisees sitting in Moses' seat, and the obligation to observe their teaching,[41] is a flat contradiction of the rest of the chapter, which bitterly denounces them, and is still more questionable. The writer is what Bacon calls a neo-legalist,[42] who seems to react from Paul, and to emphasise Christianity as a new Law. Jesus is the giver of a new Law for the practical Christian life, the teacher of a new righteousness applicable to the kingdom of God, which he is seeking to prepare and to found. It is the Law as interpreted by Jesus, not the Law as expounded and practised by the Scribes, that he strives to uphold. This Law is for him the norm of the Christian life, and in this respect he represents a more organic connection with the teaching of Jesus than in the case of Paul. With Paul's reasoning on the nullity of the Law, and its incompatibility with the new dispensation of faith and grace, the writer apparently did not sympathise. He maintains the attitude of Jesus, not of Paul, and he makes Jesus pointedly denounce the workers of " lawlessness." [43]

On the other hand, he is strongly anti-Jewish, the antagonist of the Jews of his time, who reject Christ and take their stand on the old Judaism. On them Jesus pronounces stern judgment for their rejection of his claims and his teaching,[44] and casts them forth from the kingdom.[45] The kingdom shall be taken from them and given to another.[46] The Gentile Church, as founded by Jesus, is the inheritor of the Jewish Church. It is the embodiment of the kingdom of God that has displaced the

[40] Matt. v. 17-18. Luke has only the saying about the tittle, xvi. 17.
[41] Matt. xxiii. 2 f.
[42] " Jesus and Paul," 2.
[43] ἀνομία, vii. 23 ; xiii. 41.
[44] Matt. xi. 20.
[45] Ibid., viii. 12.
[46] Ibid., xxi. 43.

old. The Law and the prophets were until John, the herald of a new dispensation, which began with the Gospel of the kingdom.[47] The author is strongly influenced by the growing ecclesiastical spirit of the late first century. He explicitly makes Jesus the founder of the Church as it had developed in the writer's day, and stresses the leadership of Peter, on whom Jesus confers the keys,[48] with the power to loose and bind, while at the same time conferring it on all the disciples and recognising the corporate authority of the Church.[49] The ascription to Peter of this distinctive authority, which is nevertheless limited by the autonomy of the community, seems a later addition in the interest of a Petrine party. Such a party undoubtedly already existed in Paul's lifetime, in opposition to his masterful spirit and his claim to independence of all apostolic authority. Whilst joining his fellow-evangelists in relating the institution of the Eucharist, he alone ascribes baptism to the institution of the risen Christ. The addition of the triune formula, as part of this rite, clearly proves that in so doing he was guilty of a glaring anachronism. In common with Mark and Luke, he reads back into the message of the Baptist the primitive Christian baptism with the Spirit. Similarly, the lengthy discourse in which Jesus sends out the Twelve, contains passages [50] which are palpably a reflection of the later Gentile mission.

In all three evangelists the main interest is in the acts and teaching of the historic Jesus, as the norm of Christian faith and life. The writers seek to relate the faith and life of the believer to the real source of both. They aim at depicting the Gospel in its pristine form and thus bringing their readers into contact with the Master, as he lived and taught and suffered on earth. This Gospel might be made to fit, in their minds, with the later modification of it crystallising in the Church at large. But it might also represent a less mystic and individual, a more concrete type than that specifically represented by Paul and some of his successors. These narratives are a striking evidence of the keen interest in the

---

[47] Matt. xi. 13 ; Luke xvi. 16, who amplifies.
[48] Matt. xvi. 19.
[49] *Ibid.*, xviii. 15 f.
[50] *Ibid.*, x. 17 f.

earthly Jesus on the part of many believers,[51] whose faith was centred in him rather than in the Christ of Paul. They seem to reflect a simpler and distinctive type, which is also observable in the Acts of the Apostles, the Epistle of James, and in the Apostles' Creed, and is distinguishable from that of Paul, the Epistle to the Hebrews, and the Johannine Writings, which culminated in the Nicene and later creeds. Back to the Source —to fact in contrast to speculation—might be, to a considerable extent, their motto. Making allowance for the later subjectivism of the writers, which they undoubtedly reveal, they possess the inestimable merit of portraying for us Jesus as he was in the flesh, in contrast to the Pauline and the Johannine representation of him. They thus enable us the better to estimate the development that had taken place in the long interval between the actual mission of Jesus and the period of their final composition, late in the second half of the first century. They are a needful caveat against the tendency, still too dominant among theologians, to read the Synoptic Gospels, in the light of the Fourth, to regard the later views of the fourth evangelist about Jesus as merely a fuller expression of certain ideas imperfectly expressed in the first three. There is a more substantial difference than this between the two presentations, and from the historic point of view it is very hazardous to conclude, in this fashion, that the Jesus of the Synoptics is substantially the Logos-Christ of the Fourth. The broad fact is that the latter is largely abstract and subjective ; the former largely concrete and actual. Whether the Christ of this later faith is identical with the Christ of actual history depends on the validity we assign to this faith as a guarantee of historic reality. For the historian, at least, there is a real difference. Can we, with complete assurance that we are in accord with this reality, as the early record embodies it, thus evade the difficulty, on the assumption that historically the one is as factual as the other ? The religious conceptions of, say, A.D. 100 are

[51] Prof. Burkitt concludes from his study of the early tradition, as represented by Mark, that " the interest of the nascent Church was not in the least directed towards the past." " Gospel History and its Transmission," 264. Cf. " Earliest Sources for the Life of Jesus." Professor Creed forcibly opposes this contention in an article in The Expositor, 1922. J. Weiss also emphasises the interest of the early Church in Jesus' life as reflected in Mark, " Urchristenthum," 544.

hardly an infallible standard for the facts of, say, the years 28-29, especially with the simpler, and what is, on the whole, the authentic record of these facts before us.

It is said that the simpler tradition of Jesus, as contained in this record, was in danger of eventuating in a barren belief, compared with the richer and fuller faith of the developing Church. Less mystic and theological the belief might be, but it seems a strange perversion of fact that can posit of this simpler tradition such an eventuality. Nobody can read these simpler narratives of the actual Jesus with a receptive mind and not experience the fascination and the power of them. They do indeed suggest puzzling problems, but not by a long way to the same extent as the more abstract figure and teaching of the Fourth Gospel, with its enigmatic historic setting, which, for many, hamper rather than strengthen its appeal as a Gospel. The Sermon on the Mount, for instance, grips and thrills where the theological discourses of the Fourth Evangelist only mystify and perplex. For the moral and spiritual life there is no barren belief in these simpler Gospels, but a perennial power, which brings us into actual touch with a unique personality and displays to us this personality as a historic reality. This reality Christianity cannot afford to ignore, unless we are content to substitute for it a mere noumenology without concrete foundation. Paul and the Johannine writer may have contributed to enrich the Gospel in their own subjective fashion, but their contribution should not be allowed to overshadow, much less to displace, in theological thought, the perennial message of their Master and ours. From this point of view there is some force in von Hofmann's dictum, " Paul has had his day ; it is time the Gospels had theirs." [52]

VI. The Johannine Gospel—The Incarnate Word

The Fourth Gospel and the First Epistle of John, which were apparently written by the same person,[1] reveal the influence

---

[52] Quoted by Somerville, " St Paul's Conception of Christ," 257.

[1] On the question of the identical authorship of the Gospel and the Epistle, see Brooke, " The Johannine Epistles, International Critical Commentary," 1912. As the result of a detailed and judicial discussion, he concludes in favour of the identical authorship. See also Windisch, " Die Katholischen Briefe, Handbuch zum N.T.," iv. 2 (1911). He concludes that the identity is probable, 125.

of Pauline thought. But, like the Epistle to the Hebrews, and in a more formative degree, they have distinctive features which not only reflect the developing thought of the Church of the end of the first century, but contributed to this development out of a meditative and mystic mind. To understand this contribution we must take into account the culture, temperament, and religious experience of the writer, the age in which he lived, the stage of development which Christianity had reached, the particular problems which confronted it. Who the writer was is one of those debatable questions which has long divided the critics. Some still think that he was the Apostle John, whom they identify with the beloved disciple, who figures in the second half of the book, and they accept the Gospel as substantially an accurate presentation of the historic Jesus, though perhaps coloured, to some extent, by later reflection. Others think of a disciple of the apostle, who wrote down and elaborated what he had learned from him, and whom they identify with John the Elder, mentioned by Papias.[2] Others regard it as the product of an unknown genius, not necessarily connected with the apostle, of the early Catholic Church, who gave expression to his ideas under the form of a history. Some are inclined to see in it the product of a school rather than of an individual. Personally, I should say that the author was not an immediate follower of Jesus, as we know his disciples in the Synoptic Gospels. The Gospel is evidently an end of the century production, and the later testimony to the longevity of the apostle and the ascription to him of the Gospel are open to serious objection. The most likely supposition is that it is the work of John the Elder, who was not necessarily a disciple of the apostle, and who made use of a source, or sources, in addition to the Synoptic Gospels, whilst imparting to the book his own thought and style. He seems to have been a Jew of the Diaspora who had an intimate knowledge of Palestine and of Hebrew religious thought and customs.[3]

[2] Eusebius, " Hist. Eccl.," III. xxxix. 4.
[3] On the Gospel and its distinctive place in early Christian thought, see my " Historic Jesus," with references to recent literature. A cogent statement in favour of the authorship of the Elder will be found in Charles' Introduction to his " Commentary on Revelation," 29 f. (1920). For the recent discussion of problems of " Introduction," see also Bernard's

He unreservedly accepted Christianity, as he understood it, as the absolute truth, and he impressed on it the stamp of a meditative mind, responsive in a high degree to the culture influence of his time, and of a mystic religious experience. He plainly lived in an age in which Christianity has become a Gentile religion, and has left the controversy with the Jewish-Christian party of Paul's time far behind. The controversy is now with the non-Christian Jews, who are its embittered and active opponents and defamers, and with whom accommodation is absolutely impossible. These Jews, for instance, deny the divinity of Christ as incompatible with Jewish monotheism. They strenuously object to the claim made, in the writer's time, of the equality of Jesus with God. They reject as an absurdity the doctrine of the Eucharist as the eating of the flesh and the drinking of the blood of the Son of God in the growingly crude sense. They resent the ignoring of Jewish racial feeling and privileges in a religion which is now predominantly Gentile, and has entirely emancipated itself from Judaism. A Gnostic tendency which denied the real humanity of the Christ and made him an emanation from God, has, moreover, been developing within the Church since the days of Paul. Christianity, which has become a separate religion from Judaism in the view of the state, is also exposed to the active opposition of a hostile world, and the enthusiastic faith of the earlier time, with its spontaneous inspiration and its tense belief in the speedy coming of Christ, has been dulled by age. It stands in need of an apologetic and a reinterpretation for the times in order to vindicate it against Jewish attack, guard it against error, and commend it to the Greek mind. The Church, as an institution, with its developing organisation, its sacramental rites, and its deposit of truth also needs to be confirmed in the faith against the doubt and perplexity of its members in the face of Jewish attack, false teaching, and the anxiety caused by hope deferred.

The object of the writer is to give a version of the Gospel which shall meet the exigencies of this complex situation. His

" Commentary " (1928) and MacGregor's (1929). A convenient summary is given by V. Taylor, " The Gospels " (1930), and a more elaborate one by Howard, " The Fourth Gospel in Recent Criticism and Interpretation " (1931). I have found E. F. Scott's exposition of the thought of the writer (" The Fourth Gospel," 1906) specially helpful.

method, in the Gospel, is the appeal to history—to the life and teaching of Jesus himself. Unlike Paul, he is not content with the appeal to his experience of Christ, though this experience forms a cardinal part of his work. He writes a life of Christ, which for Paul was a secondary matter. It is, however, not a life in the more factual manner of the Synoptic writers. It is professedly written with the intention of proving a thesis and with a purely religious purpose. " These (signs) are written that ye may believe that Jesus is the Christ, the Son of God, and that believing ye may have life in his name." [4] It is at once apologetic and propaganda. He has confessedly selected his material with this object in view—with a view, particularly, to the needs of those for whom he writes. Christianity has become a universal, pronouncedly Greek religion. It is surveyed from the Greek standpoint, and though the Hebrew element in the writer's thought is patent, it is strongly coloured by ideas current in his Greek environment. Though a Jew, he lives in a Greek environment and has assimilated much from it in his own religious experience. Environment and experience are, therefore, reflected in the Gospel. The Greeks are, in fact, brought into contact with Jesus.[5] Paul had spoken to the Greek world, but in terms largely of Jewish thought, especially of Phariseeism, as well as his personal religious experience. The author of the Fourth Gospel speaks to the Greek world in terms of the incarnate Logos-Christ and his experience of him as the light and life of the world. His Gospel is, accordingly, largely a subjective treatment of the life and teaching of Jesus, as we know them more objectively from the Synoptists. He makes use of the Synoptic account, whilst modifying it to suit his purpose, and freely omitting data that will not square with his own conception of Christ. He thereby tends to create a misleading impression of his historic person and life. At the same time, there is a framework of history in it, though even the purely historic element varies at times, in striking fashion, from that of the other evangelists. The account of the Judæan ministry of Jesus is a really valuable supplement of the Synoptic one, and he seems, in some particulars, to correct as well as expand the Synoptic data. It may be granted, too,

[4] xx. 31.   [5] xii. 21.

that in some respects this later interpretation of the mind of Jesus, hampered as it was by its purely Jewish environment, gives explicit expression to some ideas which are only imperfectly expressed, or are merely latent in the Synoptic account.   The mind of Jesus was really larger than its environment, and in the wider sphere of the Fourth Gospel the moral and spiritual verities proclaimed by him found, as it were, their proper atmosphere.

At the same time, the author allowed himself a questionable freedom in depicting the historic Jesus, and in handling historic fact, under the influence of his apologetic aim and his religious apprehension of him.   His Christ is, therefore, for the historian a problem as much as a fact.   He has more of the historic sense than Paul.   He seeks to give his conception of Christ a historic content, to bring it into touch with the historic Jesus. But the same problem arises in connection with this Gospel as in the case of the Pauline writings—the problem whether, and how far, we can accept his interpretation of Christ as historically valid.   Some theologians, whilst admitting the subjective element, reply that in effect it does not much matter.[6]

[6] Professor Bacon, for instance, seems to me to regard too indulgently the Evangelist's markedly subjective treatment of history.   " He seeks to convey truth and not mere fact."   " Jesus and Paul," 222.   See also " The Fourth Gospel in Research and Debate," 466 f.   But surely " mere fact " is of no small importance in getting at the truth of what Jesus was and taught.   His own authentic testimony is of primary value as the foundation of faith in preference to that of a later writer, who exercises the right to present this testimony in accordance with his own conceptions.   Interpretation of this kind cannot claim the same authority for faith.   There is more force in Professor Gardner's contention that it is a legitimate undertaking " to bring out the inner and spiritual meaning of the Master's life," " Ephesian Gospel," 338 (1915).   It is, however, a fair question whether the Fourth Evangelist's method of doing it is not misleading in as far as he creates a historic Christ who is obviously at times not true to reality. Mr Baker's contention that the difference between the two kinds of teaching in the Synoptics and the Fourth Gospel is explained by the assumption that the former represents the public, the latter the private teaching, is not convincing. *Expositor*, 1922, 310 f.   Others hold, too sanguinely, it seems to me, that there is no essential difference between the Synoptic and Johannine representation of Jesus.   Foakes-Jackson, for instance, thinks that the Synoptic representation " is compatible with a recognition of the claims made by the Johannine Christ."   " Problem of the Fourth Gospel," 52 (1918).   Mackintosh considers that " the Christ depicted in every part of the New Testament is radically the same Christ."   " Person of Christ," 312 (1912).   More historically minded, Rawlinson holds that " the Evangelist has . . . dramatised doctrine by representing it as being taught by our Lord; with the result that the affirmations of Christianity with regard to Him become in this Gospel His own self-affirmations."   " New Testament Doctrine of Christ," 208 (1926).   It seems clear to me that the Johannine Christ, whose mind is markedly influenced, in important respects, by Hellenist thought, cannot be regarded as an exact replica of the historic Jesus.

His interpretation is true as experience, if not as history. But it is as history, and not merely as experience that the writer would have us accept it, and in depicting the Jesus of his own thought and experience, he cannot be said to be reproducing, in important respects, the Jesus of actual history. The Gospel is really a blend of primitive tradition and Pauline Christianity with Hebrew and Greek thought and the writer's religious experience. It is more a theophany than a history, and the theophany has become more subject to Hellenist influence than in Paul or the Epistle to the Hebrews. Its "secularisation," to use Harnack's descriptive term, has made a distinct advance. It is dominated by the Logos conception. In the Prologue this conception takes possession of Jesus and retains possession of him throughout the book. Into it the writer absorbs the primitive Christology. But the combination has a certain air of unreality. The Johannine Logos, or divine Word, is hardly an exact expression of the Jesus who proclaimed the Gospel of the kingdom to the simple folk of Galilee and declared himself to the disciples and to the High Priest to be the Jewish Messiah. This Jesus was untouched by philosophy and made no claim to be the incarnation of the Logos. Even if the writer only sought by this expedient to make him intelligible to the Greek world, he ran the risk of conveying a misleading impression by associating him with a train of thought by which he did not realise or contemplate himself.

Hence the marked difference between the Johannine Christ and the Christ of the Synoptic record. Jesus is, for instance, not only recognised as the Messiah from the outset by his early followers. In the Prologue he is presented as the eternal Son of God, and in this capacity he argues throughout with the hostile Jews in a fashion very different from the Synoptic disputes with the scribes and Pharisees. Much of his teaching is concerned with this argument, as the writer himself evidently argued in accordance with the later historic situation in which he writes. The scene of Jesus' mission is placed mainly in Judæa and Jerusalem, and only very secondarily in Galilee, and a main object of it is to assert and prove his divinity as Son of God against these unbelieving Jews. Jesus himself inaugurates the mission to the Greeks, which has produced a predominantly Greek Christianity by the end of the century.

Incidents are made the theme or the vehicle of theological instruction and apologetic in accordance with this more advanced situation. The discourses in which this is done are, as a rule, strikingly different from the terse ethical sayings of the Synoptic record. They are set compositions of a mystic character, very unlike the parables in which Jesus brought home his teaching to the common folk. Symbolism and allegory take the place of parable. Though there is in the Synoptic parables treating of the kingdom an element of mystery, which " they that are without cannot understand," this element is greatly accentuated in these discourses. They mystify at times rather than enlighten, and one can understand their bewildering effect on Jewish listeners. There is something persistently enigmatic in them. The laboured argumentation in the same monotonous tone, which occupies so much of the Gospel, does not induce the conviction that the Christ of these discourses is identical with the Synoptic Jesus, who lived in closest communion with God and revealed Him out of the fullness and freshness of his ethical and religious consciousness of Him. Nor does the author hesitate to elaborate them by his own additions which, significantly enough, are in the same style, and which he does not differentiate from the words of the speaker. From the historian's standpoint, this seriously detracts from their historic value. The writer commits the mistake of representing a subjective version of what Jesus said or did as what he actually said and did, as if this were the same thing. In so doing he is doubtless convinced that his version is substantially true to the original, and that he is only amplifying, supplementing the primitive tradition, which is no longer adequate to the needs of his time. There is no conscious deception. His method is in accordance with the current, unscientific one of writing history, whether sacred or secular. At the same time, it must be said that the presentation of the historic Jesus and his teaching in accordance with the writer's theory about him is, for the modern reader at least, misleading. " John " is not really a historian, but an experimental theologian of the mystic type, even if his Gospel contains valuable historic material.

The Evangelist differs from all other New Testament writers, except the author of the Apocalypse, in thus explicitly

identifying Christ with the Logos. He might have taken this
conception of him as the Word of God from Hebrew sources—
from the creative Word in the first chapter of Genesis and other
Old Testament passages [7] and in the Targums (the Memra), or
from the conception of the Wisdom of God in the Hebrew
Wisdom Literature,[8] which had been influenced by Greek
thought. The Hebrew conception of the Word or Wisdom of God,
in its more developed form, as the instrument of His activity in
creation and redemption, might well have led him to adopt the
Logos term as a suitable one to convey the Hebrew idea to the
Greek mind. Others [9] find its source in the Platonic-Stoic
conception of the divine Reason immanent in the world, which
Philo of Alexandria engrafted on the Hebrew religion as the
intermediary between a transcendent God and the universe.
At Ephesus the various philosophies were keenly discussed,
including that of Philo, of which the Alexandrian,[10] Apollos,
may be regarded as a representative. The Epistles to the
Colossians and Ephesians show that speculations of this kind
were rife in the region, and both the term and the conception
which it represented would be familiar to the readers of the
Fourth Gospel. It is, therefore, not unlikely that the writer
of the Gospel took it over from Philo, of whose works he appears
to have had a knowledge,[11] directly or indirectly, and for whom
it had a religious as well as a cosmic significance.[12] At the
same time, there is a distinct strain of Hebrew thought in the
work, and it is a mistake to regard the writer as exclusively

[7] Ps. xxxiii. 6, 9, for instance.
[8] Prov. viii. 23 f., etc. So Westcott, " Gospel According to John " ;
Sanday, " Criticism of the Fourth Gospel " ; Loofs, " What is the Truth
About Jesus Christ ? " ; Rendel Harris, " Origin of the Prologue to St
John's Gospel " ; Bacon, " Jesus and Paul." That there is a hint of the
Logos doctrine, as derived from the Wisdom Literature, in Luke xi. 49,
" Therefore also said the wisdom of God," is not convincing. The phrase
means simply, in the Rabbinic manner of speaking, " God said." See
Strack and Billerbeck, " Kommentar," ii. 189 (1924).
[9] For instance, Wernle, " Beginnings of Christianity," ii. 148 f. (Eng.
trans., 1904) ; Moffatt, " Introduction," v., 23 f. ; Scott, " The Fourth
Gospel," 53 f. (1906) ; Heitmüller, " Die Schriften des N.T.," ii. 697 f.
(1908) ; Windisch, " Die Frömmigkeit Philos," 113 f. (1909) ; Feine,
" Theologie des N.T.," 641 f. (1910). Johnstone, after a long discussion,
concludes that he borrowed from both Jewish and Greek sources,
" Philosophy of the Fourth Gospel," 101 (1909).
[10] Acts xviii. 24.
[11] See Scott for identical passages, 58 f.
[12] For Philo the Logos is the helper and inspirer of the soul in its quest
for the higher life, as well as the medium of the divine activity in creation.

a votary of Greek culture. Philo himself, it should be remembered, represents a combination of Hebrew with Greek thought.[13]

Whilst thus taking over the Greek-Alexandrian Logos conception, he gave it a concrete, personal sense, which it does not seem to have possessed so definitely for Philo, though the personality of the Logos, as the Divine Reason, in Philo is a much-disputed question.[14] At all events, Philo knows nothing of an incarnation, and it is the Logos incarnate in Christ that the author of the Fourth Gospel introduces in the preface. It is this incarnate divine being, who is the life and the light of the world, that he depicts in the body of the work.[15] The incarnation is the fundamental fact of the writer's Christianity. Jesus is human as well as divine—no mere phantasm, as the Gnostics were beginning to teach (Docetism). The Word became flesh and dwelt among us. The miraculous birth is ignored and his generation by a human father is, in the body of the work, assumed. The real humanity is thus emphasised, though it must be said that the Logos theory, which overshadows the Gospel, tends to throw the humanity into the background and to impart a specifically superhuman aspect to the figure of Jesus. It is largely a theophany in the guise of history. Christ is God rather than man—a sublime, transcendental, isolated being, in spite of the historic setting and the realistic and human

[13] Recent attempts to find the source of the writer's thought in that of the Mandæans, a Mesopotamian sect supposed to have taken its origin from John the Baptist, are unwarranted, as Burkitt has shown (*Journal of Theological Studies*, xxix., 1928, and "The Church and Gnosis," 1932). Others (for instance, Loisy, "Le Quatrième Évangile," 1921; Dodd, "The Authority of the Bible," 1928) discover an affinity between his thought and that of Egyptian Gnosticism, as reflected in the Hermetic literature. Odeberg discovers in his mysticism an acquaintance with contemporary Palestinian thought of a mystic tenor ("The Fourth Gospel in its Relation to Contemporaneous Religious Currents," 1929). So also Schlatter ("Der Evangelist Johannes," 1930). Wetter, "Der Sohn Gottes" (1916). Dix finds the Logos doctrine of the Fourth Gospel in the Emmanuel of Isa. vii., *Journal of Theological Studies*, 1925. For a review of the various recent attempts to find a key to the writer's thought in such directions see Howard, "The Fourth Gospel in Recent Criticism and Interpretation," 161 f. (1931).

[14] See, for instance, Kennedy, "Philo's Contribution to Religion," 157 f.

[15] Harnack's view that the prologue is a mere introduction or covering letter, with no organic connection with the Gospel itself, has found no support among critics, "Ueber das Verhältnis des 4ten Evangeliums zum ganzen Werk" (1892).

touches which seem to startle the reader by their strangeness, their lack of congruity. His divine being is the main theme of his message. The Master of the Synoptists, the revealer of God and the kingdom of God, is largely transformed into the revealer of his own divine person. Whilst the Johannine Christ is built on the Pauline foundation of the pre-existent, exalted Christ, his divinity is enhanced. He is essentially God (θεός). If the designation θεός without the article, applied to him in the Prologue, may signify " divine " rather than God in the absolute sense, Thomas addresses him as " my God " (ὁ θεός μου).[16] He is timeless. He existed already in the beginning, in the depth of eternity. Not only is he the creator of all things. He possesses in himself absolute life and knowledge (light), and is capable of imparting them to man, who derives from him his rational and moral nature—the light that lighteth every man that cometh into the world. He comes forth from the inmost being of God—" the only begotten from the Father," " the only begotten son in the bosom of the Father." [17] He is from the outset of the book the Son of God, and in this character he appears throughout. He is also, as in the Synoptists, the Messiah, the Christ, the Son of Man. " We have found the Messiah," avers Andrew at the first contact with him, and Nathaniel confesses him to be the Son of God in the Messianic sense.[18] But the eschatological is largely displaced by the Logos conception. He undergoes no development, and the supernatural character of his person and his works admits of none. There is no temptation, no struggle in Gethsemane. He is absolute Master of his destiny, is entirely free from the limitations of the Jewish race and religion. He comes from above, is above all, is one with the Father, and the Father has given all things into his hand. There is no transfiguration, since, as the divine Logos, Jesus stands in need of none. He expressly declares his pre-existence and appeals to Moses and the Old Testament as witnesses of the fact. He is omniscient and omnipotent, and manifests his divine glory by his miracles, which are dramatic proofs or " signs " of his divine glory

[16] xx. 28. The phrase " the true God " in 1 John v. 20 practically seems to be applicable to Christ as well as God.
[17] i. 14-18.   [18] i. 41, 49.

rather than the outcome of sympathy with suffering humanity. The great " sign " is, in fact, Jesus himself in his incarnate divine being. He is not exalted to this supreme position by the resurrection, as in Paul. He is on earth what he had ever been—God in human flesh, Lord of the universe, though the writer uses the term Lord rather sparingly. Whilst Paul is mainly concerned with the exalted, heavenly Christ, the interest of the Johannine writer is in the incarnate Logos, in his manifestation on earth. Whilst, farther, for Paul the earthly life of Jesus is a life of humiliation, an emptying of his super-natural being, for the Johannine writer it is a majestic manifestation of the glory of the God-man. Even the Cross is but the culminating manifestation of the Son's divine glory.

In this mysterious, sublime figure the human is in danger of being absorbed in the divine. This is part of the penalty paid by the author in envisaging Jesus in the light of an idea, rather than of the primitive actuality, even if the portrait is the fruit of an experience as well as an idea. He himself is influenced by the Gnostic tendency to sublimate Jesus, which he would otherwise fain counteract. " I am from above." This is half way to the Gnostic ethereal Jesus in the semblance of a man. He has left the primitive tradition far behind. He has out-distanced even Paul, though in the Logos-Christ features of the Pauline heavenly Christ—his pre-existence, his mysterious vocation as the divine instrument of creation, the subjection of all things to him—are reproduced.[19] But even Paul would not have written that the Word was absolute God ($\theta\epsilon\acute{o}\varsigma$), or that the Father and the Son are one.[20]   At the same time, the dependence of the Son on the Father, his subordination to Him, is repeatedly emphasised, somewhat after the manner of Paul, and the distinctive personality is preserved in spite of the Son's absolute divinity. " The Father is greater than I." The Son acts by the Father's will and commandment. He does nothing of himself, but as the Father has taught him and he has seen the Father doing. He is sent, commissioned by the Father, and his teaching is not his own, but " his " that sent him. Father and Son are two distinct beings in such passages,[21] if assumed to be of the same

[19] See, for instance, iii. 11-13 ; cf. 31, and vi. 33 f.   [20] x. 30.
[21] John xiv. 28 ; xiv. 31 ; v. 19 ; viii. 28 ; vii. 16, 28-29.

nature. The writer is a monotheist. The Logos-Christ
explicitly professes belief in the only and true God, and claims
to reveal the nature of this God as life and light. But in
revealing the one, true God, he is also revealing his own
divinity as the possessor of these qualities in himself.[22] The
Evangelist, whilst retaining his monotheist faith, thus seems
to be unaware of any dissonance between this faith and the
absolute deity with which, in spite of his subordination to the
Father, he invests him. The modern reader can hardly fail
to feel that he is endangering the monotheism which he
incidentally makes Jesus profess. His creed is at times
di-theistic rather than monotheistic. He unconsciously raises
a problem which he does not concern himself to solve. The
two conceptions—the historic and the theological, the oneness
and the duality, the equality and the inequality—do not
harmonise. The discrepancy is not overcome. His creed
may, moreover, he described as tri-theistic, for the Spirit is
markedly personalised as the witness to the truth who, as
" another Advocate " or " Comforter," takes the place of the
Son as the revealer of the Father and is the indwelling inspirer
of the believer's life (chapters xiv., xv., xvi.). There is here
evidently a Trinity,[23] though it is not a Trinity in the later
developed sense of the one in three. 1 John v. 7, which teaches
such a Trinity, is spurious.

VII. The Johannine Gospel—Main Ideas

How in his incarnate existence he was the light and life of
the world, the truth, the absolute revelation of God in his
person and teaching, the embodiment of the divine life and
the imparter of it to man, is the specific theme of the Gospel
and more generally of the Epistle. The Logos-Christ unfolds
this theme in controversy with the Jews, and in intimate
converse with his disciples. His message reflects the influence
of the Pauline teaching. A number of passages show his
familiarity with Paul's Epistles as well as the Synoptic tradition.

[22] John v. 44 ; xvii. 3 ; cf. 1 John v. 20 ; John i. 4 ; viii. 12 ; cf. 1 John
i. 2, 5.
[23] " The title ' another advocate ' and phrases already quoted . . . forbid
the conclusion that the writer's thought was entirely and uniformly duali-
tarian," Rees, " The Holy Spirit in Thought and Experience," 108 (1915).

But this teaching has passed through the mould of the writer's mind and is more influenced by Greek thought. The Pauline Gospel is Hellenised and adapted to the writer's Hellenist environment. In the process, he accommodates the primitive and Pauline tradition, in accordance with his Logos conception and the more developed Christianity of his time. The synthesis is not, in some important respects, a harmony. Whilst it reveals the influence of the primitive and Pauline Gospel, it also diverges from it or combines it with later disparate elements.

He knows Paul's conception of the sin-enslaved will. The Johannine Christ, in fact, speaks of bondage to sin and freedom from sin in terms of Paul. " Every one that committeth sin is the bondservant of sin. . . . If therefore the Son shall make you free, ye shall be free indeed."[1] Whilst in the Gospel sin is distinctively unbelief in Christ—the rejection by the Jews of his claim to be the Son of God in the Johannine sense[2]—in the Epistle it is ethically conceived, as in Paul, as unrighteousness, lawlessness.[3] " Sin is lawlessness." " All unrighteousness is sin." The writer has appropriated Paul's negative attitude to the Law and its antithesis to grace. " The law was given by Moses ; grace and truth came by Jesus Christ."[4] The reference is, however, only an incidental one, and the antithesis between Law and grace, works and faith, has apparently by this time fallen into the background in the Gentile world, with the controversy of which it was the watchword. Moreover, the combination of " truth " with grace shows that the writer has characteristically in mind the Gospel as the complete revelation, of which the Law was but the imperfect anticipation. The place of the controversy between Jewish and Gentile believers over Law and grace is now taken by the conflict between Christianity and Judaism. The attitude of the writer to the Jews and their religion is throughout one of uncompromising antagonism. In agreement with Paul and the Epistle to the Hebrews, the Johannine Christ stands for spiritual religion against Jewish legalism. His antagonism to this religion finds striking expression in the conversation with the Samaritan woman. Whilst " salvation is from the Jews," Christianity, as the spiritual worship of God, has

---

[1] John viii. 34-36.
[2] xv. 22 ; xvi. 9.
[3] 1 John i. 8-9 ; iii. 3 ; v. 17, ἀδικία, ἀνομία.
[4] John i. 17 ; cf. Rom. vi. 14.

15

displaced Judaism. " The hour cometh, and now is, when the true worshippers shall worship the Father in spirit and truth ; for such doth the Father seek to be his worshippers. God is Spirit, and they that worship him must worship in spirit and truth." [5] In contrast to the respect for the Law rightly understood, which the Synoptic Jesus shows, the Johannine Christ speaks of " your law," [6] and substitutes for it his own divine law, the new commandment in place of the old, and enjoins its observance by his disciples.[7] He goes beyond even Paul, who exhorted his converts to respect the weaknesses and prejudices of Jewish believers, in dejudaising the Gospel root and branch. He is the sworn foe of the Jews and the Jews of him.

Pauline also is the idea of a propitiation for sin which is emphasised in the Epistle,[8] and is, at least incidentally, implied in the Gospel in the Baptist's emphatic proclamation, at the outset, of Christ as the Lamb of God that taketh away the sin of the world.[9] From this point of view, the purpose of the incarnation is the expiation of sin by the blood of Christ, whereby the sinner obtains forgiveness.[10] " Forgiveness of sins for his name's sake." " Forgiving our sins and cleansing us from all unrighteousness." Neither in the Gospel nor in the Epistle is there, on the other hand, explicit mention of the cardinal Pauline doctrine of justification by faith, though it may be implied in these expressions. The idea associated by the Johannine Christ with his death, in his prayer on the eve of his arrest, is, as in the Epistle to the Hebrews,[11] that of sanctification, not justification,[12] and the death is also emphasised as the crowning manifestation of his glory and the means of the extension of his mission, and the fuller revelation of the truth by the coming of the Spirit. In both the Gospel and the Epistle faith is specifically belief in the Son of God in virtue of " the witness " concerning him.[13] In both it is, generally, assent to, belief in what the Son declares and strives to prove himself to be by his miracles (" signs "), though it

[5] John iv. 23-24.
[6] x. 34.
[7] xiv. 15, 21 ; xv. 10, 12.
[8] 1 John ii. 2 ; iv. 10.
[9] John i. 29. See also vi. 51, in which Jesus speaks of giving his flesh for the life of the world. *Cf.* 1 Cor. v. 7.
[10] 1 John i. 9 ; ii. 12.
[11] Heb. x. 10, 29.
[12] John xvii. 17-19, (ἀγνίζει) ; *cf.* 1 John iii. 3.
[13] 1 John v. 1, 9-10, 13.

has also its religious side in as far as it operates in the believer the assurance of eternal life. If differently conceived, it is, as for Paul, " the work of God." [14] Only those whom the Father draws and the Son chooses can believe [15]—the Johannine form of the Pauline predestination theory.

The characteristic doctrine of the writer is not justification, but regeneration, the rebirth of the soul through water and the Spirit, the renewal of man's nature as the result of faith in the incarnate Son of God, in whom is life eternal.[16] " Except a man be born anew, or from above, he cannot see the kingdom of God." In this doctrine there is apparently a reminiscence of the Synoptic saying of Jesus, " Whosoever shall not receive the kingdom of God as a little child, he shall in no wise enter therein," or as in Matthew, " Except ye become as little children, ye shall in no wise enter into the kingdom of heaven." [17] It has also an affinity to the Pauline " new creature," the new life in Christ. As developed by the writer, it reflects, farther, the influence of the conception of the rebirth of the soul to eternal life, characteristic of current Greek thought and mystery religion.[18] From this point of view, the distinctive purpose of the incarnation is the attainment of eternal life through the Son of God, rather than the expiation of sin. The Gospel starts with the conception of the incarnate Logos as the life of man, and it closes with this conception. " These are written that ye may believe that Jesus is the Christ, the Son of God ; and that believing ye may have life in his name." [19] The same conception of eternal life through the Word dominates the Epistle.[20] Christ as the life and the light of the world is the grand theme of both. Life and light (illumination, knowledge of God in Christ, " the truth ") are interconnected. " This is life eternal that they should *know* thee and him whom thou didst send." [21] It has an intellectual (Greek) and an ethical (Hebrew) side. On the intellectual or metaphysical side this life-giving knowledge is concerned with the eternal reality behind the sensible world, true being in contrast

[14] John vi. 29.   [15] *Ibid.*, vi. 44 ; xv. 16, 19.
[16] *Ibid.*, iii. 3 f. ; 1 John ii. 29 ; iii. 1 f. ; iv. 7 ; v. 1, 10 f.
[17] Mark x. 15 ; Matt. xviii. 3.
[18] On this point see Windisch, " Die Katholischen Briefe, Handbuch," iv.² 118 f.
[19] John xx. 31.   [20] 1 John i. 1 f.   [21] John xvii. 3.

to this lower sensible existence, the ideal as opposed to the real. It is the divine, the eternal, as distinct from the phenomenal, the transient, aspect of life, which to the Greek mind constituted the true reality. As thus envisaged it is light, knowledge (gnosis) of the higher kind, and this element in it reveals the Greek-Gnostic influence on the writer's mind. It is this illumination, this higher knowledge that differentiates the children of light, who believe in the incarnate Word or Son of God, from the children of darkness, who refuse to believe in him. In becoming flesh and living a divine-human life, Christ has made it possible for the believer to participate in this higher knowledge.

But life eternal has an ethical, a religious side, and this is also an essential of it. It involves a change of heart, a new relation to God as well as a new consciousness of God, which ethically regulates his life, fosters the divine life in the soul. Believers " become children of God." [22] They have experienced the new birth—" born not of the flesh, but of the Spirit." [23] Here there seems to be a reminiscence of Paul's antithesis between the flesh and the spirit and the obligation to crucify the flesh and live after the Spirit. Hence the obligation of the children of God to live the higher life in the ethical sense. " Every one that hath this hope purifieth himself even as he is pure." " Whosoever is begotten of God doeth no sin." [24] The Son of God was manifested that he might destroy the works of the devil, and the children of God are differentiated from the children of the devil by love and righteousness. They " have passed from death into life," and the proof of this ethical transition is " love of the brethren." Love is the great test of life.[25]

As in Paul, this ethical life is mystically conceived. The Pauline idea of a mystic union with Christ reappears in the Johannine idea of abiding fellowship, oneness with Christ through the Spirit, through whom he makes his continued presence and power felt in the heart of the believer. He reproduces, too, the Pauline conception of the possession of believers by the indwelling Christ. Christ is the vine and they are the branches, and Christ organically abides in them

[22] John i. 12.
[23] Ibid., iii. 6.
[24] 1 John iii. 3, 9.
[25] 1 Ibid., iii. 10, 14.

and they in him.[26]   The writer has not, however, assimilated the mystic teaching of dying and rising with Christ, and ascribes the mystic indwelling to the gift of the Spirit.[27]   He further develops the Pauline Christ-mysticism into a God-mysticism, and speaks of the indwelling of the Father as well as the Son in the believer.   " God abideth in us and we in him in virtue of the gift of the Spirit."   " We (Father and Son) will come unto him and make our abode with him." [28]

Whilst the writer thus presupposes and develops the Pauline mysticism, the more primitive enthusiasm, the dynamic, charismatic Christianity of Paul and the primitive community are lacking.   The Spirit is predominantly the Spirit of truth,[29] as against the false teaching of the writer's time—the guarantee of the verity of the Gospel professed by the Church.   The practical Christian life is characteristically concerned with the keeping of Christ's commandments, especially the commandment of love, in accordance with the current conception of the Gospel as a new law.[30]

Very characteristic is the stress laid on baptism and the Eucharist in connection with the assimilation of eternal life by the believer.   The imparting of this life is sacramentally conceived, and the sacramental element is emphasised from a different point of view from that of Paul.   These rites have become highly important ecclesiastical doctrines in the writer's time.   Baptism, which Paul was disposed to depreciate on occasion, is now essential to the new birth.   " Except a man be born of water and the Spirit he cannot enter into the kingdom of God." [31]   The water as well as the Spirit has a mystical efficacy, though the mention of the Spirit seems to be a caveat against an undue evaluation of the rite, apart from its spiritual effects.   The ecclesiastical motive is equally apparent in the teaching on the Eucharist in the discourse arising out of the feeding of the multitude, though the omission of the institution of the Eucharist by Christ may be another tacit protest against

[26] John xv. 1 f.
[27] Ibid., xiv. 16 f. ; xv. 26 ; xvi. 7 f. ; 1 John iv. 13.
[28] 1 John iv. 12, 13 ; John xiv. 23 ; cf. xvii. 21, 23.
[29] xiv. 17, 26 ; xv. 26 ; xvi. 13 ; 1 John iv. 2 f. ; v. 7.   On his doctrine of the Spirit in detail, see E. F. Scott, " The Spirit in the N.T.," 193 f.
[30] xiii. 34 ; xiv. 15, 21 ; xv. 10 f. ; 1 John ii. 8 ; iii. 22, 23.
[31] iii. 5 ; 1 John v. 6-8.

the tendency in the developing Church to invest the rite with
a superstitious efficacy. Without participation in the Eucharist
no one can have part in eternal life. " Except ye eat the flesh
of the Son of Man and drink his blood, ye have not life in
yourselves. He that eateth my flesh and drinketh my blood
hath eternal life. For my flesh is meat indeed, and my blood
is drink indeed." [32] The words as they stand sound very
materialistic and suggest the assimilation of the Deity in the
mystery cults, and the redemption of the flesh as well as the
spirit by the eating of his body, the meat or new manna from
heaven which imparts immortality even to the flesh. No
wonder that even the disciples are perplexed by this crass
reasoning, and in response to their murmurs, Christ explains
the eating in a spiritual sense. " It is the Spirit that quickeneth ;
the flesh profiteth nothing " (v. 63). At the same time, the
reiterated eating of the flesh and the drinking of the blood
do seem to imply more than a symbolic meaning,[33] and appear
to indicate the growing tendency to materialise the symbol
and infuse into the sacraments ideas derived from the Greek
mysteries. The mystic union, the fellowship with Christ
in the Eucharist, which to Paul is spiritual,[34] and which seems
to find expression in the afterthought of the writer, is in
danger of disappearing in a crasser conception of the rite in
the view of the community, if not of the Evangelist. Here,
as in other respects, he gives expression to two distinct tendencies
of the time—the material and the spiritual—which will not
really harmonise in his thought.

Emphasis is also laid on the Church itself as the community
of God's children, in which His redemptive purpose is realised.
The growing ecclesiastical conception of the Church, as it
had developed in the writer's time, exercises a very appreciable
influence on his thought. The term is, indeed, not mentioned,
but the institution as it had developed by the end of the century,
occupies a prominent place in his mind, and is represented as
occupying an equally prominent place in that of Christ himself.
" The story of the beginnings of Christianity," says Professor

[32] vi. 53-55.
[33] Scott, "Fourth Gospel," 287-288. See also Moffatt, "Theology of
the Gospels," 194 f. The conception of the Logos as the new manna or
meat from heaven is taken from Philo.
[34] 1 Cor. x. 15 f.

Scott, " is described in such a manner as to adumbrate the later development in which an ordered community, with its set laws and sacraments, continued the work of Christ. A whole region of John's thinking becomes intelligible only when we take account of this ecclesiastical interest which underlies the Gospel." [35] The Church is the depository of the truth as against both the unbelieving Jews and the Gnostic false teachers of the writer's time. Eternal life is only obtainable by those within its pale. A narrowing tendency to equate Christianity with a certain orthodoxy, of which the Church has the monopoly and is the judge and the guardian, is making itself felt. Here, again, there is a contradictory strain in the writer's thought, which has a universalist and a particularist side, according as the emphasis falls on the universalism of the Christian message or on the contemporary conception of the Church as the exclusive vehicle of salvation. On the one hand, eternal life is free to all and is offered to all. Whosoever believeth shall be saved. God loves the world and Christ is the Saviour of the world. Hence such characteristic sayings, " I, if I be lifted up, will draw *all* men unto myself." [36] In such passagers the Pauline universalism and emphasis on the love of God in sending his son to redeem the world finds unreserved expression. On the other hand, truth, salvation is confined to the Church, outside of which there is only error, darkness, condemnation, since the world cannot receive the Spirit of truth. From this point of view, Christ dies, not for the world, but for the Church (his " friends," " his own sheep," " the brethren "), and the Church is sharply distinguished from the world. The antagonism of the Roman Government to it has had the inevitable result of rousing its antagonism to the Roman Government. The more irenic spirit of Paul and of 1st Peter which survived in the Roman community, as the Epistle of Clement shows, is disappearing in the circle to which the writer belonged.

Eternal life is not merely a thing of the future—the great possession that lies beyond the present transient existence—though its full realisation may be in the region beyond. For the writer, as for Paul, though more completely, it is an

---

[35] " Fourth Gospel," 24-25. [36] xii. 32 ; *cf.* 1 John iv. 9, 14.

experienced reality. The believer is already in full possession
of eternal life. " He that believeth on the Son *hath* eternal
life." [37] " He that hath the Son hath life." [38] The eschatological element in the primitive Gospel is present in the Fourth,
apparently as a concession to the well-established tradition
of the teaching of Jesus and the apostolic preaching on this
subject. Resurrection, even the bodily resurrection, judgment,
the speedy coming of the judge are there.[39] But the eschatological teaching in the cruder sense is merely antiquarian.
Unlike the author of the Apocalypse, the Johannine writer
spiritualises the early eschatology. It is really displaced by the
conception of eternal life as a present experience, by the
thought of the spiritual abiding of Father and Son or the Spirit
in the individual and the community. The hope of an
apocalyptic coming (Parousia) still persisted in the community,
as is abundantly evident in the Apocalypse, which stands in
such glaring contrast to the Fourth Gospel in this respect. But
to many it was seemingly illusory, and anxious questionings
as to its validity were rife. The writer reflects these anxious
questionings,[40] and modifies the more literal eschatological belief
accordingly. He seeks to allay doubt by a spiritual interpretation of this belief. The Gospel is not merely an apologetic for
Christianity against the attacks of unbelieving Jews in the
writer's time. It is meant as an apologetic for the benefit of those
who were perplexed over the question of the coming of Christ,
and who are assured that he has already come in the spiritual
experience of his followers and dwells in their hearts and in
the Church. Christ is glorified at his departure from earth,
his " lifting up," and has no need to return to manifest his
glory.[41] Judgment is already meted out to those who reject
him.[42] Though the popular view of the coming on the clouds
of heaven is retained, it is practically superseded by that of the
resurrection on the third day, in which he definitely comes
back to the disciples, and by the coming, at his departure, of
the Advocate or Comforter, who seems at times to be identified
with Christ himself. This transmutation presupposes the
Pauline indwelling Christ or Spirit of Christ, and even Paul,

[37] iii. 36.
[38] 1 John v. 12.
[39] v. 27-29 ; vi. 39-40 ; xii. 48 ; xx. 1 f. ; 1 John ii. 28.

[40] xvi. 17-18.
[41] xii. 23 f.
[42] xii. 31.

who gave such marked expression to the primitive belief in a spectacular coming and judgment, veered later to the more spiritual conception. It is also in line with the Synoptic teaching of the kingdom as present, which Jesus himself combined with the apocalyptic view of it. Moreover, the resurrection is distinctively spiritualised in contrast to the popular belief in a bodily resurrection at the last day. Christ, indeed, appears to the disciples in a body that can be touched and felt, and the dead are represented as coming forth from the tombs for judgment. But this material conception is really displaced by that of eternal life as a present possession of the believer. Those who believe in Christ are already conscious of eternal life, have already experienced the resurrection, " I am the resurrection and the life. He that believeth on me, though he die, yet shall he live ; and whosoever liveth and believeth on me shall never die." [43] The writer seems thus to share the Gnostic view of the resurrection as present and spiritual. At the same time, there again appears an incongruity in his thought in his retention of the belief in the literal coming and the bodily resurrection, whilst practically transforming them in a spiritual sense.

The emphasis is thus no longer on the traditional eschatology, but on the ethical and spiritual aspect of the Gospel, as manifested in the experience of the believer, particularly in the supreme fact of love—the love of God in Christ and the believer's love of God and the brethren. The essense of God is love, [44] and this fundamental fact finds its counterpart in the Christian life. Even here, however, there is a dissonant note which betrays the ecclesiastical influence. On the one hand, this love is universal, in accordance with the essential character of God as revealed in Christ, and the Logos is the light that lighteth every man coming into the world. On the other, it is limited to the Church in contrast to the world, to the believer as distinct from the unbeliever. " Greater love hath no man than this that a man lay down his life for his friends." [45] " Hereby know we love because he laid down his life for us, and we ought to lay down our lives for the brethren." [46] The love of God and one's fellow-believers is set against the hate of the world, and in the Gospel the antithesis is absolute.

[43] xi. 24-26.   [44] 1 John iv. 8, 16.   [45] xv. 13.   [46] 1 John iii. 16.

It prevails also in the Epistle which excludes not only the world, but all Christians whose speculative opinions are obnoxious to the writer and who belong to the world, not to the Church. Difference of theological opinion is already beginning to cleave the Christian communities into the friends and enemies of the Gospel ; orthodoxy, as represented by the writer, to claim a monopoly not only of truth, but of the love of God and righteousness. The teacher who dissents from the Christianity represented by him is an antichrist, and is necessarily a bad man, and also an outcast from the fellowship of God and the brethren. Paul was hard enough on those who differed from him. But he was not so intolerant in regard to variations of the Gospel preaching as the author of the Epistle, who would hardly have shared his joy that Christ was preached, even if the preaching was opposed to his own.[47]

The Fourth Gospel is a wonderful production. It may not be an original creation. The writer has drawn liberally on the primitive tradition, on Paul, and on Hebrew-Hellenist thought. He is not, like Paul, an original genius. But his book is far more than a compilation. It is a synthesis on which he has stamped his own meditative mind and religious experience, and it was destined to exercise a profoundly formative influence on theological thought. The synthesis was so distinctive that it seems to have aroused no little opposition even within the Church of the writer's time. From both Gospel and Epistle we can perceive that he is engaged in inculcating and enforcing a version of the Gospel which fails to appeal to many of his fellow Christians. In the Gospel, indeed, these opponents are mainly the unbelieving Jews, with whom Christ maintains a running controversy. But in the Epistle the opponents of the writer are mainly his fellow-believers, who are not prepared to accept his conception of the Logos-Christ. Many of them are addicted to Gnosticism and have adopted a Docetic view of Christ. Among these may be reckoned Cerinthus, of whom, according to tradition,[48] " the Apostle " John was the sworn antagonist. But the writer's opponents were not necessarily all adherents of the Gnostic type of thought, which denied that " Jesus Christ is

[47] Phil. i. 18.
[48] Irenæus, " Adv. Haer.," iii. 3, 4.

come in the flesh," [49] and sought to explain away his humanity
in a Docetic sense. These " antichrists " included others
who denied " that Jesus is the Christ, the Son," in the Johannine
sense.[50]   In other words, they objected to the writer's Logos
theory as applied to Jesus, and held to the more primitive and
authentic representation of Jesus as the Son in the Messianic
and filial sense, whom God had chosen to be the agent of His
redeeming purpose.   Their opposition appears to have been
based on historic, not on speculative, Gnosticising grounds.
Hence the fact that the Gospel only gradually won its way to
the allegiance of the Church.   From the writer's time
throughout the second century the opposition seems to have
made itself felt, and in the second half of the century it appears
as a party within the Church under the name of the Alogi
(deniers of the Logos).   These Alogi rejected both the Fourth
Gospel and the Apocalypse as non-apostolic writings, and
ascribed them, without convincing reasons indeed, to the
Gnostic Cerinthus.   They appear to have based their rejection
on the ground that the Johannine Gospel was incompatible
with the early tradition as embodied in the Synoptic writings,
and Harnack sees in their opposition an early attempt to test
theological speculation and belief by historic criticism.   " They
tried to refute the Logos doctrine and the Logos Gospel on
historical grounds, by a reference to the Synoptic Gospels.
The representatives of this movement were, as far as we know,
the first to undertake within the Church a historical criticism,
worthy of the name, of the Christian Scriptures and the Church
tradition." [51]

Apart from the speculative element blended with the
writer's religious experience, this experience is a striking
evidence of the power of the life and personality of Jesus
in those of his followers.   It is the measure of his magnetic
influence acting on a mystic mind, whose thought, whilst
coloured by that of the age, is vitalised by the living Christ,
with whom he is united in spiritual fellowship.   Nor is his
Gospel purely an abstract production, though the abstract
element in it and in the figure of Jesus is only too evident.
The writer is in touch with the historic Jesus, if this Jesus is

[49] 1 John iv. 3 ; 2 John 7.   [50] 1 John ii. 22-23.
[51] " History of Dogma," iii. 19 (Eng. trans.).

to him the incarnate Logos. He reproduces features, aspects of his life and teaching, if he encumbers them all too lavishly with his own reasonings. Whilst the discourses largely reflect ideas in the mind of the writer, or current in his time, they also contain not a few utterances which actually came or might actually have come from his lips. Jesus' revelation of the Fatherhood of God is there, and it is tersely conveyed in the great saying, " God is love." [52] The active outflowing of this love is movingly expressed. " Herein was the love of God manifested towards us that God sent his only begotten Son into the world that we might live through him." " God so loved the world that he gave his only begotten Son."[53] The self-surrendering love of the Son, which runs through the Gospel and the Epistle, even if it is limited to his disciples, is true to life. Jesus as a unique revelation of the Father is a historic fact. " He that hath seen me hath seen the Father." [54] This great sentence grips us as one that could have been uttered by Jesus. That God was in Christ in his God-like life and teaching, that he attained to a matchless spiritual fellowship with Him, that the kinship of the human with the divine reached in him its highest expression, none who has seriously perused the authentic record will deny. The Son of Man is also there, though he is idealised, deified as the incarnate Logos, and the incarnate Logos largely displaces the Messiah, who is to come again and judge the world. He has caught, in essential respects, the spirit of Jesus. " Let not your hearts be troubled," for instance, reminds of the " Be not anxious " of the Sermon on the Mount, and such resemblances could easily be amplified. As in the Epistles of Paul, the Spirit of Jesus is the inspiration of the highest moral and spiritual ideal and effort. It energises the life of the believer in the conflict with sin, in the pursuit of the highest good, in the practical exercise of a mystic faith and love. Christ is the great exemplar of the life of self-renunciation and service, as in the Synoptists. " If I then, the Lord and Master, have washed your feet, ye ought also to wash one another's feet. For I have given you an example that ye also should do as I have done to you." [55] Dying to live is true life here, as in the Synoptists. " Verily, verily I say unto you,

[52] 1 John iv. 8, 16.   [54] John xiv. 9.
[53] John iii. 16 ; 1 John iv. 9.   [55] *Ibid.*, xiii. 14-15.

except a grain of wheat fall into the earth and die, it abideth by itself alone ; but if it die, it beareth much fruit. He that loveth his life loseth it ; and he that hateth his life in this world shall keep it unto eternal life. If any man serve me, let him follow me." [56] " He that doeth righteousness is righteous, even as he is righteous ; he that doeth sin is of the devil. . . . To this end was the Son of God manifested that he might destroy the works of the devil." " He that loveth not abideth in death. . . . Hereby know we love because he laid down his life for us, and we ought to lay down our lives for the brethren. But whoso hath the world's goods, and beholdeth his brother in need and shutteth up his compassion from him, how doth the love of God abide in him ? My little children, let us not love in word, neither with the tongue, but in deed and in truth." [57] It is in this experienced power of a living Christ, not in its speculative element, that the real strength of the Gospel lies, as a testimony to the unique Master and Lord, even if the Master and Lord has been transformed in the alembic of the writer's mind. The metaphysic with which it works can be dropped without loss to this power. The metaphysic is the writer's. The spiritual power is the abiding heritage of Christ. If his metaphysic tends at times to mystify the reader as well as " the Jews," he understands the art of transforming it into an overmastering ethical force.

VIII. JUDE AND SECOND PETER

The Epistle of Jude professes to be written by a brother of James, who is presumed to have been the Lord's brother. This Jude was not an apostle, but an associate of the apostles [1] and an influential evangelist in the early period. If written by him, the Epistle must be dated before the reign of the Emperor Domitian, for this Jude was already dead when this emperor arrested and examined the relatives of Jesus.[2] The character of the contents seems, however, to tell against this identification. " The faith once delivered to the saints " (v. 3), the emphasis on the former teaching of the apostles of our Lord Jesus Christ (v. 17), and the antichristian and

---

[56] John xii. 24 f.
[57] *Ibid.*, iii. 7-8, 14 f.

[1] 1 Cor. ix. 5.
[2] Eusebius, " Hist. Eccles.," iii. 19-20.

immoral tendency of the heretics described in v. 4 point to a lengthy interval after the strictly apostolic period. Apart from the evidence which it affords of the current belief in the threefold Deity of the Father, Son, and Spirit, its doctrinal importance is small. It is largely concerned with Jewish Apocalyptic, and is valuable only as evidence of the existence of what, as we shall see, was evidently Gnostic and, in the view of the author at least, antinomian views in the late first or early second century Church.

It is very questionable whether we should include 2nd Peter among the subapostolic writers. Its date may probably be put beyond the middle of the second century. There can be very little question about the falsity of its professed authorship. The "Simon Peter, a servant and apostle of Jesus Christ," who professes to address Christians in general, is a pious invention after the fashion of the time. Professor Milligan rightly describes it as "a pseudepigraph written in the second century by an unknown author, who desired to gain credit for his work by issuing it under the great name of St Peter." [3]   Nor is it reasonably doubtful that he borrowed from Jude, instead of *vice versa*.[4]   It is a homily, in epistolary form, which the writer unsuccessfully tries to disguise by biographical references to Peter in the first person, and by making him foretell and denounce in lurid language the future false teachers and their teaching, which is palpably of the Gnostic type.[5]   In addition to the striving to counteract current Gnostic aberrations, he seeks to meet the prevailing scepticism as to the second coming, which long-deferred hope has discredited, and to supply a needful apologetic for the times.   Noticeable, too, is the current tendency to misinterpret Paul, owing to the difficulty of certain passages in his Epistles, though it is questionable whether the writer himself has rightly apprehended the Pauline Gospel.   Neither Paul nor Peter, we may safely assume, would have written that Christ has made us "partakers of the divine nature," [6] which is a distinctively Greek conception of salvation.   Nor, assuming that the

---

[3] "The New Testament Documents," 114 (1913).

[4] See Mayor, "The Epistle of St Jude and the Second Epistle of St Peter" (1907), against Zahn, Spitta, and Bigg, who maintain the dependence of Jude on 2nd Peter.

[5] ii. 1 f.   [6] γένησθε θείας κοινωνοὶ φύσεως, i. 4.

Revised Version gives the correct rendering, would they have spoken of "our God and Saviour Jesus Christ."[7] The designation is specifically post-apostolic.

IX. DEVELOPING GNOSTICISM

Paul's antagonism to incipient Christian Gnosticism did not avail to check the Gnostic movement within the Christian communities, as the later subapostolic literature amply shows. It is especially prominent in the Pastorals, in the Johannine writings, the Apocalypse, and in the still later Epistles of Jude, 2nd Peter, and Ignatius. In these writings "false teachers" abound, and for the most part they are evidently representatives of this accentuated Gnostic tendency. The writers strive to vindicate and commend, in opposition to them, "sound doctrine" as preserved in the Church and contained in the Old Testament Scriptures and the true tradition, handed down to the later generation of Christians.[1] There is evidently an intellectual and religious ferment in the communities to which these documents are addressed. Keen discussion on the Gospel and its implications and significance is being carried on by the more independent and enquiring minds. Christian teachers debate with one another on the nature of God, the person of Christ, the question of evil in man and the material universe, the attainment of redemption from evil, the relation of belief and conduct, etc. These writings survey the situation from the traditional, apostolic standpoint, and present and maintain this standpoint against its opponents. They give us only glimpses, in recurrent phrases, of the points at issue between their writers and the false teachers who oppose them, and whom they oppose in the interest of sound, i.e., apostolic teaching. An active religious and intellectual movement is developing out of the clash of opposing minds, which seeks, in an independent spirit, to mould Christianity in accordance with current speculation. This movement is neither specifically Jewish, nor specifically pagan. It is syncretistic. It borrows from Greek and Oriental thought and religion as well as from Judaism. It may be described as

---

[7] i. 1. [1] 2 Tim. i. 13, etc. ; iii. 15-17.

a Jewish, pagan, and Christian intermixture,[2] though there may be a predominance of one or the other element in it, according to the predilection of the individual. Harnack's description of it as " the acute Hellenising of Christianity "[3] is rather misleading, since it was strongly influenced by Oriental dualistic, as well as Greek thought and religion.

These documents are all anti-Gnostic. Their writers take their stand on the traditional, apostolic faith as it was apprehended towards the close of the first century and the early part of the second. They regard these Gnostic innovators as meddlesome sectaries and disturbers of the communities. In the Pastorals and Jude and 2nd Peter they are given to " vain talking," " profane bubbling," to " speaking great swelling words." [4] They dispute and wrangle about words, to the subverting of those that hear them.[5] They " blaspheme " God and His truth and rail at the apostolic teachers.[6] They sneak into the communities and have marked success in proselytising silly women for mercenary ends.[7] They foment foolish and ignorant questionings, engendering strife.[8] They are impostors, deceiving and being deceived.[9] They are mockers and sceptics, who set at nought all higher authority even of a heavenly nature.[10] They wrest the Scriptures, including the Pauline letters, to their own destruction.[11] They are false teachers and foment a baneful sectism.[12] The intellectual ferment is patent. There is a clash between tradition and speculative freedom, between the appeal to apostolic authority and subjective opinion, between the faith that has been handed down and the faith that is still in the making. Unfortunately, the writers of these documents, who indulge largely in denunciation and exhortation, do not give us much definite information on the actual points at issue in the controversy. They are evidently too biassed in their judgment of the movement to convey a discriminating survey of it.

---

[2] Dr Hort's contention that the false teaching is purely Judaistic, not Gnostic, is untenable. " Judaistic Christianity," 132 f. (1894).

[3] " History of Dogma," i. 230, and see Bousset, " Hauptprobleme der Gnosis," 2 f. (1907).

[4] 1 Tim. i. 6 ; 2 Tim. ii. 16 ; Tit. i. 10 ; Jude 16. ; 2 Peter ii. 18.

[5] 2 Tim. ii. 14 ; cf. 1 Tim. vi. 4.   [7] 2 Tim. iii. 6 ; Tit. i. 11 ; Jude iv.

[6] 1 Tim. i. 20 ; vi. 4.   [8] 2 Tim. ii. 23.

[9] 2 Tim. iii. 13 ; Tit. i. 10.   [11] 2 Peter iii. 16.

[10] Jude 8, 18 ; 2 Peter ii. 10 ; iii. 3.   [12] 2 Peter ii. 1.

Christian Gnosticism, as we learn from other all too scanty sources, was an earnest attempt to grapple with the problems suggested not only by current philosophy, but by the Gospel itself in its more developed form, though its solution might in part be fantastic and unhistoric. The fantastic side of it might well strike the writers of these documents as " dreamings," "mere logomachy."[13] There were, doubtless, shallow and mercenary charlatans among its protagonists, of the type described in these documents. But this is only one feature of what was in reality a serious speculative and practical movement, which sought to construct a Christian philosophy of man and the universe and promote the higher spiritual life. The earnest Gnostic thinker and moralist is there as well as the charlatan, though it is difficult to discover him in the descriptive epithets and phrases applied to the whole movement. The movement was, in fact, bound to supervene on the developed Christology of Paul and the writer of the Fourth Gospel. The pre-existent, heavenly Christ of Paul, the Johannine God-man, inevitably raised the problem of the real humanity of Jesus in relation to his divinity. They bequeathed this conception to the faith, without concerning themselves with the question whether it actually corresponded to the historic reality, or could be brought into harmony with this reality. Hence the Gnostic attempts at the solution of the puzzle.

These Gnostic sectaries profess " a knowledge falsely so called,"[14] and though it is not specifically defined, it is possible, directly or indirectly, to descry some of the characteristic ideas against which the writers pit the true apostolic faith. The emphasis on the one and only God,[15] the sovereign of the universe, seems to be an offset to the Gnostic distinction between the supreme God, who sends Christ to redeem man, and the Demiourgos or inferior creator God of the Old Testament, to whom the evil in matter is ascribable. Cognate with this assertion of Christian monotheism is the emphasis on the essential goodness of creation as the work of God, in repudiation of the dualist Gnostic theory of it as essentially evil. " For every creature of God is good and nothing to be rejected if it be received with thanksgiving ; for it is sanctified

[13] Jude 4 ; 1 Tim. vi. 4.   [15] *Ibid.*, i. 17 ; ii. 5.
[14] 1 Tim. vi. 20.

16

through the word of God and prayer." [16]   Similarly, the one mediator [17] between God and men, the man Christ Jesus, may be taken as a counterstroke to the Gnostic theory of a series of æons or emanations from the supreme God for the purpose of man's redemption, and to the Gnostic denial of the real humanity of Christ.   These æons or emanations are clearly discernible in " the myths and interminable mythologies," or genealogies concerning this series of intermediary beings or powers between the supreme God and man.[18]   In recognising this heavenly hierarchy, these false teachers are guilty of denying the only Master and Lord, Jesus Christ,[19] either in the sense of disowning his supreme and exclusive claim as Redeemer, or of explaining away his real humanity against the Johannine conception of him as the God-man.   Equally patent the Gnostic distinction between ordinary faith and the higher esoteric knowledge, and the consequent differentiation between the spiritual or pneumatic Christian, who has attained to this knowledge, and the mere natural or psychic Christian, who cannot rise above a crude faith.[20]   In repudiation of this exclusive tendency, which is incompatible with the equality of all believers in Christ, faith in the common acceptation of the term is emphasised as the true note of the apostolic Gospel, proclaimed in the current teaching of the Church.   Hence, too, the insistence on the universal appeal of this Gospel.   Salvation, the knowledge of the truth is available for all alike."   God willeth that all men should be saved and come to the knowledge of the truth." [21]   " For the grace of God hath appeared, bringing salvation to all men." [22]   God in the Pastoral Epistles is characteristically the Saviour-God, and Christ as Saviour is the agent of His saving purpose, which is unlimited by any artificial intellectualist distinction.   Salvation is a thing not of the intellect, but of the religious and ethical life.   Its real criterion is the life of practical obedience to the Gospel ethic. From the ethical point of view, these self-assumed pneumatics

---

[16] 1 Tim. iv. 1 f.

[17] μεσίτης, 1 Tim. ii. 5-6, an approximation to the representation of Christ as the mediator in the Epistle to the Hebrews.

[18] 1 Tim. i. 4 ; iv. 7 ; Tit. ii. 14 ; iii. 9.

[19] Jude 4 ; 2 Peter ii. 1.   [21] ἐπίγνωσις, 1 Tim. ii. 4.

[20] Jude 19.   [22] Tit. ii. 10.

are the real psychics, not the true spirituals. In contrast to the simple believer, they have not the Spirit of God, nor the love of God.[23]

Moreover, in their false spiritualism they are seeking to entangle the Christian life in the old legalism, in reaction apparently from the Pauline freedom. To this end they have set up as teachers of the law,[24] which they do not understand and misapply. They engage in "fightings about the law" and strive to enforce "the commandments of men." In their misdirected legalism they do not realise that law, in itself good, if used lawfully, is not made for a righteous man (the true Christian believer), but for the lawless sinners.[25] Their false spiritualism leads to a morbid asceticism, showing itself in abstinence from certain foods and prohibition of marriage.[26] They evidently regard nature and human life with jaundiced eyes, as the result of their assumption of the absolute antagonism of matter and spirit. They thus attribute their defilement of mind and conscience to God's handiwork, which He created to be received with thanksgiving by those that believe and know the truth. God has richly given us all things to enjoy. To the pure, on the contrary, all things are pure, whereas to these unbelieving legalists nothing is pure.[27] In professing a higher knowledge of God, they thus deny Him and unfit themselves for every good work.[28] Further, their ethical dualism has led them to deny the bodily resurrection and explain it in a spiritual or symbolic sense as a quickening in baptism of the higher life in man. Two of them, Hymenæus and Philetus, are specially named as representatives of this aberration from the truth, "saying that the resurrection is past already."[29] Along with it, they rejected the second coming in the apocalyptic sense.[30] The belief in the second coming was a genuine element of the primitive tradition. It was a heritage from Jesus himself. The bodily resurrection, on the other hand, was not necessarily an element in the faith of Jesus himself, who appears to have held the doctrine in the

---

[23] Jude 19-20; 2 Peter ii. 12, where they are described as "irrational creatures, born animals" (φυσικά).

[24] νομοδιδάσκαλοι.

[25] 1 Tim. i. 7 f.; Tit. i. 14; iii. 9.

[26] 1 Tim. iv. 3.

[27] *Ibid.*, iv. 3 f.; vi. 17; Tit. i. 15.

[28] Tit. i. 16.

[29] 2 Tim. ii. 18.

[30] 2 Peter iii. 4.

spiritual sense current in certain Pharisaic circles. Nor does
it seem to have been the belief of Paul who, in the fifteenth
chapter of 1st Corinthians, clearly teaches the rising in a purely
spiritual body, and towards the end of his life expected an
immediate transition of the soul to the spirit world, to be clothed
with the spiritual body prepared for it.   The belief in the raising
of the actual body of Jesus was a later apologetic development,
and in spiritualising this doctrine the Gnostics were really
upholding the older tradition.   In any case the Pauline
conception of the spiritual resurrection of the believer in
baptism would of itself ultimately tend to the Gnostic interpretation of the later materialist doctrine.

Finally, they are represented as men of very bad
character as well as heterodox [31] teachers.   For the writer
of the Pastoral Epistles morality and sound doctrine are
interdependent.   Faith and a good conscience are interlinked,[32]
and it is evident that for him a good conscience is compatible
only with his own version of the faith, which is the current
traditional, apostolic one.   The sectaries are accordingly
" men corrupted in mind and bereft of the truth." [33]
As unbelievers they are defiled in mind and conscience.[34]
Because Hymenæus and Philetus hold a spiritual view of the
resurrection they are " ungodly men," whose word eats as does
a gangrene.[35] They have a form of godliness, but deny the
power thereof, and a lengthy catalogue of vices is ascribed to
them.[36] They are, moreover, regarded as insincere and
mercenary in spirit, liars and hypocrites, " supposing godliness
a way of gain," teaching things which they ought not for filthy
lucre's sake," " with feigned words making merchandise of
you." [37]   In Jude and 2nd Peter, who largely borrows from
him, the same tendency to judge a man's character from his
creed is observable.   These Gnostics, who have crept privily
into the communities, are " ungodly men who have turned the
grace of God into lasciviousness." [38]   In their fantastic dreamings they defile the flesh.[39] Whilst they share in the common
love-feasts, they are addicted to revelry in their own meetings.[40]

---

[31] ἑτεροδιδασκαλεῖν, 1 Tim. i. 3.   [34] Tit. i. 15.
[32] 1 Tim. i. 5, 19.   [35] 2 Tim. ii. 16 f.
[33] Ibid.,vi. 5 ; 2 Tim. iii. 8.   [36] Ibid., ii. 2 f.
[37] 1 Tim. iv. 2 ; vi. 5 ; Tit. i. 11 ; 2 Peter ii. 5.
[38] Jude 4.   [39] Ibid., 8.   [40] Ibid., 12 ; 2 Peter ii. 13.

They " have eyes full of adultery that cannot cease from sin."
They entice the unwary believer to fleshly lusts, "promising them
liberty, whilst they themselves are bondservants of corruption."
They walk after the flesh in the lust of defilement and despise
dominion.[41] Both writers are given to rhetoric and are
evidently apt to be carried away into sweeping general accusations. In all these documents there is a lack of discrimination,
and an evident tendency to equate unsound doctrine with
moral perversity. There was at least one section of them
which could not be justly charged with walking after the flesh
in the lust of defilement. The ascetics were puritans, not
sensualists. Matter being evil, the believer must abjure self-
indulgence and practice a rigid abstinence. In this respect
they represent, in fact, a reaction, in an extreme form, from the
current materialism, and emphasise the higher spiritual nature
of man in conflict with the practical materialism of their pagan
environment. Their pessimistic view of the world and man
is an extreme adaptation of the Pauline antagonism between the
flesh and the spirit, the Johannine antithesis between Christianity
and the world. At the same time, it seems to have been the
case that, in a certain section, speculative freedom was, as these
writers imply, associated with moral licence, on the ground
that, matter being evil, gross self-indulgence does not affect in
the least the higher life of the spirit. At all events, we learn from
other sources [42] that among the adherents of early Gnosticism
were sects who held this theory. It is, therefore, possible that,
while the ascetics of the Pastoral Epistles narrowed the liberty
of the believer by a new legalism, the advocates of this liberty,
in the Gnostic sense, widened it into an unrestricted libertinism.

In the Johannine writings it is more particularly the Gnostic
teaching on the person of Christ that is controverted. As in
Paul, there is, indeed, in these writings a Gnostic tendency.
The resurrection is held to take place on the reception of
eternal life through Christ. Eternal life is the true knowledge
of God. The Gospel is largely equivalent to this knowledge ;
the antagonism between the light inherent in it and the
darkness of unbelief is absolute. The tendency to emphasise

---

[41] 2 Peter ii. 10, 18-19.
[42] The so-called " Second Epistle of Clement," for instance, about the
middle of the second century, c. 9 f. (Lightfoot's edition).

Christ's ethereal nature is very strong. On the other hand, there is a set attempt in both the Gospel and the first and second Johannine Epistles to counter the Gnostic tendency to reduce him to an abstraction pure and simple and explain away his humanity. In consequence of the inherent evil of matter, which could not be the vehicle of the divine, these Gnostics adopted what is known as a Docetic view of his person. They either regarded the human in the divine æon, Jesus, as merely phantasmal, his body as only a body in appearance (Saturninus and Basilides [43]) ; or, accepting his real humanity, they differentiated between the man Jesus and the divine æon or emanation which descended into him at his baptism and left him before his crucifixion, so that only the man suffered (Valentinus [44]). In the Fourth Gospel, on the other hand, the divine Word or Logos became flesh, lived a real human life, and died a real death on the Cross. Christ was real God and real man—the God-man. The Johannine Gospel thus contradicts the Gnostic assumption that matter, the flesh, being essentially evil, cannot be the real medium of the divine, and attempts, by the doctrine of the incarnate Word, to meet the danger of Gnostic unreality, which the pre-existent heavenly Christ of Paul tended to beget and for which the Johannine writer himself is to some extent responsible. In spite of the incarnation, the incarnate Logos is at times somewhat phantasmal.

This striving is also apparent in the first two Johannine Epistles, which emphasise the incarnation as a fundamental fact and denounce its gainsayers as liars and antichrists. " Who is the liar but he that denieth that Jesus is the Christ. This is the Antichrist, even he that denieth the Father and the Son. Whosoever denieth the Son the same hath not the Father." [45] In this passage the deniers may be those who reject the Johannine doctrine of the God-man, and, like the Jewish-Christian Ebionites, prefer the adoptionist conception of him in the primitive tradition. They are not necessarily Gnostics.[46] In other passages the reference is indisputably

[43] Irenæus, " Adv. Haer.," i. 24, 2 f.   [44] *Ibid.*, i. 7, 2 f.   [45] 1 John ii. 22.
[46] Possibly the liar is Cerinthus, of whom the " Apostle " John appears in tradition as the inveterate enemy, and who seems to have held the Docetic view somewhat later connected with the names of Saturninus and Basilides, " Irenæus I.," xxvi. 1.

to the Docetic view of the person of Christ. " Every spirit
which confesseth that Jesus Christ is come in the flesh is of
God, and every spirit that confesseth not Jesus is not [47] of God."
Equally patent the anti-Gnostic emphasis on the real death as
well as the baptism of Jesus. " This is he that came by water
and blood, even Jesus Christ ; not with the water only (the
descent of the divine æon into Jesus at the baptism), but with
the water and the blood " [48] (the actual death on the Cross).
Similarly the " deceivers " of the second Epistle are clearly
Gnostics. " For many deceivers are gone forth into the
world, even they that confess not that Jesus Christ cometh in
the flesh. This is the deceiver and the Antichrist." [49]

Docetism is thus emphatically condemned, though it is
not quite clear which form of it the writer has in mind. In
opposition to the pretensions of these falsifiers of the truth,
he claims for himself and his fellow-believers the true knowledge
of God. " They are of the world, therefore speak they as of
the world and the world heareth them. We are of God ; he
that knoweth God heareth us ; he who is not of God heareth
us not. By this we know the spirit of truth and the spirit
of error." [50] Whilst in the Pastorals these false teachers are
still within the Church, in the Johannine Epistles they are outside it. They have seceded, and fellowship between them and
adherents of the writer's views is impossible. " They went
out from us, but they were not of us ; for if they had been of
us, they would have continued with us." [51] The bond of this
fellowship is love of God and of one another, as well as fidelity
to the truth. The implication is that those who do not share
the writer's Christology are lacking in this supreme Christian
virtue and are incapable of doing righteousness. On the one
side are the children of God, who walk in the light ; on the
other the children of the devil, who walk in darkness.[52] The
children of God eschew sin and practice righteousness in
accordance with the nature of God, who is light, and the
example and commandments of Christ, the righteous. " Every
one that hath this hope set on him purifieth himself even
as he is pure." [53] The Gnostics, as children of the devil, are,

[47] 1 John iv. 2-3.
[48] Ibid., v. 6.   [50] 1 John iv. 5-6.   [52] Ibid., i. 5 f.; iii. 6 f.
[49] 2 John 7.   [51] Ibid., ii. 19.   [53] Ibid., iii. 3.

on the contrary, necessarily sinners, " for the devil sinneth from the beginning." Here, again, as in the Pastorals, Christian morality is dependent on correctness of creed, as the writer strives to fix it. The dividing line between righteousness and unrighteousness is orthodoxy in his sense. It is evidently impossible to differ from his view of Christ and keep Christ's commandments. In a word, " the false prophets " are necessarily bad men, though, unlike the Pastorals, the Johannine Epistles do not give us a detailed register of Gnostic vices. The writer does not specifically charge them with libertinism.

In the Apocalypse, on the other hand, the Gnostics, as represented by the sect of the Nicolaitans, are clearly Antinomian. Whilst the Church at Ephesus repudiates them and their works, they are very active in that of Pergamum.[54] There and at Thyatira the false teaching is frankly libertine, and as libertines the Nicolaitans appear in the tradition preserved by Irenæus.[55]

In the Epistles of Ignatius the Gnostic movement has become widespread and is a real menace to the faith and unity of the Christian communities in the province of Asia, to which he writes. Though they are outside the pale of the Church (" outside the altar " [56]), they are carrying on an active propaganda among its members. As in the Johannine Epistles, too, the heresy against which he inveighs is Docetic. But he leaves us in no doubt about the form of Docetism which these unbelievers [57] profess. They specifically teach that Christ was a mere phantasm. He only assumed a human body, and lived, suffered, rose again only in appearance.[58] In refutation of this unconscionable speculation, Ignatius appeals to history. He reiterates the reality of Christ's birth, life, death, and resurrection in a strain which sounds like a repetition of an early form of the Catholic creed.[59] Christ was truly born of Mary, though conceived by the Holy Ghost.[60] His humanity equally with his divinity is a reality. He was of the seed of David according to the flesh, being both the Son of man

[54] Apoc. ii. 6, 15.
[55] I. 26, 3.
[56] Trallians 7 ; Eph. 5.
[57] ἄπιστοι.
[58] Tral. 10 ; Smyr. 2 f.
[59] Tral. 9 ; Smyr. 1 ; cf. Mag. 11 ; Eph. 7.   See also Curtis, " History of Creeds and Confessions," 49-50 (1911).
[60] Eph. 18.

and the Son of God—both of Mary and of God.[61] Ignatius is a firm believer in the bodily resurrection as well as the virgin birth, which these sceptics alike impugn. Christ's bodily resurrection is attested by his appearance in his material body to his disciples.[62] He rebuts, too, the Gnostic distinction between the supreme God and the creator God, and at the same time maintains, against the Gnostic mythology, the supremacy of Christ, the eternal Word, as the sole emissary and revealer of the Father. " There is one Jesus Christ who came forth from the one Father. . . One God who has revealed Himself through Jesus Christ, His son, who is His eternal Word, proceeding from Silence, and in all things was well pleasing to Him that sent him." [63]

Similarly, he maintains the Pauline freedom from the Law against the Gnostic ethical dualism, which showed itself in the ascetic tendency to restrict this freedom by the old legalism. The Gnostic appeal to the Law in support of this asceticism is unwarranted. Judaism is incompatible with Christianity. " If we still live according to Judaism, we acknowledge that we have not received grace." [64] " It is absurd to profess Christianity and at the same time to Judaise." [65] Christ has taken the place of the Old Testament as the supreme authority and has " freed you from every bond." [66] The Gospel, which the prophets also proclaimed,[67] is the perfect revelation of God. Christ is the door to the Father, through which the patriarchs, the prophets, the apostles, and the Church enter in.[68] On the other hand, these Gnostics, who would impose the old Judaism on the Church, are opposed to the growing sacramentalism which Ignatius represents. They do not share his materialist conception of the Eucharist which is, for him, " the flesh of our Saviour Jesus Christ, which suffered for our sins and which the Father in His goodness raised up anew." [69]

The antithesis between those who " corrupt the faith of God,

[61] Eph. 7, 20.   [62] Smyr. 3.
[63] Mag. 7-8. He makes use of the Gnostic term Σιγή, silence, as denoting the unrevealed God. The οὐκ preceding ἀπὸ σιγῆς προελθών is evidently a later insertion. See Bauer in Lietzmann's " Handbuch Die Apostolischen Väter," 226 (1920).
[64] Mag. 8.   [66] Philad. 8-9.   [68] Ibid., 9.
[65] Ibid., 10.   [67] Ibid., 5.   [69] Smyr. 7.

for which Jesus was crucified, by their wicked doctrine," and the Catholic apostolic teaching is thus far-reaching. As against such wicked doctrine, this teaching is the authoritative, historic faith, the true tradition. At the same time, the appeal to history in proof of this claim is not so incontestable as the writer, in his passionate and uncompromising dogmatism, assumes and asserts. Whilst rightly emphasising the real humanity of Jesus against the Docetism of these Gnostics, it is open to question whether the virgin birth, the bodily resurrection, the crass sacramentalism, on which he insists as essentials of the Catholic faith, are in accord with the early tradition. In challenging these doctrines, the Gnostics seem, in fact, to have been in closer touch with historic reality than their opinionated opponents. Similarly, it is extremely problematic whether the evil character and motives attributed to those sectaries are true to life. Here, as in the other documents, the tendency to make creed the criterion of conduct is only too patent. They are unsparingly denounced as "wild beasts," "ravening dogs," "beasts in the shape of men." [70] Such vituperation hardly betokens the balanced judgment, the objective observer of men and things. In this fanatic, if pathetically heroic, believer, obsessed by the passion for martyrdom, we may not look for the impartial mind. At the same time, he is not quite so intolerant as the Johannine scribe, and exhorts the churches to strive to bring the heretics to repentance and thus regain them for the true faith. [71]

The growth of the Gnostic movement later in the second century threatened to transform the Gospel into a religious philosophy, and accentuated the exclusive spirit within the Catholic Church. Ultimately the Church, as the guardian of the apostolic tradition, was fain not merely to denounce it, but to barricade itself against it by a fixed tradition, a ministry claiming succession from the apostles, the Catholic creed, and a canon of recognised scriptures. Meanwhile, it is important to note it, in its early stage, as a phase of the developing faith, which has its root in the tendency, observable in Paul, to make Christianity both a philosophy of the universe and a religion of redemption. It is not an accident that the later Gnostics,

[70] Eph. 7; Smyr. 4, etc.   [71] Eph. 10; Smyr. 4.

like Marcion, claimed him as the true exponent of the Gospel, though he would certainly have repudiated much of their teaching.

X. Beginnings of Catholicism

The subapostolic period is a period of transition towards the early Catholic conception of the Gospel and the Church, which ultimately triumphed in the acute conflict with Gnosticism in the second half of the second century.

This conception was due to the circumstances of the developing Church. Diversity in the apprehension of the Gospel led to an increased emphasis on tradition. The presence of Antinomian tendencies among the Gnostic sectaries led to the increased regulation of the Christian life, in accordance with the conception of the Gospel as a new Law. The Church was increasingly exposed to persecution, and persecution accentuated the necessity of unity and the utility of an ordered ministry in the face of a hostile world. Moreover, there is observable in the Epistles of Ignatius, as well as the Fourth Gospel, a tendency to materialise the sacraments under the growing influence of the mystery religions, and consequently to transform the ministry into the medium of sacramental grace.[1]

Accordingly there gradually develops throughout the period a distinctive type of teaching, organisation, life, and spirit, compared with the strictly apostolic age.[2]

This teaching embodies the current common Christianity —the more elementary facts of the Gospel, which the writer of the Epistle to the Hebrews describes as " the first principles of Christ," and which consists of repentance, faith, baptism, and the laying on of hands, the resurrection of the dead and judgment.[3] With this is combined the more advanced teaching,

---

[1] On this factor see F. W. von Walter, " Ignatius von Antiochien und die Entstehung des Frühkatholicismus. Festschrift für R. Seeberg," ii. (1929).

[2] Dr Mason solves the problem of the rise of Catholicism by denying its existence, with a ready, but indiscriminating facility. " The Church was Catholic from the outset." " Essays on the Early History of the Church and Ministry," 56, edited by Dr Swete (2nd ed., 1921). This is a repetition of Battifol's dictum, " The infant Church is Catholic." " Primitive Catholicism," 142 (Eng. trans., 5th ed., 1911).

[3] Heb. vi. 1 f.

resulting from the development of Christian thought, which
he describes as " the solid food for full-grown men," [4] and
which itself betrays, in some respects, Gnostic features. This
more advanced teaching is also reflected in the Fourth
Gospel and enters into the current common Christianity,
though such themes as the Logos-Christ of this Gospel might
not as yet be universally professed. Speculative Christology,
for instance, was more in evidence at Ephesus than at Rome,
to judge from the Epistle of Clement, which is largely practical
and is uninfluenced by Greek philosophy, and in which
the Logos theory does not seem to be professed. This
common Christianity has completely emancipated itself from
Jewish nationalism. It recognises in Christ more than the
Jewish Messiah. It shares the enhanced evaluation of him
as the divine Redeemer of the world, whilst repudiating
extreme Gnostic speculation. It bases itself on " sound
doctrine," of which the Church is the pillar and bulwark.

It further emphasises the apostolic authority. The apostles
are the foundation of the Church. They are invested with a
special sanctity as " the holy apostles." [5] Theories of the
succession of the ministry from " the apostles " are beginning
to find expression in the Epistle of Clement to the Corinthians,[6]
and in those of Ignatius. There is a growing sense of solidarity
in the Christian communities as units of a universal body—
" the Catholic Church " in the sense of the universal Church—
the meaning of the term Catholic as first used by Ignatius.[7]
This solidarity is fostered by visits and written communications, from one community to another, such as the Epistle of
Clement, which is sent from the Church in Rome to the Church
in Corinth, and those of Ignatius, who writes to the Christians
of the province of Asia as the representative of that of Antioch.
The question of the organisation of the communities of this
wider fellowship is becoming a pressing one in the midst
of false teaching and a hostile world, as we see from the Pastoral
Epistles, the Epistle of Clement, and those of Ignatius. At
the same time variety of organisation still prevails. At Corinth
and Rome, for instance, it seems to be at a more primitive stage
than at Antioch and a number of churches of the province

[4] v. 14.
[5] Eph. ii. 20 ; iii. 5.
[6] Chapters xlii.-xliv.
[7] Smyr. 8.

of Asia, where primitive episcopacy—the emergence of one presbyter-bishop in the local community, with subordinate presbyters and deacons—begins to appear by the first quarter of the second century.

Whilst the organisation is thus still in a transition stage in the Church at large, the tendency in Clement as well as Ignatius is to emphasise an orderly ministry in opposition to the disorderly or heretical self-assertion of members of the community. To this end both urge subordination to the local office-bearers, who wield the powers of their office in virtue of a regular succession from Christ and the apostles. In Ignatius there is, in addition, a marked striving to exalt the office of the single bishop in each community to which he writes, as a divinely ordained essential of its corporate life, whilst also recognising the rights of the other office-bearers and the community itself. With him the hierarchic conception of the Church acquires a pronounced importance, though the importance assigned it is actuated by the necessity of securing and maintaining unity in the face of persecution and false teaching, rather than by purely hierarchic reasons.

The more primitive charismatic ministry of the Spirit, in and through the individual, is accordingly giving place to the official ministry, of which " the laying on of the hands of the presbytery " [8]—consecration by the presbyter-bishops of the local community—is an indispensable condition. " The gift of prophecy " is, however, still recognised as a title to the ministry and is, in the case of Timothy, associated with the laying on of hands. Moreover, the wandering prophet and teacher are still pursuing their distinctive vocation of inspired edification, alongside the local ministry, as is apparent from " The Didache " and " The Shepherd of Hermas," which reflect in this respect the more primitive conditions. But the free inspiration of the Spirit was evidently not without its drawbacks, and required supervision and control, especially as it might, and did, lead to laxity of conduct and " false " teaching. Freedom of teaching is, therefore, being limited in view of the recurring necessity of " proving the spirits." [9]

[8] 1 Tim. iv. 14. ; cf. 2 Tim. i. 6.
[9] 1 John iv. 1. See also the Epistles of Ignatius, "The Didache," and "The Shepherd."

Similarly, there is a marked tendency to regulate the life of the community, as the minute directions of the Pastorals show. The Gospel is distinctively conceived as a new Law, which the believer realises in a regulated life of obedience to Christ in this evil world, and thus attains at last to salvation.[10] There is here a certain divergence from Paul, resulting in what Wernle has called " Catholicised Paulinism," and others describe as "moralism." Paul, indeed, speaks of " the law of Christ." But his characteristic teaching is freedom from law, the antithesis of law and grace, faith and works, flesh and spirit. Salvation, both as a gospel and a life, is the operation of this antithesis in the heart and life of the believer, not merely a new Law realised by the believer in obedience to the will of God in Christ. It is the present deliverance by faith from the law, from both the guilt and power of sin in the flesh, the ethical dying to the flesh and the rising in the Spirit with Christ, the mystic indwelling of Christ and his Spirit in the believer, and the dynamic manifestation of the Spirit in the Christian community. In the incipient Catholic Church, on the other hand, salvation is the future attainment of God's promise in and through Christ, and the Gospel, on the practical side, is a new Law which conditions the believer's life, inspired by a living faith and hope. This new Law is not the mere revival of the Old Testament Law, though the Old Testament ethic forms an important element of it.[11] Nor is it the Torah of the scribes and Pharisees, from which Paul had delivered Christianity and with which Gentile Christianity since his day ceased to concern itself, except in certain extreme Jewish-Christian and Gnostic circles. It is primarily the practical Gospel as Jesus taught it, and as modified by the larger world and sphere of thought into which this Gospel has expanded, and which it strives to win for Christ. In virtue of this modification, it tends to foster a new legalism. It lays on the believers the yoke of the Lord, which is not the easy one of Jesus himself, whose more human conception of life, in opposition to the Pharisees, and his great doctrine of *filial*, and not merely legal, obedience to the will of the Father,

[10] See, for instance, James i. 12 ; 1 Tim. vi. 19 ; Hebrews i. 14 ; 1 Pet. .3 f., etc.
[11] 2 Tim. iii. 15-16.

it tends to a certain extent to ignore. The result is an ordered Christianity, in which the practical Christian ideal is to be exemplified in character and in the social relations, and discipline is to be applied and observed to this end. As we have seen, too, the ascetic tendency in the pursuit of the higher life is already discernible, though it is not an essential of it, as in certain forms of Gnosticism, and the ordinary Christian life, in accordance with the new Law, is the normal type.[12] It is maintained by the exercise of a strict discipline within the community, in the effort to raise it to a higher moral level than that of its lax and all too generally depraved environment.

This divergence is not a case of conscious antagonism to Paulinism, though explicit antagonism to the current abuse of the doctrine of justification by faith is perceptible in the Epistle of James. It is a case rather of misunderstanding Paul's distinctive Gospel, of using Pauline words and phrases without having grasped their full meaning. Law is no longer what it was to Paul—a burden and a curse, from which faith in Christ delivers the oppressed soul. It is an element of the Gospel, and the Christian life is the realising, the conforming to this element in obedience to Christ. It was the outcome of a more even moral and spiritual experience than that of Paul and a less pessimistic sense of man's moral incapacity, and it was fitted to appeal to the ordinary convert, who could not easily grasp the more spiritual and mystic Pauline teaching. It met in a more intelligible fashion the widespread striving for moral reformation in the Græco-Roman world, which is ascribable to Stoic influence. It met, too, the prevailing conviction of a moral law—whether this Law was regarded as the Law of nature or the Law of God—to which man should conform his actions. The idea of Law, as embodied in the Roman Empire, was also finding expression, in the moral and religious sphere, in the utterances of Stoic writers and wandering preachers, and contributed materially to the acceptance of the Gospel as the highest embodiment of the Law.

With the regulated life and organisation of the community there are combined in all the subapostolic writings, more or less, the hope of the coming of the Lord and the belief in a

[12] 1 Tim. iv. 4 ; Tit. ii. 1 f.

bodily resurrection. The spiritualising tendency finds, indeed, marked expression in the Fourth Gospel, which regards the Parousia as having already taken place in the resurrection. As in Paul and John, Christ or the Spirit of Christ is regarded as present in the community, preserving it from error and directing its life.[13] In general, however, the belief in the coming, in the apocalyptic sense, persists, and even in the Fourth Gospel as well as the Apocalypse it finds a place alongside the more spiritual view. But the primitive enthusiastic, charismatic spirit, which was so closely associated with the otherworldly atmosphere, declines more and more into the background of congregational life. On the other hand, the belief in a bodily resurrection which Paul interpreted in a spiritual sense, tends to become the conventional one, as in the Gospels, the Apocalypse, Clement, and Ignatius, and is widened so as to include unbelievers as well as believers, on the assumption that the wicked must be raised for judgment.[14] Connected with it is the chiliastic conception of the future kingdom, which also finds marked expression in the Apocalypse and other post-apostolic documents, and seems to have been widespread.[15]

[13] Rev. ii. and iii.
[14] John v. 29 ; Rev. xx. 11 f.
[15] See Harnack, " Hist. of Dogma," i. 167.

CHAPTER IV

THE GOSPEL IN THE EARLY FATHERS

I. The " Apostolic " Fathers

THE title of this chapter comprehends the conception of the Gospel in the writings of the so-called Apostolic Fathers—Clement of Rome, the author of the second Epistle erroneously ascribed to him, Ignatius of Antioch, Polycarp of Smyrna, Barnabas, and Hermas. In addition to these we may include Papias, and the anonymous " Didache," which belongs to this period.

These writers are post-apostolic. The designation " apostolic " has been applied to them on the assumption that they had been disciples of the apostles. They may have been, but we have no certain evidence to prove that they were. Though Origen identifies Clement of Rome with the Clement mentioned in the Epistle to the Philippians, the identification is very doubtful. Equally doubtful that of the author of " The Shepherd " with the Hermas mentioned in the last chapter of the Epistle to the Romans. Whether they could have been disciples of the apostles depends on the date to be assigned to their writings, which cannot be exactly decided. In the case of certain of them, some put the date early enough in the first century to make this description a feasible one. But the early date hardly amounts, in that of Barnabas and Hermas, to more than a suggestion. By common consent, Clement wrote about the end of the first century, and the Epistles of Ignatius are most probably assignable to the reign of Trajan, i.e., in one of the early years of the second century. The Epistle of Polycarp was written shortly after those of Ignatius. That of Barnabas, " The Didache," and the " Shepherd of Hermas " may be assigned indefinitely to the first half of the century.

These documents are of the nature of tracts for the times. They were written with a view to the instruction and guidance, in relation to existing conditions, of the communities to which they are addressed. As in the case of the New Testament writings, they reveal the individuality of the writers and show the influence of culture, religious experience, and historic conditions on their thought. As religious literature they do not, however, reach the high level of the New Testament, though they contain not a few impressive passages. They are typical of a less original, less dynamic age. " It is correct to say that between the most important constituent parts of the New Testament and the literature of the period immediately following, there is a great gulf fixed." [1] At the same time, they form only a part of the Christian literature of the age. It is highly probable that, apart from the Apocryphal Gospels, etc., more was written in this period than has been preserved. They cannot, therefore, be regarded as representing the sum total of its Christian thought, or even of all that their authors thought on the Christian faith. Even so, they are inferior to the writings of a Paul and other New Testament scribes.

As sources these early Fathers use the Old Testament Scriptures, which they regard as the specially inspired Word or Oracles of God,[2] " the Words of the Lord Jesus," [3] *i.e.*, the Gospels, which they also rate very highly, some of the New Testament Epistles,[4] the oral apostolic tradition,[5] and the germ of the later Apostolic Creed.[6] From these sources they derive the common faith in Jesus Christ as the divine revealer of God and the Saviour, who lived and died and rose in fulfilment of the divine purpose of redemption ; will reappear as the judge of the world ; is, in his life, the exemplar of that of the believer, and inspires the believer and the community through his Spirit. Whilst they share the developed evaluation of his person in the Pauline, or the Johannine sense, they have not thought out his relation to the Father. They are

[1] Harnack, " Hist. of Dogma," i. 135.
[2] The τὰ βίβλια, the Inspired Books in this specific sense.
[3] Epistle of Clement, c. 13.
[4] See " The New Testament in the Apostolic Fathers " (1905).
[5] Clement, c. 7 ; Polycarp, 7. ; *cf.* Jude 3, 2 Pet. iii. 2.
[6] Loofs, " Leitfaden," 87 ; Harnack, " Hist. of Dogma," i. 155 f.; Seeberg, " Dogmengeschichte," i. 192 f. (3rd ed., 1922).

monotheists, and their belief in the one God is made to consort with that in a threefold or a twofold Deity, according to the view taken of the Spirit. The influence of Paul and the Fourth Gospel is further apparent in their conception of the Gospel in relation to Judaism. In these documents Christianity appears as the universal, Gentile religion. It has completely separated itself from Judaism,[7] though, as the Epistles of Ignatius show, there is a tendency among a number of the Gnostic sectaries to reimpose the old legalism. The Christians are the new, the true Israel, " the third race " in contrast to Jews and Greeks. On the other hand, the specific Pauline view of faith is more or less superseded by the moralist one. For these Fathers the Gospel is a new Law, Christ the new lawgiver. Not one of them fully apprehends Paul's soteriological teaching, though some are nearer to this apprehension than others. Equally characteristic is the other-worldly spirit which links the writers with the Apostolic age, though the declension of the communities from the primitive ideal is more or less apparent. The kingdom of God is the antithesis of this world, and will displace this world in the great transformation which is imminent. The Parousia is still at hand.

Whilst there is thus general agreement, there is also diversity in their presentation of the common faith. The apprehension and experience of the Gospel varies with the individual. The heresy that is denounced in some of them should not blind us to the fact that diversity of thought existed among the adherents of the apostolic tradition, and was not confined to those who professed Gnostic views. It is a mistake to assume that the apprehension of the Gospel was uniform. Theology, if we may use the term, was in a state

[7] This appears to have been largely the case even in the Jewish-Christian communities in Palestine. These communities formed part of the universal Church. (On these communities see J. Weiss, " Urchristenthum," 530 f. ; Hort, " Judaistic Christianity," 164 f.). From Justin's " Dialogue with Trypho " (47-48) we learn, however, that there were Jewish Christians in the early second century, who continued to observe the Law, refused fellowship with Gentile Christians unless they did likewise, and while recognising Jesus as Messiah, rejected the virgin birth. They appear to have clung to the primitive Adoptionist view of him. These Palestinian Christians retained the name Nazarenes, which the Jews originally applied to the followers of Jesus (Acts xxiv. 5). They are later known, from their poverty, as Ebionites. See Weiss, 568 f. ; Hort, 194 f. ; Harnack, " Hist. of Dogma," i. 285 f. ; Loofs, " Leitfaden," 81 f. (4th Auflage, 1906).

of flux. The Christian thought of the Epistle of Clement, for instance, is not identical, in every respect, with that of Ignatius. The belief in the continued inspiration of the believer by the Spirit extends well into the second century. The exercise of the gift of prophecy, as it appears in these writings, made, in fact, a uniform, completed creed impossible. Moreover, the assumption that the Church of these early Fathers possessed and followed exactly the apostolic tradition [8] is unwarranted, if only in view of the lack of a true apprehension of the Pauline teaching.

II. Clement of Rome

Whilst in the Epistle of Clement to the Corinthian Church there is no mention of the author, it was ascribed to the Roman presbyter-bishop of this name by Dionysius of Corinth in the second half of the second century.[1] Though it is a communication from the Roman Church, not from any individual presbyter-bishop, the statement that it was actually written by this Clement has been generally accepted as reliable. As has been noted, his identification with the Clement of the Philippian Church—the fellow-worker of Paul—is very doubtful, whilst the assumption that he was identical with Flavius Clement, the cousin of the Emperor Domitian, is a very unlikely one. Lightfoot's suggestion that he was a freedman of his household is more probable.[2] The critics also differ on the question of his nationality. The impression made by the Epistle is that the writer was of Jewish race. He is not only familiar with the Old Testament, his references to it reflect the spirit of one to whom it was a sort of national literature, and who feels a kinship with its great figures, though the standpoint is that of Gentile Christianity. He was evidently a leading presbyter-bishop of the Roman Church, who writes on behalf of this Church to that of Corinth. There is nothing in the Epistle to indicate that he was sole bishop. It is only a later tradition that makes him third bishop of Rome after

---

[8] Clement 5, for instance.
[1] Eusebius, " Hist. Eccl.," iv. 11, 23 ; cf. iii. 16.
[2] " Apostolic Fathers," i. 61. He gives the additional matter discovered in a library at Constantinople and published by Bryennios in 1875 and also a Syriac version of the Epistle, now in Cambridge Univ. Lib.

the apostle Peter.[3] Though writing on behalf of the Roman-Christian community, the Epistle bears the stamp of his own personality. His personality is that of the Church leader who places the corporate interest and order of the community in the foreground, and inculcates the subordination of the individual to the whole. The keynote of his character, as well as the Epistle, is obedience to the will of God in accordance with the example of Christ, the holy men of the Old Testament, and the apostles, especially Peter and Paul, and the duty of subordinating self and selfish ends to the general weal, as befitting the Christian profession. He is the upholder of tradition in thought and usage and is apt to interpret it in the light of the present order of things. He emphasises the regular succession of the office-bearers of the community from the apostles as a guarantee of the true tradition, and even finds a proof of this succession in a misquoted Old Testament prophetic passage (c. 42 f.). His mind is that of the capable ecclesiastical administrator, rather than the independent thinker, and his thought is accordingly of the stereotyped, limited order.

Characteristic of it is the recurring emphasis on God as the Father, the Creator, the Lord or Master, the Maker of the universe,[4] whose providence and power it manifests, and who has spoken and still speaks to man through the Old Testament scriptures, which Clement quotes profusely.[5] His conception of God has in it something of the Roman feeling for the majesty and grandeur of an ordered system of things rather than the Greek sense of a supreme mind.[6] This supreme God and Father takes the chief place in his thought, and the monotheism of the Old Testament is emphasised all through. At the same time, the divine person and work of Christ, to whom these scriptures also bear witness, are dwelt upon. Whilst he does not, like Ignatius, call him God,[7] he

[3] Irenæus, "Adv. Haer.," iii. 3, 3. Hemmer not only confidently describes him as bishop of Rome, but speaks of him as "le pape Clément"! "Les Pères Apostoliques," ii. ; "Introd." iv.

[4] πατὴρ παντοκράτωρ, κτιστής, δεσπότης, δημιουργός.

[5] c. 8 ; 19 ; 20 ; 33, etc

[6] c. 19 f. ; 33. The κατὰ διάνοιαν of c. 33 seems to refer to human, not to divine intelligence.

[7] The τοῦ θεοῦ of c. 2 which Lightfoot accepts (" The Epistle of Clement," 37) should be τοῦ χριστοῦ. See Knopf, " Die Apostolischen Väter," 45 (1920), Lietzmann's " Handbuch " (1923).

has a profound sense of his divine rank. For him, as for
Paul, he pre-existed before his coming as the Suffering Servant.
He is " the sceptre of the divine majesty," " the mirror of
God's faultless and sublime countenance," [8] who abased himself in order to realise his God-appointed mission, as delineated
in Isaiah liii. He is the Lord, the Christ, who was sent forth
from God and chosen by God, the beloved Son or Servant of
God, and (in language evidently borrowed from the Epistle to
the Hebrews) the High Priest and guardian of our souls, who
brings our prayers and gifts or offerings before God.[9] Through
him believers attain the full knowledge of God and become the
elect people of God.[10] Though he came from God to bestow
this benefit, he is not the agent of creation. Whilst Clement
believes with Paul in the pre-existent Christ, he knows nothing
about his creative function, and is ignorant of the Logos
doctrine of the Fourth Gospel. This doctrine had apparently
not penetrated to Rome from Asia Minor, and there is nothing
in the Epistle to suggest Greek speculative ideas. The phrase
" the holy word "[11] means the Jewish scriptures. It is the
supreme God who creates the world. Besides the Lord Jesus,
the person and activity of the Spirit, by whose inspiration he
claims to write,[12] are emphasised. In spite of the monotheistic
stress on the creator God and Father, his terminology,
like that of Paul, to whose First Epistle to the Corinthians he
refers,[13] suggests belief in a threefold deity, and his expression
of this belief savours of tri-theism. " Have we not one God,
and one Christ, and one Spirit of grace that was shed upon
us ? "[14] " For as God liveth, and the Lord Jesus Christ liveth,
and the Holy Spirit, who are the faith and hope of the elect."[15]

Like Paul he emphasises the speedy coming and the
resurrection, which he seems to accept in a bodily sense. He
finds divine indications, as well as analogies of the resurrection,
in such phenomena as the transition of day and night, the new
life springing from the decaying seed cast into the ground,
and in the myth of the Phœnix, which he takes as literally true.[16]
Whilst he ignores Paul's mystic conception of it as the rising

[8] c. 16 ; 36.
[9] c. 36 ; 42 ; 59 ($\pi a \hat{\imath} s \ \theta \epsilon o \hat{\upsilon}$) ; 61 ; 64.
[10] c. 59.
[11] c. 56, $\dot{o} \ \ddot{a} \gamma \iota o s \ \lambda \acute{o} \gamma o s$.
[12] c. 63.
[13] c. 47.
[14] c. 46.
[15] c. 58.
[16] c. 23-25.

of the believer to a new spiritual life, he shares the Pauline universalism and has the cosmopolitan outlook of the Roman administrator, writing from the capital of a universal empire. Christian believers are the elect people of God apart from all restriction of race or religious usage.[17] With Paul he emphasises man's need of forgiveness in the exercise of God's mercy.[18] He sees in the Old Testament history the operation of the divine forgiveness in return for repentance,[19] though he does not, like Paul, bring it into connection with the prospective redemption of Christ, and in this respect shows a more historical sense in his use of Old Testament passages.[20] He re-echoes Paul's panegyric of the love of God in Christ and the love of Christ for man, who gave his blood for us, his flesh for our flesh, his soul for our souls.[21] He shares his conception of salvation as thus due to the blood of Christ, and ascribes the justification of the believer to faith, in contrast to works. " Let us fix our eyes on the blood of Christ and understand how precious it is unto his Father, because, being shed for our salvation, it was for the whole world the grace of repentance."[22] "And so we, having been called through His will in Christ Jesus, are not justified through ourselves, or through our own wisdom, or piety, or works which we have wrought in holiness of heart, but through faith, whereby the Almighty God justified all men that have been from the beginning."[23] Nevertheless, he cannot be said to have thoroughly assimilated Paul's distinctive conception of justification by faith, for this reference to it is only incidental, and his characteristic view is rather that of the Epistle of James. As in this Epistle, Abraham is justified by his obedience to the will of God, and justification by works is emphasised. " We are justified by works and not by words."[24] Salvation is the reward of works. Faith is specifically for him the manifestation of obedience to God,[25] of submission to His will in a life of goodness,[26] of the love that eschews faction and strife,[27] and also the conviction of the truth of

---

[17] c. 29-30 ; 64.   [18] c. 17 f.   [19] c. 7-8.
[20] In c. 12, however, he finds in the scarlet thread given by the spies to Rahab (Josh. ii. 18) a prophecy of the future redemption by Christ's blood.
[21] c. 49.
[22] c. 7.   [24] c. 10 f. ; 30 f.   [26] c. 34.
[23] c. 32.   [25] c. 10-15.   [27] c. 49-54.

God's promises.[28] " Let us, therefore," he concludes, " enlist ourselves with all earnestness in His faultless ordinances." [29] It is on the ethical aspect of faith, in the realisation of Christ's ordinances or commandments, that the distinctive stress is laid.

The so-called Second Epistle of Clement is neither an Epistle, nor was it written by him. It is a homily delivered to a congregation at Rome, according to the conjecture of Harnack,[30] at Corinth according to that of Lightfoot,[31] about the middle of the second century, and later ascribed to the Roman presbyter-bishop. Its author's thought has a resemblance to that of Hermas, who appears to have been his contemporary. It is, at all events, sufficiently distinctive from that of Clement of Rome to confirm the conclusion that the ascription of the work to him is unwarranted. The preacher is a leading presbyter of the community, who quotes New Testament writings as received Scriptures of equal authority with the Old Testament writings. This alone necessitates a post-Clementine date.

The preacher has a lofty conception of Christ. Christ stands for him as God, though there was evidently in the community a tendency to question such an exalted claim. " We ought to think of Jesus Christ as of God, as of the judge of the quick and the dead." [32] He is, however, not quite consistent, since, in chapter xiv., God is said to have created Christ as well as the Church. As in Paul, he is the pre-existent spirit who became flesh for our salvation. Since he is identified in a couple of passages with the Spirit, and in the concluding doxology Christ alone, as the Saviour and Prince of Immortality, is associated with God, the Father, the writer seems, like Barnabas and Hermas, to have conceived the Deity in a twofold or binitarian sense.[33] This incarnate Spirit is the sole source of

[28] c. 27.   [29] c. 37.

[30] " Zeitschrift f. Kirchengeschichte," i. 264 f.

[31] " The Apostolic Fathers," ii. 191 f. (1890). Bartlet (" Zeitschrift für N.T. Wissenschaft," vii. 123 f. (1906)), and Streeter (" Primitive Church," 238 f. (1929)) contend that it was written at Alexandria.

[32] c. 1.   The letter of Pliny to Trajan mentions a similar idea as current among the Christians of Bithynia, of which he was governor. Quod essent soliti stato die ante lucem convenire carmenque Christo *quasi deo* dicere. Letter 96, " Selected Letters," by Prichard and Bernard.

[33] c. 9; 14; 20. Seeberg holds that the pre-existent Church stands for the Holy Spirit, " Dogmengeschichte," i. 141 f. This appears to me an unwarranted inference in view of the express identification of the Spirit with Christ.

salvation, and the greatness of this salvation is emphasised by the contrast with the pagan darkness and ignorance from which Christ has delivered his Gentile hearers.[34] It is specifically the knowledge, the revelation of the Father of truth, of eternal life through him. It involves the absolute renunciation of paganism, the steadfast confession of him in the face of persecution, and obedience to his commandments in a life of active goodness, of " works " or " good works," [35] in accordance with the Christian professions.[36]

The other-worldly spirit of the preacher appears in the strongly marked antithesis between this world and the next, between life in this world and life eternal. " This age and the coming age are enemies." [37] Doing the will of Christ in an evil, perishable world is the imperative condition of salvation. We must keep our baptism (the " seal " [38] of consecration to Christ) pure and undefiled in order to enter the kingdom of God. " Who shall be our advocate if we be found not to have holy and righteous works." [39] For the preacher salvation is a thing of reward in return for righteous living, just as the successful athlete is crowned in the games.[40] Repentance, the keeping of the flesh pure, in keeping the Lord's commandments, are essential to the obtaining of the reward of eternal life.[41] Repentance and a pure life to this end is the keynote of the sermon. Hence the necessity of guarding against the Gnostic false teachers who deny the bodily resurrection, and aver that not the flesh, but the spirit is judged, and that it is, therefore, a matter of indifference how we treat the flesh. The incarnation of Christ, who was spirit before he became flesh, precludes such a perverted inference. As we were called in the flesh, we shall rise in the flesh to receive our reward. " We ought, therefore, to guard the flesh as a temple of God." Only so can we become sons of God, brethren of the Lord.[42] Only as we have wrought righteousness in the sight of God, shall we enter into the kingdom and receive the promises.[43]

For the preacher this righteousness has a markedly ascetic

---

[34] c. 1.   [36] c. 3-4.
[35] τὰ ἔργα, καλὰ ἔργα, c. 4 ; 12.   [37] c. 6.
[38] σφραγίς in the mystery religions, the mark imposed on the initiated, to which there is evidently a reference. Knopf, " Apostolische Väter," 162.
[39] c. 5-6.   [40] c. 7.   [41] c. 8.   [42] c. 9.   [43] c. 11.

character, involving the strictest self-control [44] in its pursuit,
for the sake of its eternal reward and for the purpose of disarming and winning the pagan blasphemer to Christ.[45]   The
nature of the Church also demands this active pursuit of
righteousness.   The Church in the spiritual sense has existed
from eternity, before the sun and the moon were created.
It has now become, by the manifestation of Christ in the
flesh, the body of Christ, and, therefore, he that deals wantonly
with the flesh deals wantonly with the Church.[46]   Hence,
once more, the stress laid on repentance and ascetic self-control,
and on the religious value of fasting, prayers, almsgiving
against the day of judgment—" the day of his appearing,
when he shall come and redeem us, each man according to
his works "—which they are to keep before their minds.
" Blessed is every one that is found full of these.   For alms-
giving lifteth off the burden of sin." [47]

The sermon is a classical exposition of the " moralism "
which by the middle of the second century was transforming
the Gospel into a system of morality and was acquiring a
strongly ascetic character.   With it is combined a heightened
evaluation of Christ in the direction of the later orthodoxy,
though there is still the idea of his subordination to God the
Father.   The conception of the Gospel is throughout the
legalist one, which the striving to preserve the Christian community from the deteriorating influence of its pagan environment, on its thought and life, has accentuated.   Compared
with the Epistle of Clement, there is a marked absence of the
Pauline conception of salvation in the sermon.   One may not
judge of the whole content of the writer's thought from this
comparatively short specimen of it.   At the same time, it may
be taken as typical of his pronounced moralist standpoint,
and may fairly be described as un-Pauline.

[44] ἐγκράτεια.
[45] c. 12-13.
[46] His reasoning is, in the original, not clear and is a confused serving
up of traditional matter, though he plumes himself on his argumentation.
[47] c. 16.

III. IGNATIUS OF ANTIOCH

The Epistles of Ignatius, bishop of Antioch, were addressed, most probably, towards the end of the reign of Trajan,[1] to certain churches in the province of Asia, to the Roman Church, and to Polycarp. Their genuineness has been the subject of keen controversy. Certain it is that a number of spurious epistles under his name was in circulation in the ancient Church, and the question has been voluminously discussed whether any of those ascribed to him can be received as genuine. As the result of the critical work of Zahn[2] and Lightfoot,[3] it is now generally agreed that seven of these, in the shorter Greek rescension, were actually written by him, though there are some persistent critics who regard them, or some of them, as forgeries.[4] They certainly are of a piece, and seem to me too real to be invented. They fit the character and circumstances of the impassioned martyr, who, in the face of the doctrinal division within the Church and persecution without, emphasises the clamant need for Christian unity, on the basis of the acceptance of the traditional faith and the recognition of the authority of the threefold ministry of the single bishop, and his subordinate presbyters and deacons, which has developed in these communities.

Whilst Clement specially emphasises the supreme Creator-God, Ignatius is mainly concerned with the conception of God in Christ. His teaching is largely influenced by a specific heresy emanating from a Christian-Gnostic party, which denied or questioned the true humanity of Christ. This heresy was due to the difficulty of conceiving of any contact between the divine Being and matter, which was regarded as the source of evil. It was not to the divinity, but the humanity of Christ that these Christian-Gnostic teachers took exception. That Christ was in some sense divine, they were ready to admit, but they could not conceive the possibility of the divine

[1] Harnack's conclusion that they were written in that of Hadrian ("Chronologie," i. 388 f., and "Die Zeit des Ignatius," 1873) does not seem to have gained adherents.
[2] "Ignatius von Antiochien" (1873).
[3] "Apostolic Fathers" (1885). Recent "Com. on the Epistles," by Bauer in Lietzmann's "Handbuch" (1920).
[4] For instance, Bruston, "Ignace d'Antioche," 45 f. (1897), rejects the Epistle to the Romans, whilst accepting the other six.

becoming truly incarnate in a human body, and one section of them, as we have seen, regarded the human life of Christ as a mere apparition or phantasm, and denied the reality of his birth, death, and resurrection. This was the form of Docetism, of which there were various kinds, against which Ignatius inveighed so passionately. He attacked the same tendency to explain away the human Christ that we meet in the Johannine Epistles, if not necessarily the same form of it.

His Epistles reveal the influence of the Johannine writings on his thought. If he was not a disciple of the Evangelist, as von der Golz thinks probable,[5] he had assimilated his teaching, whilst combining it with that of Paul. He represents the Greek striving to attain to a higher knowledge and life, such as the mysteries sought to ensure, and he shows familiarity with the train of ideas characteristic of these cults.[6] This knowledge and higher life he finds in a mystic faith in Christ and in a mystic communion with God in Christ. Platonic idealism is also reflected in the Epistles, though his thought is that of the impassioned believer rather than the Christian philosopher. Nothing could, in fact, be less philosophic than these letters, which are written in the ecstatic mood of one possessed by a passion for martyrdom and apt to express his thoughts and emotions in extravagant language. He is more a preacher than a thinker. His ideas on the divine-human Christ are asserted rather than argued, and these axiomatic assertions leave no room for argument to others. His purpose is not, in fact, to argue, but to confirm the faith of the churches to which he writes. Like Clement, he claims to write by inspiration of the Spirit,[7] and this is sufficient to settle the question. We may, with von der Golz, speak of the theology of Ignatius, and he certainly has strong theological convictions. But he does not develop them in the Epistles, and presents them as articles of faith, which he has evidently derived largely from Paul and the Fourth Evangelist, and from the common stock of Christian tradition.

[5] " Ignatius von Antiochien," 169 f. (" Texte und Untersuchungen," 1894.).   von der Golz thinks that the Johannine influence was the stronger. This seems to me debatable.
[6] Schlier discovers in the Epistles traces of Oriental religion and thought, which appear to have appreciably influenced Syrian Christianity, " Religionsgeschichtliche Untersuchungen zu den Ignatius briefen," 3 (1929).
[7] Philad. 7.

Whilst Christ is the Logos or Word of God, as in the Fourth Gospel, the title does not denote for Ignatius all that it means in the Prologue of this Gospel. He is specifically the revealer of God, " the mind," " the unerring mouth of the Father." [8] He " proceeds from silence," [9] and at the incarnation breaks this eternal silence by making known and executing the divine purpose of salvation, which God had planned in eternity. He is thus the Word in the Pauline sense of revealing " the mystery which hath been kept in silence through times eternal, but is now manifested," [10] rather than in the Johannine sense of the eternal, creative Logos. Whilst he pre-existed, " was with the Father before the worlds and has appeared at the end of the times," [11] he is not represented either as the agent of creation or as begotten of God, as in the Johannine writings. He does not become the active agent of God before his incarnation for the purpose of man's redemption. Though he was humanly born of Mary, he was in his divine nature unbegotten, " ingenerate." [12] Ignatius knows nothing of the later orthodox doctrine of the eternal generation of the Son, and would ultimately have been accounted a heretic for denying his eternal generation by the Father.

As the incarnate revealer of God and the agent of man's redemption, Christ has, for Ignatius, the value of God. The writer is, indeed, an adherent of the common monotheism, and speaks of the " one God who manifested himself through Jesus Christ." [13] Nevertheless, with the Fourth Evangelist, he applies to him the term " God." He speaks of " Jesus Christ, our God," of his " becoming God in the flesh," and, very crassly, even of " the blood of God." [14] He ascribes to him divine attributes,[15] and asserts his oneness with God.[16] In such passages he thus seems to identify God and Christ in a modalist sense, as if they are merely manifestations of one and the same divine Being. The inference does not necessarily follow. These expressions indicate merely his strong conviction of the divinity of Christ as the divine Word and Redeemer, not his identification with God in a modalist sense. Through-

---

[8] Mag. 8 ; Eph. 3 ; Rom. 3.
[9] Mag. 8.
[10] Rom. 16, 25, 26.
[11] Mag. 6.
[12] Eph. 7.

[13] Mag. 8.
[14] Eph. 1, 7 ; Rom. 1.
[15] Pol. 3.
[16] Eph. 5 ; Mag. 7.

out the Epistles he specifically distinguishes between the
Father and the Son, and even subordinates the Son to the
Father, who is described as " the Most High "—God in the
supreme sense.[17]   He represents Christ as " the Son according
to the will and power of God."[18]   Whilst the Son as well
as the Father is " God," as in the Fourth Gospel, they are
similarly regarded as distinct, the one from the other, and
are not merely modes of one and the same Deity.   He further
distinguishes the Spirit from both,[19] though in one passage
he is identified with Christ.[20]   His distinctive view of the
Godhead is thus the tri-theistic one, which he combines with
the current monotheism.   How this monotheism accords with
the belief in a threefold Deity, he does not explain, and leaves
us with the impression of a certain inconsistency and crudeness
in his thought.

Whilst thus asserting the divinity of Christ, he is equally
concerned to maintain his true humanity against the Docetists,
who deny it.   Christ became incarnate in a real, not a merely
illusory body.   He is " the new, the perfect man,"[21] not the
semblance of a man.   He is flesh as well as spirit—God in
the flesh,[22] though, unlike Paul and the Fourth Evangelist,
he believes in the virgin birth, which seems incompatible with
his full humanity.   He insists again and again on the reality
of his human as well as his divine nature in words that suggest
a rudimentary version of the second article of the later creed.
" Jesus Christ, who was of the race of David, who was the
son of Mary, who was truly born and ate and drank, was truly
persecuted under Pontius Pilate, was truly crucified and died
in the sight of those in heaven and those on earth ; who,
moreover, was truly raised from the dead."[23]   As man he is
generate and passible, i.e., born of Mary and capable of suffering, though as God ingenerate (unbegotten) and impassible.
He not only lived a real human life and died a real death.
He remained after the resurrection what he had been before
—flesh and spirit ; rose in the self-same body and ascended
to heaven in the flesh.   In his anxiety to repel the Docetists,
he thus urges a very materialist conception of the risen and

[17] Mag. 13 ; Rom. 1.
[18] Smyr. 1.   [20] Mag. 15.   [22] Eph. 7.
[19] Eph. 9 ; Mag. 13.   [21] Eph. 20 ; Smyr. 4.   [23] Tral. 9, etc.

exalted Jesus, and knows nothing of the Johannine resurrection
in the spiritual sense, or of the spiritual body which Paul
attributes to the risen Christ. " For I know and believe that
he was in the flesh even after the resurrection . . . ate and
drank with them (the disciples) as one in the flesh." [24]

The purpose of the incarnation is the redemption of man
and the world. In his incarnate state he inaugurates and
carries out the divine " economy " (as in the canonical Epistle
to the Ephesians), or plan of salvation which God conceived
in eternity, and which involves the virgin birth, the death,
and resurrection of Christ.[25] This " economy " has completely superseded the old dispensation. Christianity is not a
mere development of Judaism. It is a new religion, a distinct,
divine departure from Judaism, though he finds in the prophets
the precursors of Christ, who looked forward to him and
preached the Gospel of salvation through him.[26] Into this
redemptive " economy " he absorbs both Johannine and
Pauline thought.

As in the Fourth Gospel, it is concerned with the attainment
of eternal life, the true knowledge of God. " God manifested
Himself in human form for the renewal of eternal life." [27]
Christ is the door of the Father, by which the patriarchs, the
prophets, the apostles enter in.[28] He is " our only teacher,"
to whom the secrets of God have been entrusted ; " the mind
of the Father," from whom we derive the knowledge of God.[29]
True life and true knowledge are thus to be found only in
the incarnate Redeemer. Moreover, this redemption to true
life and knowledge seems to involve for Ignatius something
like the deification of the soul, not merely its regeneration, as
in the Fourth Gospel, and this deification evidently holds of
the flesh as well as the spirit. Hence the reiterated expression
of the aspiration " to attain to God," " to be full of God,"
" to partake of God." [30] In this respect the influence of the
mystery cults is more marked in the Epistles than in the
Fourth Gospel. Believers are " fellow initiates " [31] into the
mysteries of the Gospel.

[24] Smyr. 3.
[25] Eph. 18-20.
[26] Mag. 9-10 ; Philad. 5.
[27] Eph. 19.
[28] Philad. 9.
[29] Eph. 3, 15, 17 ; Mag. 9 ; Philad. 9.
[30] Ibid., 4, 12 ; Mag. 14 ; Tral. 13 ; Rom. 2 ; Smyr. 11.
[31] Ibid., 12 συμμύσται.

As in Paul, redemption is also concerned with the deliverance of man and the universe from the evil régime of the astral principalities or powers. In pictorial fashion he represents the appearance of Christ as that of a resplendent star in the firmament, which caused perturbation among the other heavenly luminaries, and portended the destruction of their power and the abolition of death.[32] In the Pauline phrase, the incarnate, divine Christ is " the new, the perfect man," the founder of a new humanity by his death and resurrection.[33] Hence the reiterated reflection of the Pauline emphasis on the Cross and the resurrection. His death is the destruction of death ; his resurrection the guarantee of life. Whilst the Cross is a stumbling-block to the unbeliever, it is salvation, life eternal, incorruption,[34] to the believer. The Gospel is the perfection of incorruption.[35]

His conception in detail of Christ's redemptive work and its appropriation by the believer is discernible in certain characteristic passages throughout the Epistles. In these passages there are also distinct reflections of the teaching of Paul. Paul is, in fact, the hero in whose footsteps he would fain tread,[36] if he does not always interpret the mind of his leader aright, and shares the current view of the Gospel as a new Law and of salvation as the reward of works.[37] As in Paul, Christ's death on the Cross is an essential of God's saving purpose. Christ, who, as God is impassible, suffered, as man, and truly suffered for man's salvation. His flesh was truly nailed to the Cross for our sakes.[38] His blood has a supreme efficacy for the believer.[39] He knows the Pauline doctrine of expiation, if he does not elaborate it in Pauline fashion. In one passage, at least, he speaks of " the flesh of our Saviour, Jesus Christ, which suffered for our sins." [40] In another, Christ " died for us that, believing, we might escape death." [41] Though he does not appear to have shared Paul's intense consciousness of sin in the face of the Law and the divine righteousness, he speaks of the need of repentance and forgiveness, of the divine wrath

[32] Eph. 19.
[33] Ibid., 20 ; Smyr. 4.
[34] Ibid., 17, 18, ἀφθαρσία.
[35] Philad. 9.
[40] Smyr. 6, ὑπὲρ τῶν ἁμαρτιῶν ἡμῶν παθοῦσαν.
[41] Tral. 2.

[36] Eph. 12.
[37] Ibid., 9 ; Rom. 1 ; Pol. 1, 2, 6.
[38] Pol. 3 ; Smyr. 2, δι' ἡμᾶς.
[39] Eph. 1 ; Smyr. 1.

and judgment. " The Lord forgiveth all men when they repent." [42] If he directs his remarks on this subject specially to the heretics, he doubtless regarded repentance and forgiveness as an essential of the Gospel for others besides his theological opponents.

For him, as for Paul, Christ's saving work is appropriated by faith. Christ is God's gift to man, and this gift is to be received in faith. Faith is, indeed, as in the Fourth Gospel, often belief in the divine-human Christ, as the writer conceives him. But it is not exclusively identical with the reception of right theological doctrine. It is also equivalent at times to trust in the grace of Christ, by which believers are redeemed, and which frees the soul from every fetter.[43] It is also the means of justification, and he disclaims justification by his sufferings for Christ.[44] Moreover, for him, as for Paul, a living faith lies at the root of the life of communion with the crucified and risen Christ, of the mystic indwelling of Christ, whose temples believers are, of the mystic dying with Christ, in order to live with him.[45] As in Paul, too, faith eventuates in love as its inseparable concomitant. " Faith and love are the beginning and the end of life—faith the beginning, love the end." [46] They are " the all in all " of the believer's life, in contrast to that of the heretics, and neither is preferable to the other.[47] Unfortunately, he shows the current tendency to claim a monopoly of both for those who share his theological beliefs. Those who differ from him can have neither. These " wild beasts " and " mad dogs " are, in Pauline phraseology, of the flesh, and they that are of the flesh cannot do the things of the spirit.[48] These heretics, who can have no part in the kingdom of God, he consigns to the eternal fire and denies them any chance of resurrection.[49] Hardly the language of faith united with love. Oh these rabid theologians !

Ignatius was not only a theologian who had learned much at the feet of Paul, if he did not always understand him, he was an ecclesiastic who, in the sphere of organisation, impressed the stamp of his ideas on the early Catholic Church. His

[42] Philad. 8 ; cf. Smyr. 5 ; Eph. 11.
[43] Philad. 8 ; 11.
[44] Rom. 5.
[45] Eph. 15 ; Mag. 5.
[49] Ibid., 16 ; Philad. 8 ; Smyr. 7.
[46] Ibid., 14.
[47] Smyr. 6.
[48] Eph. 8.

Epistles were written not only to defend the Church against heresy, but to farther the developing organisation of the three-fold ministry of the single bishop or pastor, presbyters, and deacons. In this organisation he saw the only effective guarantee of the unity of the Church and the preservation of the common faith. Hence the incessant insistence on the divine right of this ministry, in each community, in language which at times sounds very extravagant, though the main underlying motive is the practical one.

It is clear that there was a current of opposition to his exaggerated insistence on the divine right of the ministry, as it had developed in these communities. These opponents demurred to his exaltation of the episcopal organisation in its primitive form, and asked for historic proof from " the archives of the faith." " If I find it not in the archives, *i.e.*, the Gospel records," objected they, " I will not believe." [50] " It is written," retorted Ignatius. " That is just the point to be proved," was the counter retort. Whereupon, abandoning the appeal to tradition, he adduced Christ himself and the faith through him as " the inviolable archives," and his own inspiration by the Spirit. Rather a subjective method of settling a historic question.

Along with the organisation, he also lays the utmost stress on the worship of the Church, and especially on the celebration of the Eucharist, of which he seems to have a very realistic conception. He calls the bread " the bread of God, which is the flesh of Christ," and longs for a draught of His blood.[51] In a number of passages such expressions have no more than a figurative, spiritual meaning. Despite the very realistic terms, in which, in one passage, he speaks of " the Eucharist as the flesh of Christ which suffered for our sins," he does not seem to have actually anticipated the later materialist view of the elements, or to have regarded the celebration of the rite in the later sacrificial sense, as an offering anew of the real body and blood of Christ. He does repeatedly mention the altar, and thus ascribes to it a sacrificial character. But the

---

[50] Philad. 7-8. This is the reading adopted by Zahn, " Ignatius von Antiochien," 378 f. (1873), and by Funk, " Die Apostolischen Väter," 100 (1906).
[51] Rom. 7.

sacrifice seems to consist only in the offering by the community of its prayers and gifts to God. On the other hand, he seems to have associated with the rite ideas derived from the Greek mysteries. For him the Eucharist is "the medicine of immortality," "the antidote against death," [52] and these terms suggest a magical sort of substance by which the recipient partakes of Deity and attains to immortality. In view of his habitual use of metaphor, it is questionable whether he meant them to be literally construed.[53]

The Epistle of Polycarp, bishop of Smyrna, to the Philippians may be treated as a sort of appendix to those of Ignatius. Written shortly after the martyr had left Smyrna, it refers to his journey Romewards to meet his doom, and expresses heartfelt appreciation of his heroic character. It is a simple exhortation, interspersed with quotations from the New Testament writings, and reveals a diffident, if earnest, personality, in striking contrast to that of the impassioned, forceful bishop of Antioch, whose doom he was ultimately to share. He is a humble-minded disciple of the apostles, such as Irenæus represents him in his Epistle to Florinus, who is content to repeat their teaching, whilst professing his inability to rise to the wisdom of Paul.[54] He merely re-echoes, in addition, Ignatius' condemnation of Docetism and of the rejection of the resurrection, and this thoroughgoing condemnation is the most significant feature of the writer's doctrinal standpoint in relation to his times. "For every one who shall not confess that Jesus Christ is come in the flesh is Antichrist; and whosoever shall not confess the testimony of the Cross is of the devil; and whosoever shall pervert the oracles of the Lord to his own lusts and say that there is neither resurrection nor judgment, that man is the first-born of Satan." [55]

---

[52] Eph. 20.
[53] On this subject, see von der Golz, "Ignatius," 73 f.; Harnack, "Hist. of Dogma," i. 211; Seeberg, "Lehrbuch der Dogmengeschichte," i. 169 (3rd ed., 1922).
[54] Epistle 3, Lightfoot's ed. Lightfoot adduces strong arguments in favour of its genuineness against Schwegler, Zeller, and Helgenfeld, "Apost. Fathers," i. Pt. II., 564 f. See also Harnack, "Chronologie," i. 382 f.; Eng. trans. by Lightfoot, and in vol. i. of "Ante-Nicene Lib.," German trans. and Com. by Bauer, Lietzmann's "Handbuch" (1920).
[55] Epistle 7.

IV. BARNABAS

The author of the Epistle[1] of Barnabas was identified by Clement of Alexandria with the apostle of this name. The identification is highly improbable. The Epistle is anonymous, and if the author was named Barnabas, as later tradition came to believe, he must have been a different person from the apostle. Paul's fellow-missionary would hardly have presented the Jewish religion in the bitterly hostile spirit of the writer. Moreover, in the Epistle he is not an apostle, but the " teacher " of the community to which he addresses it,[2] and the deferential manner in which he refers to the apostles shows conclusively that he was not, like the companion of Paul, of apostolic rank. That it was written at Alexandria, as most critics conclude, is probable enough. Its markedly allegorical method of interpreting Scripture is Alexandrian. As the earliest notices of it come from the Alexandrian Fathers, Clement and Origen, there is a presumption that the tradition which connects it with Alexandria is reliable, and that it was directed to a Christian community in this city. The date of its composition is uncertain. The only certainty is that it must have been written after the destruction of the temple by Titus. The writer expressly states that it had been destroyed as the result of the Jewish rising against the Romans.[3] How long after it is impossible definitely to say. Perhaps the reference that follows to its rebuilding by the Jews, as the servants of the Romans, is to the construction of a temple to Jupiter on the ruins of the old one after the suppression of the second Jewish rising, under Barcochba, in A.D. 135. Though the meaning of the passage is admittedly obscure, this is at least a possible inference, and would place the composition of the Epistle in the third decade of the second century.[4] Whilst Lightfoot[5]

[1] Though it is termed an epistle, it is largely of the nature of a tract, as Windisch contends, " Die Apostolischen Väter," 411 f. (1920).

[2] chs. 1 and 4. Krüger thinks that it was not addressed to a single community, but to the Church at large. " Hist. of Early Christian Literature," 21 (Eng. trans., 1897).

[3] c. 16.

[4] See Windisch, " Die Apost. Väter," 388 f.

[5] " Apost. Fathers," ii. 509.

and Bigg [6] would date it as early as the reign of Vespasian, Harnack [7] and Pfleiderer [8] refer it to that of Hadrian. On the whole this seems the safer conclusion.

Whether the writer was a Jewish or a Gentile Christian is also a debatable point. The extreme anti-Jewish spirit seems to betoken a Gentile author, and this impression is confirmed by the misrepresentation of Jewish rites,[9] which he shares with his fellow-Christians of the second century. Moreover, he refers to the former pagan life of his hearers, among whom he apparently reckons himself,[10] and claims that the Christians are the true heirs, through Christ, of the ancient " Testament " given to Moses.[11]

His purpose is to initiate his hearers into the higher spiritual knowledge or wisdom of the Old Testament, which the Jews have totally misunderstood, and in which he professes to be an expert. This knowledge has nothing to do with the current speculative Gnosticism,[12] of which his hearers are quite incapable. The community is lacking in knowledge, though not in faith, hope, and love.

In its lack of true knowledge as to the nature of Judaism, it shows a tendency to appropriate Jewish legalism, apparently in deference to the authority of the Old Testament Scriptures.[13] As in the case of the writer of the Epistle to the Hebrews, his aim is to impart instruction on the true nature of Judaism in relation to Christianity. His Epistle is, however, rather a crude effusion, though he plumes himself on his superior knowledge. In style and culture it is greatly inferior to Hebrews. " Whilst the Epistle to the Hebrews is a master-

[6] " Origins of Christianity," 56 (1909). Both rest their conclusion on the quotation from Daniel in c. 4, in which the writer is supposed to describe the political conditions of the time of Vespasian. There is a full discussion of the authorship of the work in Donaldson's " Apostolic Fathers," 248 f. (1874).
[7] " Chronologie der altchristlichen Literatur," i. 427.
[8] " Urchristenthum," ii. 553 f. Armitage Robinson admits the possibility of the later date. " Barnabas, Hermas, and the Didache," 6 (1920).
[9] See chs. 7 and 8.
[10] ch. 16, etc.
[11] c. 15. On this question, see Knopf, " Nachapostolische Zeitalter," i. 37 f. ; Windisch, " Apost. Väter," 413.
[12] The emphasis laid in c. 5 on Christ's coming in the flesh is not directed against Docetism, but refers to the necessity of his bodily manifestation in order by his incarnation and resurrection to abolish death.
[13] c. 4.

piece, Barnabas is a sad bungler." [14]   His exposition and
argumentation are materially weakened by his excessive
proneness to a fanciful interpretation of the Old Testament.
Religion, he maintains, is spiritual, and its true understanding
demands spiritual insight.   For lack of this insight the Jews
have totally misinterpreted and perverted their own Scriptures,
which, from beginning to end, foreshadow Christianity, and
have made themselves the victims of a crass materialism.

In developing this thesis he maintains that the covenant with
Abraham had reference to the future believers in Christ, not to
the Jews, and that the later covenant with them, mediated
through Moses, was annulled through their idolatry.   For
no sooner had Moses received the Tables of the Law, on the
Mount, than he broke them in pieces, because of their infidelity.
The original covenant and the promise attached to it have
been fulfilled in the Lord Jesus, and the Christians, on whose
hearts it has been sealed through faith in him, not the disobedient Jews, are the inheritors of it. [15]   The Jews have, further,
utterly misunderstood the ceremonial Law given by Moses,
which they have interpreted in a gross material manner.   In
ordaining this Law, Moses meant it to be spiritually, not
literally apprehended and practised. [16]   The sacrificial cultus
and the ceremonial Law as practised by them are, and have
ever been, a travesty of religion and a contravention of the
revealed will of God.   Witness the continual protests of the
prophets against their false religiosity. [17]   Similarly their
Sabbath keeping, their circumcision, their veneration for the
temple are the result of a crassly material conception of God
and His revealed will.   The seventh day after the creation,
on which God rested and which He hallowed, pointed forward
to the Christian Sunday, the eighth day, on which Christ rose,
the day of Christian rejoicing, with which a new creation
began. [18]   The true temple is the renewed heart of the believer,
in which God, who has no need of any building of men, dwells.
Unlike the building which the Romans have destroyed, it is
spiritual and incorruptible. [19]   " Therefore let us become

[14] Gwatkin, " Early Church History," i. 98 (1909).
[15] chs. 4, 13, 14.
[16] c. 10.   [18] c. 15.
[17] chs. 2, 3.   [19] c. 16.

spiritual, a perfect temple unto God." [20]   " For a holy temple unto the Lord is the abode of our heart." [21]

In proof of these contentions he appeals throughout to Scripture, which he cites with a supreme disregard for the historic sense. He finds, for instance, the pre-existent Christ, " the Lord of the whole world," acting with God at the creation.[22] Scripture from Genesis onwards is made to testify to him and his future manifestation in the flesh as Son of God, whose suffering was necessary to complete the condemnation of the Jews, as well as for the remission of sin.[23] Abraham, in instituting circumcision, which has been abolished in Christ, looked forward in spirit to Jesus and the Cross.[24] Moses and the prophets similarly adumbrated baptism and the Cross for the remission of sin, as a variety of incidents and quotations abundantly proves.[25] Whilst there is no little force in his denunciation of the crass materialism of the old Jewish religion, his exegesis in proof of it can only be described as fancy roving wild over the sacred page. In his craze for a fanciful reading of Old Testament texts, he far outdoes Paul and every other New Testament writer. In his revulsion from historic Judaism, he would hardly have admitted with Paul that the Law was, at least, a schoolmaster to Christ. He has, in this respect, carried the anti-legalist and anti-Judaic spirit to the verge of absurdity. In the face of the historic testimony of the Old Testament, he stoutly maintains that the Jews have never been the people of God. In their crass religious literalism and materialism, they have ever been alien from God.[26] The Christians alone are the true people of God, radically distinct and different from the old, falsely so-called.

Whilst thus radically anti-Judaic and anti-legalist, he does not go the length of regarding, with the Gnostics, the God of the Old Testament (the Maker or Demiourgos of the world) as distinct from and inferior to the supreme God. He retains the Jewish monotheism, whilst repudiating the historical Jewish religion. He wholeheartedly recognises Moses and the prophets as the revealers of His will in the spiritual sense.

For him, as for Paul, Christ is the pre-existent Son of God

[20] c. 4.
[21] c. 6.
[22] chs. 5, 6.
[23] chs. 6, 7.
[24] c. 9.
[25] chs. 11 12.
[26] chs. 4, 16.

who participated in the creation of the world, though, in
identifying him with the Spirit,[27] he seems to ignore the
passages in which Paul teaches a triune deity, and to hold
a di-theistic or binitarian conception of the Godhead. He
came in the flesh because his humanity, though voluntary,
was necessary for man's salvation, and because mortal eye
could no more behold him, in his supernatural nature, than
the naked eye can behold the sun. He suffered and rose
again in order to abolish death, and this suffering was also
necessary for the remission of sin, and that he might be the
judge of the world. As in Paul, his death was a blood sacrifice
for sin. Christ offered his body—" the vehicle of his spirit "—
for our sins in fulfilment of prophecy and in keeping with the
typical offering of Isaac on the altar.[28] For him, as for Paul,
the Cross is the central fact of his life and of the Gospel, and,
like Paul, he passes over his early life and concentrates on the
Cross and the resurrection. He knows Paul's doctrine of the
new creation in Christ and of the sanctified body of the believer
as the temple, the dwelling of God. " By receiving the
remission of our sins and hoping on the Name, we become
new, created afresh from the beginning. Wherefore God
dwelleth truly in our habitation within us. How ? The
word of His faith, the calling of His promise, the wisdom of
the ordinances, the commandments of the teaching, He Himself
prophesying in us, He Himself dwelling in us." [29]

Whilst Christianity is a spiritual, non-ritualistic religion,
with neither temple nor sacrifice and, apparently, only one
rite—baptism [30]—it is legally conditioned. Like all those
early Fathers, Barnabas here diverges from Paul, with whose
Gospel he is, in many respects, in close touch. It is " the
new Law of our Lord Jesus Christ." [31] If, as in Paul, it has
freed the believer from the old Jewish yoke of constraint, it
becomes, in turn, a new code of conduct. This new code
consists of the commands, the ordinances of Christ. Nor

[27] chs. 6, 7, 9, 11, 12. It is very doubtful whether in c. 9 he goes beyond
Paul and applies the term θεός to him. Whilst he mentions the Spirit in
a number of other passages, it is the Spirit of the Lord operating in the
Old Testament, not the Spirit in the Christian sense. " Da Barnabas eine
Lehre vom heiligen Geist als selbständiger göttlicher Person wohl nicht
gehabt hat, so fehlt bei ihm auch die Trinität." Windisch, " Der Barnabas-
brief "; Lietzmann's " Handbuch "; " Die Apostolischen Väter," 375 (1923).
    [28] c. 7.   [29] c. 16.   [30] c. 11.   [31] c. 2.

is the writer's conception of faith the specifically Pauline one.
" As far as in us lies, let us exercise ourselves in the fear of
God. Let us strive to keep His Commandments, that we
may rejoice in His ordinances." " The doctrines of Christ
are three—hope, righteousness, love." [32] This may be a reflection of the Synoptic Gospel, but it is hardly a reflection of
the distinctive Gospel of Paul. Abraham is, indeed, said to be
justified by faith.[33] But this is merely an incidental remark,
and faith is rather the power to produce the Christian virtues
than the means of deliverance from sin and death. At the
same time, his conception of the Christian life under the
new law is free from the ascetic spirit, which its narrow interpretation tended to nurture, in spite of the fact that his view
of the world is pessimistic, and of the near approach of its end.
It is a life of joy and mutual zeal in well-doing.[34]

This new law he strives to apply in the concluding sections [35]
of the Epistle in which, after the Jewish didactic fashion, he sets
forth the " Two Ways "—that of light and that of darkness.
In this concluding part he combines the ethical teaching of
the old and the new religion in a practical spirit, and at the
same time gives an illuminating picture of the moral and
social life of the community. In the observance of these
injunctions, its members are to practise the higher Christian
morality, in contrast to that of the Gentile world. From the
practical point of view, they earn his hearty commendation.
If lacking in knowledge, they are rich in faith, hope, and love.
They observe with joy the eighth, i.e., the first Christian day
of the week, as the day of the resurrection,[36] and are exhorted
to visit one another for mutual instruction and examination.[37]
They are to beware of living a solitary, self-sufficient life and
neglecting the assembly in the common meeting-place, where
each is diligently to concern himself with the spiritual welfare
of all.[38] They are to share their goods with the needy brethren,
and to be partakers in common of the things that are corruptible,
as well as of those that are incorruptible.[39] They are to be
generous in giving and faithful in guarding what is committed
to their charge. They are to avoid division and seek to bring
the contentious together. They are to act in a Christian

[32] c. 4 ; c. 1. [34] c. 4. [36] c. 15. [38] c. 4.
[33] c. 13. [35] chs. 18-21. [37] c. 19. [39] c. 19.

spirit whatever their station, whether as subject, master, or servant, and are to strive to save souls by the word.[40]   As an incentive to this life of well-doing they are to keep constantly before their minds the resurrection and the coming judgment, which is near at hand.   " The Lord is near and His reward." [41]

V. HERMAS

" The Shepherd " of Hermas, like the Apocalypse, is the work of a Christian prophet.   It owes its title to the visionary appearance to the writer of a man, glorious in visage and dressed in the garb of a shepherd, who is described as " the angel of repentance,"[1] and communicates to him a series of mandates or commandments, and similitudes or parables, which he is directed to impart to the Church. These are prefaced by a series of visions, in which an old woman, who personifies the Church, also imparts to him a number of revelations.   The work is apocalyptic in the sense that it professes to convey a divine message to the Church through the visionary experiences of the writer.

There is no doubt about the name of the writer.   In the work he repeatedly tells us that his name was Hermas.[2]   But there is the usual difficulty about his identification and the date of the book.   His identity with the Hermas of the sixteenth chapter of Romans is inadmissible, since the work clearly belongs to the post-apostolic period.   He tells us that he was brought up by an unnamed person, who sold him to a Roman lady of the name of Rhode.[3]   He was thus apparently a castaway and his early life was that of a slave.   From the detailed description of Arcadia in the ninth similitude,[4] it has been plausibly argued that he was a native of this region.   He appears, at all events, to have been of Greek, not of Jewish descent.   According to a tradition preserved in the Muratorian fragment (late second century), he was a brother of the Roman Bishop Pius, and wrote " The Shepherd " during his episcopate (A.D. 140-154).   The statement is somewhat dubious, inasmuch as, in the work, the Roman Church is not governed by a single

---

[40] c. 19.   [1] Vis. v.   [3] Vis. i. 1.
[41] c. 20.   [2] Vis i. 1, 2, etc.   [4] Sim. ix. 1.

bishop, but by a number of presbyter-bishops.[5] Nor is such a castaway likely to have had any known relatives. The composition of the work under Bishop Pius is, therefore, rather doubtful. The mention of Clement in Vision ii. 4, to whom the old woman, who personifies the Church, directs him to give a book of revelations, suggests that, as Harnack contends, this part of it at least was written whilst Clement was still alive, *i.e.*, probably in the early second century. Harnack, assuming the accuracy of the statement about the writer in the Muratorian fragment, is further of opinion that it was concluded about the year 140.[6] From the length of the work, we may justifiably conclude that its composition extended over a number of years, and there are indications in it that this was the case. But in view of the dubiety of the evidence of the Muratorian fragment, it is not essential to extend this period to the episcopate of Pius. It may, therefore, be assigned to the early part of the second century, when the single bishop had not yet displaced the rule of a number of leading presbyter-bishops over the community. Gnosticism, towards which he does not show the embittered attitude of Ignatius, was evidently only at an incipient stage in the West. One persecution, which has cost many members their lives, has already afflicted the Church (perhaps the persecution under Trajan, which was of a general character). Another is apprehended, though the author writes during an interval of immunity, which would suit the reign of Hadrian from 117 onwards. The apostolic age lies in the past, and the state of the Church, which has a large and very mixed member-

[5] Vis. ii. 4 ; *cf.* ii. 2 ; iii. 9.
[6] " Chronologie," i. 266-267. Pfleiderer agrees as to the date, 140, for the publication of the work, but thinks that the Clement mentioned in it is not necessarily the Clement who wrote the Epistle to the Corinthian Church, since the name was a very common one at Rome. Knopf also concludes that its composition was gradual, and places it between 130 and 140. " Nachapostolische Zeitalter," 40 (1905). Turner accepts the Muratorian date, *Journal of Theological Studies* (1920). Edmundson rejects it and would place it in the late first century, *The Expositor* (1922). Streeter also rejects the Muratorian statement, but infers that the early portion of the work was written whilst Clement was still alive, *i.e.*, at the beginning of the first century, " Primitive Church," 203 f. (1929). A recently discovered MS. of "The Shepherd," now in Michigan University Library, lacks the first four Visions. Bonner infers that this part originally circulated as a separate work. *Harvard Theol. Rev.*, April 1925. Wilson considers that the remainder, as contained in the Michigan MS., was written later in the reign of Trajan. *Harvard Theol. Rev.*, January 1927.

ship, betokens a lengthy interval between this age and the writer's time.

The community addressed is evidently the Roman Church, though his message is directed mainly to the Church at large. His occupation was apparently that of a small trader, to judge from the allusions to business and its drawbacks for the spiritual life. He had some knowledge of the current popular philosophy and was gifted with a vivid imagination, of which he makes ample use to convey his message in figurative, allegoric fashion to his time. His literary gift was limited, and his work becomes at times tedious to the modern reader. Some portions are both long-winded and far-fetched.[7]

The prophetic element runs through the whole work, inasmuch as it professes to give a series of revelations in the form of visions, mandates, and parables. The writer is, however, essentially a moralist, and his message is concerned mainly with the Church as a spiritual and ethical institution, and with the conduct which is befitting in its members. The Church is showing marked signs of spiritual declension, in consequence of their worldly spirit. It needs a moral tonic in order to attain a higher standard of Christian living, and prove its steadfastness in the face of impending persecution. Hence the need of penitence for sins committed after baptism, and of the renewal of the moral life, without which salvation is impossible. Repentance and renewal form the keynote of his message throughout. His Christian thought is conditioned by this absorbing theme. Apart from his conception of the Christian life and the Church, his theology is meagre. He is imbued with the practical, not the philosophic spirit. In this respect " The Shepherd " resembles the Epistle of

---

[7] I have used the original text as edited by Funk. An exhaustive examination of " The Shepherd " is given by the late Principal Donaldson, " Apostolic Fathers," 318 f. (1874). A recent and more summary one by Armitage Robinson, " Barnabas, Hermas, and the Didache " (1920). See also Harnack, " Altchristliche Literatur," i. 49-58. Dobschütz has minutely examined its teaching from the point of view of the life of the community, " Life in the Primitive Church," 309 f. See also Baumeister, " Die Ethik des Pastor Hermas " (1912), and the older work of Zahn, " Der Hirt des Hermas " (1868). A valuable commentary, with a German translation, has been provided by Dibelius in Lietzmann's " Handbuch zum N.T.," " Die Apostolischen Väter," 415 f. (1923). English translations are available in vol. i. of " The Ante-Nicene Library," by Donaldson and Crombie (1867), by Taylor (1903), and by Lake in the " Loeb Classical Lib." (1912-13).

James, the only New Testament writing from which he quotes directly, though there are allusions which seem to show a knowledge of the other New Testament books.[8]

Like Clement he emphasises in a monotheistic tone the one Creator-God, who created, out of nothing, and for the sake of man, the universe, which is the manifestation of His power and wisdom.[9] Man is dependent on Him who comprehends all things, but cannot Himself be comprehended. He is the source of all the virtues. Both faith and repentance are His gift. Whilst He is to be feared, He is also to be trusted. If He is the enemy of sin, he is ever ready to pardon the sinner. His mercy, in spite of an all too-prevalent moral declension, is emphasised throughout. With Him is associated in the work of creation the pre-existent Son, as in Barnabas. " The Son of God is older than all the creation, so that he was a fellow-councillor with the Father in the work of creation."[10] What he has created, he sustains. " The name of the Son of God is great and immeasurable, and sustains the whole world."[11] He is also spoken of as " the holy, pre-existent Spirit that created every creature," and his incarnation is explained as the union of this Holy Spirit with a human being (" flesh "), chosen by God for the purpose of man's redemption. " The pre-existent, Holy Spirit that created the whole world, God made to dwell in flesh which He chose."[12]   " The Holy Spirit is the Son of God."   " The Son is the Holy Spirit."[13] These passages clearly teach a di-theistic conception of the Godhead, as in Barnabas, though his lucubrations on the subject are by no means lucid or consistent, and this inference has been contested.[14]

His view of the incarnation of this Son or Holy Spirit

---

[8] See " The New Testament in the Apostolic Fathers," 105 f. He evidently took what he says about the double-souled (doubting) man in Mand. ix. from James. Gregory points out other passages assimilated from James, " Canon and Text of the New Testament," 186 f. (1907).

[9] Vis. i. 1 and 3 ; Mand. i., xii. 4 ; and cf. ii., Clem. i.

[10] Sim. ix. 12.

[11] Sim. ix. 14.   [12] Sim. v. 6.

[13] Sim. ix. 1 ; Sim. v. 5. The latter text, which is regarded by Funk as doubtful, is accepted by Dibelius as authentic, " Apost. Väter," 569. See also Turner, *Journal of Theol. Studies* (1920).

[14] By Seeberg, for instance, 127 f. (3rd ed.), against Loofs, Harnack, and others, who contend that Hermas does identify the Son and the Spirit. His statement of the case against this identification does not seem to me quite effective.

has been described by Harnack as adoptionist.[15]   But it is not, as he implies, adoptionist in the primitive sense that the man Jesus was chosen, or adopted to be the Son of God or Messiah, and anointed or invested with the Holy Spirit to this end. For Hermas, on the contrary, Christ is the divine, pre-existent Holy Spirit or Son of God who became " flesh " in the man Jesus ; not, as in the primitive tradition, the man adopted to be the Son of God in the Messianic sense.   His conception is, in fact, not the primitive adoptionist one, but the Pauline conception of the pre-existent, heavenly Christ, who became incarnate in the historic Jesus.[16]

Unknown to him, as to Clement, is the conception of the Logos as applied to the Son—another indication that the Logos theory of the Fourth Gospel and Ignatius had not yet impressed itself on the mind of the Roman community,[17] in spite of the currency of Greek speculative ideas at Rome. He had evidently not read the Fourth Gospel, and the similarity of thought in a couple of passages does not warrant us in inferring literary dependence on it.[18]   On the other hand, the angels fill a large place in his imagination, and play an important part in the divine economy.   He associates them with the Father and the Son as councillors in the work of creation and redemption.   To them is committed the care of the creation,[19] and they take an active part in Christ's redeeming mission.[20]   To the archangel Michael in particular, who seems to be identifiable with Christ, is assigned the duty of watching over the conduct of Christians.[21]   This marked angelology is evidently derived from late Jewish apocalyptic sources.

The purpose of the incarnation is the redemption of man from sin.   It is unfolded in the parable of the vineyard.[22] The lord of a field, in which there was a vineyard, commissions one of his slaves to wall it round with stakes during his absence,

[15] " Hist. of Dogma," i. 190-191.   See also Lake, " Landmarks of Early Christianity," 110 f. (1920).

[16] Some have seen in this union of the divine Son or Holy Spirit with the human Jesus a foreshadowing of the later Roman doctrine of the two natures—the divine and the human—in Christ.   In this composite being a perfect humanity is partnered with, yet distinct from the pre-existent divine Christ, who unites himself with it.

[17] The founding of the Tower (the Church) through the creative word of " the name," refers to God.   Vis. iii. 3.

[18] See " The New Testament in the Apost. Fathers," 123.

[19] Vis. iii. 4.   [20] Sim. v. 5-6.   [21] Sim. viii. 3.   [22] Sim. v. 2 f.

and promises him his freedom on his return. The slave not
only does so, but clears it of the weeds that have grown up in
it, and makes it fruitful. For this service the lord not only
rewards him with his freedom, but adopts him as co-heir with
his son, and sends him many dishes from his table. The
field, explains the Shepherd, is the world; its lord is God.
The slave is Jesus in whom the Son of God is incarnate. The
vines are the people of God. The stakes are the angels who
guard this people. The weeds are their sins. The dishes from
the lord's table are the commandments which He gives through
the Son. The absence of the lord is the time that elapses before
his return.[23] The Son, adds the Shepherd, became a slave
in order to purge away the sins of the people [24] by his sufferings
and labours. Having thus cleansed them from sin, he showed
them the paths of life by giving them the Law which he had
received from his Father. In reward the human Jesus—
" the flesh " in which the pre-existent Son or Spirit dwelt, and
which co-operated with the Spirit—is assumed as a partner with
it, *i.e.*, enters on his exalted state.[25]

Such is the Shepherd's conception of the redemption
accomplished by Christ. Though he does not mention his
death, the purging away of sin is ascribed to his suffering and
his devotion to the object for which he became incarnate.
The significance of the Cross is so far recognised in harmony
with the traditional doctrine. With this is combined the
giving of the Law, which is to regulate the life of the Christian
and which the Son received from his Father. On its observance,
" life," salvation depends. Hermas entirely ignores the Old
Testament Law in its bearing on Christianity, and in this
respect differs markedly from Paul, the Epistle to the Hebrews,
and Barnabas. The Gospel is for him an absolutely
independent system of Christian ethics, of which the Son
of God is the source and the revealer, and which the Shepherd
conveys to him in a series of mandates. It starts, as far as
Judaism is concerned, with a clean slate. It has no relation
to any historic revelation. It is the expression of the divine
will manifested by the Son of God, without any attempt to
trace it by a forced and fanciful exegesis throughout the Old
Testament.

[23] Sim. v. 5.   [24] τὰς ἁμαρτίας αὐτῶν ἐκαθάρισε.   [25] Sim. v. 6.

The forgiveness of sin is operated in baptism. It is conditional on faith in the word (the Gospel) and repentance of past sins.[26] The penitent believer is baptised by immersion in the name of the Lord, and thus is symbolically saved through water.[27] The Tower which Hermas sees in one of his visions, and which symbolises the Church, accordingly appears as built on the waters.[28] Baptism is also for Hermas " the seal of the Son of God," impressed on all who bear his name, and without this seal no one can enter the kingdom of God. So indispensable is it that even the saints of the old dispensation could not enter the kingdom until they had received the seal of baptism at the hands of the apostles, who went and preached the Gospel to them in Hades.[29] In this idea of the quickening influence of baptism on the dead, there seems to be a vague echo of the Pauline conception of baptism as a dying to the old and a rising to the new life of the soul, though Hermas applies it only to the dead, not to the living. " Before a man bears the name of the Son of God," explains the Shepherd in speaking of the pre-Christian departed souls, " he is dead."

Otherwise he has not much in common with the distinctive Pauline doctrine of redemption. He, indeed, lays constant stress throughout on sin, which entails death and captivity,[30] and arouses God's anger, and on the need of renewal and restoration from sin. Repentance and faith are God's gifts, and both are necessary for the remission of sin. Faith is for him the cardinal saving virtue. " Through her the elect of God are saved." [31] He speaks of the necessity of propitiating God for sin. " How," he asks, " shall I be able to be saved, or how shall I propitiate God for my sins, or with what words shall I pray the Lord that he may be propitious to me ? " [32] He knows, too, the idea of justification in the sense of declaring righteous or making righteous in the mercy of the Lord.[33] In such passages there is a resemblance to the terminology of Paul. But the thought underlying it is, for the most part, not distinctively Pauline.

---

[26] Vis. iii. 7 ; Mand. iv. 3.   [27] Vis. iii. 3.   [28] Vis. iii. 2 f.

[29] Sim. ix. 15, 16. Perhaps an echo of 1 Pet. iii. 18, 19 ; iv. 6, in which Christ is asserted to have preached in Hades.

[30] Vis. i. 1.

[31] Vis. iii. 8 ; cf. Mand. viii., where faith is also mentioned as the first of the Christian virtues.

[32] Vis. i. 2, ἐξιλάσομαι τὸν θεόν.   [33] Vis. iii. 9 ; Mand. v. 1.

This appears clearly in his markedly legalist conception
of the Gospel and the Christian life. Even more distinctively
than in the post-apostolic writers generally, the Gospel, in
addition to its being a message of redemption, is a system of
law regulating the life of the believer. Of this law Christ is
the revealer, the legislator, and on its observance the salvation
of the believer depends. This Gospel is not, as in Paul, the
deliverance through faith from sin and death in dependence
solely on the grace of God in Christ, not on works. It is the
fulfilment of Christ's commandments in a life of penitence
and in the exercise of the Christian virtues, of which faith is
the chief. Incidentally, indeed, the remission of sin is obtainable in baptism through faith and repentance. But this holds
only of sins committed before baptism, and it is with the
remission of sins committed after baptism that the writer is
chiefly concerned. This is, in fact, the main theme of the
book. This remission is obtained only by penitence and the
practice of the commandments of the Son of God, as exemplified
in the Christian virtues. From this point of view—and this
point of view is the characteristic one—salvation from post-
baptismal sin is the result of penitential works, of righteous
living in the effort to keep the commandments ; not of faith
and grace in the Pauline sense. Hence the markedly legalist
conception of the Gospel.

In this connection he proclaims the possibility of a second
repentance for wilful sin committed after baptism. This
doctrine forms another marked feature of the work, and shows
a reaction from the more rigorist post-apostolic view, which
allowed no room for repentance for such sin.[34] In accordance
with this more liberal view, he maintains that a second repentance is possible, and emphasises throughout God's mercy in
accepting it. There is, however, no room for further repentance in the case of renewed wilful relapse into sin. " Forgiveness will be granted to all the saints who have sinned up to the
present, if they repent with their whole heart and banish doubt
from their minds. But the Lord has sworn by His glory in
reference to the elect. If any of them sin after a certain day,
which He has fixed, he will no longer have salvation. For
repentance has its limits for the righteous." [35] " There is but

[34] See Heb. vi. 4-8, for instance.   [35] Vis. ii. 2 ; *cf.* iii. 5.

one repentance (for sin after baptism) to the saints of God."[36]
" If any one, after his great and holy calling (to Christ), falls into
sin through the temptation of the devil, he has one opportunity
to repent.   But if he again and again sins and seeks to repent,
this repentance is of no avail, and he will scarcely attain to
life."[37]

There was evidently difference of opinion in the community
over the admission of penitents who had lapsed into wilful,
post-baptismal sin. We have, in fact, in the " Shepherd "
a foreshadowing of the later controversy over this question
associated with the names of Hippolytus and Novatian in
the third century. Hermas, in the early part of the second,
voices the more liberal attitude in reaction from the post-
apostolic rigorism.

The legalist conception of the Gospel is definitely expressed
in the similitude or parable of the great willow tree, overspread-
ing mountains and valleys, under which are assembled those
called by the name of the Lord. The tree, explains the
Shepherd, is the law of God given to the whole world. This
law is further particularised as the Son of God (i.e., the Gospel)
who is preached to the ends of the earth, and those assembled
under its shade are the peoples who have heard and believed
the Gospel. The glorious angel of the Lord, who stands
beside it, is Michael, who exercises dominion over the believers,
and seems here to be identifiable with Christ.[38]

The content of this law is the subject of the mandates which
the Shepherd has previously communicated to Hermas in detail.
The saving effect of its observance is emphasised throughout
the work. Salvation is the reward of the keeping of the
commandments. For Hermas, religion is a thing of righteousness and its reward, the practice of the Christian virtues
and the merits ensuing therefrom. Of these virtues the chief
are faith and self-control,[39] the daughter of faith, from which
the other virtues proceed. " Whoever devotes himself to
these and is able to cleave to their works will have his dwelling
in the Tower with the saints of God." [40] " If, when you
have heard these (commandments and parables)," the Shepherd
further explains, " ye keep them and practise them with pure

[36] Mand. i. 1.   [38] Sim. viii. 1.   [40] Vis. iii. 8.
[37] Mand. iv. 3.   [39] ἐγκράτεια.

minds, ye will receive from the Lord all that He has promised
you." [41] " You will have life if you attend to my commandments and walk in them. . . . If you do not keep them, but
neglect them, you will not be saved." [42] Even if the task is
hard, it is possible by the help of God to achieve it. " Trust
God . . . for if you return to the Lord with all your heart
and practise righteousness for the rest of your life and serve
Him rightly in accordance with His will, He will accord you
the healing of your former sins and power to master the works
of the devil." [43] Nay, it is in our power to do more than
has been commanded — to perform what later came to be
theologically known as works of supererogation. " Keep the
commandments of the Lord and you will be well pleasing
to God, and inscribed among the number of those who observe
them. And if you do any good beyond what is commanded
by God, you will gain for yourself more abundant glory and
will be more honoured by God than you would otherwise
be." [44] Fasting is an additional merit in God's sight, though
it is of no avail unless performed in the right spirit, and for
the practical purpose of alms-giving [45] (i.e., spending on others
what you have spared on yourself). " If you observe fasting as
I have commanded you, your sacrifice will be acceptable to
God, and this fasting will be written down " (to your credit).

The conception of the Christian life is the ascetic one,
and this asceticism has a redeeming value. The antagonism
between this world and the next, which is a common feature
of early Christianity, is here very marked. Hermas follows the
author of the Epistle to the Hebrews [46] and anticipates Augustine
in his doctrine of the two cities and their distinctive laws. The
Christian is a dweller in a strange land. His city is far removed
from that in which he dwells on earth, and he is bound to obey
the law pertaining to his city at the peril of losing his citizenship
for disobedience. Participation in the affairs of this world is
detrimental to the spiritual life. The acquisition of riches is,
therefore, not permissible to the Christian. He must be
content with what suffices for his subsistence, and must set
his mind on acquiring purely spiritual riches. " If, then,

[41] Vis. v.
[42] Mand. iv. 2 ; xii. 3 ; cf. vi.-viii.
[43] Mand. xii. 6.
[44] Sim. v. 3.
[45] Sim. v. 1.
[46] Heb. xi. 13 f.

ye know your city in which ye are to dwell, why do ye acquire here lands and costly establishments, vain dwellings and buildings. Take care, therefore, as one living in a foreign land, to acquire no more than what is necessary and sufficient, and when the lord of this city shall cast thee out for disobeying his law, be ready to leave it and depart to your own. . . . Instead of lands buy afflicted souls, according as each is able ; visit widows and orphans and neglect them not, and spend your riches and all you possess, which you have received from God, on such lands and houses." [47]

The distinctive note of the writer's religion is thus the legalist one. In its relation to the Christian life, the Gospel is a Law to be rigidly obeyed, and on this obedience salvation, which is its reward, depends. This Gospel is widely removed from that of Paul, which emancipates the believer from the Law and conceives the Christian life as a life of freedom from the old legalism, of spontaneous service rendered in the power of a living faith, from which the thought of reward, the possibility of merit are excluded. It is a Gospel which shows the influence of Stoic, as well as Jewish moralism. It is based on the law of nature (Epictetus), or the Law of God (Seneca), and perhaps reflects the Roman sense of Law and obedience to the Law as the indispensable condition of a universal, ordered society.[48] " The Shepherd " thus shows in a marked degree the growing influence of environment on post-apostolic Christian thought. It is a Gospel adapted to the times, and it may be said that the adaptation was a necessary development in view of the danger of the moral contamination of the Christian community by its pagan environment. The Pauline Gospel of freedom, even if ethically limited, was too idealistic for ordinary human nature. Many of the members of the Christian community were evidently in danger of being religiously enervated by the pagan society in which they lived. " Living with the heathens " has become a serious menace to the Christian life, and not a few seem to have succumbed to the temptation to do as their neighbours did. As in the Epistle of James, there is a considerable proportion of rich members, who are infected by the worldly spirit of their environment, and are

[47] Sim. i. 1.
[48] On this point see M'Giffert, " Christianity in the Apostolic Age," 451.

Hermas 293

prone to overlook their duty towards the poor and the mutual dependence of rich and poor in a Christian society.[49] The clamant need of the time was to foster and preserve strength of character, loyalty to the Gospel ethic in an age of moral declension. There was room for the moralist as well as the preacher of faith, and the insistence on the keeping of the Lord's commandments was by no means superfluous, if the idea of earning salvation thereby is questionable from the religious point of view. The Christian prophet who preaches the Gospel of obedience to the Law of the Son of God, visionary though he be, has a strong sense of the practical needs of the time.

At the same time, this Gospel had its drawbacks from the standpoint of the Christian freedom from legalism which Paul had won for the Gentile Church. We miss the note of this freedom, combined with a lofty ethical life, characteristic of the teaching of the Apostle. The reaction from this freedom to the old legalism, in spirit if not in form, seems to tend towards the later monastic development. Hermas himself belongs to the type of character that gravitates in this direction, though, in an allegorical work, the references to himself need not be taken in a strictly personal sense. At all events, the character which he introduces, under his own name, in the early part of the work, is not that of the robust Christian who can manfully be in the world, without being of the world in the un-Christian sense. This character represents the Christian with a supersensitive conscience, who is much concerned with his own sins and the sins of others. He cannot control his wife and children, who appear to typify the community, and finds it difficult to control himself. He would evidently not have suited the part of the bishop in the Pastoral Epistles. He is prone to confess and bewail his sins and to make himself a nuisance to others, though he corrects what purports to be his own tendency to querulousness by insisting on the duty of eschewing sadness and putting on cheerfulness.[50] He is only happy when he is miserable and making everybody else miserable. The Church tells him to cease praying continually about his sins and pray for righteousness,[51] and in judging his complaints over its declension, we must make

[49] Sim. ii.   [50] Mand. x. 2, 3, λύπη, ἱλαρότης.   [51] Vis. iii. 1.

allowance for the temperament and spiritual experience of the writer.

His conception of the Church vividly reflects the expanding Christianity of the first half of the second century. It has won its way, in the conflict with the state, to a strong consciousness of its vocation and power as a universal association, " the kingdom of God." It has become the Catholic (the universal) Church, though the term is not used, as in Ignatius. It has spread far and wide over the empire and is conscious of its organic unity. This organism is no recent institution. As in the so-called Second Epistle of Clement, it existed before the creation. God is its creator and for its sake was the world made. Through it His purpose in history is to be realised. From the standpoint of its age, he naïvely represents it as an old woman ; [52] from that of its membership, as a great tower which is being built up on the Son of God, the rock, who is also the only gate into it. Like the woman, the rock is old, for the Son was before the creation, whilst the gate is new, the Son having only manifested himself at the end of the old dispensation. The tower which is being built on it is the Church—" the kingdom of God "—into which no one can enter except through the Son. In the building of it the apostles, the office-bearers, and the martyrs are represented by the most beautiful and perfectly fitting stones. [53] It is thus that he pictures the prominence and the unity of the ecclesiastical class, which, by the time when he wrote, has become markedly differentiated from the ordinary members of the community, and whose members are prone to strive among themselves for " the first seats." [54] The expanding Church is also figured as a great tree overshadowing the whole earth, in which the Gospel is being preached. [55] It is a spiritual empire, and is so far from being sacerdotally conceived that, like Barnabas, he does not even mention the Eucharist, and only emphasises baptism in the name of the Lord. [56] The Church is for him, above all, a spiritual and moral institution. It exists for the development of the moral life, and its organisation and worship are touched on only in passing. He himself

[52] Vis. ii. 4 ; cf. i. 3.
[53] Vis. iii. 2-5 ; Sim. ix. 2 f.
[54] Vis. iii. 9.
[55] Sim. viii. 3 ; cf. Sim. ix. 17.
[56] Vis. iii. 3 and 7 ; Sim. ix. 16.   He ignores the Matthæan formulary.

is a charismatic and is interested mainly in the individual spiritual life, and in the further revelation of God's mind and will.

Though existing from the creation, the Church is but a temporary institution. It has no real root in this evil world, and from this point of view it is sharply contrasted with the empire.[57] The Christian is a sojourner in a strange land, and the end is not far off. The building of the tower will soon be finished, and then comes the end.[58] It contains good and bad members. There are, too, apostates and traitors, false teachers, introducers of strange doctrines,[59] though this is not emphasised, and Gnosticism is only incidentally alluded to.[60] The Church has been recently exposed to persecution for the name.[61] Persecution is in store for it in the near future, and these apostates not only renounce it in the face of such persecution, but betray the servants of God. Some have been faithful unto death— the martyrs. Others—the confessors—have endured torture, prison, confiscation; and the tendency is to exalt the martyrs and place them almost on a level with the apostles. There is, in fact, already the germ of a martyr cult and the later hagiolatry or worship of the saints.[62] But there are many waverers, and not a few have denied Christ. Some have even blasphemed his name. Among the apostates are the (spiritual) children of Hermas himself.[63] For those who have merely denied Christ a second repentance is possible. For those who have not only denied, but blasphemed his name, no second repentance is to be hoped for.[64]

VI. "THE DIDACHE" AND PAPIAS

The author of "The Didache," or "Teaching of the Lord, through the Twelve Apostles, to the Gentiles,"[1] was evidently

[57] Sim. i.
[58] Vis. iii. 8.
[59] Sim. viii. 6 ; ix. 18, 19.
[60] Sim. viii. 6 ; ix. 22.
[61] διὰ τὸ ὄνομα.
[62] Vis. iii. 1 and 2 ; Sim. viii. 31 ; ix. 28.
[63] Vis. ii. 2.
[64] Sim. vi. 2 ; viii. 6 ; ix. 26. The assumption that in Vis. iii. 7 the writer teaches the possibility of the remission of sin committed in this life, through penitential suffering in an intermediate state (purgatory), is not warranted.
[1] Διδαχὴ Κυρίου διὰ τῶν δώδεκα ἀποστόλων τοῖς ἔθνεσιν. It was discovered by Bryennios in the monastery of Phanar at Constantinople and published in 1883. It is mentioned by Eusebius (iii. 25) as among the non-canonical writings, though Clement of Alexandria reckoned it in

a Jewish Christian who had a knowledge of some of the New Testament writings, especially the Gospel of Matthew, in addition to the Old Testament scriptures. As usual, the critics differ over its provenance. Whilst Harnack finds it in Egypt, Knopf, with greater probability, prefers Syria.[2] There is also the usual discrepancy over the question of its date. In favour of a comparatively early date is the archaic caste of the writer's thought and the prominence of the ministry of apostles (in the wider sense of the term), prophets, and teachers in the Christian communities. On the other hand, the prophetic class, as we learn from the " Shepherd " of Hermas, continued well into the second century, and its prominence in " The Didache,"[3] alongside the official ministry of " bishops and deacons,"[4] does not necessarily betoken an early date. Its marked deterioration further suggests a lengthy interval between the composition of the book and the apostolic age. Moreover, if, as is almost certain, the writer borrowed his doctrine of the Two Ways from the Epistle of Barnabas, and is also to some extent dependent on the " Shepherd " of Hermas, his work must be posterior to those of both these writers. Many scholars have, indeed, accepted Dr Taylor's theory[5] that the first part of it is a Christian adaptation of a Jewish tract, " The Two Ways," for the instruction of proselytes. On this theory, the writer and Barnabas could have borrowed from the same Jewish source, and neither need be dependent on the other. But nothing is otherwise known of the assumed existence of

the canon. There has been a number of editions, including that by Harnack in " Texte und Untersuchungen," ii. (1886), with copious notes and discussions and a German translation. See also Zahn, " Forschungen," iii. (1884), and Funk, " Tübinger Quartalschrift " (1884). There are English translations by Hitchcock and Brown, Spence, Schaff, and Romestin. French edition of the text, with translations by Hemmer, Laurent, and Oger (1907). There is a recent German translation by Knopf, " Die Apostolischen Väter " (1920, Leitzmann's " Handbuch zum N.T. "), with commentary. See also Dr Armitage Robinson's discussion of its date and contents in " Barnabas, Hermas, and the Didache " (1920), Streeter in " The Primitive Church," 140 f., 279 f. (1929), and Maclean, " The Doctrine of the Twelve Apostles " (1922).

[2] " Nachapostolische Zeitalter," 43 (1905), and " Die Apostolischen Väter," 3 (1920).

[3] c. 10 f.

[4] c. 15. Streeter argues in favour of an early date, approximately A.D. 90, " Primitive Church," 140 f., and rejects its dependence on Barnabas and Hermas.

[5] " The Teaching of the Twelve Apostles " (1886).

this Jewish tract, and Dr Armitage Robinson has, on this ground, recently questioned the validity of the theory. As the result of a searching comparison of the Epistle of Barnabas and " The Didache," [6] he has adduced cogent reasons for his conclusion that the first part of the latter work is mainly an amplified reproduction of chapters 18-20 of the former. He has also found in it traces of the writer's dependence on Hermas. He accordingly postpones its composition till about the middle of the second century. He is further of opinion that it is rather an imaginative picture of the primitive Church than a representation of the Church and the ministry as it existed in the writer's time. To me this part of his argument is by no means convincing. The writer does seem to be depicting the actual conditions prevailing in the first half of the century in the communities which he addresses. In spite of Ignatius, diversity of organisation, as well as of thought, prevailed in the Church at large till far into the century.

" The Didache " consists of two parts. The first is a brief manual, under the title of the " Two Ways," for the instruction of catechumens in the practical Christian life. The second is a sort of " Book of Common Order " bearing on the worship and organisation of the community. As in Jeremiah xxi. 8, the Two Ways are the way of life and the way of death.[7] The former consists in the love of God and our neighbour and the practical observance of the Christian virtues, as enforced in the teaching of Christ, particularly in the Sermon on the Mount, and, to a more limited extent, that of Paul and James.[8] As we have seen, the contents of these chapters are largely an amplification of the three chapters in which Barnabas sets forth the way of light and the way of darkness. In chapter v. the way of death is illustrated, in more summary fashion, in the form of a catalogue of the vices which the believer is to eschew.

In the second part the apostle and prophet still exercise their function of proclaiming by inspiration the word of God, though as a class they have evidently degenerated. There are

---

[6] " Barnabas, Hermas, and the Didache," 43 f.

[7] This conception of the Christian life was known to Ignatius (Mag. 5), Hermas (Mand. vi. 1), and 2nd Clement, as well as to Barnabas and the Didache.

[8] c. 1-4.

false apostles and prophets (" Christ traffickers " [9]), who make a living out of their vocation, and whose character and message require to be tested by the community. Incidentally, the writer gives an insight into its faith and life, which are of the primitive caste. Its conception of God is that of the Father-Creator, who exercises a providential care for His children in the abundance of His gifts.[10] The sense of the divine Fatherhood also appears in the repetition of the Lord's Prayer thrice a day,[11] and in the prayers prescribed in celebrating the Eucharist.[12] Like Clement and Ignatius, it believes in the threefold Deity of Father, Son, and Spirit in the formula prescribed for baptism.[13] It applies to Jesus the titles Lord, Saviour, and Servant, and conceives the Gospel as His commands.[14] It believes in the continued inspiration of the prophets by the Spirit, in its operation in preparing the heart for faith, and in the unforgivable sin of rejecting its inspiration.[15] It recalls, in connection with the Eucharist, the life, knowledge, faith, and immortality which the Father has granted to His children through His servant Jesus.[16] It shares the current idea of seeking by alms-giving to provide " a ransom for sins." It shares, further, the subapostolic conception of the Church as the universal body of the saints, which forms the kingdom of God.[17] It reproduces the features of its life and worship, which are still those of a primitive character. It assembles on the Lord's Day for the celebration of the Eucharist, in which only baptised believers, after confession of sins and reconciliation of aggrieved members, participate,[18] and which is conceived as spiritual food and drink unto eternal life, and as " a sacrifice " (in reference to the offerings of the members).[19] There appears to be also a private week-day celebration, which is preceded by a common meal (the Agape, or Love-feast), though this term is not used.[20] Baptism is preceded by instruction and fasting, is performed by immersion in " living " (*i.e.*, running) water, or by sprinkling, if there is not sufficient

[9] c. 12.
[10] chs. 1, 3, 4, 10.
[11] c. 8.
[12] chs. 9, 10.
[13] c. 7.
[14] chs. 4, 8, 9, 10, 11, 15.
[15] chs. 4, 11.
[16] chs. 9 and 10.
[17] c. 10.
[18] chs. 9, 14.
[19] chs. 10, 14.

[20] Drews seems to be right in assuming two celebrations—one (chs. 9-10) on a week-day, which is preceded by the Agape ; another (c. 14) on the Lord's Day without the Agape, " Zeitschrift für N.T. Wissenschaft," v. 74 f.

water, in the triune name. Fasting is observed twice weekly, and the Lord's Prayer repeated thrice daily.[21] The Church is exposed to persecution and lives in the constant expectation of the coming of Christ, which shall be preceded by the appearance of Antichrist and heralded by the sign of the Cross in the heavens, the blast of the last trumpet, and the resurrection of the saintly dead.[22]

Of the teaching of Papias, who may also be reckoned among the "Apostolic Fathers," we know almost nothing, since his "Expositions of the Lord's Sayings" have not survived, except in some extracts in Irenæus[23] and Eusebius.[24] From Eusebius we learn that he believed in a millennium after the resurrection from the dead, when the material reign of Christ would be established on the earth. The loss of his work is all the more regrettable, for, on his own confession, he was a diligent collector of the traditions of the elders, who had known the apostles, and of two, who, he says, somewhat problematically, had been disciples of Christ—Aristion and the presbyter John.[25] Eusebius, however, who tells us that he was bishop of Hierapolis, in Phrygia,[26] did not rate his production very highly, and concludes, from his knowledge of it, that he was "of very limited understanding."[27] He seems, however, to have possessed a considerable knowledge of early tradition, and Eusebius quotes from him the statements that Mark wrote his Gospel on the information of Peter, and that Matthew wrote the "Logia" of Christ in the Hebrew language.[28]

[21] c. 8.
[22] c. 16.
[23] "Adv. Haer.," v. 33, 4.
[24] "Hist. Eccles.," iii. 39.
[25] Some critics have identified this John with the apostle, but Papias himself mentions two Johns in the same sentence, and clearly distinguishes the Presbyter from the Apostle John.
[26] "Hist. Eccles.," iii 36.
[27] Ibid., iii., 39. Translations of the "Fragments of Papias" are given in I. "Ante-Nic. Lib." See also De Boor, "Neue Fragmente des Papias, Texte und Untersuchungen," v. (1889).
[28] Ibid., iii. 39.

CHAPTER V

THE APPEAL OF THE GOSPEL

I. THE DEVELOPING GOSPEL

FROM this lengthy survey it is sufficiently evident that the Gospel in the early Church has undergone a process of development. This development reveals the influence of the individual apprehension of the teaching and person of Jesus, of the religious experience of the believer, and of the larger environment into which the Gospel erelong expanded.

The Gospel, as reflected in the New Testament and other early writings, was not, in important respects, fully and finally proclaimed by Jesus during his brief ministry in Galilee and Judæa. It is a growth extending over a century and a quarter, and to this growth the Christian thought and experience of other minds besides his materially contributed. Moreover, whether as a message or a movement, it was conditioned by its environment as it expanded into the Græco-Roman world and came into touch with the religion and culture of this wider environment. From this environment, as well as from individual thought and experience, it absorbed much that did not at first form a constituent element of it. It is a mistake to regard it, in this developed sense, as a thing purely superterrestrial, independent of historic conditions and forces. Even in the original form in which Jesus proclaimed it, it was to a large extent a product of Judaism, since the main ideas of this proclamation were derived from the Jewish religion. His mind was steeped in the Jewish scriptures, and he appears to have been familiar with the train of thought of the later Jewish Apocalyptic, and with the rabbinic teaching of the synagogues, though in his public ministry the interest in this teaching is largely that of antagonism. By Hellenist thought he seems to have been untouched. The original Gospel shows, indeed, distinctive features from the outset, which it derived from the personality and religious experience of Jesus himself. These impart to it an originality, an uniqueness which elevate it above its historic setting and constitute something new, supremely great. To ignore this is to turn on it the blind eye. At the same time, to focus only these features and survey it in the light of a preconceived theory of the Gospel, whether as proclaimed by Jesus or developed by his later followers, as something purely superterrestrial, independent of historic conditions, is equally mistaken. It is not an abstraction of this kind that presents itself to our view in the New Testament and other early writings, though there is an abstract element in them. What they show is a historic process by which the Gospel rose and developed within the first century and a half, and, as later Christian history shows, the development was by no means complete within this period.

The first stage of it is represented by the mission and teaching of Jesus himself. This stage is of limited duration, and is confined to the small region of Galilee and Judæa. But it is of infinite importance, whether as the germ or the inspiration of what was to become a universal religion. The Gospel starts as an obscure movement within Judaism. It is concerned specifically with the religious enlightenment and betterment of a petty folk among the hills of Galilee and Judæa. But as Jesus proclaimed it, it has both a sublime character and a far-reaching purpose. It is concerned with the establishment of the kingdom or rule of God, primarily among the Jews as God's people, to whom he proclaims the kingdom in the ethical sense. But the kingdom in the ethical sense is but a preparation for the kingdom in the eschatological, transcendental sense, and this aspect of it has a universal bearing. In this sense, its realisation involves the divine transformation of the world, the inauguration of the new age or æon, though his message and his mission are concerned mainly with his own people, and only incidentally with those of non-Jewish race. It really transcends locality and race. It contemplates the universal rule of God, which is at hand and which the Jews will reject and the Gentiles will inherit. " Many shall come from the east and the west and shall sit down with Abraham and Isaac and Jacob in the kingdom of heaven ; but the sons of the kingdom shall be cast out into the outer darkness." [1]

There is a presage here of a far larger movement. Practically, however, the mission of Jesus is kept within the limits of Judaism, is confined within the boundary of Palestine, and as effective influence, makes itself felt only within a small area even of Palestine. From the point of view of its later development, it is the day of small things. Jesus is the Master only of a small community of disciples. The Church, as we know it even in the primitive phase succeeding his death, does not exist, though the germ of it is there in the circle of his disciples. He appears as a teacher and a prophet, preaching the kingdom of God and the Fatherhood of God ; forms an inner circle of disciples ; wins by his preaching and his works of healing, and by the missionary propaganda of these disciples, many followers ; becomes fully conscious of his filial relation to the Father, and his Messianic vocation and destiny, and is ultimately recognised by his disciples as the promised Messiah ; is publicly acclaimed as the Messianic king by his followers on his entry into Jerusalem ; is opposed from the outset by the Scribes and Pharisees, and ultimately, in virtue of a sudden revulsion contrived by them and the priesthood, becomes the victim of the bigotry and intolerance of his opponents. He dies on the Cross as the suffering Messiah and Servant of God, leaving to his disciples the conviction of his triumph over death, of salvation through him, and his coming in glory to judge the world. This, in the most general terms, is the Gospel in its earliest form.

After his death a new stage is reached in the early preaching of his disciples, with its distinctive proclamation of him as the Messiah who has risen and been exalted through suffering to glory, through whom salvation is available to those who repent and believe in him and are baptised in his name, and who will speedily come as the judge of the world. This preaching results in the establishment of the Church in its primitive Jewish form, and the tentative extension of the mission to the Gentiles.

The work and teaching of Paul constitute a farther stage, of vast formative importance. As the result of his missionary

[1] Matt. viii. 11.

activity and that of his disciples or his fellow-apostles, in the larger sense, the Church strikes permanent root in the Gentile world, the disruption between the Law and the Gospel is definitely made, the Gospel is emancipated from its Jewish limitations and becomes a universal faith, and the conservative Jewish opposition ultimately dwindles into insignificance. From the mould of his Christian faith and experience, his knowledge of Jewish Apocalyptic and theology, and, in a lesser degree, of Hellenist thought, Paul further stamps on the Gospel a heightened conception of the person of Christ and his cosmic significance, and of his redemptive function as the divine deliverer from sin, corruption, and death. Whilst he works out his cardinal doctrine of justification by faith in virtue of the death of Christ, in terms of the rabbinic theology, he combines with it a magnificent ethic as the fruit of faith and the working of the Spirit in the heart, and makes of the Gospel an emancipating and transforming power. He further infuses into it his distinctive mysticism, which is based on the death and resurrection of Christ, and shows traces, in diction at least, if not, perhaps, in substance, of the influence of Greek mystery religion. He starts the conflict with incipient Gnosticism with which his own conception of the pre-existent, cosmic Christ has a certain affinity, and the influence of which is discernible in his terminology.

In the next stage—that of the subapostolic period, in which we may include the early or so-called " Apostolic " Fathers, the anti-Judaic tendency of Paul is continued and developed in the Epistle to the Hebrews, the Fourth Gospel, the Epistles of Ignatius, and the Epistle of Barnabas. The Gospel, as the absolute religion, has completely superseded Judaism, and the Christians have displaced the Jews as the people of God, the true Israel in the divine redemptive " economy," or scheme. On the other hand, whilst the anti-Judaic spirit is accentuated throughout the expanding Gentile Church, the Pauline Gospel is being gradually transformed into a new Law in accordance with the moralising spirit of the incipient Catholic Church, under Stoic influence, and the growing need for the regulation of the Christian life in its pagan environment. To a certain extent, as in the Epistle of James, it represents a reversion to the ethic of Jesus as the norm of the believer's life. With few exceptions, the moralist conception of the Gospel thus displaces the distinctive Pauline faith mysticism. In spite of this and other divergences, however, there is observable a growing tendency to emphasise the importance of tradition, as derived from the apostles (Paul included), in opposition to the rising Gnostic movement within the Church, and to enhance the importance of the ecclesiastical office in the Christian community.

Very marked within this period is the enhanced influence of Hellenist, or, more correctly, in the case of Ignatius at least, Hellenist-Oriental thought on the development of the Gospel. This influence makes itself felt very strongly in the Johannine and the Ignatian writings. In these writings Christ definitely appears as the incarnate Logos, and is equated with God in the absolute sense. The Gospel specifically becomes the true revelation or knowledge of God through the Logos Christ, and the means of eternal life in virtue of the regeneration of the soul, as in the Fourth Evangelist, or of its ultimate deification, as in Ignatius. Combined with this distinctive conception of Christ and his redemptive function is the accentuated sacramentalism, which shows the influence of Greek mystery religion, as well as Hellenist thought, in moulding the Gospel in its Johannine and Ignatian form. At the same time, there appears alongside it a tendency to revert to the more concrete Jesus of the early tradition, as reflected in the Synoptic Gospels. In the Johannine and Ignatian writings themselves there is distinct evidence of dissent, on historic grounds, from the fully fledged theory of the incarnate Logos-Christ. This dissent is also traceable in the second century, and the theory only ultimately won its way to supremacy in the period which lies beyond the scope of this study.

II. The Preparation for the Gospel

In the period under review the Gospel was a message and a mission to the world, rather than a theology. We speak of a New Testament theology. Bulky volumes have been written under this title. Their authors trace the development of the content of the Gospel and construct out of the available Christian literature a synthesis of the theology of these writings. The task is a legitimate one, and its performance by capable theologians has enriched theological literature and materially contributed to elucidate the origin of Christianity on its doctrinal side.

Specifically, however, the Gospel of the period is not a theology, but a message. The aim of this message is primarily to convert and to edify, not to construct a religious philosophy. Whilst speculation—philosophy enters into it—it is largely incidental and subordinate to the aim of commending the Gospel as a revelation and a redemption. Paul, the Fourth Evangelist, the writer of Hebrews embody the speculative element in their teaching. But they do so mainly for practical and apologetic purposes. The apostles and teachers of the early period are primarily missionaries of the faith in Jesus Christ, whether preaching to the heathen or edifying the Christian believer.

In important respects the ancient world was prepared for the appeal of the Gospel. Paul speaks of " the fullness of the time,"[1] and it is true that there was a variety of factors tending, at least indirectly, to the favourable reception of the Christian message in the Græco-Roman world. The external conditions in the first Christian century were, it may be said, so far favourable as to make the Christian mission possible, and at least potentially effective. The universal rule of Rome, the far-reaching Roman Peace (the *Pax Romana*), the intermingling of peoples, the far-flung system of highways, the common Greek language, spoken over a large part of the empire, made for the rapid expansion of the Christian message. In the intellectual sphere Greek thought, with its tendency towards monotheism and its emphasis on the things of the spirit, provided points of contact with the Gospel. Similarly, in the sphere of religion there was a preparation for the Gospel in the widespread aspiration for the deliverance of the soul from the things of sense, its regeneration to life eternal, as reflected in the Greek mysteries. In virtue of this community of ideas, the ancient world was, we may say, ready for the appeal of the Gospel, with its sublime conception of God, its doctrine of redemption, its lofty ethic.

On the other hand, the factors making for the reception of the Gospel were only of relative, and therefore of limited

[1] Gal. iv. 4.

value, and we must be careful not to overestimate their efficacy.
The strength of the appeal was offset by its difficulty. There
was antagonism as well as response to the Gospel, and for long
the antagonism is more in evidence than the response. In
the case of Judaism it did not necessarily follow that, because the
Gospel had so many points of contact with the Jewish religion,
the result would be the Christian transformation of this
religion. As a matter of fact, the Jews as a race rejected the
Gospel. Among the peoples of the empire it is equally vain
to look for the spontaneous acceptance and the speedy triumph
of the Gospel. Nearly three hundred years elapsed between
the first preaching and the conversion of the head of the Roman
State. Another three centuries of conflict with paganism
intervened before its triumph was complete, even within the
empire. Such facts warn us against generalising too facilely
on the strength of the Gospel appeal, or the extent of the
preparation for it in the ancient world.[2] All movements which
aim at transforming human society and inaugurating a new
era in human progress, even in cases when conditions—what
is called the spirit of the age—are tending in this direction,
only achieve their aim through conflict with the conservative
forces of the age. Only as they are endowed with an inherent
vital power, do they succeed in overcoming the opposing force,
and, as a rule, they do so only gradually. Sometimes the
revolution wrought by them may appear swift and decisive,
the conflict short and sharp. Even so, the result is achieved
only in virtue of a long period of preparation, which makes
the revolution but the final stage of a lengthy process. Christianity was no exception to this law of human progress. The
transformation which it effected in the religious sphere was
the work of centuries of struggle and suffering, and its final
triumph, when it came at last, with effects akin to a revolution,
through the conversion of Constantine and its elevation to
first place as the imperial religion, was only the last act of a
long-drawn-out drama of heroic effort and endurance.

[2] On the preparation for the Gospel I have in manuscript a general
survey which I intended to serve as an Introduction to my " Historic Jesus,"
and also to this volume. For reasons of space I have been compelled to
omit it in both cases. I may yet publish it separately.

III. STRENGTH OF THE APPEAL

At the same time, it may be said that the appeal of the Gospel was destined to prevail in virtue of its inherent merits, compared with every other religion in the ancient Roman world. It bore within it the germ of its own predominance.

In the first place, it had an immense advantage over its rivals in possessing a historic founder, whose claims to the allegiance of the ancient world, in the moral and spiritual sphere, were based on the solid fact of a unique personality. Apart from the later dogmatic interpretation of his person, Jesus, as revealed in the authentic record of his mission and character as prophet, teacher, healer, and saviour, was a unique figure in this sphere. He was overwhelmingly worthy of the supreme claim made for him on moral and spiritual grounds. No mythical figure, like Attis, or Sarapis, or Mithras, not to mention the Græco-Roman hierarchy of mythological or state deities, could approach him as the historic, and, at the same time, the highest manifestation of the divine in the human. The personal impression which he made on his followers may be gauged from the Gospel about him, which they preached, and the writings in which they conveyed this impression to posterity. Apart from this preaching, there is the still more powerful impression of the actual figure of Jesus, as he taught and toiled and suffered in the prosecution and consummation of his mission. Here was the concrete answer to the Stoic quest for the ideal wise man, the perfection of character. Never man spoke as this man, and communicated so powerful a religious and moral inspiration. In keeping with the historic personality, is the teaching on God and the kingdom of God. In its elevation and simplicity it comes to the soul with a compelling force, in spite of its Jewish apocalyptic colouring. In the mission preaching of his disciples in the apostolic and subapostolic periods it underwent a gradual development. The Jesus of the early tradition was transfigured, in accordance with the resurrection experience of the immediate disciples, into the exalted Lord. Into the thought of Paul and John about him the speculative element intruded itself. Even so, the Gospel retains the basic features of that of Jesus himself in its conception of the Father-God and His infinite love ; of His redemptive purpose and its achievement in Christ ; of the fact of evil as sin and of responsibility and judgment for sin ; of the possibility and the actuality of a new life here and life eternal hereafter ; of the imminent end of the present æon or order of things, which held out the prospect of the deliverance of man and the universe from their thraldom to the demonic power of evil. This was the Gospel in its missionary content, and with this Gospel Christianity could start on its mission with an appealing power that no rival cult could approach. Compared with it, every other faith, not excepting even the Jewish faith, with its burdensome ceremonial law, its nationalist limitations, could be weighed in the balance and found wanting. In the moral and spiritual sphere it was, in its more practical form, a unique Gospel, if only because it was based on a personality and a life and a teaching which could not be gainsaid, except by ill-informed or prejudiced opponents, as the highest possible manifestation of God in and to humanity.

Second only to the appeal of the Gospel itself was the appeal of the Christian life. The Christian life at its best was the most effective missionary agent of the Christian faith. There can be no doubt whatever about the new moral and spiritual power that operated within the Christian communities. They were, indeed, far from realising the standard which Paul and his fellow missionaries set up and strove to keep up. Among the Gentile converts there were lacking the high moral standard and training, which the Jewish Christians inherited from the law and the prophetic teaching of the Old Testament. There was, in fact, throughout the Gentile world a deep sense of the low moral tone prevailing in the great cities, and the widespread pessimism of the age was due, in part at least, to the consciousness of this fact. It found expression especially in Stoicism, with its emphasis on the need of regeneration from the life of sense, of self-renunciation, and self-discipline. The early Christian mission to the Gentiles was conducted in the cities, and the terrible picture of city life which St Paul gives in the first chapter of the Epistle to the Romans, as reflected in cities like Antioch and Corinth, is sufficient to show how difficult was the task of creating a moral sense, a mode of life worthy of the Gospel. These Gentile converts had to be weaned from old associations and habits formed in this polluted atmosphere, and in cities like Corinth the process was a slow and arduous one. Moreover, they consisted at first largely of persons of the lower class, predominantly perhaps of the slave class, and the moral and spiritual elevation of this class, with the debasing vices and deteriorating influences inherent in ancient slavery, might seem an almost hopeless enterprise. Paul's description of the social and moral declension of even the higher classes in these cities, where the mission activity was mainly carried on, might seem to preclude the possibility of a moral regeneration. The apostle was, however, apt at times to write in very absolute terms, and there is some reason to infer that this description, whilst generally accurate as an indication of the widespread presence of revolting vice, was too absolute as a literal reflection of the moral condition of pagan city life. Moreover, he himself provides the corrective in the second chapter of the Epistle, in which he reminds the Romans that " the Gentiles, which have no law, do by nature the things of the law, those having no law being a law unto themselves in that they show the work of the law written in their hearts, their conscience bearing witness therewith." [3] The fact of conscience as a testimony to sin implies the sense of sin, and it was in this fact that the Christian Gospel of the regenerated life found the possibility of an effective response, even in such an apparently hopeless environment.

Thus the Christian life, the training in the ethical and spiritual teaching of Jesus, the regeneration of the soul by the Spirit of God, the elemental power of a newborn faith, working in even the most degraded heart, could become a reality. In spite of the blemishes which too many of these converts carried over into the Christian communities, as the New Testament and later writings remind us, these early communities could and did become the nurseries of a moral and spiritual life, of an enthusiasm in well-doing, of a spirit of service and self-sacrifice, of a strength of character in enduring and suffering, of a passionate devotion to the highest ethical ideal, unparalleled in the religious history of the time. They shone as so many stars in the moral firmament of the ancient world, and pointed

[3] Rom. ii. 14-15.

to many the way out of the darkness to the light of the Gospel. They were, in virtue of this fact, especially after the great missionaries had disappeared, the main instrument of the spread of the Gospel in their environment, and their power of attraction was by no means inconsiderable. The history of early Christianity is the history of a power not only of religious revolution, but of moral regeneration, even if the real fell short of the ideal depicted in the New Testament writings and in the early apologetic writing known as the *Epistle to Diognetus*. The Christian life was, in fact, the most powerful argument used both in defence and in propagation of the Christian faith. Even the ordinary Christian life was essentially the missionary life. The command " Go ye and make disciples of all nations " applied to every Christian as well as to the apostles. Christianity could not help being an aggressive faith. Every convert must strive to win others to Christ. He must devote himself heart and soul to the cause, seize every opportunity to impart to others the blessing of salvation, to save not only his own soul, but the souls of others. Christianity might be a faith centred in the unseen, concerned with the world to come, but it was in close touch, in this respect, with the world around it, with at least the eternal interest of the man next door and of men everywhere. And the time was short. " The Lord is at hand." Hence the intensity of this individual effort to bring all and sundry into the fold of Christ, in which alone salvation from the wrath that is speedily coming is to be found.

Next in importance we might perhaps place the influence of the Christian Scriptures as a magnet to draw men to Christ. These Scriptures were at first the Old Testament, especially the Law and the prophetic writings. But erelong the Gospels and the Epistles took rank beside these, and ultimately exceeded them in importance as the Word of God. The Gospels and some of the Epistles, especially the more ethical and spiritual parts of them, lent an enormous strength to the claim of the Christian faith to the sole supremacy of the world. Where in all the literature of the ancient world is there anything to compare with them in the religious sphere ? Where, even in modern literature, is there anything in this sphere so heart-searching, so compelling as the idealist sayings and parables of

Jesus, the idealist ethical utterances of Paul, as in the thirteenth chapter of First Corinthians ? And this literature was available in a language that was widely current in the west as well as the east, in the speech of commerce as well as culture, the everyday speech (κοινή) of a vast area of the ancient world. No wonder that its missionary influence was effectively operative. We know from their own explicit statements that converts like Tatian and Justin Martyr were led from Philosophy to Christianity by reading the Old Testament, and they had many predecessors and successors who, like them, could not resist the unique message of these books. In spite of their " barbarian," *i.e.*, non-Greek origin, they were impressed by the simplicity and antiquity of this message, by the moral verve and spiritual soar of the prophets, if also by its authoritative tone and by the power of prophecy, on which these early apologists lay such stress. The Old Testament bulks largely in the early Christian writings, including those of the New. It is *par excellence* " the Scriptures " referred to in the New Testament literature. But the quotations from the Gospels and Epistles in the early Fathers show that the sayings and deeds of Jesus were comparatively early in circulation, and the letters of the apostles were known and read in connection with churches as far apart as Lyons and Antioch. The adoption of the Old Testament as a Christian book gave to Christianity an antiquity and a prestige which it could not derive from the apostolic writings. Here was unrolled the authoritative record of the divine activity and the divine will in creation and history, such as no other document, however ancient, could supply, and in comparison with which the myths and philosophy of Homer and the ancient Greeks seemed to be of yesterday. It lent great weight to the claim of Christianity to be regarded as the authoritative religion above all its rivals. It tended to meet the craving for an assured revelation of God and eternal life.

For the type of mind concerned to believe rather than to reason and know—the mood of the large mass of mankind in a world, in which the mass was ignorant and held in contempt, and knowledge was the prerogative of the few—this authoritative note was of the utmost practical importance. In this connection illumination by the Spirit of God is the essential and the potent thing. Faith, not reason, conviction, insight by the Spirit, rather than knowledge as the result of inquiry and argument—this, in the early period at least, was, generally speaking, the method of the Christian appeal, though in the hands of one so exceptionally gifted as Paul, Christianity could also be presented as " a reasonable service of God." [4]   With such " Scriptures " as the authoritative basis of faith, this appeal brought with it a new light and a new life to those predisposed, by habit of mind, to give ear to it.   Even for the more educated class there was in this message from God about God—its sublime monotheism and its spiritual power, for instance— something so essentially superior to every other message, so compelling by its inherent worth, that the authority of faith might well triumph over reason.

In the next place we may rank the tendency of Christianity to adapt itself to its environment.   It developed this tendency in a remarkable degree, and it did so from a very early period, though the full development only came later.   This was a tribute to the syncretistic spirit which it could hardly escape paying, and in certain respects it profited thereby, even if the tendency had its drawbacks.   The process began with the universalism of Paul, the Hellenist Jew, who, once he decided to pass from a narrow Pharisaism to Christianity, broadened his new faith into a universal religion.   Only such a religion could conquer the Græco-Roman world, with its medley of races and peoples, and Paul was the special instrument in transforming Christianity, in the spirit of Jesus, from a sect within Judaism into the religion of humanity, though he had some tentative predecessors and many fellow-workers.   There was, indeed, an indispensable limit to the process of accommodation. There could be no accommodation with the polytheistic principle of Græco-Roman religion, which Paul and the later exponents of Christianity denounced as idolatry to be destroyed root and branch, like the Canaanitish gods of old.   Christianity is the absolute as well as the authoritative religion, and in this respect can make no terms with any lower form of religion. Nor could there be any accommodation with the lax pagan morality, though the Jewish ceremonial law, with its scrupulous externalism, was discarded along with Pharisaism.   Within

[4] Rom. xii. 13.

such definite limits the process of accommodation took an ever-larger scope. It was continued by the authors of the Fourth Gospel and the Epistle to the Hebrews in respect of the Logos doctrine which, though it substantially appears in Paul, seems to be drawn by him from a Hebrew rather than from a Greek source. In the Fourth Gospel and Hebrews, on the other hand, the Greek source is more evident, and a decided step is taken in the direction of conveying to the Greek mind Christian beliefs in a manner fitted to make them more easily comprehensible. But the tendency to assimilate, as well as make formal use of Greek thought, in the course of this process of accommodation is patent. Paul himself makes use of Stoic and Platonic ideas in his representation of God and the spiritual world to the Greek reason. The Fourth Gospel shows the play of this subtle influence still more strongly in its doctrine of the Logos-Christ as the source and the imparter of life eternal, life conceived as the eternal reality in and beyond the sensible world.

The tendency was further developed by the later apologists, who proclaimed Christianity as the true philosophy, as the complete revelation of the eternal Reason or Logos, which has operated in less direct form in the best of the Greek thinkers. It was a risky thing to embody in Jesus a philosophic concept, and involved a radical transformation of the historic reality. The historic figure of Jesus is really irreconcilable with this later Logos-Christ, for his significance, his supremacy, lies in the moral and spiritual sphere, not in that of rational speculation. The prophet of Nazareth, the Messiah who suffered on the Cross, is not the supreme head of a philosophic school, as Justin and others, in virtue of a sanguine but unhistoric assumption, tend to make him. Moreover, paganism tended to react on Christianity in spite of the radical difference between the two. In its tendency, for instance, to seize on Christian beliefs and rites and impart to them a sensuous, materialistic significance and content. More especially it tended to materialise, mystify the sacraments in accordance with ideas associated with the mystery religions, to transform the symbol into the thing symbolised. These semi-pagan Christians discarded the old blood sacrifice along with the priestly ritual and polytheistic practice. But ultimately the tendency is

The Gospel in the Early Church

Eucharist, for instance, as the offering anew of the very body
and blood of Christ, in contrast to the simple spiritual rite of
a more primitive time. The sensuous craving in worship
inherited from the past not only thus debased the original
sacramental rites of baptism and the Lord's Supper, it added
new ones as material vehicles of the Grace of God. Jesus was
thereby transformed into the supreme mystagogue of a mystery
religion as well as into the supreme head of a philosophic
school. Even the taint of the polytheistic conception of God
which the Athanasian theology, with its doctrine of the con-
substantiality of the Son, was a determined, if dubious, attempt
to eliminate, as far as the person of Christ was concerned,
ultimately made its leaven felt in the practice of saint and
image worship, of transforming the old gods in this fashion
into intermediaries between God and His worshipper. The
accommodating tendency might thus in course of time have
very questionable effects, might more and more deform the
original Gospel and infuse into it extraneous elements from
philosophy or the mystery religions. But its missionary value
for the spread of the Gospel in its more developed form is evident.

Another powerful factor of the success of the Gospel
appeal is to be found in the personality of some of the Christian
missionaries, and for the Apostolic age this was one of the
first importance. The man was, in fact, almost as important
as the message in the case of a Peter, a Paul, the mystic author
of the Fourth Gospel, and in a lesser degree the outstanding,
though nameless writer of the Epistle to the Hebrews, James
the Lord's brother, Barnabas, Silas, Titus, Timothy, Apollos,
Epaphroditus, Onesiphorus. Among women, Priscilla and
Phœbe are also conspicuous for their forceful activity among
the apostles in the wider sense of the term. Peter occupies
the first place in the earliest mission work in Palestine, and
ultimately he seems to have extended his labours far beyond
the bounds of Palestine. His impulsive zeal, his initiative
within the limited sphere of the Jerusalem community, his
authority as the most prominent of the Twelve, who had
formed the inner circle of the disciples of Jesus, secured him
the leadership in the early stage of the mission. But he was
ultimately overshadowed by Paul and later appears but furtively

on the scene of the wider movement, which owed so much to the greater of the two apostles. He had not the culture, or the creative genius, or the persistent driving force of Paul, who, in virtue of his larger experience and training as a Jew of the Diaspora, his extraordinary powers of mind, his qualities as the born propagandist, which his career as a zealous Pharisee had already developed, has been not unjustifiably termed the second founder of Christianity. To call him the real founder of it, as some have done, is to ignore the fact that he was, after all, but the product of Christ as he understood him, and as he had been transformed by his vision of him into the " new creature in Christ Jesus." Paul could never have replaced Jesus, because in the moral and spiritual sphere Jesus was unique. Without him he would have remained a Jewish Rabbi, though he might have attained a fame superior to that of any other contemporary Rabbi. " When it pleased God to reveal His Son in me." " To me to live is Christ." Such utterances give us the key to the secret power operating in the Pauline mission. Christ-possession is the secret of Paul's superlative missionary initiative and achievement, the hidden spring that quickens his genius as a religious thinker. At the same time, the genius, the character, the temperament were there, and were operative, in formative fashion, even before he was transformed on the road to Damascus from the Apostle of Pharisaism into the Christian Apostle of the Gentiles. Without the personality of Paul, Apostolic Christianity would have been a much smaller thing, though, even apart from Paul, it was already making headway, as a world religion, towards Asia Minor and the west in the mission work of those who preceded him in preaching to the Gentiles. But without the brain of Paul this Gospel would have lacked its characteristic apologetic as a religion independent of Judaism. It could not have won so decisively and so speedily in the conflict with the Judaisers, who would have confined it within the cramping shell of Jewish legalism. Its expansion would certainly have been much more limited in what is the crucial stage of every great movement—the stage when it has to prove its power not only to exist, but to grow. From this point of view, Paul is the greatest man of the movement—the man with whom the movement could not afford to dispense.

Next in importance to Paul is the mystic author of the Fourth Gospel. If he was not an original thinker, like Paul, he possessed the power to adapt to the Greek mind the free Pauline Gospel of the divine Saviour of the world. A very characteristic element in Paul's teaching—his doctrine of the Law and works—erelong fell into abeyance with the controversy that produced it, only to be recreated by Augustine and revived by Luther. It really did not impress itself on the Christianity which took a grip of the Græco-Roman world—the Christianity of the ancient Catholic Church. This Christianity was cast in the Greek mould, and in the casting of it the Fourth Gospel exercised a decisive and permanent influence. " John " is an enigma, and even the advocates of its apostolic origin are fain to admit the difficulty of ascribing it to John the Apostle. The author chose to be anonymous, and he remains a problem. We can only say, on the understanding that the Johannine Epistles were written by the same person, that he described himself as " the presbyter "—probably the equivalent of John, the presbyter *par excellence*, to whom Papias refers. He was at any rate, next to Paul, the great formative influence of the early age, one of the elect among its " apostles, prophets, and teachers," known and unknown. In this category, though hardly in the same rank as Paul and John, is the author of the Epistle to the Hebrews, who might quite well have been the Alexandrian Apollos, to judge from the description of him as " a learned man mighty in the Scriptures."

Beside this elect trinity the other figures of the Gentile mission are only of secondary importance. But in forceful activity there was a host of apostles, prophets, and teachers eminently fitted to be their fellow-workers in the sustained missionary effort which carried the Gospel, within a generation, from Jerusalem to Rome. This forceful activity continued beyond the more strictly Apostolic age. It is traceable in the Pastoral Epistles,[5] in the Third Epistle of John (v. 7), in the Epistles of Ignatius, in " The Didache," and other documentary evidence right through the second and third centuries. These men appear under the general term " evangelists," [6] and to these evangelists, nearly all of them unknown to us by name, was

[5] 2 Tim. iv. 5.
[6] For references see Harnack, " Expansion of Christianity," i. 435 f.

due the establishment of churches in regions like Egypt and
North Africa, Gaul, and Spain, where the beginnings and early
progress of the Christian mission are wrapped in obscurity.
Even beyond the confines of the empire in the far south and
east—in Armenia, Persia, and " India "—these evangelists
penetrated. The apocryphal " Acts of the Apostles," which
detail the mission activity of the apostles in the restricted
sense of the Twelve in these distant regions, are largely
romances. But there seems to be credible evidence for the
mission in at least what is now Afghanistan, and the later
activity of evangelists like Irenæus in Gaul, Pantænus of
Alexandria in S. Arabia, and Gregory the Illuminator in
Armenia, is authentic and symptomatic.

There is, indeed, a distinct drop in the intellectual level
and the spiritual power of the second century as compared
with the first. Men like Justin, Tatian, Athenagoras, who strive
to defend Christianity and enforce its claims as apologists, are
distinctly of inferior calibre, both intellectually and spiritually.
The intellectual level rises again in Clement of Alexandria,
Irenæus, Tertullian, Origen—and Tertullian was certainly a
man of genius of the ill-balanced, erratic type. All four
were men of powerful personality and intellect, and from the
third century onwards the personal element, as a missionary
force, made its power ever more widely felt with the increasing
culture of the Christian clergy and the firmer grip of Christianity
on the higher classes. It was, however, from the moral and
religious, rather than the intellectual side of personality that
Christianity derived its power to conquer the world—from the
passionate devotion of heart and will which braved and even
welcomed martyrdom for the sake of " the name." From
Nero to Diocletian the martyrs were the greatest missionaries.
" The oftener we are mown down by you, the larger our numbers
become," cried Tertullian triumphantly. *Semen est sanguis
Christianorum.* The persecutions were a blessing in disguise
to the suffering Christians. Their persecution proved the power
of their creed and won far more converts than their persecutors
destroyed. Moreover, they served as a moral and spiritual
tonic to the later Church, whose growing expansion involved
to a certain extent a loss of spiritual power.

Finally, the organisation of the Christian communities lent

a powerful force to the Christian mission. In the earliest period the charismatic ministry—the co-operation of the various gifts of the members in the service of the Gospel under the direct inspiration of the Spirit—was a working substitute for a definite organisation. The members spoke and served in these communities, or carried the Gospel from place to place as the Spirit moved them. The apostles, prophets, and teachers were an itinerant class, " speaking the Word of God " from city to city, from Antioch to Rome. This itinerant class continued to exist till well into the second century, and in the form of " the evangelist " till much later. But even in the early period organisation became a necessity, and the necessity became ever more clamant in the face of a hostile state and the ferment of life and thought which the movement developed, and which gave rise to divergent interpretations of the Gospel, devisive tendencies, especially the Gnostic tendency, to which the term heresy in the early sense was applied. We have seen these tendencies already at work in the New Testament Epistles. Their influence is still more strongly reflected in the Ignatian Epistles, in which the primitive episcopacy appears as an indispensable countercheck. Hence the development of organisation and the struggle with Montanism, which was an attempt to preserve or revive the more primitive religion of the Spirit, and with Gnosticism, which sought to transform Christianity into a theosophy and an aristocracy of intellect. Hence, too, the tendency to link up the local communities by means of provincial synods, and, ultimately, the whole Church by means of the General Synod or Council. The germ of this tendency is observable, even in the apostolic age, in the informal cohesion of the communities founded by a single apostle like Paul, to whose single authority they were amenable. It was further involved in the Pauline conception of the Church as one body—the body of Christ—with many members, the Church as conceived in the universal, as well as the particular sense. There was hardly anything in the Græco-Roman world resembling this corporate life, which was at the same time local and universal. The Jewish synagogue has some resemblance to it. But the synagogue was a local religious and racial organisation, and was not linked in the common fellowship of the Christian communities under the authoritative leadership of their apostolic founder, or in the same intensive degree of the cohesive influence of a common faith, which begets a strong consciousness of their oneness. The secular guild has also some features in common with the Christian ecclesia. But the common features are largely formal. In its common faith, worship, activity, fellowship, making every unit a part of the whole, and the whole the collective power of the units—like an army engaged in a campaign—the Christian organisation is unique from the outset. And the organisation possesses the power to develop with the growth of the movement. From being a more or less informal league of separate communities, whose bond was spiritual rather than constitutional, it developed, through the clerical order, into a highly organised league like that which the empire represented in the political sphere. Its practical efficacy was especially great in times of persecution. It was the rallying power when the battle was sorest and in danger of being lost.

This developed organisation was largely modelled on that of the empire, and finally resulted in the concentration of authority and administration in the official class of bishops and their assistants, the presbyters and deacons. It applied within the Church, in some of its features at least, the system of organisation by which the Roman genius for government ruled and welded together the empire. The Church thus borrowed from the State the system which materially contributed to enable it, ultimately, to conquer the State. Whatever its drawbacks, compared with the more democratic system of an earlier time, it had the unquestionable advantage of concentrating the energy and increasing the power of the Church as a missionary force. From this point of view, it is hardly too much to say that the Church was, in the religious sphere, what the Roman army and the Roman administration were in the political sphere. And the efficacy of this organisation became irresistible when both spheres were allied, and Church and State united in the prosecution of the same end. The Church had, indeed, to pay tribute for this alliance in the loss of freedom, the lowering of its ideal of a kingdom not of this world, the blending of morality and religion with secular aims, interests, and methods. The State, in fact, in the long run conquered the Church and held it captive. Even so, this questionable process contributed to its ultimate triumph over paganism. *Tandem vicisti Galilæe* !

IV. DIFFICULTY OF THE APPEAL.

Such, it seems to me, were the main factors to which the Christian Gospel owed its advance to supremacy. But, as has been noted, the advance was slow and very gradual. It took 300 years from the Advent of Jesus to win this supremacy, and even then paganism was but half conquered. Why this tardy, for long comparatively limited success, despite the inherent merits of the Gospel and the influences tending to prepare the world for its favourable reception ?

In the first place, there was the magnitude of the task itself. Was anything more unlikely than that a movement so insignificant in its origin, so idealist and otherworldly, should become the exclusive religion of the Roman Empire ? The Christian missionary everywhere came up against the moral inertia, the degrading conditions prevailing in the large centres of population. St Paul draws a terrible picture of the moral condition of the age. It is, as I have noted, a onesided, temperamental delineation. But it was far from being merely censorious. Slavery was universal and the moral as well as economic effects were disastrous. The stage was coarse and licentious ; the shows of the arena brutalising in the highest degree. Family life was lax. Abortion and the exposure of infants were conventional expedients for shirking the duties of parenthood. Unnatural vice (male prostitution, *paiderastia*) was prevalent " with a shamelessness beyond belief." Moral corruption is not the monopoly of any age. Its germ is in human nature and it is active in every age. It would be easy to draw a picture of the social life of all large modern centres of population that might stand as a parallel to Paul's delineation, if one restricted attention to its darker side. But in the modern world the moral standard is high, the moral sense sensitive in the circles that count for the general moral judgment. We regard as degenerate, perverted, the judgment that lowers this standard to the level of the brute in human form. In the ancient world, on the other hand, brutish sensuality was regarded as a matter of course, or only lightly condemned.

Some of the great emperors, some even of the great philosophers, were addicted to it.   Among the higher classes in the cities the moral atmosphere was poisoned by this and other evils, and in this poisoned atmosphere it was desperately difficult to bring into effective operation the antidote of the Gospel appeal on behalf of the Christian ideal of individual and social morality. The slavery, the ignorance, the poverty, the misery, the degradation of the masses made it exceedingly difficult to find in the lower classes any general understanding of, or interest in the things of the spirit.   To offer anything loftier than a crass and formal superstition seemed like casting pearls before swine.   To appeal to the higher side of human nature when common human nature was so obtuse, so incapable of response to such an appeal, must have been futile in nine cases out of ten.   The Gospel might be a religion for the publican and the sinner, for the mass of miserable humanity, but it demanded a certain moral sense, a certain capacity of moral and spiritual elevation for its reception, and it was only where this condition existed in some appreciable degree that it could count on a hearing.   Though its adherents seem at first to have been drawn from the lower classes, the proportion of these classes won for the Gospel was small, compared to that which remained heedless or hostile.   When the mob broke into tumult and raised the cry, " The Christians to the lions," the impression for long made by the narratives is that this proportion forms but a small minority of the population of any given place.   Moreover, the Gospel did not hold out the lure of any material improvement in the worldly lot of these classes.   It did not preach a social revolution.   Its kingdom is not of this world.   It taught a doctrine of political and social quietism.   " Submit yourselves to every ordinance of man."   The New Testament writings, with some exceptions, reiterate the injunction to be subject to constituted authority, to submit to the prevailing social order. The Gospel is quite compatible with slavery.   Spiritual freedom does not involve either political or social liberty, though the doctrine of Christian brotherhood demands the humane and equitable treatment of inferiors, and tends to transform the spirit of a harsh and degrading social system. It holds out the prospect of a higher and better state for the weak and the oppressed.   But it is attainable only in the world to come. This might be consoling. But such a doctrine was not fitted to appeal to more tangible interests, to produce an upheaval of the lower social strata.

In the second place, the Christian ideal of life was too high to be generally attractive for average human nature. It demanded a degree of self-sacrifice, moral courage, an intensity of will power, devotion, of which we of this age have but a faint conception. Convention, habit, prejudice, environment, were all against the Christian ideal of the consecration of the whole life to God. It involved a radical breach with old associations, customs which it was painful to renounce, the renunciation of which involved, besides, social disability and even material loss. It meant division in the family, estrangement from friends, social ostracism. It did not pay, for it was impossible to be a Christian and practise any trade connected with the conventional polytheism. It was highly unpopular, and, more serious, it was dangerous. To be a Christian was to be treated as an outlaw, to be exposed at any moment to arrest, a summary trial, and laceration by the wild beasts in the arena. It required heroism to profess such a religion in the days of a Nero, a Domitian, or even a Marcus Aurelius and a Septimius Severus. And even if these risks were taken with impunity and the general persecutions were few in number —though local persecution was an oft-recurring contingency— there was the constant odium of being regarded and treated as a suspect. Christianity, in the popular view at least, was associated with hideous practices in consequence of the calumnies circulated by its enemies, especially the Jews. The Christian worshipped an ass's head and other monstrosities, and in their secret conventicles gave themselves up to abominable orgies. They were the votaries of a debased and maleficent superstition. They were, besides, outside their own circle, unsocial, querulous, gloomy bigots—" the enemies of the human race "—conscientious objectors who shirked their duty as citizens, and made themselves, by their fanaticism, a nuisance to their neighbours. They constituted a danger to the common welfare. It certainly required no little heroism to be a Christian in this environment of calumny, ill-will, suspicion, constant personal danger, and it is not surprising that average human nature was not equal to this heroism in common life.

In the third place, Christian idealism was ill-fitted to appeal to the practical, utilitarian Roman spirit. The Roman tended to apply to religion the utilitarian standard, to value it as an expedient for ensuring his prosperity—warding off blight from his crops, securing protection for his household, keeping the masses in subjection, increasing the power and maintaining the order of the Roman state. The gods were useful and therefore necessary. They accorded admirably with the instincts of a hard, practical race, whose right and mission it was to conquer the world by force of arms, and impose on it an iron rule for the benefit of Rome and the glory of the Roman name. There was, indeed, in Stoicism and in the Roman law, as influenced by Stoic teaching, an idealist, humanitarian strain. It is observable in the tendency towards a larger and more equitable conception of human right, in the case of conquered nations, the slave, of women. But there is always a large mass of opinion more or less hostile to such a tendency in every age, including even our own, and the insistent propaganda of an idealist religion like Christianity might easily provoke it into active opposition and nurture the spirit of resistance. To such a hard, egotistic race, a God who required his votary to lose his life in order to find it, to love his neighbour as himself, to love even his enemies, to treat the slave and the outcast as a brother of equal value in the moral and spiritual sphere ; a God who was no respecter of persons, in this sphere at least, whose kingdom was not of this world, who ruled His kingdom by love and not by force, who had, in His infinite love, even died to redeem it—such a God was a mere old wife's fable. To model the individual life and the government of the state in accordance with this ideal God was, for the ordinary, practical Roman, visionary drivel. When Christianity did succeed in converting the emperor it was, in part at least, because the emperor had the insight to discover from various motives that the God of the Christians, with an organised Church at his disposal, might, after all, be a very present help in time of trouble, in the struggle with his rivals for supremacy in the empire, for instance, and might be of considerable utility for the government of the empire. Unfortunately, this opportunism was by no means an unmixed gain for the triumphant Church. It had, in fact, disastrous effects on its spiritual life, which seems to thrive best in opposition. It led, in the east at least, to the virtual absorption of the Church by the state, the repression of spiritual liberty, its secularisation as the adjunct and prop of imperial policy and interests.

In the fourth place, Christianity ran clean counter to the dominant polytheistic principle in religion. Polytheism might be bankrupt as far as the educated intelligence of the age was concerned. But if to the philosopher the Deity was a unity, it manifested itself in a variety of forces and forms, and even the later philosophers of the Stoic and Neoplatonic schools were devoutly addicted to a sort of spiritualised polytheism. For the mass, especially in the rural districts, the principle in its crasser form was still the only possible principle. For the government, the imperial cult, in particular, was the indispensable adjunct of political order, of the majesty of the Roman state as embodied in the emperor. To deny this principle was, therefore, to renounce religion as the age conceived it. Christianity was thus equivalent to atheism. The Christians deny the existence of the gods. They have no temples, no statues, no sacrifice, no ritual worth speaking of, in the early period at least. They are accordingly atheists. Moreover, they are traitors. Their atheism involves treason, disloyalty. They refuse to take part in the imperial cult. They flout, in particular, the state religion along with the worship of the gods in general. They profess allegiance to another king, and they prate about a kingdom superior in extent and grandeur to the Roman Empire. They are, therefore, traitors, disloyal to the emperor and the empire, which has grown up by the favour of the gods. This was the crucial test between the Christians and their fellow-citizens, the insuperable barrier to the profession of Christianity as far as the state was concerned. The political outweighed every other consideration in its eyes. They are otherwise unprofitable and disgruntled citizens. Their atheism is further responsible for the evils that afflict the Empire from time to time and threaten its collapse—for the invasions of the barbarians, for the calamities in the form of pestilence, famine, floods, earthquakes that periodically scourge it. What is the cause of these calamities? Undoubtedly the atheism of the Christians. "To the lions," therefore, with these atheists and traitors.

The apologists might adduce powerful arguments to disprove these accusations and inferences. They might array against the polytheistic mythology the objections of the philosophers themselves. They might make much of the ridiculous tales told of these old gods, and demonstrate the folly of worshipping the creature instead of the Creator. They might disclaim the charges of atheism and emphasise the fact that the Christians worshipped the one and only God in spirit and in truth. They might protest against paying any part of the worship due to the one and only God to these false gods, who were really demons in disguise and tricked foolish people into a false worship. They might asseverate their loyalty to the emperor and appeal to the sterling character of their fellow-Christians, in proof of their fidelity and their devotion to duty in ordinary life. They might remind their detractors that they prayed for the emperor and were the most prompt in paying their taxes. They might appeal, in the name of justice, against the injustice of trying and punishing them merely for the profession of Christianity, without specific evidence of any criminal act. They might retort on their opponents the charge of being the authors of the decay of the Roman power, and even claim some of the emperors as their benefactors. These arguments were mostly forcible enough, but they could avail little against the dominant superstition and misrepresentation, which made it difficult to arrive at a common understanding or discuss such matters on their own merits.

In the fifth place, Christianity found a formidable obstacle in the intellectualism of the age. It was this more particularly that hindered its progress among the educated class. Its real strength lay in the moral and spiritual sphere. Here it was *facile princeps* among all the religions of the age. It could, too, give a reason for its faith even on the intellectual side of it, and it certainly won men of notable intellectual power from a comparatively early period—Justin, Irenæus, Clement of Alexandria, Tertullian, Origen, Cyprian, Lactantius, for instance, before it became the official imperial religion, and therefore, being fashionable, the true religion for many even among the intellectuals. But its doctrines of the incarnation, the Cross, the bodily resurrection, had their difficulties for this class, and it is questionable whether the apologists, even the ablest of them, like Tertullian and Origen, handled such controversial topics in the manner best fitted to commend them to the intellectual inquirer, or succeeded in really disarming their critics. Whilst the deification of man was a characteristic Greek conception, the incarnation of God in a material body and the bodily resurrection was a stumbling-block to the philosophers, to whom matter was essentially evil and only spirit is immortal. Moreover, a great deal of this ancient apologetic, with its emphasis on prophecy in the sense of prediction, as the supreme test of truth, its claim in behalf of Christianity, as they understood it, as the absolute philosophy as well as the absolute religion, its conception of Jesus as the embodiment of the Greek Logos, its unscientific and unhistoric exegesis, its tendency to treat faith as the enemy of reason, is, for the modern Christian, quite unconvincing.[1] Its method and content are often weak, and its exponents do not show an accurate or a critical knowledge of past conditions. Even in the brilliant pages of a Tertullian it was more fitted to provoke opposition than force assent. He was so far right when, in opposition to the philosophers, he demanded what Jerusalem has to do with Athens ? Right, in so far as the significance of the religion of Jesus did not lie in its being a new philosophy after the Greek model, but a faith to live and die on. Wrong, in so far as religion cannot be defended or commended by an imperious and impatient contempt of reason as an enemy of the truth. He might have learned better from Paul in this matter, though the tendency to disparage reason versus faith might be traced back to the apostle of the Gentiles. The fact is, that these apologists, in virtue of their training in an atmosphere of thought so different from that which Jesus breathed, a conception of God and the universe and human life so different in some respects from his, were not the best fitted to expound and enforce the elements in the Gospel that can alone carry conviction to the mind as well as the heart. Even Origen does not always score against

---

[1] For a recent attempt in English to estimate the second century apologetic, see Carrington, " Christian Apologetics of the Second Century " (1921). I should be disposed to be more critical at times of the statements of these Apologists and to avoid the orthodox bias of the author, who, like them, insists, as an axiom, on " the cosmic Lordship of Christ," in virtue of the Logos theory, which they borrowed from Greek philosophy.

Celsus, because he is as much a Gnostic philosopher as a follower of Jesus.

In addition to the weakness of much of this Christian apologetic, there was, in the sixth place, the deterrent effect of the difference of view and the bitter controversies, especially on the person of Jesus, that too often rent the Church into warring factions right down the centuries. Monarchian contended with Trinitarian, in one form or other, long before the Council of Nicæa and long after it. Practical questions like those of Rebaptism and the Lapsed, more purely ecclesiastical questions arising out of the conception of the Church and its proper government, even the chronological question about the date of the celebration of Easter fomented strife, confusion, and schism. This clash of opinion might betoken both fervour and freedom of thought, for speculative opinion, apart from the Gnostic extravagances, was comparatively free in the first centuries within the ancient Church. It might be a symptom of the vitality of the body ecclesiastical. It might be the inevitable concomitant of growth within the movement, which can only exist where ferment takes place. But it might also betoken an excrescence, a morbid growth. Certainly it tended to bring into discredit in pagan eyes (as we learn from Celsus, among the earlier witnesses, and Ammianus Marcellinus, among the later) a religion that claimed to be an infallible revelation, and yet produced so much contention, disagreement over its content, that proclaimed the doctrine of brotherhood, and yet gave rise to so many warring sects, that professed peace on earth and goodwill among men, and yet was so addicted to strife and mutual hatred. " See how these Christians love one another," was a pagan gibe that was not unmerited, though happily it was not due to the Gospel in itself, but to the perversion of it, and did not apply where the spirit of Jesus prevailed. Where this spirit prevailed, self-sacrifice, love of the brethren, love of all men, helpfulness, the forgiving spirit, patience under persecution, steadfastness in well-doing prevailed. On this side the Gospel could disarm its critics and teach even philosophy the secret of the true life, the practical power of faith.

INDEX

A

Aaron, 178
Abel, 122
Abraham, 90, 93, 95, 122, 129, 132, 145, 185, 263
Acts of the Apostles, 3-4, 7, 10, 13, 15 f., 17, 23, 26 f., 31, 34 f., 170-171, 183, 192, 194, 212
Adam, 60, 69, 121-122, 145
Adoption, 94, 103
Adoptionist, 10, 209, 246, 286
Afghanistan, 317
Africa, North, 317
Agape, the, 17-18, 133, 298
Alexander the Great, 52
Alexandria, 220, 276
Alogi, the, 235
Ammianus Marcellinus, 327
Amos, 96
Ananias of Damascus, 29
Andrew, apostle, 222
Angelology, 43, 58-59, 286
Antichrist, 161-162, 187, 246-247, 275
Antioch, 12, 33, 51-52, 55, 61, 133, 257, 267, 275, 308, 311, 318
— (Pisidia), 10
Antiochus Epiphanes, 20, 92
Apocalypse, the, 187 f.; the Antichrist, 187-188; its author, 188-189; its thesis and its development, 189-190; its Christology, 190-191; subordination of Christ to God, 191; redemptive work of Christ, 191-192; universalism, 192-193; resurrection and millennial reign of Christ, 193-219, 232, 235, 239, 248, 256
Apocalyptic, 2, 14, 23 f., 32, 43, 54, 60, 64, 71, 111-112, 136-137, 161-162, 187 f., 201, 232, 300, 303
Apocryphal Gospels, 258
Apologists, the, 313, 325-327
Apollos, 143, 173, 220, 314, 316
Apostates, 295
Arabia, 317
Aramaic, 48
Arcadia, 282
Aristion, 299

Armenia, 317
Asceticism, 265-266, 291-292
Asia Minor, 12, 168, 171, 262, 315
Asia, Province of, 155, 163, 248, 252-253
Athanasius, 314
Athenagoras, 317
Athens, 10, 141
Attis, 307
Augustine, St, 62, 291
Augustus, Emperor, 165
Aurelius, Marcus, 322

B

Baptism, 15 f., 28, 70, 113 f., 158, 164, 175, 186, 209, 211, 229, 265, 288-290, 298, 314
Bacon, 210
Barcochba, 182, 276
Barnabas, 173, 257, 264, 276 f., 285, 287, 294, 296, 303, 314
Bartlet, 37
Basilides, 246
Benjamin, 41
Bethany, 23
Bigg, 277
Binitarian, 264, 285
Blakeston, 56
Blunt, 37
Bousset, 12, 49, 114
Bread, breaking of, 17
Bultmann, 195

C

Cadbury, 35-36
Cæsarea Philippi, 18
Caiaphas, 20
Cain, 122
Calvary, 8-9
Catholic Epistles, 153
Catholicism, early, 153, 156, 158, 160, 164, 214, 250, 251 f.; causes of its development, 251; its teaching embodies common current Christianity, 251; combines

329

pagan source, 11-12 ; enhanced consciousness of the person of Jesus, 12-14 ; compatible with monotheism, 13 ; salvation, 14 f. ; understood in the Messianic sense, 14-15 ; its conditions—faith, repentance, baptism, remission, 15-17 ; connected with the death of Christ, 17-18 ; Jesus regarded his death as a vicarious sacrifice, 18-20 ; Was it also act of expiation, propitiation ? 20 ; the Suffering Servant of Isaiah liii., 20-21 ; self-sacrificing service for the sake of the kingdom, 21-22 ; "hanging him on a tree," questionable exegesis, 22 ; the death vicarious, not propitiatory, in the primitive preaching, 22 ; the Pauline development is not discernible in it, 22-23 ; the coming of the Christ, 23 f. ; the belief in the Ascension a later pictorial addition, 23 ; that in the coming of Christ a genuine trait of the primitive tradition, 23-24 ; the Messiah and his coming in Jewish thought, 24 ; the Christian innovation, 24-25 ; tense expectancy and its practical effect, 25 ; the transcendental conception of the kingdom, 25 ; to include the Gentiles, 25-26 ; the inspired community, 26 f. ; the inspiration by the Holy Spirit; the Spirit a divine power, not a person, 26-27 ; a dynamic experience, 27 ; the Spirit's operation in the mission of Jesus and that of his disciples, 28 ; its characteristic effects, 28-29 ; the primitive Gospel and Judaism, 29 ; Stephen and the incipient reaction from Judaism, 29-30 ; an experienced Gospel, 31 f. ; the Jewish atmosphere, 31 ; based on personal conviction about Jesus, 31-32 ; modern thought and the primitive preaching, 32 ; the Apocalyptic element, 33 ; the new spiritual life, 33-34.

Gregory, the illuminator, 317

H

Habakkuk, 93, 95
Hades, 172, 191, 288

Hadrian, Emperor, 182, 277, 283
Hagar, 122
Harnack, 27, 35, 40, 47, 49, 77, 181-182, 218, 240, 264, 277, 283, 296
Harrison, Mr, 163
Harvard Theological Studies, 35-36
Hawkins, 35
Hebrews, Epistle to, 154, 172 f. ; its authorship, 172-174 ; addressed to Roman community, 174 ; the Gospel viewed in the light of sacrificial cultus, 175 ; its Logos doctrine, 176-177 ; Christ the High Priest, 177 ; his essential humanity, 177-178 ; supersession of the old covenant, 178 ; his propitiatory death and his intercession, 178 ; the Gospel the absolute religion, 178 ; an interpretation and an apologetic, 178-179 ; agreement with and divergence from Paul, 180-181, 212, 214, 225-226, 251, 262, 277, 287, 291, 303, 313-314, 316
Heitmüller, 114
Hellenism, 48, 112-113
Hermas, " Shepherd " of, 253, 257, 264, 282 f., 296
Hierapolis, 299
Hippolytus, 290
Hofmann, von, 213
Holtzmann, H. J., 36
Hosea, 96, 130
Hymenæus, 243-244

I

Ignatius, 159, 239, 248 f., 251-253, 256-257, 259, 267 f., 286, 298, 303-304, 316
Immortality, 141, 264
Imperial cult, 189
Incarnation, 213 f., 246-247, 265, 268 f., 285 f., 304
Inge, Dean, 57
Inspired community, 26 f.
Intolerance, 47, 50, 234
Irenæus, 31, 248, 275, 299, 317
Isaac, 122, 129
Isaiah, 5, 17-18, 20 f., 24, 28, 41, 43, 45, 69, 92, 95-96, 125, 127, 130, 179
Ishmael, 122
Israel, 92, 94, 96, 115, 122, 127 f., 145, 171, 181
Italy, 174

Printed in Great Britain at THE DARIEN PRESS, *Edinburgh*

[7]